Wordsworth
and the
Enlightenment

Wordsworth and the Enlightenment

Alan Bewell

Nature, Man,
and Society in the
Experimental Poetry

YALE UNIVERSITY PRESS

NEW HAVEN AND LONDON

Designed by Jo Aerne and set in Baskerville
type by Brevis Press, Bethany, Connecticut.
Printed in the United States of America by
Vail-Ballou Press, Binghamton, New York.

Library of Congress Cataloging-in-Publication Data
Bewell, Alan J., 1951–
Wordsworth and the Enlightenment : nature,
man, and society in the experimental poetry /
Alan Bewell.
p.   cm.
Bibliography: p.
Includes index.
ISBN 0–300–04393–7 (alk. paper)
1. Wordsworth, William, 1770–1850—
Criticism and interpretation.
2. Experimental poetry—History and
criticism.   3. Anthropology in literature.
4. Philosophy in literature.   5. Nature in
literature.   6. Enlightenment.   I. Title.
PR5888.B47   1989   88–20644
821'.7—dc19   CIP

The paper in this book meets the guidelines
for permanence and durability of the
Committee on Production Guidelines for
Book Longevity of the Council on Library
Resources.

205513

10 9 8 7 6 5 4 3 2 1

For my parents,
Mary E. Bewell and Charles E. Bewell

Contents

Preface

This book seeks to demonstrate how Wordsworth reshaped the language of Enlightenment anthropology as he set out to write a history of the origins and development of the human mind—his own and that of the human race. At the core of Wordsworth's poetry is an anthropological vision, explicit in the notion of *The Recluse* as a "philosophical poem, containing views of Man, Nature, and Society," a concern with how human beings, individually and as a species, made the transition from a state of nature to society. At once our first and greatest anthropological poet, Wordsworth found in Enlightenment anthropology a new kind of narrative on human origins, and as he explored its possibilities and limitations, he found his own distinctive voice and style. In the shorter poetry and narratives originally intended for *The Recluse*, Wordsworth took up the "experimental" language of eighteenth-century moral philosophical inquiry, with its explicit focus on the observation of marginal individuals—idiots, children, villagers, and women, the blind, the deaf, and the mute—and "savage races" described by missionaries, colonial administrators, and travelers, and made it a primary vehicle of self-representation and self-understanding:

> I breathed (for this I better recollect)
> Among wild appetites and blind desires,
> Motions of savage instinct, my delight
> And exaltation. [*Home at Grasmere*, MS. B, lines 912–15]

Wordsworth saw himself as a poet speaking from the margins of English society—from an outpost of culture whose way of life was threatened; the methods and stance of Enlightenment anthropology could thus be applied to his own situation, as a "native" of the Lake District, and to his own intellectual development. Anthropological inquiry provided him with a pattern and justification for autobiography, for an account of the origin and progress of his mind.

The working thesis of this study is that Wordsworth's major objective as a poet was to write a series of poems that together would constitute a general history of the imagination, of the forms that it has taken over the course of human history and the role that it has played in the genesis and development of social institutions such as language, poetry, religion, property, and civil government. The different fields that comprised Enlightenment anthropology provided him with a model for how such a history might proceed. In eighteenth-century ethnography, geology, environmental theory, and biblical studies, in philosophical inquiries into the genesis of myths, the supernatural, and the idea of death, and in the speculative use of marginal individuals and cultures, Wordsworth found discursive models for talking about human origins.

Rather than applying modern anthropological approaches to Wordsworth's poetry, I have attempted to provide a historical reconstruction of the various concerns and rhetorical forms that shaped eighteenth-century anthropological thought. I hope that readers, once conversant with this discourse, will be able to extend it to other poems that were neglected in this study.

Unless otherwise noted, the translations that appear in this book are mine.

As is the case with anyone who writes today about Wordsworth, I am greatly indebted to a distinguished body of scholarship, critical, textual, and historical. During the years that this book was in progress, however, I have benefited directly from the encouragement, support, and advice of many individuals. I am grateful to Robert Dunham, Jared Curtis, Robin Blaser, and Michael Steig of Simon Fraser University, and to Albert Wlecke, Homer Brown, and Robert Folkenflik of the University of California, Irvine, for their continued interest and assistance. James R. Holstun and Alan Liu read significant portions of the manuscript and have been a constant resource for criticism, commentary, and suggestions. James K. Chandler offered extensive and valuable criticism of the entire manuscript. Others read parts of the manuscript and contributed to subsequent revisions: my thanks to Kenneth Johnston, Patricia Meyer Spacks, Michael Cooke, Cristina Malcolmson, David Marshall, Jerome J. McGann, James McKusick, and Geoffrey Hartman. To Ellen Graham, Harry Haskell, and Jo Aerne, of Yale University Press, and to Joseph Black, who helped in the preparation of the manuscript, my special thanks. Finally, this book owes much to my family—to my wife Sharon Haughian and my daughters Carmen and Janet—who continually demonstrated the wisdom of an "hour of feeling."

I am grateful to Yale University for a junior faculty fellowship, which allowed me to complete the manuscript. Parts of chapter 2 appeared in a slightly different form in *English Literary History* 50 (Summer 1983):321–46; a portion of chapter 4 was originally published in *English Literary History* 53 (1986):357–90.

Abbreviations

BL	*Biographia Literaria; or Biographical Sketches of My Literary Life and Opinions.* Ed. James Engell and W. Jackson Bate. 2 vols. in 1. Princeton: Princeton University Press, 1983.
Borderers	*The Borderers.* Ed. Robert Osborn. Ithaca, N.Y.: Cornell University Press, 1982.
BWS	*Bicentenary Wordsworth Studies in Memory of John Alban Finch.* Ed. Jonathan Wordsworth. Ithaca, N.Y.: Cornell University Press, 1970.
DWJ	*Journals of Dorothy Wordsworth.* Ed. Ernest de Selincourt. 2 vols. London: Macmillan, 1959.
EY	*The Letters of William and Dorothy Wordsworth: The Early Years, 1787–1805.* Ed. Ernest de Selincourt. 2d ed., rev. Chester L. Shaver. Oxford: Clarendon Press, 1967.
Home at Grasmere	*"Home at Grasmere": Part First, Book First of "The Recluse."* Ed. Beth Darlington. Ithaca, N.Y.: Cornell University Press, 1977.
LY	*The Letters of William and Dorothy Wordsworth: The Later Years.* Ed. Ernest de Selincourt. 2d ed., rev. Alan G. Hill. Oxford: Clarendon Press, 1978–79.
Moorman	Mary Moorman. *William Wordsworth: A Biography.* 2 vols. Oxford: Clarendon Press, 1965.
MY	*The Letters of William and Dorothy Wordsworth: The Middle Years.* Part 1, 1806–1811. Part 2, 1812–1820. Ed. Ernest de Selincourt. 2d ed., rev. Mary Moorman. Oxford: Clarendon Press, 1969–70.

Peter Bell	*Peter Bell.* Ed. John E. Jordan. Ithaca, N.Y.: Cornell University Press, 1985.
Prelude	*The Prelude 1799, 1805, 1850.* Ed. Jonathan Wordsworth, M. H. Abrams, and Stephen Gill. New York: Norton, 1979.
ProseW	*The Prose Works of William Wordsworth.* Ed. W. J. B. Owen and Jane W. Smyser. 3 vols. Oxford: Clarendon Press, 1974.
PW	*The Poetical Works of William Wordsworth.* Ed. Ernest de Selincourt. 2d ed. Oxford: Clarendon Press, 1952.
Reed *EY*	Mark L. Reed. *Wordsworth: The Chronology of the Early Years, 1770–1799.* Cambridge, Mass.: Harvard University Press, 1967.
Reed *MY*	Mark L. Reed. *Wordsworth: The Chronology of the Middle Years, 1800–1815.* Cambridge, Mass.: Harvard University Press, 1975.
STCNB	*The Notebooks of Samuel Taylor Coleridge.* Ed. Kathleen Coburn. 3 vols. to date. New York: Pantheon Books and Princeton: Princeton University Press, 1957–.
STCL	*Collected Letters of Samuel Taylor Coleridge.* Ed. Earl L. Griggs. 6 vols. Oxford: Clarendon Press, 1956–71.

Wordsworth
and the
Enlightenment

The Recluse as a
Beginning Intention

How shall I seek the
origin?
—1850 *Prelude* 2.346

There is little question
that the central event
that shaped Words-
worth's mature poetry
was his determination
to write *The Recluse,* the
"philosophical poem, con-
taining views of Man, Na-
ture, and Society" (*ProseW*
3:5). This decision, made
early in 1798, extended well
beyond those poems that have
customarily been considered
part of this project, in ways
that have not been adequately understood. Most discussions of *The Prelude* and the
related shorter lyrics and narratives
written between 1798 and 1805 tend,
with some justification, to treat these
poems as if they were opposed to or departed from the concerns of *The Re-*
cluse.[1] This view, however, is based upon

the assumption that *The Recluse* had a preconceived structure, against which the shorter poems can be judged as deviations. In fact, during its early stages the "philosophical poem" was at best an evolving encyclopedic intention.

The original design for *The Recluse* was significantly different from what has come to be its received form: a tripartite structure that, by John Alban Finch's conservative estimate, would have required at least thirty-three thousand lines of poetry.[2] In Wordsworth's first announcement of the project, in his letter to James Tobin of 6 March 1798, he declares that his object is to "give pictures of Nature, Man, and Society" and that he cannot imagine "any thing which will not come within the scope of my plan." And yet he still hopes to complete the poem in "a year and a half" (*EY* 212). Either Wordsworth was here showing much greater confidence than Coleridge, who was willing to set aside twenty years for a similar kind of poem ("ten to collect materials and warm my mind with universal science . . . the next five to the composition of the poem—and the five last to the correction of it" [*STCL* 1:320–21]), or the structure of the project was originally much less extensive than we have come to believe. Furthermore, Wordsworth does not commit himself to large discursive and narrative poems, but instead to a series of "pictures" of nature, man, and society.

The textual history of the early *Recluse* poems also indicates a changing conception of its structure. "The Old Cumberland Beggar" passed from being among the first of the "philosophical poems" to a fairly undistinguished location at the head of the "Poems Referring to the Period of Old Age" in the 1815 classification of the poetry. "The Discharged Soldier," which strongly echoes the opening cantos of Dante's *Divine Comedy*, was probably first written as an introduction to *The Recluse*. Yet like its namesake, the poem was discharged from duty and lingered for six years before being taken back into service for book 4 of *The Prelude*. Wordsworth, it seems, shelved the poem when it appeared that a reworking of "The Ruined Cottage," expanding on the role of the Pedlar as a Virgilian guide, might prove a better beginning. But despite extensive reworkings and revisions, this poem also proved unsatisfactory, and Wordsworth eventually used it to introduce *The Excursion*.[3] The experimental challenges and the frustration associated with the early stages of *The Prelude* hardly need emphasizing. What should be stressed is that during the period when Wordsworth wrote (or began writing) his best poetry, approximately 1798–1802, the form of *The Recluse* was not at all clear to him, so there was a great deal of uncertainty about how and which of his poems would eventually fit into its evolving structure.

Given these uncertainties, it is useful to think of *The Recluse* less as a poem than as a governing intention. The shorter narratives and lyrics can then be seen as part of this encyclopedic poem, because each was composed with the assumption that it would eventually find a place in its main structure—each was nominated, though few were confirmed. As Thomas Kuhn has remarked, certain texts in the history of science have played a major role in initiating and defining the specific character and objectives of subsequent scientific research and writing: "Aristotle's *Physica*, Ptolemy's *Almagest*, Newton's *Principia* and *Optics*, Franklin's *Electricity*, Lavoisier's *Chemistry*, and Lyell's *Geology*— these and many other works served for a time implicitly to define the legitimate problems and methods of a research field for succeeding generations of practitioners."[4] *The Recluse* served a similar purpose as it opened up a new field of poetic inquiry that was materially different from the poetry being written at the time; it established the questions and problems the poems were to take up, the subjects to be addressed, and the methods to be employed in doing so; it also indicated the theoretical relationships that were to pertain among the poems. Michael G. Cooke has argued that "romanticism must be construed as more than the presence of divers data and alternative schemes. It entails an impulse and a demand for a principle of comprehension. It takes the form, characteristically, of an act of inclusion."[5] *The Recluse* constituted a poetic paradigm by introducing a principle of inclusion, a set of problems, and a mode of writing appropriate to solving them.

In reconstructing this paradigm, one confronts a number of difficulties. Unlike the works cited by Kuhn, which inaugurated clearly defined fields of inquiry by their existence as texts, the idea of *The Recluse*, even as it instituted the appearance of a unique kind of poetic "experimentalism," did not achieve a satisfactory textual form. Furthermore, though Wordsworth frequently claimed that all his poems were part of this system, he just as frequently avoided describing it. In the preface to *The Excursion* (1814), he declares that the reader only needs to be apprised of the structure of *The Recluse* and he "will have no difficulty in extracting the system for himself " (*ProseW* 3:6). Instead of systematic statement, we are given an architectural metaphor. *The Prelude* has the same relation to *The Recluse,* he writes, "as the ante-chapel has to the body of a gothic church. Continuing this allusion, [the poet] may be permitted to add, that his minor Pieces, which have been long before the Public, when they shall be properly arranged, will be found by the attentive Reader to have such connection with the main Work as may give them claim to be likened to the little cells, oratories, and sepulchral recesses, ordinarily included in those edifices" (5–6).

A similar pattern of assertion and deferral can be seen in other descriptions of *The Recluse.* In the preface to *Poems* (1815), Wordsworth declares that his "guiding wish was, that the small pieces of which these volumes consist, thus discriminated, might be regarded under a two-fold view; as composing an entire work within themselves, and as adjuncts to the philosophical Poem, 'The Recluse.'" Once again, however, this announcement is accompanied by reticence; the philosophical unity of the poems is asserted, but the task of discovering it is left to the reader. "For him who reads with reflection," Wordsworth writes, "the arrangement will serve as a commentary unostentatiously directing his attention to my purposes, both particular and general" (*ProseW* 3:28). In the 1800 preface to *Lyrical Ballads,* Wordsworth stresses that it is the systematic character of his poetry that makes it "materially different" (*ProseW* 1:120) from his contemporaries'. In fact, the ostensible reason for the preface in the first place was that certain friends (Coleridge undoubtedly among them), who were interested in a poetry "not unimportant in the multiplicity and in the quality of its moral relations" had encouraged him "to prefix a systematic defence of the theory, upon which the poems were written" (120). Yet Wordsworth no sooner asserts a system than he puts off its exposition, arguing that "the Reader would look coldly upon my arguments, since I might be suspected of having been principally influenced by the selfish and foolish hope of *reasoning* him into an approbation of these particular Poems." And even if he were willing to engage in "reasoning," theory is an ineffectual form of special pleading: "to display my opinions and enforce my arguments," to present the system "with the clearness and coherence, of which I believe it susceptible, it would be necessary to give a full account of the present state of the public taste in this country, and to determine how far this taste is healthy or depraved: which again could not be determined, without pointing out, in what manner language and the human mind act and react on each other, and without retracing the revolutions not of literature alone but likewise of society itself " (*ProseW* 1:120).

Matters would be simplified if one could argue that Wordsworth's mature poetry was a direct expression of this unarticulated system. But this combined assertion and deferral of any theoretical exposition of the idea of *The Recluse* and the work's fragmentary status suggest that Wordsworth himself was not entirely satisfied with it, and that readers are justified in seeing the lyrics and shorter narrative poetry as divergences from the "philosophical poem." As I hope to show, Wordsworth's best poems had their genesis in his antagonism toward this philosophical model, in his attempt to write within and at the same time to displace, submerge, or repress the very paradigm that had initially authorized them. Especially between 1798 and 1805, Wordsworth was simultaneously engaged in launching and in scuttling that "Great Work" in which he was to "sail; on an open Ocean, & a steady wind; unfretted by short tacks, reefing, & hawling & disentangling the ropes" (*STCL* 2:1,013). The poems are written by landlocked narrators, who get caught up in the "short tacks," in the "reefing," "hawling," and "disentangling" of textual "ropes," showing by so doing that they are "all unfit / For such high argument" (*Peter Bell,* lines 979–80). This dynamic process of taking up and employing—while at the same time counteracting, concealing, and displacing—the philosophical modes of inquiry and subjects of concern that had originally sponsored these poems gives rise to many of their more remarkable qualities and to many of their mysteries. The history of Wordsworth's poetry can thus be seen as the history of his struggle against a discursive paradigm. With each new poem, the project became more fixed, more substantial, and more powerful in its control over Wordsworth, even as it became more dogmatic, cumbersome, and contradictory, less flexible to change or revision, less able to deal with contradictions and anomalies, and less dynamic in structure. Consequently, the relative poverty of some of the later poetry may have less to do with a falling away of poetic power than with the poet's weakening resistance to this paradigm.

The "Philosophical Poem" and the Exile of Moral Philosophy

One reason for the ambivalence registered in Wordsworth's remarks about the *Recluse* project is that the idea of an encyclopedic poem on nature, man, and society was not a new one, but very much a product of the Enlightenment—and Wordsworth, as he took it up, clearly felt the weight of an older poetic and philosophical program. During the eighteenth century, the first and foremost "philosophical poem," frequently referred to as such, was Lucretius's *De rerum natura*.[6] For poets writing in the shadow of Milton, this poem was more than a set of disparate ideas: it represented a powerful narrative about human origins that could compete with Milton's great Christian epic. Yet the real impetus for such an encyclopedic poem came from the extensive anthropological speculation of the Enlightenment. From Pope onward, poets dreamed of combining poetry with moral philosophical inquiry to produce a full-scale "history of the species, in its progress from the savage state to its highest civilization and improvement," a vast anthropological epic that would show, through an analysis of human nature and its powers, how mankind, left on its own, had advanced from a state of nature to society.[7]

There was Pope's massive, though incomplete, project in ethics, for which he wrote the *Essay on Man,* the *Moral Essays,* and *The Dunciad.* In the "Design" of the *Essay on Man,* Pope writes that his goal is to provide "a *short* yet not *imperfect* system of Ethics" based on "the science of Human Nature."[8] As William Mason informs us, Gray's *Alliance of Education and Government* was also to have been an "Ethical Essay," similar to Montesquieu's *Spirit of Laws* and "as extensive as human nature."[9] Wordsworth, when asked, in 1838, why he did not finish *The Recluse,* placed himself among the sons of Gray: "Why did not Gray finish the long poem he began on a similar subject? Because he found he had undertaken something beyond his powers to accomplish. And that is my case."[10] Other "philosophical poems" on the progress of mankind might be cited, from the poet laureate Henry James Pye's particularly dull *Progress of Refinement* (1783) to Erasmus Darwin's *Botanic Garden* (1792) and *The Temple of Nature; or, The Origin of Society* (1803).[11] One of the more interesting of these histories is Richard Payne Knight's *Progress of Civil Society* (1796), which Wordsworth was actually reading during the spring of 1798.[12] Explicitly patterned on book 5 of *De rerum natura,* the poem shows how Lucretius was read through the template of the stadial theories of human development popularized over the previous half century by French and Scottish philosophers. The titles of its six books—"Of Hunting"; "Of Pasturage"; "Of Agriculture"; "Of Arts, Manufactures, and Commerce"; "Of Climate and Soil"; and "Of Government and Conquest"—indicate the kind of anthropological model, divided into progressive stages of society, that engaged Wordsworth's attention during this period and was of crucial importance to his conceptualization of human origins. During the 1790s, this genre of narrative, with its explicit intellectual links to the Enlightenment, was so well known that it was even the object of satire, as in the *Anti-Jacobin's* parody of Knight's poem, entitled "The Progress of Man," published between 19 February and 2 April 1798. In the changing political climate of the late 1790s, the genre became increasingly unpopular because of its association with radical thought.

Coleridge sketched out a fragmentary history of man as part of the revolutionary prophecy of *Religious Musings* (lines 198–295). However, it was not until late 1797, while being scrutinized by Alfoxden neighbors and a government detective, that Coleridge began his own philosophical poem "on men, nature, and society" (*BL* 1:196).[13] "The Brook" was to have used the progress of a stream as a metaphor for the progress of human society. Moving from a source through a "first break or fall" that creates language ("audible" drops) and history (a "channel"); to the shelters of hunters (where a "natural" relationship— the "same dark squares"—exists between nature and mankind), the sheepfold of pastoral society, and the "first cultivated plot" of agricultural society; and concluding with civil and commercial life, Coleridge's poetic history would have repeated, allegorically, the familiar stages of a conjectural history. He must have soon realized, however, that this kind of allegory, so much like Pye's, held little likelihood of real success. Also, as he suggests by his ironic claim that the poem was to be dedicated to the "then committee of public safety as containing the charts and maps, with which I was to have supplied the French Government in aid of their plans of invasion" (*BL* 1:196–97), he could not but have been aware of the genre's links to what the *Anti-Jacobin* called "the *Jacobin* Muse" (20 November 1797).

Though it has frequently been suggested that *The Recluse* was foisted

on Wordsworth by Coleridge, when "The Brook" turned out to be
little more than a freshet, there is ample evidence that it represented
Wordsworth's own sophisticated response to his previous moral concerns and an expression of his changing political commitment. Prior
to 1798, he had been actively engaged in moral and political thought,
first in France with Michel Beaupuy, discoursing "about the end / Of
civil government, and its wisest forms" (*Prelude* 9.329–30), and later
as a member of the London Godwin circle. From 1792 to 1795, he
and William Mathews were planning a journal called the *Philanthropist,*
which was to have included among its political and literary concerns,
as Wordsworth notes, "essays upon morals and manners, and institutions whether social or political." Biographical essays on "the characters and opinions of eminent men," particularly those who had
argued for liberty, such as Ann-Robert-Jacques Turgot, Milton, Al-
gernon Sydney, Machiavelli, and Cesare Beccaria, would be included
and organized to "form a series exhibiting the advancement of the
human mind in moral knowledge" (*EY* 125–26). Kenneth Johnston
has suggested that Wordsworth probably took an active role, at least
in the early stages, of the *Philanthropist; or Philosophical essays on politics,
government, morals and manners,* which was published for eleven months
in 1795–96.[14] In the 1794 revisions to *An Evening Walk,* Wordsworth
identifies himself with moral philosophers, with

> those to whom the harmonious doors
> Of Science have unbarred celestial stores,
> To whom a burning energy has given
> That other eye which darts thro' earth and heaven,
> Roams through all space and [   ] unconfined,
> Explores the illimitable tracts of mind,
> And piercing the profound of time can see
> Whatever man has been and man can be . . .   [*PW* 1:13n]

Similarly, in *Descriptive Sketches,* a poem heavily influenced by Montesquieu and by Gray's "Alliance of Education and Government," Wordsworth transforms a journey through the Swiss Alps into an
anthropological movement back in time; in the mountains, "by vestal
Nature guarded," he claims that "the traces of primaeval Man appear"
(1793 version, lines 528–29).

In *The Prelude,* the poet describes himself during this period as a cold anatomist, dissecting society, piercing through superstition, "ancient institutions," and "old opinions" (10.850, 861) in an effort to discover a rational basis for society:

> I took the knife in hand,
> And, stopping not at parts less sensitive,
> Endeavored with my best of skill to probe
> The living body of society
> Even to the heart. I pushed without remorse
> My speculations forward, yea, set foot
> On Nature's holiest places.   [10.872–78]

This cold, rationalistic inquiry caused a moral crisis, and Wordsworth claims that he "yielded up moral questions in despair" (10.900). Yet, as James K. Chandler has convincingly argued, if he ceased moral questioning, he did not do so for long: this crisis was as much an expression of a major shift in Wordsworth's ideological and philosophical position, from the radicalism of the French Enlightenment to the more conservative attitudes represented by Edmund Burke.[15] Equally importantly, this questioning of moral philosophy gave rise to a new conception of the role that poetry might play as a medium of moral argument.

The claim that *The Recluse* was modeled on the forms and concerns of moral philosophical argument is likely to be greeted, by some, with a degree of skepticism, because Wordsworth's later opposition to moral inquiry is well known. Geoffrey Durrant, for instance, has argued that in his poetry there is "a firm rejection of the moral and psychological 'science' of Wordsworth's day."[16] It is not by coincidence that the Machiavel of *The Borderers*, Oswald, is associated with moral philosophy:

> We dissect
> The senseless body, and why not the mind?—
>
> . . . .
> Were I a Moralist
> I should make wondrous revolution here;
> It were a quaint experiment to show
> The beauty of truth—.   [1842 *Borderers*, lines 1,166–67, 1,621–24]

In language not much different from that of the *Anti-Jacobin*, Wordsworth equates the "Moralist" (the "speculator in morals" and "empiric" [*Borderers*, p. 65]) with "revolution" and "experiment." The most famous example of this antagonism is in "Expostulation and Reply" and "The Tables Turned," where Wordsworth singles out a friend's (Hazlitt's) unreasonable attachment "to modern books of moral philosophy" (*ProseW* 1:117). The intimate link between philosophy and the dialogue form in these two poems should alert us, however, not to dismiss moral philosophy too quickly. The fact that they are replete with their own precise philosophical vocabulary ("will," "Powers," "impress," "mind," "wisdom," "Nature," "impulse," and "of moral evil and of good") suggests that they are not so much distanced from moral inquiry as set against a certain kind of stay-at-home, noninteractive philosophizing, which retreats from nature and social dialogue. Like Plato's attack on the sophists, Wordsworth's criticism is directed toward a specific use of the language of moral inquiry, and this criticism serves as a preliminary to his own declaration of a commitment to "spontaneous wisdom" and wise passivity.

Wordsworth adumbrates his major criticisms of moral philosophy in a prose fragment that has unfortunately recently been given the working title of an "[Essay on Morals]." A better title would be "Against Moral Inquiry," because the fragment opens with an appeal for a moratorium on systematic philosophic statement: "I THINK publications in which we formally & systematically lay down rules for the actions of Men cannot be too long delayed" (*ProseW* 1:103). Rather than being part of an essay on morals or, perhaps, an introduction to a collection of moral essays, I would suggest that the essay was originally drafted as part of a preface explaining why Wordsworth was taking up moral issues in verse. As its complicated transitions, abrupt shifts, and digressions indicate, arguing systematically against systematic statement was not without its attendant difficulties and anxieties. The opening is strong: "I consider such books as Mr Godwyn's, Mr. Paley's, & those of the whole tribe of authors of that class as impotent" to good purposes and likely to produce bad ones. But hesitation follows: "This sentence will, I am afraid, be unintelligible." After a further page of elliptical and inadequately developed arguments, the essay breaks off with: "we shall find that I have erred when I said that . . ." (103–04). Notwithstanding these difficulties, the essay does offer a coherent argument, primarily indebted to Burke and

Hume, that the major agency in the formation of moral sentiments is not reason or the understanding, but passion and habit: "Our attention ought principally to be fixed upon that part of our conduct & actions which is the result of our habits. In a [?strict] sense all our actions are the result of our habits" (103). The appeal to reason is a rationalization or subterfuge that allows passions and habits "to work, / And never hear the sound of their own names" (*Prelude* 10.812–13); "we repair to systems of moral philosophy for arguments in defence of ourselves."

Working within an explicitly moral context, Wordsworth gives his position a rhetorical turn by insisting that language or "eloquence" plays a central role in the formation of moral sentiments and beliefs. Moral philosophers, he suggests, set an "undue value . . . upon that faculty which we call reason" and, therefore, appeal to us in "lifeless words, & abstract propositions," which are "impotent over our habits." Rather than standing apart from its readers, the text should "melt into our affection[s]" and "incorporate itself with the blood & vital juices of our minds" in the act of reading, so that language can assist in "forming those habits." Only a language directed toward the body can reshape how we habitually feel. "Can it be imagined by any man who has deeply examined his own heart," the poet asks, "that an old habit will be foregone, or a new one formed, by a series of propositions, which, presenting no image to the [?mind] can convey no feeling which has any connection with the supposed archetype or fountain of the proposition existing in human life?" A language void of images cannot act upon habitual feelings. It cannot be, as Wordsworth argues poetry is in the 1850 preface, "truth . . . general, and *operative*" (*ProseW* 1:139, my emphasis). Furthermore, because moral philosophical texts "contain no picture of human life," because "they *describe* nothing," they cannot inform "us how men placed in such or such situations will necessarily act . . . thence enabling us to apply ourselves to the means of turning them into a more beneficial course."

Wordsworth's critique of the language of moral philosophy not only served a negative purpose, but also constituted the raison d'être of *The Recluse* as a moral project in poetry. The idea of addressing moral topics with "eloquence" and through "images" emerged in the space left vacant by his expulsion of moral philosophical inquiry. This process of displacement is obvious in the first announcement of the project: "My object is to give *pictures* of Nature, Man, and Society. Indeed I know not any thing which will not come within the scope of my plan . . . The work of composition is carved out for me, for at least a year and a half to come. The essays of which I have spoken to you must be written with eloquence, or not at all. My eloquence, speaking with modesty, will all be carried off, at least for some time, into my poem" (*EY* 212, my emphasis).

The *Recluse* appears to have supplanted plans for a series of "essays," probably on education and moral subjects. The "eloquence" that these essays required was "carried off " to the "philosophical poem." To Wordsworth in 1798, the idea of presenting "most of the knowledge of which I am possessed" in a comprehensive work, comprised of a series of poetical "essays" on moral subjects, must have seemed at once a viable structure for a philosophical poem and an improvement upon the experimental language of moral philosophy. The philosophical poem, then, was not a wholly new departure from Wordsworth's previous moral and political concerns; instead, it grew out of his sense of the impotence of moral philosophical rhetoric. He did not relinquish the political and ethical concerns that had occupied him for almost a decade; instead, he relinquished his earlier faith in philosophical rhetoric, as he moved from arguments directed toward the understanding and reason, to arguments proceeding through "images" and "eloquence," aimed at incorporating themselves "with the blood & vital juices of our minds."

Moral philosophical discourse was thus exiled from a poetry that found its genesis and justification in its explicit avoidance and wholesale suppression of philosophical statement. Wordsworth could describe *The Recluse* as "a moral and Philosophical Poem"; he could speak "at length on the connection of poetry with moral principles as well as with a knowledge of the principles of human nature"; he could claim that "he had given twelve hours thought to the conditions and prospects of society, for one to poetry"; yet, simultaneously, because the very existence of this poetry was predicated upon its displacement of the language of moral philosophy, the "purpose" of each poem could not justifiably be indicated anywhere but in the poem itself.[17] Moral philosophy, however, did not simply disappear from the poems; it went underground and remained the silent, informing impulse of a poetry whose systematic preconditions could never be explicitly stated. Returning to a passage from the preface to *Lyrical Ballads*, cited earlier, we can see that it represents not only a strategy of deferment, but also an oblique statement of the encyclopedic goal of Wordsworth's poetry: "To display my opinions and fully to enforce my arguments . . . to treat the subject with the clearness and coherence, of which I believe it susceptible, it would be necessary to give a full account of the present state of the public taste in this country, and to determine how far this taste is healthy or depraved: which again could not be determined, without pointing out, in what manner language and the human mind act and react on each other, and without retracing the revolutions not of literature alone but likewise of society itself" (*ProseW* 1:120). If we are to understand these poems adequately, Wordsworth asks us to retrace "the revolutions not of literature alone but likewise of society itself."

Shaping Moral Concerns

When one recognizes that Wordsworth's poems are more than vaguely philosophical, that they had their genesis in his ongoing critical engagement with Enlightenment moral philosophy, one can begin to appreciate that the coherence of *The Recluse* did not lie in its formal structure, but instead in the experimental discourse that shaped individual poems. This suggests that Wordsworth would have felt it necessary to take up, in individual poems or series of poems, the topics and speculative concerns that normally fell within moral philosophy's purview.

Nowadays, we are likely to think of moral philosophy primarily in terms of abstract ethics, without realizing that, as Gladys Bryson has observed, "from the time of Socrates until the emergence of the separate social sciences in the nineteenth century . . . the scope of its interests was bounded only by the limits of the activities of men."[18] Wordsworth was writing at exactly that moment when the immense field of moral philosophy, the "science of MAN," as Hume termed it, was about to break up into the modern disciplines of anthropology, sociology, psychology, philosophical ethics, economics, history, and political science.[19] This situation provided him with many opportunities: for instance, he could still claim, "I know not any thing which will not come within the scope of my plan." But it also meant that *The Recluse* was subject to the same forces that led to the fragmentation of moral philosophy.

Since moral philosophy could deal with anything relating to mankind, the formal structure of these texts is interesting. They present a loose architecture of concerns, comprehensive, heterogeneous, often redundant, and yet also fluid, to the point of eclecticism. Usually they are divided into three major categories: first, synchronic analyses of the mind and passions; second, historical accounts of the origins and development of mankind and social institutions; and third, the postulation of ethical principles derived from these studies. A contemporary reader, looking into a text in moral philosophy, would expect to find, in varying degrees, analytic descriptions of the different faculties of the mind and the passions; discussions of primitive customs, economic processes, social forces, law and jurisprudence, aesthetics, education, and ethics; accounts of the origin and progress of civil government and of human institutions, such as language, the family, religion, property, justice, and affluence; and, of course, the articulation of principles of conduct.

Adam Ferguson's *Institutes of Moral Philosophy* (1796), originally written as a course in pneumatics (essentially psychology) and moral philosophy, usefully summarizes, as Gladys Bryson has observed, "what a teacher would regard as the essentials of his subject matter and method" (*Man and Society* 31). After the introduction, the *Institutes* begins as follows: part 1, "The Natural History of Man"; part 2, "The Theory of Mind"; and part 3, "Of the Knowledge of God." The "Natural History of Man" is divided into two chapters: "The History of the Species," which deals with anthropological concerns relating to the human form and aspect, habitations and modes of subsistence, varieties of races, life duration, population, arts and commerce, civil inequalities, political establishments, language and literature; and "The History of the Individual," which treats of consciousness, animal sense and perception, observation, memory, imagination, abstraction, reasoning, foresight, propensity, sentiment, desire, and volition. Here we see the complementarity of the history of the individual and of the species that was of such importance to Wordsworthian autobiography. Part 2, "The Theory of Mind," sets out its laws. Part 3, "Of the Knowledge of God," deals with the idea of God and our notion of a future state. Following part 4—"Of Moral Laws, and their most general Applications"—Ferguson takes up in part 5, "Of Jurisprudence," the rights of mankind, those of possession, property, and command, and how they are acquired and defended. The final two divisions, parts 6 and 7, deal with casuistry and politics.

This extraordinary range of subjects and concerns was usually beyond the structural limits of a single work. Consequently, a complete system of moral philosophy was rarely a single text, but instead a multitextual structure, composed of individual works of varying forms (treatises, essays, dissertations, abstracts, and lectures) on diverse subjects. Adam Smith, for instance, wrote on moral sentiments, on the origin of languages, on ancient astrology, on jurisprudence, and on the nature and causes of the wealth of nations. Hume, in his *Treatise of Human Nature* (1739), originally intended to develop a full system of logic, morals, criticism, and politics. However, after writing the first two books, in which he provided a systematic description and classification "of the understanding" and "of the passions," he limited his discussion, in the third and final book, to an examination of morals. Here, the synchronic classifications of the first two books give way to hypothetical genealogies of the origin and development of justice, promises, allegiance, civil government, laws of nations, and chastity and modesty. Hume never completed this massive philosophical project; however, in his philosophical essays, in which he rewrote portions of the *Treatise* and added essays on the origin of natural religion, on enthusiasm and superstition, and against miracles, one can see how he endeavored to produce a coherent system in which each essay would contribute to the larger framework of concerns announced in the *Treatise*. Lord Kames's work can serve as a final example of the scope of moral philosophical concerns. After his *Essays on the Principles of Morality and Natural Religion* (1751), he turned, in the *Historical Law-Tracts* (1758), to a history of the origin and development of law. Then, taking up Hume's suggestion that criticism could be reduced to a science, Kames wrote the *Elements of Criticism* (1762). In 1774 he concluded his system with an expansive "anthropology of morals," the conjectural *Sketches of the History of Man.* [20] As its title suggests, the work consists of a series of "sketches" of the historical development of various social institutions.

Regardless of the textual configuration that moral philosophical texts finally took, it is important to stress that their very existence was of major importance to Wordsworth, because it showed that an encyclopedic project of the scope of *The Recluse* was possible (at least in prose) and not merely, as many critics have assumed, one of Coleridge's many "Bright Bubbles of the aye-ebullient brain!" (*STCL* 1:209). The vast systems of Kant and Hegel were not anomalous, but were culminating expressions of the totalizing vision of late eighteenth-century moral philosophy. Moral philosophy provided Wordsworth with a model for how one might write a coherent, encyclopedic, multitextual poem, built upon a loose grouping of discrete poems of varying lengths, on different subjects, and in diverse genres. It suggested how collections of "short essays," as Wordsworth speaks of *Lyrical Ballads* in his 1800 preface, might be linked to larger treatises, such as *The Prelude, Home at Grasmere,* and *The Excursion,* and how analytical discussions of the mind (both of the individual and of the human race) could be seen in relation to narratives about the genesis and stage-by-stage development of human society and institutions. In short, it indicated what concerns should engage Wordsworth's attention, how he might approach them, and how such a heterogeneous set of poems, when "properly arranged," might be viewed as part of "the main Work" as the "cells, oratories, and sepulchral recesses" function in "a gothic church" (*ProseW* 3:6).

One could examine, at this point, Wordsworth's various classification schemes in order to show that he sought to organize the poems according to the characteristic concerns and principles of moral philosophy. In his classification of 5 May 1809, for instance, he organizes the poems into an eight-stage history of the human mind, combining a history of the individual with that of the species (*MY* 1:334–35). Coleridge also described the project in moral philosophical terms, as a poem that would combine a history of the progress of sensation— from feeling, to touch and taste, to seeing and then hearing—with a history of "the Human Race in the concrete . . . Fallen men contemplated in the different ages of the World, and in the different states— Savage—Barbarous—Civilized—the lonely Cot, or Borderer's Wigwam—the Village—the Manufacturing Town—Sea-port—City—Universities." This history, he believes, would illustrate the necessity for "a general revolution in the modes of developing & disciplining the human mind" (*STCL* 4:574–75).[21] However, my purpose is not to reconstruct *The Recluse* as an eighteenth-century moral philosophical text, thus pouring new wine into an old bottle. A knowledge of these moral philosophical concerns will serve a better purpose if it allows us to recognize the distinctive ways that Wordsworth took up these concerns in individual poems. On one hand, we will see the poems in a different light: as poetic "essays" on specific moral subjects, not only on the faculties of the mind (as in the 1815 classification of *Poems*), but also on the origin and progress of social institutions such as the family, property, religion, myth, poetry, and language. On the other hand, it will allow us to discern how the poems achieved their modernity in their departures from and displacement of this textual paradigm.

The Moral Experiment

Moral philosophy was not simply a heterogeneous collection of ideas, topics, and concerns. It also constituted a recognizable rhetoric, with a specialized vocabulary, specific modes of inquiry, methods of argumentation, and narrative forms. If we are to understand the implications of Wordsworth's assertion in the Advertisement to *Lyrical Ballads* that "the majority of the following poems are to be considered as experiments" (*ProseW* 1:116), we need to go beyond examining the ways in which he took up the subjects of moral inquiry in order to explore how he reshaped its "experimental" language. Though the goal of moral philosophy was to become a science of moral conduct, the equation of principles with beginnings during the Enlightenment led to the development of an extensive discourse on human origins. "Before we can ascertain rules of morality for mankind," Adam Ferguson declares, "the history of man's nature, his dispositions, his specific enjoyments and sufferings, his condition and future prospects, should be known."[22] In this book I do not attempt to examine the full extent of Wordsworth's employment of moral philosophical language, which would have meant writing my own version of *The Recluse*. Instead, I have restricted myself to one aspect of its concerns that is roughly equivalent to anthropology—the study of the origins and development of mankind in its widest sense.[23]

Rousseau's *Discourse on the Origin of Inequality*, a text that was exceedingly influential in Romantic accounts of human beginnings, is

typical of Enlightenment anthropological argument. "IT IS OF MAN that
I am to speak," he writes, "and the question I examine informs me
that I am going to speak to men; for such questions are not proposed
by those who are afraid of honoring the truth."[24] Writing as one man
speaking to all mankind, without appealing to divine authority, Rousseau promises to go beyond myth, to tell the "truth" about human
beginnings, a story that has remained hidden since the beginning of
time. "O man," he declares, "whatever country you may come from,
whatever your opinions may be, listen: here is your history . . . It is,
so to speak, the life of your species that I am going to describe to you"
(*Discourses* 103–04). Unlike sacred history, which explained the origin
of mankind by telling how human institutions had passed from God
to man through the reason of Adam, Rousseau's history describes how
primitive human beings, left to their own devices, invented the social
and cultural institutions that make thought and society possible.

Enlightenment philosophy faced a major difficulty when it came to
applying the "experimental method" to the study of human origins,
because these beginnings were no longer observable, having long been
lost in the darkness of time. "Like the statue of Glaucus," Rousseau
writes, "which time, sea, and storms had so disfigured that it looked
less like a god than a wild beast, the human soul, altered in the bosom
of society by a thousand continually renewed causes, by the acquisition
of a mass of knowledge and errors, by changes that occurred in the
constitution of bodies, and by the continual impact of the passions,
has, so to speak, changed its appearance to the point of being nearly
unrecognizable" (91). A new science was required, the "study of original man" (96).[25] But how is one to separate, Rousseau asks, "what is
original from what is artificial in the present nature of man," when
there is nobody on earth who has not already passed the threshold
separating man from nature? How can one gather substantial facts
concerning the origin of these institutions when their very existence
was a precondition of remembrance, record, and history? How is one
"to determine exactly which precautions to take in order to make solid
observations on this subject?" "*What experiments would be necessary to
achieve knowledge of natural man? And what are the means for making these
experiments in the midst of society?*" (92–93, author's emphasis). "Moral
experiments," proposed to provide "solid observations" of "natural
man," were thus a complicated desideratum, yet one of such impor-

tance that "the greatest of philosophers will not be too good to direct these experiments, nor the most powerful sovereigns to make them" (93).

Rousseau's appeal for an "experimental method" in moral philosophy echoes the concerns of his contemporaries. Hume first drew attention to the difficulty of making adequate "moral experiments." He argues that moral philosophy has a "peculiar disadvantage" in comparison with natural philosophy: "In collecting its experiments, it cannot make them purposely, with premeditation, and after such a manner as to satisfy itself concerning every particular difficulty which may arise. When I am at a loss to know the effects of one body upon another in any situation, I need only put them in that situation, and observe what results from it. But should I endeavour to clear up after the same manner any doubt in moral philosophy, by placing myself in the same case with that which I consider, 'tis evident this reflection and premeditation would so disturb the operation of my natural principles, as must render it impossible to form any just conclusion from the phaenomenon." Experiments in the moral sciences cannot be grounded in self-reflection, as Descartes would have argued, because the observer's "premeditation" and knowledge of the experiment interferes with the laws he is analyzing, vitiating his findings. Hume's answer to this problem is to make history his laboratory: one must first observe others, to establish moral principles, before one can make the circuitous journey back to the self. "We must therefore glean up our experiments in this science," he writes, "from a cautious observation of human life, and take them as they appear in the common course of the world, by men's behavior in company, in affairs, and in their pleasures. Where experiments of this kind are judiciously collected and compared, we may hope to establish on them a science, which will not be inferior in certainty, and will be much superior in utility to any other of human comprehension" (*Treatise* xviii–xix).[26]

The recognition that the principles of this science could not be established through self-reflection, but had to proceed through the observation of "others," made a burgeoning quantity of ethnographic material, supplied by travelers, missionaries, traders, and colonial administrators, of major importance to this new science.[27] Central to Enlightenment interpretations of these texts was the notion, summarized by William Robertson, that "in every part of the earth the prog-

ress of man hath been nearly the same," even though every nation
did not progress at either the same rate or to the same degree.[28] This
unequal, yet uniform, development meant that, at least in theory, almost all of the stages of human history were still available to the moral
philosopher. Properly interpreted, travel narratives and other ethnographic sources could provide a complete history of the human mind.
As Baron Turgot remarks, "The present state of the world, marked
as it is by these infinite variations in inequality, spreads out before us
at one and the same time all the gradations from barbarism to refinement, thereby revealing to us at a single glance, as it were, the
records and remains of all the steps taken by the human mind, a
reflection of all the stages through which it has passed, and the history
of all the ages."[29] If all cultures progress according to a universal
pattern, then the customs and values of other present-day peoples
could be used to understand earlier stages in the history of one's own
society, and vice versa. This principle, which was later to be called the
"comparative method," was integral to eighteenth-century anthropological inquiry. It was given its first enunciation in Joseph François
Lafitau's *Customs of the American Indians* (1724), when he speaks of the
"conformities" between North American native culture and classical
myth. "I have not limited myself," he writes, "to learning the characteristics of the Indian and informing myself about their customs
and practices, I have sought in these practices and customs, vestiges
of the most remote antiquity . . . I confess that, if the ancient authors
have given me information on which to base happy conjectures about
the Indians, the customs of the Indians have given me information
on the basis of which I can understand more easily and explain more
readily many things in the ancient authors."[30] The French anthropologist Joseph-Marie Degérando, writing at approximately the same
time as Wordsworth, argues that the observation of savage peoples
would contribute to the construction of "an exact scale of the various
degrees of civilization," exhibiting "what needs, what ideas, what habits are produced in each era of human society." He adds that such
studies are of central importance, because in these societies

> the development of passions and of intellectual faculties is much
> more limited, [so] it will be much easier for us to penetrate their
> nature, and determine their fundamental laws. Here, since dif-

ferent generations have exercised only the slightest influence on each other, we shall in a way be taken back to the first periods of our own history; we shall be able to set up secure experiments on the origin and generation of ideas, on the formation and development of language, and on the relations between these two processes. The philosophical traveller, sailing to the ends of the earth, is in fact travelling in time; he is exploring the past; every step he makes is the passage of an age. Those unknown islands that he reaches are for him the cradle of human society. Those peoples whom our ignorant vanity scorns are displayed to him as ancient and majestic monuments of the origin of ages: monuments infinitely more worthy of our admiration and respect than those famous pyramids vaunted by the banks of the Nile. They witness only the frivolous ambition and the passing power of some individuals whose names have scarcely come down to us; but the others recreate for us the state of our own ancestors, and the earliest history of the world. [*Observation of Savage Peoples* 63]

Degérando's assertion that savage peoples are even greater "monuments" than the "famous pyramids vaunted by the banks of the Nile" strikingly demonstrates how moral philosophy monumentalized other peoples. Reconstituted as anthropological artifacts, atavistic relics of "the earliest history of the world" (later known as "survivals"), they were read as "secure experiments" for the moral philosopher "exploring the past" and observing human origins. Every step that the traveler made over the earth could thus represent "the passage of an age."

The idea of conformities had two major consequences. First, though it is true that early modern ethnography banished the "monstrous races of men" from travelers' tales and philosophical texts, and the "opposite-footed" Antipodes, mouthless Apple-Smellers, man-eating Anthropophagi, Cyclops, Dogheads, and Giants were removed from the margins of texts and maps, where they originally appeared, now relegated to the status of fictions; it should equally be said that a new family of "savage" peoples appeared in the space vacated by these races.[31] Indians, Laplanders, Eskimos, Arabs, Hottentots, Patagonians (and Tierra del Fuegians), Kafirs, Caribs or Cannibals, South Sea Islanders, and black Africans were refashioned so that they could function as observable or empirical figures of human origins—savages, noble or otherwise. Second, though "conformities" implicitly valorized the culture of those who did the observing, they were not strictly a one-way street. Since the observer and the observed were part of the *same* history, "others" were a primary means of self-reflection, a way of recovering aspects of the self that could no longer be easily recognized. Where late nineteenth-century anthropologists, comforted by the idea of "race," could distance themselves from the cultures they observed, Enlightenment anthropology, even if it was guided by an ethnocentric belief that all cultures were on the way to becoming European, nevertheless assumed a greater degree of reciprocity in this relationship. Distance, however, was maintained in other ways. Since the moral philosopher constructing his "science of man" was usually far removed from the societies that provided the raw materials of his theories, moral inquiry was primarily a textual activity. The frontispiece to Lafitau's *Customs of the American Indians* emblematizes the laboratory of early eighteenth-century ethnography (fig. 1). Amid the clutter of medallions, statuettes, maps, and books, fragments of other cultures, mostly from the New World, Greece, and Egypt, a female writer, guided by the father-figure Time, is engaged in transcribing a divine vision of human beginnings, portrayed in a wall painting whose covering curtain has only recently been drawn aside.

When, in the Advertisement to *Lyrical Ballads,* Wordsworth declares that they were "to be considered as experiments . . . to ascertain how far the language of conversation in the middle and lower classes of society is adapted to the purposes of poetic pleasure" (*ProseW* 1:116), he is indicating the influence of another important aspect of eighteenth-century anthropological thought: its interest in language as a key to reconstructing human origins. Philology and etymological study developed, from Locke and Leibniz, through Vico and the philosophes, to the work of Horne Tooke in the latter part of the century, as an endeavor to read language as a document of the history of mankind. "Nothing is more useful for approaching the origin of all our notions and knowledge," writes Charles de Brosses in the *Traité de la formation méchanique des langues et des principes physiques de l'étymologie* (1765), citing Locke.[32] Turgot gives a fuller account: "The study of languages, well carried out, would be perhaps the best of logics: in analyzing, in comparing the words of which they are composed, in

Fig. 1. Frontispiece to the 1724 edition of Joseph François Lafitau, *Customs of the American Indians Compared with the Customs of Primitive Times*. Courtesy of the Beinecke Rare Book and Manuscript Library, Yale University.

following them from their formation up to the different significations
that have since been attributed to them, one would discover the thread
of ideas, one would see by what degrees, by what nuances mankind
passed from one to the other; one would apprehend the connection
and analogy which exist between them; one would succeed in discovering which ideas first presented themselves to man, and what order
they kept in combining these first ideas." This kind of study, Turgot
suggests, would be an "experimental metaphysics," "the history of
spirit of the human race and of the progress of its ideas, always pro-
portioned to the needs which have called them forth."[33] Don H.
Bialostosky has recently cogently argued that Wordsworth did not
view the poet as "a maker in the medium of language but a maker of
poems representing speaking persons."[34] The idea that Wordsworth
is concerned with demonstrating how the thoughts of particular individuals are embodied in the distinctive ways they speak can be usefully placed in this anthropological framework. The history of the
imagination is also a history of language, and Wordsworth, as he
sought to "enshrine the spirit of the past / For future restoration"
(*Prelude* 11.341–42), paid close attention to the languages of those
people in which this spirit was documented.

   In addition to history, comparative ethnology, and philological speculation, another aspect of the experimentalism of moral philosophy
must be considered before we turn to Wordsworth. Rousseau, when
he spoke of "experiments" that would give "solid observations" on
"natural man," probably also had in mind the proposals of Condillac,
Maupertuis, and Diderot that "metaphysical experiments" be constructed that would provide empirical evidence concerning human
origins. In a *Letter on the Deaf and Dumb* (1751), Diderot argues that it
is unnecessary "to go back to the birth of the world and to the origin
of language" in order to know how language was originally formed
and what is the natural order of syntax, because equal results can be
obtained by postulating a "Mute by Convention," someone who would
voluntarily forgo the use of articulate sounds and speak only by gestures. Such a person, Diderot remarks, "would be an excellent subject
of experiment," from whom one could infer what "order of ideas
would have appeared the best to the first men for communicating
their ideas by gesture." Diderot no sooner postulates this philosophical
fiction, however, than he has second thoughts about its validity, be-

cause this "Mute by Convention" might be tempted to model the arrangement of his gestures on the arrangement of linguistic signs,
which for him would be habitual. He therefore proposes that philosophers instead seek out a *real* mute, someone who had been "deaf and
mute from birth." Reflecting on the singularity of the idea of "turning
to one whom nature has deprived of the faculty of hearing and of
speaking in order to obtain true notions of the formation of language,"
Diderot explains that a deaf mute would be an ideal experimental
subject because he would not be prejudiced (by language) in the formation of his ideas; instead, he would pattern them according to the
laws of nature alone. And unlike "wild children," "those fictional
beings who exhibit no sign of culture, have very few perceptions and
almost no memory, and might easily pass for two-footed or four-footed
animals," a deaf mute could be readily observed.[35] Maupertuis, in a
section of the *Letter on the Progress of the Sciences* entitled "Metaphysical
Experiments" (1752), advocated the artificial fashioning of "wild children." Several children could be raised in isolation so more might be
learned about the origin of languages and whether linguistic differences were natural or cultural.[36] In each of these cases, eighteenth-
century philosophy takes up a specific stance toward marginal individuals, viewing them as keys for unlocking otherwise insoluble problems about human origins. Speculation proceeds primarily in one
direction, from text to observation, from a speculative problem to a
subject that will be the empirical means of its solution, from the theoretical construction of a *hypothetical* subject of observation to the seeking out of a *real* person who will live the theory that a hypothetical
subject can only act out.

It is ironic that empirical philosophy was preeminently a discourse
about marginal people. In its attempt to explain the normal functioning of the mind and senses and to establish general and universal
principles governing human nature and knowledge, it invariably
turned to individuals who suffered from one deficiency or another.
Consequently, there appeared in these texts a large number of marginal individuals who came to be subject to specific kinds of speculation and played a significant role in empiricist arguments about the
nature of man. This new family of marginal figures, observed within
society, complemented the moral philosophical interest in other cultures. The idiots, wild children, savages, hermaphrodites, hysterical

women, witches, fanatics, melancholics, the deaf, the mute, and the
blind may not originally have been subjects of philosophical investigation, but as they were sought out by philosophers and their stories
were circulated in philosophical texts, they were used to lend support
for empirical speculation. In describing these "remarkable cases," in
transforming marginal peoples into living laboratories where theories
about the origin of mankind could be tested and corroborated, medical, philosophical, and literary writing found a domain of shared
concerns, a place where fact and fiction, theory and observation, the
fantastic and the everyday could intermingle.

Many of these domestic marginal figures existed in texts before the
Enlightenment. Social outcasts, for instance, had played an essential
part in the demonstration of Christ's message in the Gospels. But the
advent of empirical philosophy changed how these people were represented, the kind of text in which they appeared, the authority that
made them speak, and the questions they promised to answer. In these
first "case histories," theory precedes the subject of observation, because the precondition for a marginal individual's being recognized
as significant, as being worth writing about in the first place, is that
empirical speculation has made him so. "Idiots," for example, had
long occupied an important place in biblical literature, and "wild children" were popular folkloric figures in classical, medieval, and renaissance literature; but they did not enter writing as subjects of
intensive observation until Locke's *Essay* initiated debates concerning
human development and innate ideas. Locke's theory of the mind as
a tabula rasa made them emblems of the mind in its natural state.
Consequently, they figured largely in the polemical debates concerning the status of innate ideas.[37] Similarly, melancholics, hysterical
women, witches, hypochondriacs, enthusiasts, fanatics, and the insane
belonged to a class of individuals whose spectacular "diseases of the
imagination" formed the basis of the empirical discourse on the nature and power of imagination and language. In peasants and children, giants and criminals, moral philosophers searched for surviving
elements of the mind, behavior, and physiognomy of primitive man.
It may be a coincidence that there were major advances in cataract
surgery in the decades immediately following Locke's hypothesis concerning what a man who had been born blind, but regained his sight,
might see. But this philosophical context made these operations fa-

mous and the case histories of blind people who had received these operations a focus of extensive discussion and writing. When William Cheselden published his "Account of some observations made by a young gentleman, who was born blind, or lost his sight so early, that he had no remembrance of ever having seen, and was couch'd between 13 and 14 Years," he was not simply announcing a new kind of empirical subject; he was also well aware that Lockean experimentalism had made such an individual worth watching and writing about. He was right. The "account" became famous and was cited by, among others, Voltaire, Diderot, Condillac, Buffon, Burke, Kant, Itard, and Anselm Feuerbach; and, of course, it was echoed by Wordsworth in "Tintern Abbey":

> These beauteous forms,
> Through a long absence, have not been to me
> As is a landscape to a blind man's eye.[38]   [lines 22–24]

Because textual concerns supervene upon life in a direct, though subtle and concealed, way in empirical discourse, we should be careful not to confuse the lives these individuals led in texts with the lives they led in the world (even if one objective of the experimental method was to try to make the two identical). In fact, except for the more famous wild children, Peter of Hanover, Victor of Aveyron, and Kaspar Hauser, we know very little about these people beyond what we learn of them through these philosophical accounts. These cases represent a specialized narrative form, which functioned as an integral part of empirical philosophical discourse. Like legal cases, which constitute a body of interpretations and precedents through which the legal profession thinks the law, or the case histories of psychoanalysis, which provide models for psychoanalytic interpretation and theorizing, these narratives, especially in the sphere of medicine, were more than simply illustrative examples. They were learned and passed from one philosopher/doctor to another as a vital element, part of the working grammar, of empiricist argument and knowledge. They were places where various texts converged upon and combated each other, where ideas were exchanged, and where philosophical hypotheses were tested on the bodies and minds of the observed. Often, when a more famous case was not repeated, it nevertheless provided the model for the structuring and interpretation of subsequent cases.

Through these cases, philosophers learned how to look at marginal individuals, what to observe, interpret, and write about. They learned how to transform marginal individuals into figures invested with clearly articulated speculative concerns and interpretations.

Eighteenth-century empirical philosophy was the means by which a specific group of marginal and otherwise anonymous people entered into writing and history. Philosophy made them significant, but it also exacted concessions. First, their lives were structured to meet the demands of these texts and to function as an idiom or working grammar within the language of empiricism. If they seem superficial, it is not because they actually were so, but because their cases sought to epitomize, simplify, illustrate, and clarify philosophical issues through their legibility. They were made to live for theory. To see one of these figures in a moral philosophical text, then, is already to know, even before the issue has been broached, what theoretical problem or problems are being developed within it. Cheselden, for instance, ostensibly records the impressions and conversation of the young man whose cataracts he removed, but these have been so edited and abridged that his life is presented less as biography than as a philosophical argument supported by biographical citation. Second, because these figures were brought to life in the crucible of the moral philosopher, we rarely hear a voice or come upon an idea that has not been anticipated. In the hands of Diderot, blindness can serve as a powerful tool to criticize our normal epistemological, moral, and metaphysical assumptions. Yet even when the marginalized speaker is a person like the Cambridge professor of mathematics Nicholas Saunderson, blindness remains an unhappy weakness until it has been taken up by the philosophe. "It is evident," writes Diderot, "that . . . Saunderson, with all his intelligence, did not understand the full force of the terms he employed, since he perceived only a part of the ideas attached to them. But who has not, from time to time, done the same? This accident is common to idiots, who sometimes make excellent jokes, and to wits, who say a foolish thing, neither one nor the other being aware of it." A similar instance of this denial of the marginal individual's ability to understand the discursive context and philosophical meaning of his statements occurs earlier in the letter, in Diderot's remarks on a blind man from Puiseaux. "I perceive well, gentlemen," said the blind man, "that you are not blind. You are surprised at what I do, but why are you not also astonished that I speak?" The man's obvious use of irony is lost on Diderot, who responds that "there is more philosophy, I believe, in this answer of his than he intended."[39] Another point should be stressed. Unlike the New Testament, Enlightenment philosophy did not seek to lessen the separation of these individuals from society. It did just the opposite, as it emphasized and accentuated their difference in order to increase their speculative value. The wholesale seeking out and marginalization of discursive subjects was an intrinsic part of anthropological inquiry.

Wordsworth's Domestic Anthropology

When Wordsworth, writing poetry that would show "how men placed in such or such situations will necessarily act" (*ProseW* 1:104), began to observe marginal individuals, he could not but have been aware of the important role that such figures played in Enlightenment speculation. He also must have been tempted to use them for similar purposes. In *The Prelude*, having recounted how he left the "heart-depressing wilderness" of the city to turn to the "sights" of the "public road" (12.145)—a passage that leads up to his assertion of his distinctive task as a poet—Wordsworth pauses, as he does before his own imagination in book 6, to reflect on his fascination for such people:

> Awed have I been by strolling bedlamites;
> From many other uncouth vagrants, passed
> In fear, have walked with quicker step—but why
> Take note of this?

His answer shows that this interest is fundamentally linked to moral inquiry:

> When I began to inquire,
> To watch and question those I met, and held
> Familiar talk with them, the lonely roads
> Were schools to me in which I daily read
> With most delight the passions of mankind,
> There saw into the depth of human souls—
> Souls that appear to have no depth at all
> To vulgar eyes.   [12.158–68]

Wordsworth's employment of the language of moral speculation is
explicit, as he emphasizes the need to "inquire / To watch and question" these individuals, as the means by which the "passions of mankind" and the "depth of human souls" can be "daily read." But
Wordsworth also subtly reshapes the emphases of this kind of inquiry
and its customary stance toward these people. In fact, the passage can
be seen as a critical rejoinder distinguishing his own anthropology
from that of the eighteenth century.

The most obvious difference is in the assumed relationship between
the observer and the observed: in this instance, it is the poet, rather
than the "uncouth vagrants," who is educated. These people are common or "vulgar" only to those who have not yet been "school[ed]" in
the art of reading others properly and so look on them with "vulgar
eyes." Another difference is that rather than drawing on the ethnographic descriptions of other peoples provided by travel narratives,
Wordsworth restricts his observations to people with whom he held
"familiar talk." His anthropology is conducted in a domestic context
and represents a knowledge formed from "daily" encounters on "public road[s]" (145). These "wanderers of the earth" are accorded all of
"the grandeur which invests / The mariner who sails the roaring sea,"
and yet they are born of an English landscape (153–56). In a famous
passage in the preface to *Lyrical Ballads,* Wordsworth writes that "low
and rustic life was generally chosen because in that situation the essential passions of the heart find a better soil in which they can attain
their maturity, are less under restraint, and speak a plainer and more
emphatic language; because in that situation our elementary feelings
exist in a state of greater simplicity and consequently may be more
accurately contemplated and more forcibly communicated" (*ProseW*
1:124). If we hear echoes, in this passage, of Degérando's assertion
that the simplified "passions" and "intellectual faculties" of savage nations allow the observer "to penetrate their nature, and determine
their fundamental laws," this is not by accident. It indicates the extent
to which Wordsworth draws on the same discursive context, but
through the monumentalization and observation of a different population of people—the marginal individuals he encountered in villages and in the public way. Readers have had no difficulty
interpreting statements such as this one as expressions of primitivism.
What they have not addressed is the scientific and anthropological

basis of such claims, in the assertion that through these individuals Wordsworth could "contemplate" and "forcibly communicate" an "emphatic" image of human origins.[40]

Though Wordsworth did not journey to Bali, Brazil, the African Sudan, Zambia, or Melanesian New Guinea, though he does not describe the customs of the Tupi-Kawahib, the Nambikwara, the Azande, the Ndembu, or the Trobriands, he nevertheless did bring an anthropological vision to the Lake District and the people who made up this society. His is a *domestic* anthropology, which seeks to give a "substance and life" to a specific way of life that he knew was disappearing. The motivation for this project certainly came from dissatisfaction with the way that these people had previously been represented. "Books mislead us," he writes, because "they debase / The many for the pleasure" of the wealthy "few" (*Prelude* 12.207–10). Criticizing "the utter hollowness of what we name / The wealth of nations" (the "hollowness" both of Adam Smith's book and of what it described), Wordsworth wanted to go beyond moral philosophy to speak

> Of man, no composition of the thought,
> Abstraction, shadow, image, but the man
> Of whom we read, the man whom we behold
> With our own eyes.   [12.79–87]

The confusion in this passage over whether this "man" is to be "read" or "beheld," "read" and "beheld," or first "read" and then "beheld"— an ambiguity compounded by the subsequent claim that "this glorious creature [is] to be found / One only in ten thousand" (12.90–91)— should warn us not to accept too easily a binary that places philosophical descriptions of "man" on one side and Wordsworth's observations on the other. What needs to be examined is the manner in which these "compositions" assisted Wordsworth in writing a domestic anthropology, even as he argued against them.

As I indicated earlier, eighteenth-century moral philosophy was primarily concerned with two marginal populations: other societies and marginal individuals observed within society., If we leave the more difficult issue of domestic marginals for later, one can argue that "savage peoples" generally enter Wordsworth's poetry through displacement and naturalization. A key goal of *The Recluse* project was to transfer the anthropological schemas and concerns that had been used to observe other cultures from texts to the poor and dispossessed of England. Dressed in homely attire, figures who would otherwise have been found in travel narratives (which were Wordsworth's favorite reading) are frequently transferred to new settings where, in a less explicit fashion, they support the same kind of inquiry as did their exotic counterparts.[41] Traces of this process of displacement are still discernible in many of the early experimental poems. Only one poem in *Lyrical Ballads,* "The Complaint of a Forsaken Indian Woman," depicts a figure who has not undergone transformation, its sources in Samuel Hearne's *Journey from Hudson's Bay to the Northern Ocean* (1795) being all too explicit. (Not surprisingly, this poem has not been appreciated by most readers.) Many of these figures undertake or have undergone some kind of journey, often a transatlantic crossing. They share with the Ancient Mariner the need to tell a tale; they speak a "theme" of "importance," even if, as in the case of the Discharged Soldier who had recently come from "the tropic islands," they feel "it no longer" (*Prelude* 4.446, 477–78). The narrator of "The Mad Mother" tells us that "she came far from over the main" and attests that she speaks "in the English tongue." Yet our need for such reassurance suggests that this woman, herself a figure of displacement, has far more exotic origins than one might initially assume. Geographical crossings often serve as metaphors for textual crossings. When the young Georgian youth of "Ruth" is introduced, wearing a "gallant" casque of feathers that "nodded in the breeze," the narrator observes that "from Indian blood you [might] deem him sprung." "But no!," he asserts, "he spake the English tongue, / And bore a soldier's name." Wordsworth indicated, in a note to the poem, that he had drawn his description of the flora of Georgia from William Bartram's *Travels through North and South Carolina, Georgia, East and West Florida* (1791). What he did not say, as E. H. Coleridge first observed, was that the frontispiece of the book (fig. 2) depicts a chieftain dressed remarkably like the Georgian youth (*PW* 2:510n). Instead of an outward movement, into the sphere of the exotic or into romance, Wordsworth returns these wanderers homeward and binds them to an English place. Other journeys display a similar domestic reworking of travel narratives and of the anthropological concerns that were developed in them. Among these, one might mention Peter Bell's moonlit ride; Johnny's "travel's story" ("The Idiot Boy," line 453); the instructions, by a re-

MICO CHLUCCO the LONG WARIOR
or KING of the SIMINOLES

Fig. 2. Frontispiece to William Bartram, *Travels through North and South Carolina, Georgia, East and West Florida* (Philadelphia, 1791). Courtesy of the Beinecke Rare Book and Manuscript Library, Yale University.

tired "Captain of a small trading vessel" (*PW* 2:512n), of how and
when one should make a journey to see a thorn; the return of a
brother from "the Indian Isles, / To his paternal home" ("The Brothers," lines 67–68); a blind Highland Boy launching a turtle shell from
the shores of Loch Leven; the reflections of "a traveller under open
sky" when, on returning from a twelve hours' journey, he comes upon
a group of gypsies he had seen before, "the same unbroken knot / Of
human Beings, in the self-same spot"; a poet revisiting a spot "a few
miles above Tintern Abbey" after a five years' absence.

Wordsworth's emphasis on an interactive, participatory mode of
observation also represents a qualitatively different notion of what
anthropology is. His ethnographic observations commonly are done
at close range, outside the security of Lafitau's cluttered study, with
all the possibilities of dynamic (also threatening) interchange and of
the subversion of stereotypes that close encounters imply. James Clifford has argued that "before the late nineteenth century the ethnog-
rapher and the anthropologist, the describer/translator of custom and
the builder of general theories about humanity, were distinct." It was
Malinowski, he argues, who "gives us the imago of the new 'anthropologist'—squatting by the campfire, looking, listening and questioning, recording, and interpreting Trobriand life."[42] Wordsworth's
anthropology does not claim the scientific authority that Malinowski's
did. Yet it does represent one of the most sophisticated and richest
descriptions of the values and beliefs of a locality that we have—and
it is probably the first text in the history of anthropology to pay as
much attention to the observer as to what he observes.

Wordsworth viewed the Lake District both with the eyes of an anthropologist, observing its people, customs, and beliefs with the detachment of a traveler visiting a different society, and with the eyes of
a man inhabiting its horizon of values. The same poet who tells us
that in the vale of Grasmere there can be no solitary response to
nature, because "look where we will, some human heart has been /
Before us with its offering" (*Home at Grasmere*, MS. B, lines 659–60),
is also the poet whom Hazlitt describes as scanning "the human race
as the naturalist measures the earth's zone, without attending to the
picturesque points of view, the inequalities of surface. He contem-
plates the passions and habits of men, not in their extremes, but in
their first elements."[43] Wordsworth writes that he felt a "wide . . . va-

cancy" separating himself from his past, yet nevertheless he felt that "those days" had

> such self-presence in my mind
> That sometimes when I think of them I seem
> Two consciousnesses—conscious of myself,
> And of some other being.   [*Prelude* 2.28–33]

Wordsworth's claim that he had a "double" self, an identity split into two parts, each vividly self-present, suggests that his anthropological reflection on "others" had an autobiographical component; it was the means by which he recovered that "other being" within himself. The outward glance was simultaneously a way of looking inward.

"Tintern Abbey" is typical of the manner in which Wordsworth relocated the customary site of anthropological inquiry into a domestic sphere. Though the poem has often been read as a private, strongly egotistical, almost mystical exploration of the poet's mind, he actually sought to make a much more universal statement, by using the history of a locality and a complementary autobiographical account of the genesis, growth, and education of his mind as the basis and pattern for a major moral philosophical statement of what humans have been, what they are, and what they ideally might become. "Tintern Abbey" is first and foremost an anthropological history, a synoptic version of *The Recluse*. Though Wordsworth concentrates on the differences between the "two" landscapes and the "two" selves manifested by his revisit to the Wye, the poem goes far beyond these two visits—as it points into the distant past, to a time that preceded the appearance and destruction of the abbey, and into the future, as the poet imagines Dorothy's return. It sets both the landscape and the observer within a larger interactive history, embodied in the site, of what humans have been and are through what they have done and do to nature. Like *The Prelude*, the history is sweeping in its simplicity, as it traces how, from loving a nature felt "all in all" (line 75), the poet, a representative of mankind, has learned

> To look on nature, not as in the hour
> Of thoughtless youth; but hearing oftentimes
> The still, sad music of humanity.   [89–91]

One should add that language is the implicit middle term of this tran-

sition, as is emphasized by the shift from "looking on" nature as a
"thoughtless youth" to "hearing . . . humanity." "Tintern Abbey" is
thus more than a history of landscape and a history of mind: it is also
a history of the mediating role that language plays in that relationship,
as a landscape made significant to a savage eye is displaced by one
constructed for the social ear.

The poem's relation to the picturesque tradition has often been
noted, especially Wordsworth's cribbing from William Gilpin's *Observations on the River Wye*. It also has sources in "topographical" or "revisit" poems, best exemplified by Denham's "Cooper's Hill" and Pope's
"Windsor Forest."[44] What makes it distinctively Wordsworthian, however, is the manner in which these traditions are set within an anthropological framework. James A. W. Heffernan has insightfully
noted that one reason why Wordsworth placed the site of the poem
"a few miles above Tintern Abbey" is that he wanted "the landscape
of the opening passage" to be "prehistoric rather than unhistoric,
prefiguring the abbey that is not so much absent entirely as not yet
there, waiting downriver in the flow of time."[45] Numerous instances
might be cited in which the speaker actively erases or ignores all signs
of culture in the landscape and uses language to construct a "wild
secluded scene" in Wales: "hedge-rows" becomes "hardly hedge-
rows"; "plots of cottage-ground . . . lose themselves"; "little lines / Of
sportive wood run wild"; and "pastoral farms" are "green to the very
door." Many readers have seen the "wreaths of smoke / Sent up, in
silence, from among the trees" as an imaginative idealization of landscape, but one might equally note that this smoke screens a disturbing
and almost complete disappearance of human society from the landscape. The twice-repeated word *wild* takes on its darkest meaning by
the end of the first verse paragraph as Wordsworth, from his vantage
point, sees this spot as a wilderness and finds only "some uncertain
notice" of human life in its least developed form: either "vagrant
dwellers in the houseless woods," an image that evokes Rousseau's
idea that primitive humans led "a wandering and vagabond life,"
everyone taking up lodging at random, "often for only one night,"
because there were "neither houses, nor huts, nor property of any
kind" (*Discourses* 120–21); or an equally popular eighteenth-century
image of man in an asocial state, a "Hermit's cave, where by his fire /
The Hermit sits alone."[46]

Though strong arguments have been made that the erasure of history in this opening passage expresses Wordsworth's evasion of politics, a fairer understanding of the poem can be reached by placing it within the context of what might be called "political anthropology."[47] Most political and moral arguments, especially of the more radical sort during the eighteenth century, were based on a notion of "natural rights," which led to their being inextricably bound up with reconstructions of an idea of a "natural state." For most theorists, Locke's declaration that "in the beginning all the World was *America*" made the New World the matrix of republican ideology and of beginnings.[48] For instance, Thomas Paine transforms America into an observable beginning for all governments: "The case and circumstances of America present themselves as in the beginning of a world; and our enquiry into the origin of government is shortened, by referring to the facts that have arisen in our own day. We have no occasion to roam for information into the obscure field of antiquity, nor hazard ourselves upon conjecture. We are brought at once to the point of seeing government begin, as if we had lived in the beginning of time. The real volume, not of history, but of facts, is directly before us, unmutilated by contrivance, or the errors of tradition."[49]

Wordsworth also wanted to move beyond "the obscure field of antiquity" or the hypothetical sphere of "conjecture" to "anchor" his thought "in nature and the language of the sense" ("Tintern Abbey," lines 108–09). And certainly the initial gesture of "Tintern Abbey" is to transform the Wye Valley into a domestic version of America, a prospect on "the beginning of time" that would provide the "case," "circumstances," and "facts" of a political and philosophical commitment, a "real volume . . . unmutilated by contrivance, or the errors of tradition." In practice, however, this project faced serious difficulties: only by a visionary stretch of the imagination could one consider Wye Valley, whose woods had long been artificially maintained to support the local industries, as nature in a "wild" state. Wordsworth might have ignored this difficulty, in the same way as Locke and Paine ignored the institution of slavery in America; he could have made the landscape "a few miles above Tintern Abbey" an empirical image of a state of nature. But what is extraordinary about the poem is that it makes the failure of the landscape to meet his philosophical and experiential needs—this "sad perplexity"—the actual motivation for the composition of the poem. By the end of the poem, Wordsworth's communal faith is not grounded in the site, but in the "lines" he offers to Dorothy and, by extension, to his readers.

Margaret Homans has rightly observed that Dorothy "enters the poem not in her own right but in answer to the poet's and the poem's needs."[50] Appearing after Wordsworth has admitted that he "cannot paint / What then I was" (75–76), when he has recognized that "that time is past" (83), Dorothy performs the same role for Wordsworth that savage peoples did for Degérando. Her "wild eyes" (119, 148) link her directly to the "wild secluded scene" that Wordsworth can no longer adequately experience. Drawing on the Enlightenment idea that all people pass through the same stages of development, Wordsworth claims that there are "conformities" between her present "wild ecstasies" (138) and what he once felt, when "like a roe / I bounded o'er the mountains" (67–68). He finds a way out of the impasse he had earlier reached, by reading *her* present experience as a "survival" of *his* past feeling:

> For thou art with me here upon the banks
> Of this fair river; thou my dearest Friend,
> My dear, dear Friend; and in thy voice I catch
> The language of my former heart, and read
> My former pleasures in the shooting lights
> Of thy wild eyes. Oh! yet a little while
> May I behold in thee what I was once,
> My dear, dear Sister!   [114–21]

This passage is a classic statement of the doctrine of conformities: as if Wordsworth were standing not on the banks of the Wye, but instead on the banks of the Susquehanna, as if the person were not his sister (only one year younger than he), but an American native, he claims that he can "catch / The language of my former heart" and "read" his "former pleasures" in her eyes. Wordsworth's stress on the semiotic character of his observation—that he is actually recovering a *language* that has been lost to him—reinforces the dichotomy between the two worlds of the poet and his sister, and suggests that what is being celebrated and documented in the poem is the meeting or "self-presence" (*Prelude* 2.28) of these two worlds and the discovery of the historical and educational framework linking them. The relationship is reciprocal: if Dorothy has allowed her brother to recover an experience that he has passed beyond, Wordsworth offers his sister the possibility, when her ecstasy has "matured / Into a sober pleasure" (138–39), of recovering in his absence her own history, now in a textual form, in the poem.

I do not want to underemphasize the ambiguities of this relationship, but I would also point out that one can overemphasize the marginalizing procedures of the poem. One can say that the poet's repeated expressions of love and friendship for his sister ("my dearest Friend / My dear, dear Friend . . . My dear, dear Sister!") framing this speculation are only a veneer that needs to be stripped away to expose what Wordsworth has really done: that is, made his sister into a marginalized object of observation, an English savage. But this form of interpretation proceeds in the wrong direction. Instead of seeing the poem as one that confronts and critiques the exoticism of eighteenth-century anthropology, as it brings the marginalized person as close as possible to the self, this kind of criticism returns the poem to the discourse that it emerged from. A marginal comment on a passage in Richard Payne Knight's *Analytical Inquiry into the Principles of Taste* dealing with the syntax of primitive speech makes Wordsworth's antagonism toward such inquiries quite clear: "What means all this parade about the Savage when the deduction as far as just may be made at our own firesides, from the sounds words gesticulations looks &c which a child makes use of when learning to talk. But a Scotch Professor cannot write three minutes together upon the Nature of Man, but he must be dabbling with his savage state, with his agricultural state, his Hunter state &c &c."[51] This comment is valuable because it indicates not only Wordsworth's familiarity, to the point of irritation, with the anthropological methods of the Scottish Enlightenment, but also his belief that the same results can be achieved at home, "at our own firesides," by observing "the sounds words gesticulations looks" and so on that a child makes in learning to speak.

So far, I have concentrated on the manner in which Wordsworth opposed the textualism and exoticism of eighteenth-century moral philosophy by resituating its characteristic concerns and figures in a domestic anthropology. He displays a similar stance toward the other group of marginal people, the "idiots," "wild children," blind, deaf, and mute people whose case histories formed a vital part of moral

philosophical speculation. It should be stressed that even though
Wordsworth's eye was drawn, almost involuntarily, to these figures,
and even though moral philosophy provided him with a system and a
vocabulary for interpreting these encounters, what is most remarkable
about his poetry is the degree to which it *resists* this fascination. These
individuals simply do not speak in the same way that their predecessors in moral philosophy did. They do not draw attention to themselves as philosophical figures or artifacts, laden with speculation.
Frequently, the link between them and the concerns that first made
them worth writing about is broken, so that they take on the appearance of emblems or allegories of a forgotten language or illustrations
to an absent text. What we call their sublimity is actually our "dim
and undetermined sense" that they represent "unknown modes of
being" (*Prelude* 1.419–20). We know that they are not commonplace,
that they speak with strange voices; but because their genealogical
lines of descent have been erased, they are difficult to decipher. Often
they seem to come from nowhere, like the leech-gatherer, who seems
a figure "met with in a dream" (110). At other times, they appear to
have forgotten who and where they are. Like the Discharged Soldier,
they seem so immersed in themselves that they forget to draw attention
to their sources and genealogies. Others, like the Blind Beggar and
the idiot boy Johnny, promise to clear up human mysteries that have
been hidden since the beginning of time. But such expectations are
never fulfilled. To Betty and, implicitly, to the narrator's urgent questions, Johnny, "a traveller bold," only replies, "'The cocks did crow
to-whoo, to-whoo / And the sun did shine so cold!'" And that is "all
his travel's story" (448–53)! The Blind Beggar is portrayed as "a type /
Or emblem of the utmost that we know" (*Prelude* 7.618–19), yet this
knowledge is no more than a simple history, scratched on a scrap of
paper.

It is not, however, from lack of attention that readers have failed to
recognize the philosophical genealogy of these figures. It is in the very
nature of a Wordsworthian poem that it comes into being by erasing
this genealogy. By not seeing the textual predecessors of these marginal figures, however, we remain unaware of the critical status of
their silence. We do not recognize that they have been silenced and
that this silence represents Wordsworth's resistance to the textual marginalization that these individuals underwent during the previous cen-

tury—in short, his attempt to write the Enlightenment discourse on
marginality out of existence by seeking to undo its pleasure in producing marginals and in taking rhetorical advantage of those who
cannot speak or who suffer from physical or mental hardships. Their
silence disrupts the moral, anthropological, and political framework
that brought the Enlightenment into contact with marginals and the
lower classes, allowing philosophers to speak through them by ven-
triloquism. Rather than unique stories, they tell the tales of those who
participate in the common life of everyone.

Wordsworth occasionally succumbed to the temptation of writing
moral philosophy through empirical figures. And even as he sought
to make these figures speak a new language and took up a different
speculative stance toward them, he was also developing his own rhetoric of marginality. Often he assumes a more elevated moral vantage
point than the less privileged people he describes. Even so, Wordsworth is more aware and more wary than most writers of the powers
that are brought into play when we describe others. If we frequently
feel uneasiness when reading his poems, this discomfort is part of
their meaning. Clifford Geertz's observation that the anthropological
absorption with the exotic—with Berber horsemen, Jewish peddlers,
French legionnaires—was "essentially a device for displacing the dull-
ing sense of familiarity with which the mysteriousness of our own
ability to relate perceptively to one another is concealed from us"
might equally be applied to Wordsworth's poetry.[52] By observing these
individuals, Wordsworth sought to uncover the mysteriousness of human relationships and of the self.

A Prophet of the Past

The Enlightenment representation of human origins was grounded
in a twofold activity. First, one had to reconstruct the physical characteristics and social organization of the primitive world, a project
supported by the anthropological reinterpretation of history, myth,
and Scripture, by the study of other cultures and the observation of
marginal individuals, and by Enlightenment geology. Then the philosopher placed himself imaginatively in this world, attempting to see
it through the eyes of the first humans. As Robert Lowth argues, it is

not "enough to be acquainted with the language of this people, their manners, discipline, rites and ceremonies; we must even investigate their inmost sentiments, the manner and connexion of their thoughts; in one word, we must see all things with their eyes, estimate all things by their opinions: we must endeavour as much as possible to read Hebrew as the Hebrews would have read it . . . He who would perceive and feel the peculiar and interior elegancies of the Hebrew poetry, must imagine himself exactly situated as the persons for whom it was written, or even as the writers themselves."[53]

Nicolas-Antoine Boulanger explains that "notwithstanding the obscurity into which it seems we must necessarily plunge by bounding over the limits prescribed to us by history; we shall want neither flambeau nor a sure guide to enlighten our research beyond them; to wit, when we penetrate into periods of darkness, which are by most people looked upon as imaginary, but where we shall find natural facts and human institutions. In order to clear up truth thus fallen into darkness, and force in their turn to be absorpt therein all the revered chimeras, that owe their existence to ignorance and imposture, there needs but to imagine ourselves for an instant, coexistent with those who were witnesses to the calamities the world was afflicted with; to examine how they were affected thereby, and to animadvert upon the natural impressions which those disasters must have caused in them, and the sentiments with which they were thence affected."[54] In order to penetrate "into periods of darkness" that had previously been looked on as "imaginary," the philosopher reconstructs the primeval world and then inserts himself into it.

This twofold activity is central to Wordsworth's poetry of origins. In book 12 of *The Prelude*, he argues that every poet, like every prophet, has a particular "sense / By which he is enabled to perceive / Something unseen before" (12.303–05). Then follows an extraordinary vision that the poet had during the dark months of 1793 when he was wandering across Salisbury Plain—Volney's reverie on the ruins of Palmyra raised to apocalyptic dimensions:

> While through those vestiges of ancient times
> I ranged, and by the solitude o'ercome,
> I had a reverie and saw the past,
> Saw multitudes of men, and here and there

A single Briton in his wolf-skin vest,
With shield and stone-ax, stride across the wold;
The voice of spears was heard, the rattling spear
Shaken by arms of mighty bone, in strength
Long mouldered, of barbaric majesty.
I called upon the darkness, and it took—
A midnight darkness seemed to come and take—
All objects from my sight; and lo, again
The desart visible by dismal flames!
It is the sacrificial altar, fed
With living men—how deep the groans!—the voice
Of those in the gigantic wicker thrills
Throughout the region far and near, pervades
The monumental hillocks, and the pomp
Is for both worlds, the living and the dead.   [318–36]

Wordsworth believed he had a special sense that enabled him to "look into past times as prophets look / Into futurity" (*PW* 2:480) and to hear in the distant winds "the ghostly language of the ancient earth" (*Prelude* 2.328). This idea of the power of imaginative reverie may seem an unusual one, but it represents a logical poetic response to the basic principles of Enlightenment anthropology. Since our understanding of early human life depends on our ability to imagine and set ourselves within this world, anthropological method would seem particularly suited to a poet. Through a method that is overtly theatrical ("I called upon the darkness, and it took"), Wordsworth sought to recover "the voice" of those victims that pervades the "monumental hillocks." Human beings were thus not removed from the present, but could be recovered experimentally in those times when he felt that he was walking in the world of the past and once more seeing it through savage eyes.

Wordsworth's special "sense" justified what was to become his central concern as a poet: the task of writing a history of the imagination. Eighteenth-century philosophers accorded the imagination a privileged role in the history of early mankind. Degérando observes, "The imagination is the first faculty to be studied in the Savage, since it is the one which nourishes all the others. The imagination is always the first faculty to develop in the individual; thus the development of this faculty will be the easiest indication for ascertaining the level occupied by that individual in the scale of intellectual advancement" (*Observation of Savage Peoples* 85–86). The ultimate anthropological goal of *The Recluse* was to show how the imagination "nourishes all" the other faculties, to represent this "scale" of imagination in all its complexity, the story both of what souls "do within themselves while yet / The yoke of earth is new to them" and of how passion shapes us into social beings (*Prelude* 3.179–80). Where Enlightenment philosophers organized their histories in terms of the progressive stages of economic and material life (hunting, shepherding, agriculture, industry, and so on), Wordsworth's "history of the human species" is keyed to the progressive powers and forms taken by the imagination. It is a history *of* the imagination, one that seeks to show the central role that it has played in the genesis and history of mankind and the transformations that it has undergone (and will undergo) in time. It is a history of how the imagination has entered into and shaped human institutions, such as property, family, language, and religion. It is also a history *by* the imagination, an imagination that could reflect "in its solemn breast / The works of man, and face of human life" (*Prelude* 13.171, 180–81). Wordsworth conceived this history in dialectical terms, as the story of how we become linked or bound to nature and to others through the power of the imagination to discipline itself. Thus, we are "framed / To bend at last to the same discipline" (*Prelude* 6.265–66).

The purpose of this book is to show how many of Wordsworth's shorter narratives and lyrics contributed to this anthropological history. Its major thesis is that many of the most distinctive and significant features of Wordsworth's poems emerged from the manner in which he took up, revised, and often submerged the characteristic rhetorical elements, forms, and concerns of Enlightenment moral philosophy and anthropology. Instead of employing a modern anthropological approach to these poems, I have treated them as anthropological narratives, indebted to, yet simultaneously at odds with, Enlightenment anthropology—as narratives in which the imagination constructs scenes, situations, or modes of feeling that have the status of experiments, contributing to a general history of the imagination and charting its importance in each stage or phase of human life and development. Though at times the nature of this enterprise requires that some little-known intellectual groundwork be laid, my objective is not simply to do intellectual history; my hope is that the reader's patience will be rewarded by the recognition of the specific ways in which Wordsworth, as he reflected on human origins, consistently drew upon and transformed the anthropological methods he inherited from the Enlightenment. The introductory sections of the chapters should not be understood as establishing sources, then, but instead as adumbrating the general outlines of specific discourses that Wordsworth confronted as he began to write about human origins. Since Wordsworth is primarily concerned with the question of how humans first made the transition between nature and culture, I have not organized the chapters as a progressive chronology, but as an examination of the institutions that Wordsworth felt were most important to that transition: specifically, language, poetry, myth, religion, death, and property. I have not attempted to answer the question "Which came first?" because Wordsworth considered them as being reciprocally intertwined. Since the imagination in all of its historical forms is both the subject and the source of this history, all of Wordsworth's poems are implicitly documents in that history, and I hope that this book will encourage others to recognize how other poems, which I was unable to mention, were connected to this discursive project.

It should be obvious to any reader that the prehistoric past that Wordsworth saw so vividly and with such immediacy there on the lonely plains of Sarum was a fiction. Like the subsequent reverie, born of his discovery of an "intricate profusion" of Druidic shapes, lines, and circles on Salisbury Plain, the scene that rose before his inner eye was "an antiquarian's dream" (12.342, 348), derived from an imaginative response to his reading. Wordsworth's special "sense" of the past was achieved, as it were, on the rebound, as he saw in his encounters with nature and with others a significance that his reading had originally buried there. Though this reverie is not characteristic of Wordsworth's mature poetry, this is not because the later poems are fundamentally different, but because in them Wordsworth developed a more sophisticated understanding of the past and of the ways in which he could represent it in poetry. One of the major arguments of this book is that Wordsworth's anthropological concerns lay behind his turn to autobiography. Notwithstanding the importance of Augustine and Rousseau, past criticism, by placing *The Prelude* within the traditions of spiritual autobiography and confession, has ignored the

poem's affiliations with conjectural histories. It is clear that Wordsworth understood the poem in anthropological terms, as a "progress
poem," recording "in verse, the origin and progress of his own powers" (*ProseW* 3:5). When he writes, "with my best *conjectures* I would
trace / The progress of our being" (*Prelude* 2.238–39, my emphasis),
he is stressing that autobiography is a key to the conjectural history
of the human species in general, "the progress of our being." By
reading his individual life as a recapitulation of the intellectual history
of the human species, Wordsworth was able to make the history of
"the discipline / And consummation of the poet's mind" (13.270–71)
an epitome of the anthropological history of the human imagination.
The division between anthropology and autobiography, between *The
Recluse* and *The Prelude*, should consequently be seen as a false one,
because the "experimental" language Wordsworth developed in reaction to moral philosophy also provided him with the vocabulary,
speculative framework, the categories, and the narrational structure
by which he organized his life and made sense of it. Anthropological
speculation made his life worth writing about, and conversely, his
greatest achievement lies in the ways he used autobiography as the
basis for a universal inquiry into the nature and powers of mankind.
The precondition for the appearance of the author himself in his
poetry, then, was the same as for the appearance of the marginal
people he observed: what Wordsworth saw in the people he talked
with, he also discovered in himself. The textual activity and modes of
discourse that motivated *The Recluse* were not removed from *The Prelude*: they were the fundamental language out of which Wordsworth
fashioned himself.

   This close link between autobiography and anthropology explains
why Wordsworth was best able to write about those times in his childhood and early adult life when he considered himself to be marginal.
In *The Prelude*, for instance, Wordsworth, having described a mad
Bedouin's scheme to save the fundamental elements of culture from
an impending flood, confesses that he "could share the maniac's anxiousness, could go / Upon like errand" (5.160–61). Wordsworth derived his sense of vocation and of poetic origins in an anthropological
project that proceeded through the observation of and identification
with marginal people. This productive identification suggests that it
is not by accident that the poetry we most prize is integrally and am-

bivalently bound up with marginality. It also indicates that the decided differences between *The Prelude* and *The Excursion* may have less to do with a decline in the poet's powers than with a change in his sense of his social position and, with it, a change both in the kinds of discourses he found available to describe himself and in the discursive relations he took up with the people he described.

The Origin of Language

Retrospective Tales of Idiots, Wild Children, and Savages

His language consisted mostly of tears, moans, and unintelligible sounds, or of the words, which he frequently repeated: "Reuta wahn, wie mei Votta wahn is."
—Anselm Feuerbach, concerning Kaspar Hauser

Sometime late in 1797 or early in 1798, Wordsworth, in the company of Coleridge and Thomas Poole, came upon a relatively uncommon sight, a moldering gibbet high among the Quantock hills. The circumstances that gave rise to this gibbet were unique: Poole related the gruesome story of the savage murder of a harmless idiot named Jenny by her husband, John Walford, in Dodington Common. Though the incident might seem to have been too crude and sensational to have had a lasting effect on Wordsworth's poetry, its powerful apposition of idiocy and violence was not easily dismissed. His first response was

51

moralistic. In "The Somersetshire Tragedy" and in parts of "The Idiot Boy," he criticized those unsympathetic representations of idiots that made them vulnerable to such cruelty, and he used poetry to compensate for what they might lack in feeling, appealing to the sympathy and passion of those who observe them. As the poet declares in his letter to John Wilson of 7 June 1802, the feelings delineated in the poem are "such as all men *may* sympathize with. This is enough for my purpose."[1] At the same time, however, Wordsworth was just beginning *The Recluse,* so there was also the temptation to use this story as a vehicle for inquiring into the origin of memory and language, speculation that previously had had little to do with sympathy.

"The Somersetshire Tragedy," probably written shortly after Wordsworth's receipt of Poole's written account, "John Walford," in March 1798, was destroyed in 1931.[2] It appears to have followed Poole's account fairly closely.[3] Walford was a tough charcoal burner, forced by his trade to "live day and night, except Sunday, in our mountainous, solitary woods, and most commonly alone" ("John Walford" 170). Poole emphasizes his "wildness" and—anticipating Wordsworth's description of the wild Georgian youth of "Ruth"—argues that constant exposure to the severity of nature had imparted "a kindred impulse" ("Ruth," line 130) to Walford's mind. Even his clothes have become like a second skin or animal covering: "The worse the weather was, the more he was obliged to be exposed to it: he never took off his clothes more than once a week, and it frequently happened that those clothes were wetted with the snow and rain, and frozen stiff on his back: but the heat of his body unfroze them, and the keen northeast wind, as they hung on his limbs, dried them" ("John Walford" 170).[4]

While working in the woods, this illiterate man met Jenny, "a poor stupid creature, almost an ideot . . . an ordinary squat person, disgustingly dirty, and slovenly in her dress" (170). Extant lines of "The Somersetshire Tragedy" emphasize her idiocy and place it within a context of education and discipline: "Her face bespake a weak and witless soul / Which none could think worth while to teach or to controul." Jenny bore Walford an illegitimate child, but by then he was attracted to Ann Rice, a miller's daughter. Walford's mother opposed their marriage, so Walford, in obstinacy and spite, returned to Jenny and, after once more making her pregnant, married her. Though outwardly their marriage was tranquil, Jenny received the brunt of his resentment. On Saturday nights, when he came home, she would linger in neighbors' houses, afraid to meet him. Wordsworth describes her suffering in what remains of "The Somersetshire Tragedy":

> Ill fared it now with his poor wife I ween,
> That in her hut she could no more remain:
> Oft in the early morning she was seen
> Ere Robert to his work had cross'd the green.
> She roamed from house to house the weary day,
> And when the housewife's evening hearth was clean
> She linger'd still, and if you chanc'd to say
> "Robert his supper needs," her colour pass'd away.

One night, less than three weeks after their marriage, while on a road to a public house, the two had an argument, and in a wild and lonely spot Walford murdered Jenny and left her corpse by the roadside. Upon interrogation, he claimed that after he struck her, "the devil put it into my head that now I might get rid of her at once, and I tried to drag her and tumble her into a deep mine shaft which was nearby: but I could hardly move her." Like the ass in *Peter Bell*, which is so heavy that Peter "might as well have tried to stir / The abbey huge of Westminster,"[5] Jenny "was as heavy as a church, and I took out my knife and cut her throat" (173). The supernatural thus appears as an excuse for the bloodiest of actions. Surprisingly, when one considers the extent to which Poole considered himself a humanitarian, he reflects very little on the brutality of the attack. With the neutral tone of reportage, he comments on Walford's dispatch: "He did it effectually; for all the muscles and great vessels on one side of the neck were divided, and a torrent of blood gushed out from the body . . ." (173). Idiots, it seems, count for little in either marriages or murder stories. The rest of the narrative recounts in detail the events that led to Walford's conviction, his journey in the cart to the place of execution, and finally—reaching its climactic conclusion with his passionate encounter with Ann Rice—his gallows confession, execution, and gibbeting:

She was lifted up into the cart; and, as she knelt on the straw, he bent down his head over her shoulder. They talked together nearly ten minutes, or rather he talked to her. No one heard what passed, nor do I find that she ever mentioned it to any one. The people, intensely interested, had their eyes fixed on them. He raised up his head for a moment, and then bent down, endeavouring to kiss her. The officer, who was by, held his arm, and said, "You had better not—it can be of no use." He then snatched her hand, and as she was drawn back, kissed it; some tears for the first time rolling down his cheeks. She was removed; and he, after recollecting himself for a few minutes, wiped his face, and said, "I am now ready" (178).

By the end of the narrative, Jenny has been all but forgotten.

From what remains of "The Somersetshire Tragedy," it appears that Wordsworth did not just identify with Walford, but also was troubled by the cruelty that Jenny had suffered. In "The Idiot Boy," written at approximately the same time, the issue is once more addressed, in terms of the effect that unsympathetic representations of idiots have upon the ways they are treated. In this poem, Walford's cruelty can be seen as only a more violent expression of a general indifference throughout society toward the suffering of idiots; unfeeling representations, by the rich and in law, philosophy, medicine, and literature, justified their increasing exclusion and confinement. Responding to John Wilson's criticism, Wordsworth writes that "the loathing and disgust which many peo[ple] have at the sight of an Idiot, is a feeling which, though having som[e] foundation in human nature is not necessarily attached to it in any vi[tal] degree, but is owing, in a great measure to a false delicacy, and if I [may] say it without rudeness, a certain want of comprehensiveness of think[ing] and feeling. Persons in the lower classes of society have little or nothing [of] this: if an Idiot is born in a poor man's house it must be taken car[e of] and cannot be boarded out, as it would be by gentle folks, or sent to [a] public or private receptacle for such unfortunate be[in]gs." His object in "The Idiot Boy" is to replace this "loathing and disgust," with a more traditional view of idiocy, which can still be observed among "the lower classes of society" and, as he further notes, in Switzerland and "in several parts of the East." There, idiots are often worshipped or considered "as a blessing to the family to which they belong," because they are seen as being closer to God. "I have often applied to Idiots, in my own mind, that sublime expression of scripture that, *'their life is hidden with God,'*" he writes. In opposition to predominant representations of idiocy, Wordsworth makes the idiot a figure of mystery, and thus of our own limits of understanding. Furthermore, he encourages his readers to learn from the lower classes to show greater sympathy toward idiots: "I have indeed often looked upon the conduct of fathers and mothers of the lower classes of society towards Idiots as the great triumph of the human heart. It is there that we see the strength, disinterestedness, and gra[n]deur of love."[6]

In "The Idiot Boy" humor is a defense against the ominous threats facing Johnny—his name is possibly a condensation of "Jenny" and "John." Anxiety is localized in his mother, Betty Foy, and her friend Susan Gale as part of a poetic strategy for displacing the real threats that faced an idiot separated from his family. The representations of a mother and an aging widow are set against the pre-established interpretive codes of the contemporary reader, the sleepy-eyed indifference of a country doctor who confesses, "What, Woman! should I know of him?" (260), and the thwarted efforts of the narrator who, as a would-be poet, seeks to transform the adventure into a sentimental or supernatural ballad.[7]

Betty's images of her son are imbued with passion and arise either from a vain, yet loving, overestimation of his abilities or from fear for his welfare:

> "Oh saints! what is become of him?
> Perhaps he's climbed into an oak,
> Where he will stay till he is dead;
> Or sadly he has been misled,
> And joined the wandering gipsy-folk."

> "Or him that wicked Pony's carried
> To the dark cave, the goblin's hall;
> Or in the castle he's pursuing
> Among the ghosts his own undoing;
> Or playing with the waterfall."   [222–31]

Where superstition leads Betty to produce an anxious fiction about Johnny's encounter with ghosts, the supernatural ballad of the novice poet relies upon the reader's willingness to turn him into one:

Perhaps he's turned himself about,
His face unto his horse's tail,
And, still and mute, in wonder lost,
All silent as a horseman-ghost,
He travels slowly down the vale.

And now, perhaps, is hunting sheep,
A fierce and dreadful hunter he;
Yon valley, now so trim and green,
In five months' time, should he be seen,
A desert wilderness will be!

Perhaps, with head and heels on fire,
And like the very soul of evil,
He's galloping away, away,
And so will gallop on for aye,
The bane of all that dread the devil!   [322–36]

In the narrator's trial forays in the popular supernatural ballad genre, Johnny is depicted as a threat, "a fierce and dreadful hunter," "the bane of all that dread the devil!" Rather than leading us to sympathy, the poet uses supernaturalism to distance us from idiocy, to marginalize Johnny, making us view him as a fearful otherness. The same superstitions that transform isolated and ostracized female beggars into witches—a subject that Wordsworth would later take up in "The Mad Mother," "Goody Blake and Harry Gill," and "The Thorn"—also transform the idiot into an apotheosis of evil. Rather than fearing for the lost boy, we are taught to fear for our possessions and to seek to exclude him. And these less than admirable attitudes are confirmed when the narrator, progressing beyond the initial image of a Skimmington Ride, treats us to an image of idiocy in flight—"He's galloping, away, away."

If Wordsworth's moral goal of replacing the exclusionary indifference and aggressivity of contemporary views of idiots with those based on sympathy and love is a relatively straightforward aspect of the poem, his attitude toward the philosophical interest in idiots is not. On one hand, the poem can be seen as a devastating burlesque of the "high seriousness" with which idiocy entered into the philosophical debates of the eighteenth century. Yet despite the comedy, Wordsworth was not immune to such seriousness, of which we perhaps catch a glimpse in the narrator's (and, later, Wordsworth's) insistence that Johnny's words are being transcribed verbatim ("His very words I give to you" [449]). We should not understand "The Idiot Boy," therefore, simply as a parody of the eighteenth-century speculative use of idiots. It is also a highly ambiguous narrative in which Wordsworth partly succumbs to the temptation to contribute his own philosophical discourse on idiots—a seriousness concealed in comedy.

Hypothetical Histories and the Enlightenment Discourse on Idiocy

It is probably not too great an exaggeration to say that the philosophical discovery of the idiot took place in the eighteenth century. Throughout the seventeenth century, he frequented the margins of knowledge, in the shadowy, undifferentiated world of Folly and Unreason, often unrecognized, often ignored.[8] Only with Locke's *Essay Concerning Human Understanding* does he suddenly emerge in philosophy as someone worth writing about—an observable approximation of human origins, a "blank page" or tabula rasa.[9] As one who, like the mute, stands outside language and exhibits only a rudimentary power of memory, the idiot occupies the threshold between nature and man, and could be seen as a figure linking the two states. Consequently, he was a privileged object of observation and commentary in the heated arguments of philosophers and theologians concerning the origins and conditions of language and memory and their role in defining man. Very much a treatise on memory, concerned with showing that all memory is a product of education and culture, Locke's *Essay* set the pattern for subsequent empiricist texts by using idiocy critically, as a central example supporting the polemic against the doctrine of innate impressions. "All *Children,* and *Ideots,*" Locke writes, "have not the least Apprehension or Thought of them" (1.2:49). The absence of these impressions indicates that no memories are "natural" or innate to man, but instead each must be produced; idiocy, then, is a state deriving from the inability to produce or retain memories. Locke further argues that if these individuals had such memories, they would "shine out in their full Lustre, and leave us in no more doubt of their being there . . . But alas, amongst *Children, Ideots, Savages,* and the grosly *Illiterate,* what general Maxims are to be found? What universal Principles of Knowledge?" (1.2:64). Locke designates here a family of privileged epistemological subjects—of which the idiot is but one member—who can play, through what they in varying degrees lack, a central role in the empiricist discourse on the human conditions of memory. The conventional explanation for the appearance of marginal people in Wordsworth's poetry, which ascribes it to sentimentalism, primitivism, or romantic nostalgia, is therefore only partly true—as true as it was for Locke, who also assumed their "simplicity." We need also to recognize that Wordsworth's interest in observing and writing about idiots, children, savages, and illiterates works within, even as it works against, the philosophical procedures of the Enlightenment.

The empiricist insistence on observation and experience was not without its own paradoxes, especially when it came to giving an account of the origin of human memory. Idiocy, as a state of forgetting in which sensations pass without being retained more than momentarily, would seem to be common to all humans, before they developed the ability to remember and then record events and impressions. But how this capability came into being, how mankind moved from a state of nature to culture, language, and memory, was unavailable to either observation or reflection. In the opening lines of his *Treatise on the Sensations,* a text that can serve as a model of how empiricists dealt with this problem, Condillac writes: "We cannot recollect the ignorance in which we were born. It is a state which leaves no traces behind it. We remember our ignorance only when we remember what we have learned. We must already know something before we can attend to what we are learning. We must have ideas before we can observe that we were once without them. Reflective memory which makes us conscious of the passage of one cognition to another, cannot go back to beginnings: it supposes them . . ."[10] How is one to give an account of the genesis of memory and the various faculties when such an account presupposes the existence of the very faculties it would seek to explain? In seeking to recover its origin, memory suffers from a structural infirmity, for its very existence indicates that it has already passed beyond the period of its genesis. Memory alone, then, cannot remember the conditions that made it possible.

This admission might seem a strange way to open a lengthy empiricist treatise adumbrating just such a history. However, it plays an important role in justifying Condillac's recourse to what was one of the most popular and characteristic of eighteenth-century empiricist discursive genres: the "hypothetical," "conjectural," or "natural" history. Dugald Stewart, in his discussion of Adam Smith's *Dissertation on the Origin of Languages,* summarizes the problem: "When, in such a period of society as that in which we live, we compare our intellectual acquirements, our opinions, manners, and institutions, with those which prevail among rude tribes, it cannot fail to occur to us as an interesting question, by what gradual steps the transition has been made from the first simple efforts of uncultivated nature, to a state of things so wonderfully artificial and complicated." Unlike earlier sacred histories, which explained the origin of human culture by referring to the biblical account of the divine dispensation of language and culture to Adam in Eden, these histories set out to explain how mankind, left to itself, might have invented human institutions. Yet the philosophical historian who would write such a history faces a conundrum, for "long before that stage of society when men begin to think of recording their transactions, many of the most important steps of their progress have been made." Though travelers' observations of "rude nations" can provide him with "a few insulated facts" about these beginnings, they are not enough to make up a "regular and connected detail of human improvement."[11] Consequently, the philosopher must have recourse to conjecture and surmise.

There was, indeed, an attempt to maintain the scientificity of these histories through an emphasis on method (they were to conform to reason and fact; they were to recount the *natural* history of human beings, without recourse to divine intervention; events were to be explained through their psychology and situation; and great effects were to be explained as the consequence of multifarious small and gradual changes). Nevertheless, it is clear that the empiricist quest for origins opened a space for a new kind of imaginative narrative. To recall Vico's story of the *giganti* wandering in fear on the mountain heights, astonished by the first advent of thunder and lightening, caused by the exhalations of the earth drying after the Flood; to read Boulanger's or Buffon's account of postdiluvian man, walking through the ruins of the world, traumatized by the Flood and feeling himself the continual object of vengeance and persecution by an irritated nature;

or to listen to Rousseau's tale of natural man, a mute and docile beast, unaware of death or disease, devoid of sexual drives, fearful, lazy, and concerned primarily with self-preservation—is to recognize the imaginative range of the hypothetical history. This kind of narrative presents a special and complex fusion of fact and fiction, textual speculation and observation. Adam Ferguson adumbrates what was later to become the standard criticism of these histories:

> The progress of mankind from a supposed state of animal sensibility, to the attainment of reason, to the use of language, and to the habit of society, has been . . . painted with a force of imagination, and its steps have been marked with a boldness of invention, that would tempt us to admit, among the materials of history, the suggestions of fancy, and to receive, perhaps, as the model of our nature in its original state, some of the animals whose shape has the greatest resemblance to ours . . . If there was a time in which he had his acquaintance with his own species to make, and his faculties to acquire, it is a time of which we have no record, and in relation to which our opinions can serve no purpose, and are supported by no evidence.[12]

Ferguson's uneasiness about the role of imagination in these histories anticipates the misgivings of modern sociologists and anthropologists, who, since the nineteenth century, have sought to distinguish themselves from their eighteenth-century predecessors by wholesalely rejecting the imagination. Yet by the end of the Enlightenment, these narratives were far more sophisticated theoretically than might be supposed. Though Michael Kearney, in 1775, criticized the role of the imagination in these histories, he nevertheless admitted their fascination:

> It hath ever been a favorite employment of the human mind to trace backwards events to an unfathomable obscurity; imagination hath here been indulged to an excess almost as romantic as in exploring futurity, and hath created a field of seemingly more probable, though equally illusive speculation; forcing its researches far beyond the limits of any means of information. Something however there is highly captivating in the earliest history even to sober minds . . . As the individual rises from the imbecility

of infancy to the strength of manhood, and thence sinks into
decrepitude; so has the species its stages of perfection; and to
retrace the steps by which a nation, now perhaps in the fullness
of refinement, ascended from barbarism to its present state, gives
a pleasure irresistibly engaging.[13]

Kearney's ambiguous attitude toward hypothetical histories, his
"sober" recognition of their "captivating" and "romantic" excess, suggests that writers in this genre were not unaware that they were bal-
ancing facts and fictions. Wordsworth's simultaneous fascination with
the fictional possibilities of the hypothetical history and his desire to
go beyond "a mere fiction of what never was" (*Home at Grasmere*, MS.
D, line 804) should not, therefore, be seen as solely a result of his own
sophistication, but was very much a reflection of the complexity of
these narratives by the end of the eighteenth century.

Condillac's "hypothetical history" is an account of the education of
the individual. Condillac puts forward the hypothesis of a statue that
is successively given its senses and then seeks to demonstrate, in an
imagined history of what the statue feels and knows at each stage in
the birth of its senses, the progressive genesis of all our faculties out
of sensation. But since empiricism understands itself as a philosophy
grounded in facts, he is unwilling to base his arguments solely upon
hypothetical demonstration and seeks empirical support in the story
of a "wild child" found in the forests of Lithuania in 1694. By so
doing, he allows us to see, in his movement from a hypothetical to an
empirical subject of inquiry, the experimental form that idiocy took
in eighteenth-century philosophy.

Idiocy did not enter philosophical writing unchanged, but instead
appeared in this exotic form, in accounts of wild children. An idiot
by situation and lack of education, rather than by nature, the wild
child was seen as a being whose feral isolation had prevented him
from learning or had led to his forgetting those cultural mechanisms,
notably language, necessary for thinking and remembering. Since his
idiocy was not congenital, it appeared that he was a "teachable idiot"
and could thus provide a crucial empirical link between the state of
nature and man: by tracing his education, one might recover the lost
stages in the history of man. Speaking of Peter of Hanover, one of
the most famous and controversial of eighteenth-century wild chil-

dren, Lord Monboddo declares that he considers Peter's history "as a
brief chronicle or abstract of the history of the progress of human
nature, from the mere animal to the first stage of civilized life."[14]
Throughout the eighteenth century, the wild child was inseparable
from hypothetical histories. Not only did he inhabit these texts, as an
empirical supplement to speculation, but his very nature was understood through them; they, in turn, were embodied by him: he was
read as a "brief chronicle or abstract," a recapitulation in miniature,
of the history of man. As a wild child, therefore, the idiot was every
bit a textual creature, a product of empirical theorizing, even as the
interest in this figure was sponsored by the desire to go beyond texts.

Though Condillac uses the Wild Child of Lithuania as an example
of a state of nature, he insists upon his subordination to the hypothetical history. He draws our attention to the fact that after the child
learned to speak, he was unable to give a retrospective account of
what happened in the forest: "As soon as he could speak he was
questioned concerning his former state, but he could remember no
more about it than we can remember what happened to us in the
cradle." Since memory is produced by culture, "it was perfectly natural for him to forget his first state . . . His life was a sleep interrupted
only by dreams" (*Treatise* 225, 226). The wild child suffers, as does a
normal person, from the structural infirmity of memory: once he has
been recovered from the forest, he cannot give a retrospective account
of "what he has heard" and "what he has seen." If even a wild child
cannot remember how he moved from a state of nature to society,
then the philosopher is justified in having recourse to the hypothetical
history to fill in those details. Not surprisingly, the chapter on the
Wild Child of Lithuania introduces a final chapter entitled "The Memory of One Who Has Been Given the Use of His Senses in Succession."
In it, Condillac's imaginary statue finally gives a complete account of
that dark scene in which memory and consciousness struggle into
being out of the pleasure and pain of pure sensation. Accounts of
wild children, therefore, can be seen as empirical supplements to the
hypothetical and imaginative reconstruction of a "primal scene" of
memory.[15]

The discovery of a wild child was usually an event of international
significance. This was certainly the case with Peter of Hanover. Caught

in a tree in the woods outside Hameln in 1724, Peter was an instant celebrity. He was brought to England, where he was placed under the observation of Dr. Arbuthnot, who wished to educate him and study his development. When, after two months, the project proved futile, he was lodged with a Hertfordshire farmer, with whom he lived, an aged child, until his death in 1785. Soon after his appearance, it was learned that he was a congenital idiot, the son of a widower named Krüger, who had recently remarried. Probably responding to a changed family situation (a home life that is certainly quite different from the one Wordsworth depicts in his letter to John Wilson), Peter had run away from home, and his new stepmother, it seems, would not allow him to return. So he was left to fend for himself in the woods. Regardless—that is, in disregard—of the true facts of the case, many philosophers and natural scientists saw Peter as exactly the person they were searching for.

In one of the better accounts of Peter, in *Mere Nature Delineated* (1726), Daniel Defoe is reluctant to label him a wild child and argues against stories in circulation that he ran on all fours and climbed trees like a squirrel. Nevertheless, alluding to *Macbeth*, Defoe insists that those interested in Peter had not "brought an Ideot upon the Stage, and made a great something Out of Nothing."[16] Regardless of where he came from, the boy could answer important questions about the interrelation between language, thought, and feeling. He is, Defoe writes, "the very Creature which the learned World have, for many Years past, pretended to wish for, *viz.* one that being kept entirely from human Society, so as never to have heard any one speak, must therefore either not speak at all, or, if he did form any speech to himself, then they should know what Language Nature would first form for mankind."[17] Defoe's thesis, one shared by those who followed Locke, is that Peter is a being devoid of soul, that is, of rational intellect, feeling, passions, and desire, because he is devoid of language. "Words are to us, the Medium of Thought," Defoe writes, "we cannot conceive of Things, but by their Names, and in the very Use of their Names . . . we cannot muse, contrive, imagine, design, resolve, or reject; nay, we cannot love or hate, but in acting upon those Passions in the very Form of Words, and we have no other way for it" (39). The idiot's inability to feel is an issue, therefore, not simply of education, but also of language. If language is necessary for thought, feeling, and perception, idiocy can be viewed as a failure to acquire or a loss of language.

The centrality of language in Defoe's essay on human development is more apparent in his explanation of why Peter never developed beyond idiocy. He describes a person unable to produce or maintain impressions, unable to perceive or remember: "Nature seems *to him,* like a fine Picture to a Blind Man, ONE UNIVERSAL BLANK . . . He sees the Surface of it but seems to receive no Impression from it of one Kind, or of another" (27). Seeing without being able to feel or recognize is partly a result of aging; the mind loses its malleability in time. Defoe argues that it is only through language, acquired at an early age, that the mind retains its plasticity. Whereas a mute girl, who had developed a finger language, was eventually brought to speech through a painstaking discipline, Peter, now almost mature, demonstrates "the Necessity of early Education of children, in whom not the Soul only, but the organick Powers are, as a Lump of soft Wax, which is always ready to receive any impression; but if harden'd grow callous, and stubborn; and, like what we call Sealing Wax, obstinately refuse the impression of the seal unless melted, and reduced by Force of fire; that is to say, unless moulded and temper'd to instruction, by violence, Length of Time, and abundance of Difficulty" (61). The wild man presents a more complex educational problem than the wild child, because his memory has lost the ability to be readily molded and developed and requires a special kind of discipline, over and above that accorded wild children, if he is ever to be able to see and to feel—a discipline of "fire . . . violence, Length of Time, and Abundance of Difficulty."

An Idiot's Comic Rejoinder

Despite Defoe's denial, people familiar with the true circumstances of Peter of Hanover, as Wordsworth appears to have been, would have recognized that the Enlightenment had in fact "brought an Ideot upon the Stage, and made a great Something out of Nothing."[17] The idiot was a "blank page" in more than one sense, for he provided the crude material upon which was inscribed the language of philosophers. "The

Idiot Boy" is about this fictionalizing process, as it functions not only in the imaginations of mothers and supernatural balladeers, but also in empiricist philosophy. Through burlesque, Wordsworth undercuts the massive textual machinery, the carefully formulated questions and procedures, that transformed the idiot into an exotic being who held within his silence fundamental truths about human nature. Betty's fear that perhaps her son has "climbed into an oak, / Where he will stay till he is dead" (223–24) is not unfounded, for it appears—in the journalism that supported philosophical investigation—that any idiot found wandering alone in the woods was *made* into a wild child and did just that! In "The Idiot Boy," our expectations concerning the importance of this "case" are increasingly amplified until the final lines when, upon being denied these "truths," we realize that the poem has been about this process of amplification itself. In its fervor to show that nature and isolation were the causes of idiocy, the Enlightenment rejected the obvious possibility that the wild child found in the woods might simply be a "lost idiot." By insisting upon this alternative, Wordsworth allows us to see the wild child for what he is: an exotic invention of empiricist philosophy.

Wordsworth's debunking of the Enlightenment, however, does not prevent him from engaging in his own discourse on idiocy. The framework is clearly a domestic one, and we are not allowed to forget that Johnny is an "idiot" and not a "wild child." Furthermore, the account of his education moves in the opposite direction to that of Enlightenment philosophy, as Johnny learns rather than forgets to speak through his journey into nature. By breaking the conventional association of nature with idiocy, Wordsworth is thus able to argue for nature as an educative power. The poet's interest in education is apparent in the introductory lines. Betty Foy indulges in a romantic vision of her son as a quixotic hero on a quest and seeks to give him the finishing touches in horsemanship. Set somewhat topsy-turvy on his steed, he receives "o'er and o'er" a carefully ordered set of instructions:

Both what to follow, what to shun,
What do, and what to leave undone,
How turn to left, and how to right.   [52–56]

But Betty's "most especial charge," one that she strives to impress upon him through sheer repetition, is that he should come home:

> "Johnny! Johnny! mind that you
> Come home again, nor stop at all,—
> Come home again, whate'er befall,
> My Johnny, do, I pray you, do."   [57–61]

Throughout this lesson, Johnny has been brandishing his holly bough and shaking his head and the bridle, in a state bordering on ecstasy. Seeking some confirmation of his having understood her, Betty fastens upon these gestures and projects her own meaning into them. In a masterful construction of an incomprehensible statement, Wordsworth comments on Betty's claim that she comprehends her son: "his words were not a few, / Which Betty well could understand" (65–66). He shows that traditional pedagogy fails to teach Johnny how to remember; moments after she has finished, Johnny has "quite forgot his holly whip, / And all his skill in horsemanship" (84–85). Without memory, he lives entirely within the moment—his only feelings are pleasure and pain of an intensity unknown to those who can escape immediate sensation by remembering past sensations or anticipating future ones. Even his horse knows more than he; born with the innate knowledge that Johnny lacks—instincts, as the eighteenth century understood them—it "thinks" (112). As Angus Easson has observed, Betty will later find Johnny because she follows the horse's "thought processes as even she cannot follow Johnny's."[18]

Johnny's relation to language is at once a fundamental paradox and a major interpretive crux of the poem. In March 1798, at the same time as Wordsworth was reading Poole's "John Walford" and composing "The Idiot Boy," he writes:

> Why is it we feel
> So little for each other but for this
> That we with nature have no sympathy
> Or with such things as have no power to hold
> Articulate language.[19]

Here Wordsworth specifically addresses the basic weakness of eighteenth-century empiricist language philosophy: that in its insistence on language as a necessary precondition of thought and feeling, it cuts us off from nature (from "such things as have no power to hold / Articulate language") and from "each other." Wordsworth treats language as a primary social institution; but he also recognizes that if we deny its roots in nature and preverbal feeling, we deny ourselves the basis of community. Wordsworth was well aware, as any critic nowadays would be, of the difficulty of demonstrating the limits of a linguistically based philosophy. Frequently, as in the *Intimations Ode,* where the "deaf and silent" child is nevertheless portrayed as a "best Philosopher," he resorted to paradox to assert these limits. In "The Idiot Boy," we are placed in the similar position, as we are denied access to what Johnny knows. Instead, we are given a drama of conflicting interpretations.

In keeping with her loving overestimation of her son's abilities, Betty attributes speech to him. She has no difficulty understanding his "burr, burr, burr" as "the noise he loves" (100), a pure expression of joy:

> And Johnny burrs, and laughs aloud;
> Whether in cunning or in joy
> I cannot tell; but while he laughs,
> Betty a drunken pleasure quaffs
> To hear again her Idiot Boy.   [377–81]

It is crucial to recognize that the basic function of language in this joyful reunion is not to represent ideas, but to create *contact.* [20] Talking is like touching, and the "drunken pleasure" that Betty draws from hearing her son speak again is returned as she "holds" onto him tightly, kisses him "o'er and o'er again," cries, and "pats the Pony" (376–92). Inasmuch as the phrase "o'er and o'er again" recalls Betty's earlier attempt at pedagogy, it suggests that her mistake, at that time, lay in her assumption that her repeated instructions were being understood as more than simply the loving touch of words. It is only at the conclusion of the poem, on their return home, that she asks Johnny to use language for a different purpose, as representation:

> "Tell us, Johnny, do,
> Where all this long night you have been,
> What you have heard, what you have seen:
> And, Johnny, mind you tell us true"   [438–41]

Johnny's answer is famous for its brevity: "'The cocks did crow to-whoo, to-whoo, / And the sun did shine so cold!'" (450–51).

To the philosophical reader, familiar with the speculative interest in idiots found in the woods, this statement—an idiot's retrospective account of what happened to him in the woods—would have had a much different import. To an age that saw idiocy as a state excluded from language and memory, its very existence would have seemed to offer rare empirical support for an investigation of the origin of language and memory. For such a reader, the narrative's significance would not lie in its romance structure, but in its ability to document the events that preceded and made possible the appearance of these words. The importance of this statement is twice registered: by the narrator, when he parenthetically remarks that we are being given "his very words" (449), and by Wordsworth, when he commented that these words recorded verbatim were "the foundation of the whole" (*PW* 2:478). When the poem is read as a hypothetical history, using an idiot boy's journey into nature as the basis for speculation on the origin of language, narrative emphasis must be placed on the difference between Johnny's original powers of mind before he enters the woods, and the speaking and remembering idiot boy who concludes the poem. One can read through Betty's impassioned exaggeration of her son's abilities to recognize his utter lack of language and memory. His "burring" does not need to be understood as communication or play, but can equally be seen as a somatic and involuntary "noise" that his lips make, bypassing any intentions on his part: "his lips with joy they burr at you" (14), "now Johnny's lips they burr" (97), and "Johnny's lips they burr, burr, burr" (105). It is well to remember that the inability to feel the cold was a condition proverbially ascribed to idiots. The fact that Johnny loves this noise suggests that either "he is cold and does not know it" or "he says he is cold and does not know it." In either case, the orders of language and feeling are confused. In the former, Johnny suffers without being aware of it, because language is required if we are to know as well as to communicate pain; while in the latter, he stands outside the language he uses. It therefore comes as a surprise, when we next encounter Johnny, that he is now able to communicate his coldness: "'The cocks did crow to-whoo, to-whoo, / And the sun did shine so cold!'" The language is highly metaphorical, for a few words must achieve all his purposes. And the history is confused (the pun on "to who[m]? to who[m]?" captures brilliantly the fumbling emergence of personal identity; Johnny is not quite clear about either what happened or to whom it happened). But he nevertheless does display powers of mind and language that were previously absent. Thus, Johnny's "strange adventures" (341) in the woods constitute an educative process that is set against Betty's failed pedagogy.

It might be said that Johnny's nonsensical answer brings an age of interrogations of idiocy, aimed at recovering the "truth" of human nature, to a parodic end. Repeating the obstinate refusal of the Muses to satisfy the indentured poet's desire to "tell / But half of what to him befell" (339–40), it reduces the anthropological project of recovering a state of nature ("where man has been" and "what man has heard and seen"), through an idiot's retrospective account of himself, to pure metaphor—despite Betty's motherly admonition: "Mind you tell us true." Yet, as we have seen, in Condillac's account of the Wild Child of Lithuania's infirmity of memory, the inability to "go back to beginnings" (*Treatise* xxix) is itself a philosophical position that justified the recourse to hypothetical histories. "The Idiot Boy" does, indeed, allow us to draw conclusions about the state of nature and human development from Johnny's answer. It suggests that the world that first appears to human perception is fundamentally metaphoric. Only later, as language (and with it knowledge) develops, do "moons" and "owls" displace the cold suns and hooting cocks of primitive perception.

"The Idiot Boy" illustrates the complex manner in which Wordsworth, as he began to write a history of imagination, took up the philosophical questions raised by moral philosophical inquiry. In the poem, Wordsworth engages in a similar kind of inquiry, but one that is built on a critique of the marginalizing aspects of Enlightenment modes of anthropological observation. Instead of a wild child, we are given a village idiot boy named Johnny. The scientific claim of a disinterested observation of such individuals is countered by a powerful alternate view of Johnny's capacities, provided by his mother, and much of the tension and comedy of the poem derives from their opposition. Where the Enlightenment moral philosopher would transform him into an empirical key to universal human origins,[21] Betty sees her son as a village hero, a figure in a romance. "The Idiot Boy" is patterned on the role that lost idiots played in Enlightenment speculation, yet, like *Peter Bell,* which we will examine in the next chapter, it is a poem that is best understood as a *comic* hypothetical history. The resulting narrative, mixing irony, low comedy, satire, and burlesque with a philosophical reflection on human origins, has perplexed many readers who are unfamiliar with its discursive context. With a knowledge of this background, however, one can begin to recognize the extraordinary dramatic complexity and tensions within Wordsworth's early experimental poems.

First Encounters of the Primitive Kind

In Words-worth's poetry, encounters often proceed according to a clearly defined narrational pattern, as they make possible for their participants a passage between two worlds, from one that speaks immediately to the eye and ear—a wild and haunted world of mute fear and animal ecstasy—to another, whose sympathetic depths, like those of the heart, are built up and evoked by words. In "The Thorn," in the old mariner's recollection of his unexpected meeting with Martha Ray, this pattern is explicit:

"I did not speak—I saw her face;
Her face!—it was enough for me;
I turned about and heard her cry,
'Oh misery! oh misery!'"   [lines 188–91]

This passage encapsulates a specific kind of narrative progression: a speechless state, producing fear and allied with sight ("I did not speak—I saw her face") gives way to a new one in which emotion is conveyed in language, in the crude, passionate cry "Oh misery! oh misery!" Wordsworth emphasizes that a radical change has taken place, one that is arguably the origin of the sailor's ability to speak and remember, for this transition occurs only after he has "turned about," away from the image. Other poems exhibit a similar narrational movement. The speaker of "The Ruined Cottage," for instance, meets an itinerant peddler and by listening to his tale passes, as James Chandler has argued, from "the world of Rousseau's natural man, a world of sensations and inferences motivated alike only by animal appetite," to a perception of nature purveyed and informed by language (*Wordsworth's Second Nature* 128). "I see around me here / Things which you cannot see" (MS. D, lines 67–68), the Wanderer declares, as he begins the story that will teach the narrator the importance of narratives in conveying moral values. This narrative pattern, with its explicit anthropological significance, is built into most of the poems in which Wordsworth, as a speaking poet, stands out from the world and people he observes, as in "Tintern Abbey" or the *Intimations Ode.* Wordsworth's frequent use of this structuring pattern was not fortuitous, however, but suggests that he was reworking a topos not uncommon in eighteenth-century anthropology: the fiction of the "primitive encounter."[1]

The primitive encounter developed within the context of Enlightenment hypothetical histories. In a strategy that allowed these histories to accommodate and, at the same time, to circumvent the traditional Mosaic account of human origins, these histories begin after the Flood, when humans, scattered over the face of the earth and wandering alone in the great forests, were said to have forgotten the divine institutions that were originally given to Adam (the family, social laws, discursive reasoning, and language) and to have fallen (back?) into a state of nature. "All was forgotten, everything became unknown," writes Charles de Brosses. "This new state of so great a part of the human species, which has its necessary cause in a unique event, is a state of infancy, a savage state from which many nations have raised themselves little by little, and many others have but only partially emerged."[2] Vico also stresses that history begins "with the universal flood," when the sons of Noah, wallowing naked in their own filth and absorbing the rich nitrous salts of the early world, grew to the stature of giants, yet "were reduced, at the end of a long period, to the condition of beasts" (*New Science* 8–9). In Enlightenment hypothetical histories, the Flood (or, in some instances, the myth of Babel) is conventionally used as a device to divest humans of culture. It can therefore be seen as a textual strategy for conciliating "the authority of Scripture with the monuments of antiquity," a way of starting again from scratch, rewriting sacred history in anthropological terms without contradicting it (Rousseau, *Essai sur l'origine des langues* 520). The fact that these narratives begin with the Flood should not be seen, then, as a sign that the writer is engaged in a theological discourse on origins; in most cases, these beginnings served an antithetical purpose as they authorized and inaugurated a new kind of history that sought to shed light on those primal events, before the dawn of history, by which human beings as we know them came into being through their own actions, rather than God's.

Since postdiluvian solitaries repeated on a global scale the feral isolation of wild children, it is not surprising that they gave rise to interesting, if hypothetical, questions about how two of these nomadic strangers would act towards each other when, by accident, they met. How would another member of the human species appear to someone whose experience of "man" was limited to his own dreadfully weak self-understanding? What effect would such an encounter have upon his understanding of himself? How would the two communicate? And what role would passion and metaphor play in their encounter? Supported by questions of this kind, the primitive encounter developed into an elaborate philosophical fiction, useful for epitomizing in narrative terms the manner in which human society, language, and moral sentiments might have developed in the early postdiluvian world. In accounts already fraught with perplexities, the primitive encounter, like the notion of a "social contract" (whose hypothetical status was equally apparent to eighteenth-century philosophers), provided a useful theoretical model—a new kind of narrative form—for speculating on and conveying ideas about social and linguistic origins. It had the philosophical advantages of a scientific model, as it reduced society to its simplest terms, dramatizing how "the social sympathies, or those laws from which as from its elements society results," as Shelley ex-

plains, "begin to develope themselves from the moment that two human beings exist."[3] It also allowed the philosopher to depict origins
that might otherwise elude representation, because they must have
taken place over vast periods of time or because they defied logic. A
description of the progress made by two such individuals—from
speechlessness to language—could thus stand as an abstract of the
progress of mankind.

Enlightenment "Primitive Encounters"

> *Horatio.* Pray what Language did your wild Couple speak, when
> first they met?[4]

Mandeville's account of how a "wild Couple," initially brought together by sexual need, might have progressed from a language of
looks and gestures (the "Language of the Eyes" and of motions) to
speech first introduced the primitive encounter as a special philosophical narrative used to explain the origin of language.[5] Since Condillac incorporates many of Mandeville's ideas in his *Essay on the Origin
of Human Knowledge* (1746), a work that represents the most influential
speculative use of the primitive encounter, and since Wordsworth is
almost certain to have been familiar with it, a discussion of this essay
will be sufficient to indicate the general structure of this topos.[6] Beginning with the supposition "that some time after the deluge two
children, one male, and the other female, wandered about in the deserts, before they understood the use of any sign," Condillac seeks to
show how, by meeting one another, they might have invented language
(*Essay* 169). "Who knows," he asks, "but some nation or other owes its
original to an event of this kind?", a conjecture that authorizes his
own hypothetical history of the process whereby "this nation first invented language" (170). Viewing his *Essay* as a development of Lockean epistemology, Condillac argues that the intellectual operations of
the mind (those of analysis, fixing, linking, combining, reflecting
upon, and disposing of ideas) are only possible because of signs. Just
as many mathematical ideas and operations would be impossible without mathematical symbols, language allows us to *decompose,* and thus
to represent to ourselves successively, the elements that make up

thought or sensation. Therefore, as Condillac argues in the "Preliminary Discourse" to his *Course of Studies for the Instruction of the Prince
of Parma,* thinking can be said to be "an art, and this art is the art of
speaking."[7] "By gestures, by signs, by sounds, by cyphers, by letters,"
he writes; "by instruments so foreign as these from our ideas, we set
them to work, in order to raise ourselves even to the sublimest knowledge" (*Essay* 122). The progress of the human mind, as well as the
inequalities among individuals and cultures, depends entirely on the
proficiency we demonstrate in the use of signs. Limit someone to sight
and gestures, and you also circumscribe what he is capable of thinking.

Condillac's depiction of the encounter and progress of two postdiluvian wanderers aims at demonstrating, through the necessary inter-
linking of thought and speech, how human thought and, with it,
society came into being with the invention of language. Prior to meeting, the savage couple's thoughts would be limited to ideas produced
by either *accidental signs*—the habitual associations made between a
perceived object (an apple hanging from a tree) and an internal perception (the sensation of being hungry)—or *natural signs,* "the cries
which nature has established to express the passions of joy, of fear, or
of grief, etc." (51). Because these two kinds of signs lay outside of
their control, each being a product of the situations in which the
children found themselves, neither could be used to cultivate knowledge or to communicate. To recall, to compare, or to communicate
ideas voluntarily, the children would need signs that they could draw
upon at will, signs of their own making, whose meanings could be
institutionalized, and these "instituted signs," born of convention,
could only come into being through a sustained encounter.

Like Mandeville, Condillac stages the primitive encounter in a specific way, as a scene of specular instruction, in which one savage stands
before another who acts out his suffering: "He who suffered, by being
deprived of an object which his wants had rendered necessary to him,
did not confine himself to cries or sounds only; he used some endea-
vours to obtain it, he moved his head, his arms, and every part of his
body. The other *struck with this sight, fixed his eye on the same object,* and
perceiving some inward emotions which he was not yet able to account
for, *he suffered in seeing his companion suffer.* From that very instant he
felt himself inclined to relieve him, and he followed this impression
to the utmost of his power" (172, my emphasis). Suffering is here

communicated through a complex series of mimetic exchanges. The
one savage involuntarily signifies his suffering, with inarticulate cries
and with the movement of "his head, his arms, and every part of his
body" toward the desired object; meanwhile, the other, "struck with
this sight," involuntarily imitates the gestural expression of suffering,
fixes "his eye on the same object" and, suffering from "seeing his
companion suffer," seeks to relieve him. Sympathy, in its first form, is
neither an emotion nor a conscious act, but a bodily propensity to
imitate and thus repeat what is perceived long before the mind reflects
on it. The onlooking savage is "not yet able to account for" the feelings
born of this imitation, quite understandably, because their source is
foreign to him. Through frequent repetition, however, each learns "to
connect with the cries of the passions and with the different motions
of the body, those perceptions which were expressed in so sensible a
manner" (173). Having made this association, that is, having discovered the relation of sign and referent, the children would then be able
to mimic voluntarily the passions, in cases where they wished to communicate the circumstances that might give rise to a passion (for instance, to indicate danger one would mimic fear). By so doing, they
would institute arbitrary signs. The major philosophical problem of
explaining the origin of language is in this way surmounted.

Condillac's primitive encounter describes a theatre for the eyes that
initiates and becomes a theatre of speech. Handicapped by a tongue
that "was so inflexible," Condillac writes, "that it could not easily articulate any other than a few simple sounds" (174), the postdiluvian
couple would have generally resorted to bodily gesture (initially consisting of "contortions and violent agitations" [174]), and to intonation,
the raising and depressing of their voices by sensible intervals. In fact,
their facility in gesture and intonation would have been one of the
greatest obstacles to the development of speech, for these children
would have been reluctant to relinquish these languages, notable for
their power and expressivity, for speech, at a time when neither the
need for speech nor its vast possibilities would have been apparent.
For a long time afterward, therefore, conversation would have been
"sustained by a language intermixed with words and gestures" (176).
But eventually, as each succeeding generation increased its stock of
words and acquired a greater skill in articulating sounds, speech

would supplant the early languages of mankind, those of eyes, cries, action, and gestures.

Sympathy, manifested in specular mimesis, is the pivotal term in Condillac's account of the origin of language. Both a natural, prelinguistic, and prereflective mode of communication and the means by which spontaneous gestures or cries of passion are reproduced as signs, sympathy makes possible the transition from natural to instituted signs. A similar point is made by Adam Smith, when he argues that a "wild child," because he lacks the "mirror" provided by others, also lacks an idea of self: "Were it possible that a human creature could grow up to manhood in some solitary place, without any communication with his own species, he could no more think of his own character, of the propriety or demerit of his own sentiments and conduct, of the beauty or deformity of his own mind, than of the beauty or deformity of his own face. All these are objects which he cannot easily see, which naturally he does not look at, and with regard to which he is provided with no mirror which can present them to his view. Bring him into society, and he is immediately provided with the mirror which he wanted before."[8] "Who we are," as well as "who we think we are," depends on our ability to see ourselves reflected in the actions and eyes of others. Others provide us with the means of seeing ourselves, which we "cannot easily see" or which we "naturally" do "not look at." Conscience is also a product of our identification with what we imagine to be the sentiments of the spectators of our actions. "We suppose ourselves the spectators of our own behaviour," Smith observes, "and endeavour to imagine what effect it would, in this light, produce upon us. This is the only looking-glass by which we can, in some measure, with the eyes of other people, scrutinize the propriety of our own conduct" (*Theory of Moral Sentiments* 112). Self-reflection, then, always comes from the outside; it is always intrinsically social, as it is mediated by others.

What neither Condillac nor Smith addresses is the fact that sympathy, even if it is a primal human form of imitation, is dependent on an imagination that has already been domesticated. To sympathize with another person, one must first see him as being similar to oneself. Condillac minimizes and downplays the figural aspects of the imagination and passions in his version of the primitive encounter. Each child stands before the other as a mirror-image because his or her imagination does not distort the other, but instead acts *socially*, seeking, when confronted with differences, to produce resemblances.

Wordsworth's experimental poetry, with its explicit focus on marginality and the relationship between self and other, confronts this question directly. If sympathy is the expression of an already socialized or humanized imagination, then what is absent from Condillac's primitive encounter is an account of the origin of sympathy, a hypothetical history of the series of events, now lost in time, that first disciplined the imagination and made sympathy possible.

Rousseau and the "Giants" of Primitive Perception

Rousseau's account of the origin of language was of major importance to Wordsworth.[9] In the *Discourse on the Origin of Inequality*, Rousseau begins both with an acknowledgment of Condillac, who "perhaps gave me the first idea of it" (120), and with the criticism that the latter presupposed "a kind of society already established among the inventors of languages" (*Discourses* 120). As a corrective, he adds an earlier chapter to human prehistory by imagining what encounters would have been like before the appearance of sympathy. Like other "hypothetical histories," Rousseau's begins with an imaginative reconstruction of the postdiluvian world. "Having neither houses, nor huts, nor property of any kind," he writes, "everyone took up his lodging by chance and often for only one night. Males and females united fortuitously, depending on encounter, occasion, and desire, without speech being a very necessary interpreter of the things they had to say to each other; they left each other with the same ease" (120–21). The natural abundance of the primeval world easily satisfied human needs, so they wanted neither society nor language. The same persons "would perhaps meet hardly twice in their lives, without knowing or talking to each other" (119). As Rousseau declares, "Adam spoke, Noah spoke; Adam had been instructed by God himself. In scattering, the children of Noah abandoned agriculture, and the communal language perished with the first society" (*Essai sur l'origine des langues* 519).

Though sympathy, or pity, is the mainspring of human passion, a

law to both nature and man, Rousseau stresses that it would remain
"eternally inactive without the imagination, which sets it in play." Furthermore, it depends on our recognition of the likeness or conformities between ourselves and others. "How would I suffer in seeing
another suffer," Rousseau declares, "if I do not even know myself that
he is suffering, if I am ignorant of what there is in common between
him and me?" (*Essai* 517). As Hume had earlier declared, the "minds
of men" can stand as "mirrors to one another," because the imagination cooperates by producing similitudes. It is only because another
person "resembles ourselves," Hume writes, that he "has an advantage
above any other object, in operating on the imagination" (*Treatise* 365,
359).[10] Rousseau insists that postdiluvian solitaries, because of their
mutual avoidance of each other, were deprived of the means of comparison that make knowledge of oneself and others possible, so consequently, their "fellow-men were not . . . what they are for us"
(*Discourses* 144). "As soon as one man was recognized by another as a
sensible, thinking being, similar to himself, the desire or need to communicate his sentiments and thoughts made him seek the means" (*Essai* 501). This recognition, however, did not come easily or
immediately, but only after climatic and geographical conditions had
forced human beings to associate with one another.

Far from being sympathetic, the first human encounters would have
been governed by fear, ignorance, and violence. Lacking a general
idea of "man," so devoid of sympathy, knowing little, so fearing everything, early humans looked on others as enemies: "a stranger, a beast,
a monster were to them the same thing" (517). Though myths tell us
that the first world was a "golden age," Rousseau tells us it was "not
because men were united, but because they were separated . . . Human beings would attack each other when they met, but they rarely
met. A state of war reigned everywhere, and all the earth was at peace"
(518). Rousseau describes a primitive encounter:[11]

> Upon meeting others, a savage man will initially be frightened.
> His fear will make him see them as bigger and stronger than
> himself; he will give them the name *giants*. After many experi-
> ences, he will recognize that these supposed giants are neither
> bigger nor stronger than he, and that their stature did not cor-
> respond to the idea that he had originally attached to the word

giant. Therefore, he will invent another name common to them and to himself, such as, for example, the name *man,* and will leave *giant* for the fictitious object that had impressed him during his illusion. This is how the figurative word is born before the literal word, when passion enchants our eyes, and how the first idea it offers us is not the truth. [506]

Rousseau's suggestion that first encounters were not between "men," but between a fearful savage (who has not yet conceived of himself as a "man") and a "giant," shows clearly how Enlightenment anthropology took up and revised sacred history. Rousseau reinterprets the scriptural account of the "giants in the earth," the Nephilim, "mighty men . . . men of renown," born of the union of the sons of God with the daughters of men (Genesis 6:4), in order to make it yield a clue to primitive myth and perception. The book of Genesis is reinterpreted as a document of the psychology of first encounters, when the eye, enchanted by fear, euhemeristically transformed the other into a "giant." So the miscegenation between the sons of God and the daughters of men, which gave rise to the Nephilim, was not a physical but a perceptual event, involving supernatural and humanized ways of seeing. Postdiluvians, among them the ancient Hebrews, lived with giants because of the metaphoric nature of their perception, the distorting medium of "illusion"—the figures, imaginings, and supernatural myths—engendered when they fearfully scrutinized each other. Before sympathy and language could appear, "man" (both the word and the being signified by it) had to emerge from this perceptual twilight: the "giant" of primitive perception had to be banished, so that "man" could take his place.[12]

In order to explain how societies were first formed, Rousseau, anticipating Wordsworth, draws on catastrophist geology, arguing that the physical world in remote antiquity was radically different from the world of modern times. "Human associations," he writes, "are largely the work of accidents of nature: particular floods, extravasations of the seas, volcanic eruptions, earthquakes, fires sparked by lightning which destroyed forests, all were bound to frighten and disperse the savage inhabitants of a country and were bound to bring them together to make up their common losses: the legends of the calamities of the earth, so frequent in ancient times, indicate what instruments Providence uses to force humans to reunite" (522). Because early humans did not associate from choice, but from need, the beginnings of language and society are not to be found in the fertile regions of the earth, where they could survive alone, but instead in its more wretched areas, where human beings had to assist one another to survive. Necessity was, indeed, the mother of invention and passion the originator of language: in northern regions, where fire brought people together and need gave rise to passion and speech; and in the desert regions of the south, where a scarcity of water encouraged humans to associate in order to sink wells and build canals.

In the south, where families were originally formed and propagated solely by inbreeding, instinct rather than passion gave rise to preferences, and children "became husband and wife without ceasing to be brother and sister" (526), so it was not possible, in these primeval families, for a passion to be born that would incite its members to speak. To explain its appearance, Rousseau imagines another early scene, which took place at the wells long after the giants had been banished from the earth: "There the first ties among families were formed, there the two sexes made their first rendezvous. Girls would come to seek water for the household, young men would come to water their herds. There, eyes accustomed to the same objects from infancy would begin to see with increased pleasure. The heart is moved by these new objects, an unknown attraction renders it less savage, it senses the pleasure of not being alone . . . Under old oaks, conquerors of the years, an ardent youth will gradually lose its ferocity: little by little each became less shy with the other; in trying to make oneself understood, one learns to explain oneself " (525). Speech arose when passion made humans aware of the need for it—in that moment when a young man, having come to the wells to water his herd, first saw the strange figure of an unfamiliar woman from another family who had come to the well for water ("A girl who bore a pitcher on her head"? [*Prelude* 11.305]). At that moment, each felt the first stirrings of desire, an "unknown attraction," and the pleasure of no longer being alone (525).

"The Discharged Soldier"

"The Discharged Soldier" represents Wordsworth's first use of the primitive encounter as a narrational form. Though the poem was

ultimately incorporated in book 4 of *The Prelude,* it was first written
in the crucial period leading up to his announcement of the *Recluse*
project and made up, along with "The Old Cumberland Beggar" and
"The Ruined Cottage," the thirteen-hundred lines of *The Recluse* mentioned in his March 1798 letters to James Webbe Tobin and James
Losh. As I remarked earlier, it is likely that Wordsworth initially wrote
the poem as an introduction to *The Recluse,* one that proved unsatisfactory as the project developed and he turned his attention to *Lyrical
Ballads.* The major evidence for this view lies in the poem's extensive
textual allusions to the opening cantos of *The Divine Comedy.* For a
poet whose early political sympathy with the French Revolution had
undergone significant changes in response to events in France and to
a radical suppression of republican thought in England, Dante might
have seemed a kindred spirit. A fictional journey through an English
hell, in which the poet would converse with people living and suffering
in a land of sorrows, might have seemed an appropriate form for a
critique of statesmen "so restless in [their] wisdom" ("The Old Cumberland Beggar," line 68) and for a reevaluation of his political beliefs.
Whether we view "The Discharged Soldier" as the original introduction to *The Recluse* or not, however, the poem demonstrates in valuable
terms the manner in which Wordsworth, as he worked toward defining
his own distinctive poetic project, drew directly on the visionary tradition represented by Dante and reinterpreted it to conform with the
patterns of inquiry and concerns of eighteenth-century anthropological inquiry.[13]

There are substantial differences between the original version of
the poem and the revision that became part of *The Prelude,* so I will
primarily focus on the earlier text, which has been published by Beth
Darlington.[14] A brief examination, however, of the transitional passage
introducing the episode in *The Prelude* will be of value in providing a
framework for that discussion:

> Strange rendezvous my mind was at that time,
> A party-coloured shew of grave and gay,
> Solid and light, short-sighted and profound,
> Of inconsiderate habits and sedate,
> Consorting in one mansion unreproved.
> I knew the worth of that which I possessed,

> Though slighted and misused. Besides in truth
> That summer, swarming as it did with thoughts
> Transient and loose, yet wanted not a store
> Of primitive hours, when—by these hindrances
> Unthwarted—I experienced in myself
> Conformity as just as that of old
> To the end and written spirit of God's works,
> Whether held forth in Nature or in man.   [4.346–59]

Though caught up in the distractions of Cambridge life, Wordsworth claims that he nevertheless experienced "a store of primitive hours." As the editors of the Norton edition of *The Prelude* have suggested, these can be interpreted loosely to mean those "times at which Wordsworth responded with his original immediacy" (142n). I believe, however, that the poet is making the much stronger claim that in certain rare and privileged moments, he actually experienced a "conformity," in a strict anthropological sense, between himself and the primitive past—"conformity as just as that of old." Since "The Discharged Soldier" is offered as an illustration of one of these "primitive hours," it allows us to see how, at the point when Wordsworth was shifting toward an anthropological problematic, these moments were imaginatively reconstructed out of past experience.

In the preamble, Wordsworth depicts himself as a solitary wandering along a deserted "public way," which in the darkness and quiet of the night has been transformed into a primal region of "deeper quietness / Than pathless solitudes." The moonlight reinforces this illusion, for the road seems a "watry surface," reaching "to the ridge," as if the world were just emerging from the Flood, its dark, ebbing waters having only just receded, exposing the higher parts of the landscape (lines 2-7). Like the wandering Bedouin's identification of "glittering light" with "the waters of the deep" (*Prelude* 5.129–30), the idea of a flooded world is an optical illusion, a moonlight spectacle. Yet it is by means of illusions such as these that Wordsworth imaginatively entered into, and felt what it was like to live in, if only for a short while, an anthropological fiction. As readers of the Climbing of Snowdon and the Simplon Pass episodes of *The Prelude* have long recognized, mountainous ascents are frequently figures in Wordsworth's poetry for the recovery of origins. Mountains, especially the Swiss Alps and

Scottish Highlands, were seen by most eighteenth-century philosophers after Montesquieu as the last bastions of "genuine liberty" and the site of "earliest visitations" (*Prelude* 13.122–24).[15] Wordsworth's emphasis on the surrounding quiet, the "deserted . . . silence," the "silent road," "stealing with silent lapse to join the brook / That murmured in the valley" reinforces the impression that his upward journey, following the streaming road, is toward a source, a primal spot: "Above, before, behind, / Around me, all was peace and solitude" (3–25).[16] Moreover, his mention of the "steep ascent" (6) echoes Milton's description of "th' ascent of that steep savage Hill" that leads to Eden.[17] "Drinking in" (22) the stillness, almost as if it were a soporific or Lethean drug, the solitary poet succumbs to reverie, described by Rousseau as a state of "perfect, and full happiness . . . Nothing external to ourselves, nothing if not ourselves and our own existence."[18] It would seem that if Paradise is ever to be recovered, it must be discovered within, in that "happy state," bordering on a complete state of nature, in which images seem to rise "as from some distant region of my soul," bringing with them "a consciousness of *animal delight*" and "a self-possession felt in every pause / And every gentle movement of my frame" (28–35, my emphasis).

"Man's first sentiment was that of his existence," Rousseau declares, "his first care that of his preservation" (*Discourses* 142). Alone, the poet inhabits the "golden world" of Rousseau's postdiluvian wanderer. But this "first sentiment" of animal delight is short-lived and gives way to the "first care" of self-preservation, when, following a turn in the road, he comes upon an "uncouth shape" (38). Instead of being "disposed to sympathy" (16), he quickly hides behind "a thick hawthorn," so close "I could mark him well, / Myself unseen" (40–41). Few, to my knowledge, have remarked on just how odd this scene is, with the poet timorously peering from behind a bush. The emphasis upon his fearful vantage point, his "prolonged . . . watch" (84), and the successive transformations that take place in the "uncouth shape" first presented to his view, recall the specular staging of the "primitive encounter." Not only do we see what the poet sees, but we also see him actively and fearfully constructing this image. Only from a safer prospect, as his anxiety subsides, does he begin to see it more clearly:

> He was in stature tall,
> A foot above man's common measure tall,

And lank, and upright. There was in his form
A meagre stiffness. You might almost think
That his bones wounded him. His legs were long,
So long and shapeless that I looked at them
Forgetful of the body they sustained.   [41–47]

The observing poet sees both a "giant" ("A foot above man's common measure tall") and a ghastly spectre of Death, a "meagre" skeleton (because he attends to "his bones . . . / Forgetful of the body they sustained"), so weak that it can stand only by propping itself against what seems to be a gravestone.[19] The literary sources of this encounter are not difficult to discern. As Hugh Sykes Davies has observed, Wordsworth first saw figures such as these illustrating the pages of fairytales and books of romance:

> wooden cuts,
> Strange and uncouth, dire faces, figures dire,
> Sharp-knee'd, sharp-elbow'd, and lean-ancled too,
> With long and ghostly shanks, forms which once seen
> Co[uld never be forgotten.]   [*The Pedlar*, MS. E, 171–75][20]

The sources in Dante are equally clear. Halted in his life's journey by three fearsome animals—a leopard, a lion, and a wolf—Dante writes that he was thrust back "to where the sun is speechless." Then, "before my eyes there suddenly appeared / one who seemed faint because of the long silence"—the shade of Virgil. The Discharged Soldier is equally weakened and spectral, yet where the voice of Dante's under-world guide is a "fountain / that freely pours so rich a stream of speech,"[21] Wordsworth's sends forth only "a murmuring voice of dead complaint / A groan scarce audible" (79–80). Many readers have noted that the passage echoes another encounter in Hell: Satan's meeting with the dart-brandishing spectre of Death, that "other shape, / If shape it might be call'd that shape had none" (*Paradise Lost* 2.666–67). Yet what is equally obvious is that these visionary encounters are being subsumed within the larger anthropological framework of the primitive encounter. Since Wordsworth is not only looking back on his own past but also reflecting on literary tradition (specifically on the language of the sublime), we can see in this displacement the characteristic strengths and strategies of his poetry as it takes up and

revises inherited literary forms in the new terms provided by eighteenth-century anthropology.

Wordsworth is writing the same kind of history as Rousseau, for he
uses the primitive encounter to show how "the poor unhappy man"
(171) of the final lines of the episode replaces the "uncouth shape,"
the "giant," the ghastly skeleton of the first encounter. We see how
"man" first emerged from the impassioned figurations of primitive
perception. But rather than using the Bible as evidence of this process
of naturalization, he uses an actual encounter he once had with a giant
(who loses, incidentally, approximately three inches of height between
the 1805 and 1850 versions of *The Prelude*) as a staging ground for
recovering this experience within himself. The typical anthropological
methods of the Enlightenment are thus replaced by an autobiographical method, which focuses on the recollection of "primitive hours,"
each duly reinterpreted to emphasize their conformities with an anthropological fiction, when the poet "experienced in myself / Conformity as just as that of old." In these autobiographical fictions, the
narrator thus occupies at least three temporal registers: 1) as an autobiographical subject, 2) as an active agent seeing and doing things
in a staged drama whose setting is mankind's primordial past, and
3) as an observer/narrator using himself as an "experimental" subject
to support speculation about that past. It should be stressed that these
memories were not intrinsically significant; they did not press the poet
to seek appropriate anthropological forms. It was, instead, the concern
for origins that made them significant.

Using the phrase "I could mark" to signal a shift in the language
influencing his perception of the figure, Wordsworth tells us that the
man "was clad in military garb, / Though faded yet entire" (54–55).
During the 1790s, the reference to war and the West Indies would
have had an obvious political significance. It also reflects the traditional biblical association of giants with violence. Yet this emphasis on
the military dress of the soldier also introduces, in explicit terms, the
anthropological language that has been shaping the poem. In this
isolated man, no longer simply registering humanness by being "upright," but now seen as "half-sitting & half-standing," the poet sees
the survival, "faded yet entire," of Hobbesian man, for whom the
"state of nature" *is* the "state of war": "during the time men live without a common power to keep them all in awe, they are in that condition

which is called war; and such a war, as is of every man, against every
man" (*English Works* 3:112–13). A man found alone in the forest, apparently suffering from intense, feral isolation, he represents, as did
Johnny in "The Idiot Boy," an obvious subject of anthropological interest:

> He appeared
> Forlorn and desolate, a man cut off
> From all his kind, and more than half detached
> From his own nature.   [57–60]

"Long time I scanned him," Wordsworth writes, once more emphasizing that what is being described is not the man himself, but a certain
way of seeing him, how "he appeared." Transformed into one of Degérando's human "monuments" of early ages ("I wished to see him
move, but he remained / Fixed to his place"), the man is depicted as
lacking everything that might make him human:

> He was alone,
> Had no attendant, neither dog, nor staff,
> Nor knapsack—in his very dress appear'd
> A desolation, a simplicity
> That appertained to solitude. I think
> If but a glove had dangled in his hand
> It would have made him more akin to man.   [61–67]

The man seems to have no voluntary control over language: "from
his lips meanwhile / There issued murmuring sounds," a "murmuring
voice," and a "groan scarce audible" (70, 79, 80). We are thus brought
to the crucial moment in the primitive encounter when one man stands
before the other, as a figure of inarticulate suffering, seeking the sympathy that underlies and makes possible language.

   At this point, the poet, having through "prolonged . . . watch" sub-
dued his "specious cowardice," hails the figure, who is now seen as a
"Stranger" (84–87).[22] Language enters the narrative for the first time,
dramatically awakening him from his self-absorption:

> From his resting-place
> He rose, & with his lean & wasted arm
> In measured gesture lifted to his head
> Returned my salutation.   [87–90]

Wordsworth emphasizes the semiotic aspects of this encounter, as an exchange of two kinds of language, the poet's words and the soldier's silent "measured gesture." This meeting indicates the social and intellectual importance of language. "Speech alone," writes Herder, "has rendered man human" (*Outlines of a Philosophy of the History of Man* 233). The poet's questions about the soldier's "history," after "discourse on things indifferent / And casual matter" (91–95), can be seen as having the same speculative motivations as the interrogation of Johnny, ambiguously satirized in "The Idiot Boy." As the two men retrace their steps, the journey takes on the symbolical resonances of a classical catabasis, a descent into the Underworld. Wordsworth notes with "ill-suppress'd astonishment" the "tall / And ghostly figure moving at my side," as the soldier tells him a tale of "war & battle & the pestilence" (124–39). But in all he says

> There was a strange half-absence & a tone
> Of weakness & indifference, as of one
> Remembering the importance of his theme,
> But feeling it no longer.   [143–46][23]

The infirmity of the soldier's memory, his inability to speak with "feeling" about what he has undergone, reaffirms Condillac's assertion that we cannot, except hypothetically, go back to beginnings. The inaccessibility of such origins is further emphasized by the fact that by the time the two men reach the wood, "discourse had ceased. Together on we pass'd / In silence through the shades gloomy & dark" (148–49)—Dante's *selva oscura*. Nevertheless, like the highly metaphoric language of Johnny, the old soldier's account of how he was halted on his journey by the strange, unearthly howling of a dog does convey some information about the preconditions of language:

> He replied, "In truth
> My weakness made me loth to move, and here
> I felt myself at ease & much relieved,
> But that the village mastiff fretted me,
> And every second moment rang a peal
> Felt at my very heart. There was no noise,
> Nor any foot abroad—I do not know

> What ail'd him, but it seemd as if the dog
>
> Were howling to the murmur of the stream."   [128–36][24]

Both the poet and the soldier have passed from tranquil reverie into states of consciousness that correspond to the sublime. Though the soldier does not describe this prior state, it was documented by his "murmuring voice" (79) when the poet first encountered him; he seems to have imitated the "murmurs" of the brook in the same manner in which the dog "howled to the murmur of the stream."[25] Sublimity and the fear it occasions, "felt" to the "very heart," would seem to be a major precondition of consciousness. Unlike the poet, however, the soldier has not been able to pass beyond the sublime; he has fallen victim to it, becoming a figure "fixed to his place" (78), his murmuring voice now a "voice of dead complaint" (79), a dead language, yet one he cannot relinquish.

"The Discharged Soldier" is fairly typical of the kind of anthropological progress that Wordsworth began writing as he endeavored to recount the history of the imagination. It follows a movement (like Johnny's from the safety of the home into the dangerous wood and back again) from the beautiful ("harmonious imagery," "animal delight"), through a threatening state of sublimity and death, to a domesticated nature grounded on sympathy. Just as the soldier passes through a series of figural transformations, so too the poet's seeing undergoes a similar process of education and socialization. When he finally reaches his destination, a laborer's cottage door, the history would seem to come to its appropriate end, as he stands on the threshold of human society and we hear him speak for the first time, in a tone of "reviving interest, / Till then unfelt" (169–70). However, at this point a unique reversal takes place that calls into question the anthropological narrative that has framed this encounter and tells us much about Wordsworth's attitude toward the anthropological observation of marginal people. Having been reproved for not seeking "relief or alms," demanding from others "the succour which his state required," the soldier counters with an allusion to Lamentations 1:12: "My trust is in the God of Heaven, / And in the eye of him that passes me" (160–65). With the soldier's assertion that he depends on the sympathetic "eye" of passers-by, the charity and humanity of strangers, we are made to recognize that the social deprivation suffered by the stranger—"his state"—is not attributable to "savagery" within himself, but to the lack of charity, the sublime incivility, of the poet's "eye," which has repeatedly deprived him of human status. In a radical inversion of the customary Enlightenment relationship between the observing philosophe and the observed population of silent marginalized people, Wordsworth makes the observer the observed and admonishes him for his dehumanizing fictions. This critique extends not only to the poet's first impressions, when he hid behind the hawthorn, but also to his subsequent activity of selectively divesting the man of cultural attributes in order to increase his conformity with an anthropological idea of primitive man. It is not by accident that Wordsworth, having first declared that the man "was alone, / Had no attendant, neither dog, nor staff, / Nor knapsack" (60–62), having stressed that "if but a glove had dangled in his hand / It would have made him more akin to man," then adds, in the *Christabel* manuscript, that the man *did* have a staff,

> By me yet unobserved, a traveller's staff,
> Which I suppose from his slack hand had dropp'd,
> And, such the languour of the weary man,
> Had lain till now neglected in the grass,
> But not forgotten.   [117–21]

The final clause "neglected . . . but not forgotten" makes a forceful contrast between what the man *was* and *is*, and what the poet chose to see. A similar ironic moment occurs when the soldier, now addressed as "my comrade," "touched his hat again / With his lean hand" (156–67). Since the "again" refers us back to their first meeting, when "with his lean & wasted arm," the soldier "in measured gesture lifted to his head / Returned my salutation," we again see that the impact of the original description was as much dependent on what the poet and his readers did not see (in this case, the hat) as on what was described.

In an important essay Geoffrey Hartman has argued that many of the spectral qualities that we associate with figures like the Discharged Soldier derive from their genealogical link to the world of ballads and romance. "The archaic or literary forms subsumed by Wordsworth," he writes, "are the literal spooks of Gothic ballad or tale, and the etiolated personifications endemic to poetic diction."[26] From this perspective, we can see the Discharged Soldier as a figure of superseded fictions, a belated version of the Dantesque and Miltonic sublime. Written at a crucial moment in Wordsworth's career, the episode thus incorporates an idea of literary history that justifies the notion of a poetry of everyday life. For the "man" that speaks in Wordsworth's poetry to appear, "a man speaking to men" (*ProseW* 1:138), he had first to pass through the sublime underworld of a fear-enchanted past, whose vestigial traces and echoes can still be found in dreams and the fictions of romance. But the Discharged Soldier is also a shade from the Enlightenment, a figural relic of eighteenth-century anthropological method, which constructed figures like these in its quest for origins. In the poet's encounter with him, therefore, we are also given an allegory of Wordsworth's relationship to the obsolescent figures of Enlightenment philosophy.

Though it would be an exaggeration to say that anthropologists have not, until recently, begun to reflect systematically on the rhetorical and narrative aspects of anthropological inquiry, it is true that the current crisis in the concept of anthropological authority has led to extensive discussion of this issue and has brought contemporary anthropology much closer to the context in which Wordsworth wrote, where the division between science and literature was not clearly defined. This makes Wordsworth's anthropological methods of great interest. First, as I mentioned in the Introduction, Wordsworth's anthropology is distinct from most of the work done prior to the twentieth century in that it is grounded on direct observation and participation in fieldwork, not on the distanced synthesis of ethnographic documents. The public ways and pathways were Wordsworth's experimental laboratory. Second, Wordsworth denies any neutral form of observation or description. All display varying degrees of figural investment and blindness; all take a certain privileged stance toward the people they observe; all assume varying degrees of power over what they see. Whether by placing his observers behind hawthorn bushes or by employing the device of an intrusive narrator, Wordsworth continually draws our attention to the place, function, and intellectual limits of the observer in anthropological narratives. These narratives thus function in a complex, self-conscious manner, with a full recognition of the fictional status of the beginnings they portray. A third aspect is encapsulated in Jonathan Wordsworth's assertion that the Discharged Soldier is not foreign to the poet, but is "a curious version of himself " (*Borders of Vision* 12). Especially during the period of *Lyrical Ballads*, a close link is established between the observer and the observed, as both usually undergo an educative process. Wordsworth shares with the Enlightenment the notion that there is a single history for all humankind, an idea that in its positive form leads him to see aspects of his own development in others. What differentiates the poet and the soldier, a gap that grew larger in later years, is that there is a historical point beyond which the soldier, like Virgil in *The Divine Comedy*, cannot go. In the 1850 *Prelude* the anthropological distance separating the poet's world from that of the soldier is emphasized:

> And so we parted. Back I cast a look,
> And lingered near the door a little space,
> Then sought with quiet heart my distant home.   [4.466–68]

The passage draws heavily on the concluding lines of *Paradise Lost*:

> In either hand the hast'ning Angel caught
> Our *ling'ring* Parents, and to th' Eastern Gate
> Led them direct, and down the Cliff as fast
> To the subjected Plain; then disappear'd.
> *They looking back,* all th' Eastern side beheld
> Of Paradise, so late thir happy seat,
>
> . . . .
>
> The World was all before them, where to choose
> Thir place of rest, and Providence thir guide:
> They hand in hand with wand'ring steps and slow,
> Through Eden took thir solitary way.   [12.637–49, my emphasis]

In the image of the poet lingering near the cottage and casting a backward glance at a door no longer open to him, then turning toward his "distant home," Wordsworth repeats the gesture of Adam turning away from Eden, with a heart that has been made "quiet" by the discovery of a providential purpose operating in history. Only now the backward glance is that of the anthropological poet. The tale told by the Discharged Soldier functions, then, in many ways like the vision of history recounted by the Archangel Michael.[27] Here we see how anthropology defines Wordsworth's modernity, as the providential progress of human history displaces the providential divine history

set out in *Paradise Lost*. The final sentence, which (after being repeatedly questioned by copyists) was omitted from the first edition of *The
Prelude*, nevertheless indicates how uncomfortable Wordsworth was
with his own "High Argument" and the difficulties he found in arguing for it in any systematic way:

> This passed, and he who deigns to mark with care
> By what rules governed, with what end in view,
> This Work proceeds, *he* will not wish for more.   [4.469–71]

Though the language echoes Dante, the ambiguous italicized pronoun
reference (this is not Dante's "He") and the deferral of any explanation
of "rules" and "ends" reflect the way "this Work" belongs to the uncertain world of Wordsworth.

Descending to the Crude Metaphysics of Peter Bell

"In the night of thick darkness enveloping the earliest antiquity, so
remote from ourselves, there shines the eternal and never failing light
of a truth beyond all question: that the world of civil society has certainly been made by men, and that its principles are therefore to be
found within the modifications of our own human mind. Whoever
reflects on this cannot but marvel that the philosophers . . . should
have neglected the study of the world of nations, or civil world, which,
since men had made it, men could come to know" (*New Science* 96). In
this passage, Vico sets out a fundamental principle of eighteenth-
century anthropological thought, one that is central to the notion of
a "natural history of the human species": the idea that because social
institutions are "made by men," their origins and laws are to be found
in human psychology, in the historical "modifications of our own human mind" brought about by the institutions we create. Vico repeatedly criticizes social contract theorists, who make early man a
philosopher before he had become human and project back upon
mankind their own ideas and concepts. As an alternative, he insists
that the scientific treatment of beginnings should begin where its subject matter began, "from the time [man] began to think humanly."
Historiography requires a difficult intellectual descent. "To discover
the way in which this first human thinking arose in the gentile world,"

he writes, one must "descend from these human and refined natures of ours to those quite wild and savage natures," to the minds and experience, the "vulgar metaphysics" (100–01), of pre-human mankind, the "first men, stupid, insensate, and horrible beasts . . . the giants" (116). Vico stresses the difference between the primitive mind and our own: "It is . . . beyond our power to enter into the vast imagination of those first men, whose minds were not in the least abstract, refined, or spiritualized, because they were entirely immersed in the senses, buffeted by the passions, buried in the body. That is why . . . we can scarcely understand, still less imagine, how those first men thought who founded gentile humanity" (118). To the abstract, refined, and spiritualized eighteenth-century mind, the anthropological recovery of the contours of a world limited only by the vast bodily imaginations of its founders required a power of imagination that was clearly visionary, but also radically antithetical to the visionary tradition.

Though we have seen how, in "The Idiot Boy" and "The Discharged Soldier," Wordsworth began to take up the question of human origins, it was not until on or about 20 April 1798, after the majority of *Lyrical Ballads* had been completed, that he began writing a full-scale hypothetical history of the origin and development of human society, in *Peter Bell.* Here there is no nostalgic, primitivistic idealization of the powers of figuration of the world's first poets. Instead, Wordsworth attempts to sink "deep into the mind of Man," into "the darkest Pit / Of the profoundest Hell, chaos, night" (*Home at Grasmere*, MS. B, lines 984–89) bred by superstition and fear, to reconstruct imaginatively the "vulgar metaphysics" of the world's first humans.

Though the poem has not wanted readers who have appreciated its distinctive qualities, it is nevertheless true that they have not been great in number. Parodied and ridiculed during the nineteenth century, notably by J. H. Reynolds, Shelley, and Byron, it has largely been ignored during the twentieth, despite the fact that Wordsworth devoted an unusually great amount of attention to it.[28] There are a number of reasons for this critical disregard. The interpretation of comic narrative has never been a strong suit of romantic criticism. Nor has a criticism that has largely drawn its metaphysics and poetics from German and American transcendentalism and from Milton been much comforted by the strongly empiricist orientation of the poem—

its powerful image of the superstitions and violence of the primitive mind. Its employment of a bumbling narrator-persona, whose material seems to be always eluding his grasp, and its rollicking meter have also disturbed many readers. But even in the many excellent studies that have been done of Wordsworth's narrator-personas, *Peter Bell* often goes unmentioned.[29] This suggests that another reason for the poem's neglect is that readers have been unfamiliar with the genre of the hypothetical history, which it parodies. Few readers have wished to join Wordsworth in his visionary descent; few have wished to use their imaginations, as Vico argued, to see, through the fearful and aggressive eyes of Peter Bell, an image of their postdiluvian origins. The most important source of these misunderstandings, however, lies in Wordsworth's own ambiguous attitude toward the anthropological materials he develops in the poem. Where few readers have any difficulty appreciating *The New Science,* because Vico actually has faith in the narrative he is presenting, *Peter Bell* poses greater interpretive difficulties, because in it Wordsworth is simultaneously writing within and gleefully and ironically subverting eighteenth-century anthropological method.

The narrator-persona no sooner begins his tale than he becomes embroiled in a conflict with the preconceptions and interpretive assumptions of his audience—a small domestic circle consisting of nine people, among them a squire; his "pretty little daughter Bess" (124); Harry, the churchwarden; Parson Swan and his wife; and Stephen Otter:

> All by the moonlight river side
> It gave three miserable groans;
> "'Tis come then to a pretty pass,"
> Said Peter to the groaning ass,
> "But I will bang your bones."   [lines 156–60]

He is immediately taken to task. Mistress Swan cries that he has somehow "got at once into the middle," while little Bess queries, "who is Peter?" The Squire, thinking that his friend has gotten lost in the thickets of storytelling, attempts to help him onto the right path by reminding him of biblical origins—"'Sure as Paradise / Was lost to us by Adam's sinning / We are all wandering in a wood'"—and insists that he "begin at the beginning" (166–70). The inability of these listeners to see that the poet is starting in medias res points up both their ignorance of epic form and their differing expectations concerning how a story should properly proceed. The Squire's interruption introduces a different set of concerns, because it represents a criticism of the kind of beginning that the narrator has chosen. A tale that begins with so terrible and brutal a scene of violence in the wood is threatening, so his hasty admonishment of the narrator—"Begin at the beginning"— is at least partly aimed at reassuring himself and others that it will conform to their Christian expectations and to Genesis. It should be stressed that his anxieties are not without foundation: for more than a century, Enlightenment philosophers had been engaged in just such a task of providing, through hypothetical histories, alternative and often scandalous conceptions of human origins. This disruption thus serves an important purpose, as it reminds us that even though the tale is being delivered to a small, provincial gathering, it nevertheless is part of a context of competing views of human origins, each exerting its own pressure on its interpretation.

It would be easy to conclude that this story is exactly the kind of narrative that the Enlightenment was looking for: it moves from an account of the "origin of language" in Part First (which I will deal with in this chapter) to a "natural history of religion" (which takes up the remainder of the narrative and will be addressed in chapter 3).[30] In one sense, then, the tale is an expanded version of the idiot boy Johnny's verbatim report of his midnight adventure; it can be traced back to a wild vagabond's own account of what once happened to him in the woods. What must be stressed, however, is that the tale fits into and corroborates the interpretive schemas of eighteenth-century anthropology just too easily. In fact, it is so orthodox that it verges on wholesale parody. Like "The Idiot Boy," *Peter Bell* does not provide us with a simple "hypothetical history," but instead achieves its goals with destructive and parodic merriment. As a comic compendium of eighteenth-century anthropological method, the poem has its own fascinations and pleasures. Equally importantly, the poem merits our attention because it offers us the easiest access to the anthropological paradigms that Wordsworth began with and ultimately displaced in his mature work.

Tales do not become hypothetical histories without interpretation. A brief mention of these techniques is, therefore, in order because they make possible the movement, in Wordsworth's poetry, between fictional and anthropological paradigms. An obvious requirement is that the events of any narrative be seen as simultaneously occupying two temporal registers: as particular incidents in an anecdote, adventure, or tale, and as events typifying a larger anthropological drama that brought mankind into being. Selection is necessary because some narrated incidents may have been possible only at a certain place or time, while others must be emphasized as demonstrating human origins. This mode of interpretation also makes the sequential patterning of the narrative of major importance. First, the specific point when an institution or event is introduced into a story also indicates its origin and place in history. Second, narrative functions as a mode of historical explanation: earlier events serve as explanations for the genesis of subsequent events. From this perspective, the chronological disposition of events and institutions in *Peter Bell* is not unimportant, but allows the *tale* to serve as a *history,* making a journey through *space* into a journey through *time.* It is not by accident that the poem begins with a solitary individual wandering in the woods, who almost totally lacks any cultural affiliations, and that it concludes with Peter's socialization as he comes upon religion, a family, and community: it is through its chronological presentation of these events that the narrative explains the genesis and history of these institutions. When the particular events of Peter Bell's moral and intellectual development are generalized and projected back into the past, they can come to serve as reenactments of human origins.

Another aspect of this interpretive method, which I discussed earlier, is the employment of the concept of conformities. In *Peter Bell* the textual process that underlies the use of conformities is manifest. Peter can serve as a figure drawn from his listeners' past only after he has been stripped of culture to increase his conformity with the fiction of a postdiluvian wanderer. He is a composite figure, ostensibly drawn from observation, but fashioned to fit an anthropological template, a construct of Wordsworth's imaginative response to Thomas Poole's gallows-tale "John Walford," his memories of "a wild rover with whom I walked from Builth, on the river Wye, downwards nearly as far as the town of Hay" and who "told me strange stories," and his knowledge of a "lawless creature who lived in the county of Durham" (*PW* 2:527).[31] A "wild and woodland rover" (177), Peter is accorded the

"savage wildness . . . of a dweller out of doors," a "savage character"
in "his whole figure and his mien." His "unshaped half human
thoughts" (266–71), his cowardice, combined with his ferocity, cunning, and laziness, all suggest a prehuman being suffering from direct
contact with nature and the harsh effects of feral isolation. Not satisfied with describing the psychology of feral man, Wordsworth emphasizes the conformities between Peter and the animal world:

> He had a dark and sidelong walk
> And long and slouching was his gait;
> Between his looks so bare and bold
> You might perceive his spirit cold
> Was playing with some inward bait.
>
> His forehead wrinkled was and furred,
> A work one half of which was done
> By thinking of his whens and hows
> And half by wrinkling of his brows
> Beneath the glaring sun.   [281–90]

In his "long and slouching" gait, his "sidelong," crab-like walk, his
"wrinkled" and "furred" forehead, his furrowed skin (the product of
years of direct contact with winds, storms, and the "glaring sun"), his
cold, bare look, and even, in a marginal passage, his "snarling face"
(MS. 2, 44ᵛ), we are given an image of Peter as an atavistic survivor
of primitive man. He has no fixed lodging:

> He roved among the vales and streams,
> In the green wood and hollow dell;
> They were his dwellings night and day.   [211–13]

Nor does he show any idea of the importance of the family as a social
institution, for he has "a dozen wedded wives" (250). And families, as
Adam Ferguson observed, "are the nurseries of men; the basis of
empires, as well as of nations and tribes; and the compartments of
which the greatest fabrics of political establishment are composed."[32]
His is "a lawless life" (246). "To see him," as the narrator observes,
"was to fear him" (260). Prior to the events narrated in the story,
Peter's imagination has remained dormant—and with it, the power to
sympathize with nature or man. Having "never felt / The witchery of
the soft blue sky" (234–35), Peter has remained oblivious to the im-

pulses of nature, "never . . . a hair / In heart or head the better" (209–10). The awakening of his imagination will therefore play a crucial role in his education, as it leads him to sympathy for nature and mankind.

As if Wordsworth were unsatisfied with presenting us with his own version of Neanderthal man, on the night recounted in the tale Peter undergoes a further series of textual divestments. Usually he travels with his panniered asses and a semidomesticated "lurcher" named Ruffian, peddling his wares. Writers such as Count Buffon had argued that the domestication of animals was "the first mark of human civilization," so it should not surprise us that Wordsworth represents Peter, this night, as wandering alone.[33] Peter turns off the road and follows a sidepath through a "tall wood" to where it "ends" (325–40). The journey into these ancient woods, itself an anthropological reinterpretation of the Squire's idea a "wood of error," represents a movement back in time towards origins, just as, conversely, his later journey out of the woods symbolizes a historical progress. Reminding us of Degérando's "philosophical traveller," who in "sailing to the ends of the earth is in fact travelling in time" (*Observation of Savage Peoples* 63), Peter's is a journey back in time "with all the sail that he can carry" (338). The pathway ends in an old quarry, whose "huge rough stones," with their "black and massy shadows" and their unearthed "dark," "cold," and "yawning fissures old" (346–49), evoke the sublimity of a primeval world. Peter, responding to his environment, finds a corresponding language:

> "What back again, old grim-face? No!
> I'll grapple with the devil first;
> Stretch like a yawning wolf your paws
> But dam'me if by any laws
> Of yours I'll ever be coerced."   [341–45]

Though Wordsworth's contemporaries, as Henry Crabb Robinson noted, complained about the violent, "over-coarse expressions" (*Books and Their Writers* 1:241), Wordsworth dramatizes language in its crude metaphoric beginnings. With hardly a pause, Peter plunges through the sublime world of the quarry into a beautiful meadowland, its beauty wasted on him. This "deep and quiet spot" (376), with its "silent stream" (390), is not only a primal landscape, but also, as is indicated by the absence of sound (and a corresponding emphasis on sight) and by the narrator's emphatic "name it not" (358), a prelinguistic world: only a "strong and stormy gale," the violent passions that Peter, like the young child of "Nutting," brings to this bower, can bring sound to "that green spot, so calm and green!" (363–65); "All, all is silent, rocks and woods, / All still and silent—far and near" (first edition, lines 446–47). It is here, in this place without cottage, house, or hut, that Peter, "turning round his head," sees "the solitary Ass" (379–80).

As in "The Discharged Soldier," we are given a revisionary reworking of the fiction of the primitive encounter. Only now, in the meeting of wild man and ass, the topos is travestied. As we might have expected, the fundamental obstacle facing man and beast is their inability to communicate. Peter confronts a mute ass that, like Condillac's suffering primitive, resorts to a language of gesture, as "he hangs his head / Over the silent stream" (404–05), hoping that Peter will recognize his bodily stance as a sign, as pointing. But this visual gesture, this "station[ing] (415), proves ineffective. Peter faces similar difficulties. Resorting to the language of action, he seizes the halter, plies "with his staff and heels . . . The little ass on either side" (413–14), threatens the ass with a "new peeled sapling" (422), grabs the halter and gives it "another jirk" (431), attempts unsuccessfully to budge him, with each moment becoming more infuriated by its apparent lack of comprehension. So he deals the ass a blow, the first of many. The beast groans and drops to his knees; but as he does so, he turns "his shining hazel eye" toward Peter, as if to seek sympathy. Then he turns "the eye-ball in his head [itself less seeing than a *sign* of seeing] / Towards the river deep and clear" (first edition, lines 470–75), hoping that Peter will discover by imitating its gesture the reason for its suffering.

"How could it be? how could it be," the narrator asks in MS. 1 (thus drawing our attention to the absence of sympathy),

> That while the poor ass thus did lie
> On Peter's heart on Peters brain
> Not one impression did remain
> Of his large and shining eye.   [lines 326–30]

The ass's "large and shining eye," the specular image that should engender sympathy, has no effect upon Peter. Rather than being an innate passion, sympathy would seem to be a specific mode of human imitation that must be learned, by reading oneself out of an other's gaze. And within this discipline—the school of hard knocks—sound and language, the ear rather than the eye, are primary.

At this point the narrator finally reaches what was originally the beginning of his tale—that point when, having been beaten more furiously, the ass finally yields "three miserable groans" (477). It is the first appearance, though hardly a spontaneous overflow, of the language of passion. And these groans do affect Peter, who sees for the first time, as an 1820 revision indicates, the ass's "sharp his staring bones" (*PW* 2:349). Yet stare as much as they will, they do not incite sympathy: "No word of kind commiseration / Fell at the sight from Peter's tongue" (first edition, lines 492–93). Instead, he swears an "impious oath" (first edition, line 501) to murder the ass. And significantly, these words, invested with supernatural and sublime menace, have a greater effect upon the ass than did the language of action. In fear, epitomizing Hugh Blair's assertion that the "inflexions of voice . . . in the infancy of Language were no more than harsh or dissonant cries,"[34] the ass sends forth "a loud and horrible bray" (500). And this terrible cry, made human by Peter's imagination, "on the heart of Peter knocks." But rather than fostering pity, it strikes "like a note of joy" (502–03). Significantly, however, a vague sense of fear, close to sympathy, is conjured by "all the echoes south and north / And east and west" (498–99). "In the echo of the rocks / Was something Peter did not like" (504–05), "something" fearsome and threatening. Yet Peter, suffering from the weak memory of a wild man, returns to his "blind work" (first edition, line 515). Once more the ass lengthens out "the long dry see-saw of his horrible bray" (515), and once again it is not the immediate cry of passion but its echoes, sent back to Peter from "among the rocks and winding crags, / Among the mountains far away" (511–12), that elicit a response.

Peter's fear of echoes is not the fear of someone familiar with these phenomena, but instead of someone who is apparently ignorant of their causes, as if he were hearing them for the first time. Like Vico—who speculates that religion was born with the first appearance of lightning and thunder, caused by the exhalations of a drying earth when the giants, "frightened and astonished by the great effect whose

cause they did not know . . . raised their eyes and became aware of
the sky" (*New Science* 117)—Wordsworth rewrites the myth of Narcis-
sus and Echo in anthropological terms, attributing the origin of sympathy to the powerful effect that a misinterpretation of natural causes
has upon the ignorant mind—in this instance, the fearsomeness of
echoes.[35] As Mandeville argued, primitive man assumed that an "invisible enemy" lurked behind

> every Mischief and every Disaster that happens to him, of which
> the Cause is not very plain and obvious; excessive Heat and Cold;
> Wet and Drought, that are offensive; Thunder and Lightning,
> even when they do no visible Hurt; Noises in the dark, Obscurity
> itself, and every thing that is frightful and unknown . . . When a
> Man once apprehends such an invisible Enemy, it is reasonable
> to think, that he would be glad to appease, and make him his
> Friend, if he could find him out; it is highly probable, likewise,
> that in order to this, he would search, investigate, and look every
> where about him; and that finding all his Enquiries upon Earth
> in vain, he would lift up his Eyes to the Sky. [*Fable of the Bees*
> 2:208–12]

"What is there now in Peter's heart?" asks the narrator. "Or what's the
power of that strange sound?" (516–17). Peter begins to look around,
seeking what he initially takes to be an "absent speaker," the "absent
owner" of the ass, mimicking the ass's cry. In MS. 1, he imagines he
hears "a barking cur," "a sound of human voices," and then, from the
quarry, the cry "Thief! Thief!" (MS. 1, lines 349–55). Strikingly, it is
while he is furtively searching for this owner that he notices nature
for the first time as the "agent *invisible*" (Hobbes, *English Works* 3:95)
of these cries. Peter concludes that the moon, the heavens, and the
rocks are in sympathy with the ass and have become quickened by its
cry:

> The moon uneasy look'd and dimmer,
> The broad blue heavens appear'd to glimmer,
> And the rocks stagger'd all around.   [518–20]

As in the case of the child of *The Prelude*, nature makes its first appearance as a property relation, as a figural "absent owner": "a huge
cliff, / As if with voluntary power instinct," uprears its head to assert

the claims of the owner of a boat; "low breathings . . . among the solitary hills" follow the child that has stolen another's woodcock; "the strange utterance" of a "loud dry wind" is heard by the child when he steals raven eggs; a "calm lake," a fish snapping the "breathless silence," and a heap of clothes left by the side of Esthwaite Water tell the "plain tale" of an "absent owner"; "silent trees" and an "intruding sky" speak of "the wealth" gained by the "merciless ravage" of a hazel bower. Peter's education is not unlike Adam Smith's description of the isolated murderer who is compelled to return to society to face the judgment of others, because his "exposure," as David Marshall has noted, "before the imagined spectators the man must personate in his solitude" is more frightening than a real court of justice.[36] But it is significant that Wordsworth, in reworking the primitive encounter, makes nature, rather than the onlooking savage Peter, the source of the repetition that transforms natural or accidental signs into the arbitrary signs of language. The echoes break the natural or immediate connection between language and its speaker. Furthermore, unlike the Enlightenment context of sympathy, in which a *present* agent stands as a sign to be imitated, sympathy emerges for Wordsworth in the search for an *absent* speaker, whose voice is witnessed by nature. Since the transformation of an echo into "nature's voice" is an instance of prosopopoeia, the figurative representation of an absent person as speaker, Peter is mistakenly attributing to nature sympathies that reside in himself. Therefore, his search for the "absent owner" of this voice, speaking within the shadows, will ultimately lead him to himself and to an understanding of the depths of the human heart and imagination. Yet further, it will bring him to the knowledge, which remains the shadowy ground of human sympathy, primitive figuration, and the fearsomeness of echoes, that he too can become this absent and spectral voice. As Wordsworth's poetry repeatedly demonstrates, sympathy is fundamentally bound up with a search that leads to the genesis of the idea of death, the subject of chapter 5.

The climactic scene of Part First of *Peter Bell,* when Peter's eye, continuing its search for the "absent owner" of the ass, finds a dead man in the stream, brings the primitive encounter to its conclusion and shows emphatically that behind Wordsworthian nature, despite all its fearsome manifestations, lies the displaced figure of man. Combining philosophical seriousness with burlesque, the narrator describes how Peter, finally imitating the stance of the ass, "o'er the stream . . . hangs his nose" (618) and spies "an ugly sight, I trow / Among the shadows of the trees" (529–30). It is unclear whether what scares him is the dead man or his own reflection, whether he sees only the surface of the stream or its depths. In either case, however, we are given both an encapsulated allegory and a literal enactment of Wordsworth's history of the imagination, as we see the emergence of man from the enchanted, phantasmic waters of Peter's imagination:

> Is it the moon's distorted face?
> The ghost-like image of a cloud?
> Is it a gallows there pourtray'd?
> Is Peter of himself afraid?
> Is it a coffin,—or a shroud?
>
> A grisly idol hewn in stone?
> Or imp from witch's lap let fall?
> Or a gay ring of shining fairies,
> Such as pursue their brisk vagaries
> In sylvan bower, or haunted hall?
>
> Is it a fiend that to a stake
> Of fire his desperate self is tethering?
> Or stubborn spirit doom'd to yell
> In solitary ward or cell,
> Ten thousand miles from all his brethren?
>
> . . . .
>
> A throbbing pulse the Gazer hath—
> Puzzled he was, and now is daunted;
> He looks, he cannot choose but look;
> Like one intent upon a book—
> A book that is enchanted.   [first edition, lines 541–65]

The "humanization" of this image, Peter's eventual recognition that it is a man beneath the water, is equally a humanization of the man who beholds it. Yet the supernatural aspects of romance (the ghosts, idols, imps, witches, fairies, and fiends) intimately connected as they are with the fear of death (the gallows, the coffin, the shroud, the stake, and Hell) are not simply displaced. They perform a vital role in engendering "literal" perception. Only after Peter has been scared almost to death, only after he has mimicked being what he sees, does he recognize the owner of the image reflected in the waters as a dead man:

> Quoth he, "that is a dead man's face
> Among the shadows of the trees;
> Those are, no doubt, a dead man's knuckles
> And there you see his brass shoe-buckles
> And there his breeches' knees."   [611–15]

The highly metaphorical character of Peter's initial encounter with this image gives way to language that is almost anatomical in its literalness. And finally Peter begins to understand that the ass has been attempting to communicate with him:

> That Peter on his back should mount
> He's shewing all the wish he can.
> "I'll go, I'll go if life forsake me;
> No doubt he to his home will take me,
> The cottage of this drowned man."   [681–85]

With the problem of language surmounted, this comic version of the primitive encounter reaches its formal conclusion. Peter Bell, mounted on the ass, can now make the journey that will lead him out of the woods and into society.

PART TWO

The Origin of Poetry, Myth, and Religion

THREE

The "Wonders of a Wild Career"

Peter Bell and the Natural
History of Religion

In the previous two chapters I have examined the paradoxical manner in which Wordsworth, as he sought to write a poetic alternative to moral philosophical discourse, criticized eighteenth-century anthropological methods, standpoints, and concerns even as he found ways to engage in a similar kind of inquiry. As anthropological narratives, the poems I have been discussing are not wholly successful and are best viewed as experiments in anthropological narration; rather than representing human origins, they are more frequently the site of a conflict over how such representations should be done. They nevertheless played an important role in laying the foundations for Wordsworth's later poetry, especially for the philosophical breadth of *The Prelude*. During this period, Wordsworth's poetry everywhere points to a crisis of authority, a continual questioning of what he had to say and his right to say it. In this and the next chapter, I would like to examine the issue of poetic authority more fully, to suggest how Wordsworth found his voice through his observation and identification with marginal individuals. Since the concept of poetic authority was closely linked with speculation about primitive myth and religion, a new set of concerns must be addressed, relating to the origin and function of the supernatural.

The Contradictory Discourse on Methodism

At a climactic point in *Peter Bell*, the protagonist, full of despair, his memory and his ride having brought him to a recognition of his guilt, comes upon a methodist chapel and hears a heated sermon by a methodist preacher:

> "Repent, repent," he cries aloud,
> "God is a God of mercy,—strive
> To love him then with all your might;
> Do that which lawful is and right
> And save your souls alive."   [1,196–1,200]

Peter assumes that these "joyful tidings" of repentance, mercy, and love, intertwined as they are with the more secular concern of doing "that which lawful is and right," are specially meant for him. He undergoes a New Birth; "his nerves, his sinews . . . melt" and his "iron frame" returns to its original malleable state:

> And all the animal within
> Was weak, perhaps, but it was mild
> And gentle as an infant child,
> An infant that has known no sin.   [1,208–20]

When the poem was first published, in 1819, many of Wordsworth's contemporaries were disturbed by this conversion; perhaps, too, by the fact that almost everyone in the "tale" told by the village poet is a Methodist. Leigh Hunt, who had written a virulent antimethodist pamphlet ten years earlier entitled *An Attempt to Shew the Folly and*

Danger of Methodism (1809), showed that he could be equally censorious about poets who seemed to be siding with the methodists. The poem recounts a "Methodistical nightmare," he writes, and is "another didactic little horror of Mr. Wordsworth's, founded on the bewitching principles of fear, bigotry, and diseased impulse."[1] The anonymous reviewer for the *Eclectic Review*, only slightly less depreciatory, declares that "a more extraordinary conversion never excited the scorn of a sceptic, in the annals of what is termed Methodism." Nevertheless, he shrewdly observes that "it is, perhaps, the first time such an incident was pressed into the service of poetry, and we give Mr. W. credit for venturing upon something like an honest reference to the fact of the efficacy of such preaching, although we cannot commend the manner in which he has made scripture to jingle in his verse."[2] The reviewer's case is slightly overstated: the powers of methodist preaching had frequently been a subject of debate and "scorn" in the enormous flood of controversial literature about, and mostly against, Methodism that began to appear during the 1740s and did not begin to ebb until the first two decades of the next century.[3] His remark does indicate, however, that the appearance of a methodist preacher in literature was an unusual event, so the discursive preconditions of this appearance deserve some attention.

Prior to the extraordinary growth of Evangelicalism near the turn of the century, when it seemed "as if the Church of England was on the verge of becoming a minority religious establishment," Methodism was primarily the religion of a large, neglected, and marginal population: the working class of the manufacturing villages and the newly formed mining towns, like Kingswood, or of industrial cities, such as Bristol, Newcastle, and London.[4] As the following remark, recorded by Robert Southey, suggests, the notion of missionary conversion was easily transferred to Methodism's spiritual dealings with this largely illiterate domestic population. When George Whitefield, before his embarkation to America, "spoke of converting the savages, many of his friends said to him, 'What need of going abroad for this? Have we not Indians enough at home? If you have a mind to convert Indians, there are colliers enough in Kingswood.'"[5] Wesley's conversion of the prisoners at Newgate early in his career set the pattern for subsequent methodist preaching, as the early ministry brought "a message of concern and compassion and personal salvation to people who had stood alone."[6] As Elie Halévy rightly observed: "The despair of the working class was the raw material to which Methodist doctrine and discipline gave a shape" (*Birth of Methodism* 70).

Because Methodism was the religion of the working class, it was an object of fear and misrepresentation throughout the eighteenth century.[7] Until early in the nineteenth century, when it underwent extensive reorganization aimed at suppressing its earlier emotionalism, reducing the power of itinerant preachers, centralizing the organization of church government, and breaking its close connection to working-class radicalism, Methodism was seen by its opponents as a threatening form of religious enthusiasm, inextricably linked to superstition, fanaticism, and even witchcraft.[8] As Michael MacDonald notes, Anglican pamphleteers transformed the claim that "Nonconformists were victims and the carriers of mental disease into a ruling-class shibboleth."[9] William Huntington tells of being regarded as a carrier of a "religious infection."[10] While to participants at religious rallies the sobs, tears, and wild fits of laughter, the emotional transports, sudden convulsions, paroxysms, and quakings were signs of God's spirit working in their midst, wounding and healing, to doctors, rationalists, and, especially, the more conservative members of the established Church, who were well-versed in the philosophical and religious representation and critique of "enthusiasm," these were manifestations of a particularly virulent and contagious "disease of the imagination," associated with melancholy, hysteria, and hypochondria. To squire and clergy, Methodism was not an authentic religion but a new psychological disorder. "The two great causes of Methodism," writes Hunt, in language that explains his dislike of *Peter Bell*, "are ignorance and hypochondria."[11] Robert Southey agreed. In his famous *Life of Wesley* (1820), which he was writing when Wordsworth dedicated *Peter Bell* to him, wishing him "to complete the many important works in which you are engaged" (*Peter Bell* 42), Wesley and his ministers are represented as having produced a sort of "spiritual influenza, a new disease, and he accounted for it by a theological theory instead of a physical one. As men are intoxicated by strong drink affecting the mind through the body, so are they by strong passions influencing the body through the mind. Here there was nothing but what would naturally follow when persons, in a state of spiritual drunkenness, abandoned themselves to their sensations, and such sensations spread rapidly, both by voluntary and involuntary imitation."[12]

Accounts of individuals who had undergone conversion were as strange, as fascinating, and as popular as stories of witchcraft. Wordsworth's inclusion, in the invocation and prologue to Part Third, of an apparently authentic story ("I've heard of one . . . And, for the fact I'll vouch") of how "a gentle soul, / Though giv'n to sadness and to gloom," saw, when reading late at night from a "pious book," a "wondrous word" suddenly form "into large letters bright and plain" on the page, which "brought full many a sin to light / Out of the bottom of his heart" (926–50), reflects the contemporary interest in these cases. Nor were such incidents rare. John Wesley's *Journal,* for instance, includes a thirteen-year-old girl's account of how she suffered from sudden blindness while reading from a Catholic missal: "I continued blind, just able to discern light from darkness, but not to read or do any work; till, after three months, casting my eye on a New Testament, I could read clearly. I said to myself, 'I won't read this Protestant book, I will read my own book.' Accordingly I opened the mass-book, but could not see one word: it appeared all dark and black. I made the trial thrice over, holding the mass-book in one hand and the Testament in the other. I could not see any thing in the mass-book, but could read the Testament as well as ever. On this I threw away the mass-book, fully resolved to meddle with it no more."[13]

Stories such as these suggested that the traditional discourse on witchcraft and possession might easily be applied to a religious group. John Pawson's father, for instance, told him that "Methodists are the most bewitching people upon earth: when once a person hears them, there is no possibility of persuading him to leave them again."[14] Methodism was even more threatening than witchcraft, because it was an observable phenomenon—Methodists actually *did* exist—and because it affected large groups of people. "There are passions which are as infectious as the plague," Southey declares, "and fear itself is not more so than fanaticism" (*Life of Wesley* 1:220). In comparison with Methodism, witchcraft was a local phenomenon, linked to individual hysteria and to the powers of lonely, ostracized women. Methodism (and other evangelical religions usually classified with it) was "mass hysteria," the madness of a much larger and more dangerous marginal group.

The efficient cause inevitably cited in explanations of the extraordinary success of Methodism was the effect that the language of methodist preachers had on the imaginations and, through them, the minds and bodies of their listeners. It was alleged, for instance, that George Whitefield's first sermon had driven fifteen persons mad (Knox, *Enthusiasm* 524). The theatricality of methodist preaching, the morbid fascination with death, Hell, and judgment, the pervasive emphasis on desire, the language of "trials, temptations, heart sinkings, doubts; struggles, heaviness, manifestations, victories, coldnesses, wanderings, besetments, deliverances, helps, hopes, answers to prayer, interpositions, reliefs, complaints," made it a potent drug.[15] "Like empirics," writes the anonymous reviewer of *Hints to the Public and the Legislature, on the Nature and Effect of Evangelical Preaching*, "they have but one drug. The same powerful medicine which restores the confirmed sinner to health by searching his very bones till the joints open and the teeth are loosened, they administer in all cases, and in those who have weak nerves and warm imaginations, madness is frequently the result" (499). Methodist preaching was thus viewed as a powerful rhetoric, particularly suited to a certain class of people, those who had become hardened and insensitive to gentler modes of religious persuasion—people like the ruffian Peter Bell. "The methodist preached especially to the nerves," writes the nineteenth-century historian W. E. H. Lecky: "With the most impassioned tone and gestures, with every artifice that could heighten the dramatic effect of his words, he expatiated upon the certainty of death, upon the terrors of judgment, upon the undying agonies of hell, upon the lost condition of mankind. These were the almost constant subjects of his preaching, and he dwelt upon them till he scared his hearers to the verge of insanity, and engendered a nervous disease, which propagated itself rapidly through the congregation."[16] The antimethodist literature can be seen, then, as an extensive discourse, replete with examples, on the transformative powers of language and the imagination, structured along class lines.

Since in Wordsworth's poetry there is a close affiliation between psychopathology and poetics, it should not surprise us that at the same time that he was writing poems on witchcraft (which I will discuss in the next chapter) he would also turn to the phenomenon of Methodism as a means of observing the power of language to shape directly the mind and bodily "nerves" and "sinews."[17] This interest in language is emphasized by his repetition of the word *voice* and his linking of the preacher's words to the echoing cry of the ass: "It is a voice just like a voice / Reecho'd from a naked rock" (1,191–92). In the Fenwick note to the poem, Wordsworth emphasizes this power: "In both the psalmody and the voice of the preacher there is, not infrequently, much solemnity likely to impress the feelings of the rudest characters under favourable circumstances" (*PW* 2:527). The mention of "rudest characters" suggests an equally important dimension of the contemporary discourse on Methodism: the issue of social control. Wordsworth was no less ambivalent toward the language of Methodists than he was toward that of witches, but where the witch demonstrates how communal stereotyping can give isolated women powerful modes of speech, methodist preaching raises the more explicitly political issue of the role that impassioned language (poetry and preaching) and charismatic leaders play in either controlling the poor or inciting them to disorder and violence. It thus initiates a reflection on the close relationship between revolutionary rhetoric and poetic language that was to be a major preoccupation of his major poetry, especially *Resolution and Independence* and the Revolution Books of *The Prelude*.

Peter Bell is closely linked to the religious and political controversies of the 1790s. If it had been published in 1798, when it was first written, rather than twenty years later, at a time when the Methodists had clearly sided with the status quo against radicalism, this discursive context would have been more obvious. At this time, contradictory views were held of Methodism's political objectives. Many saw it as a major threat, a revolutionary religion, secretly in league with the Jacobins and set on undermining Church government (and perhaps even the state), just as the French had toppled the ancien régime.[18] Edmund Burke's attack on Richard Price in *Reflections on the Revolution in France* reflects a longstanding paranoia on the part of gentry and clergy, going back to the Civil War and the Commonwealth, about the close connection between evangelical dissent, working-class radicalism, and republicanism. As John Walsh has observed, Methodism exacerbated these anxieties in two ways: "First, in an age when the agencies of government were decidedly weak and decentralised, Methodism looked the more sinister because of its highly articulated and nationwide organisation. Secondly, it addressed itself primarily to the poor, whom it drilled into disciplined cadres which owed their allegiance to leaders far beyond the reach of any local authority" ("Methodism and the Mob" 218). Walsh adds that the Methodists "looked alarmingly like the harbingers of a second and perhaps a more proletarian puritan revolution" (218).

Rev. T. E. Owen's remarks, in *Methodism Unmasked*, are typical of the more extreme establishment responses to Methodism in the 1790s. Citing his earlier pamphlet *Hints to Heads of Families*, he argues that Methodists are "'either blind instruments, or wilful tools, in the hands of Anarchists and Atheists,' that their aim is not a reform in religion, but a total overthrow of our Religious and Political Constitutions, and a revolution in these dominions, similar to that which has deluged France with blood, and brought upon many millions irreparable ruin."[19] Richard Polwhele voices a similar concern: "The *mania* of Methodism has seized the West of England, and is now spreading at this instant through its remotest parts . . . The feelings of the moralist revolt at the prospect; and to the politician also such a view of the Methodists as is here given must be truly alarming. To him are exhibited a vast body of people, many enthusiasts, and many infidels, all alienated from the Church-government, all looking for some great emergencies to liberate them from its restraints, and consequently all ripe for rebellion."[20] Given the paranoia of the 1790s and the outright suppression of all modes of radicalism after 1795, Wordsworth's reluctance to publish a poem that was likely to be viewed as aligning itself with "a large body of people" who were "alienated from the Church-government" probably had more to do with a fear of the political reaction it would occasion (Leigh Hunt's being typical) than with dissatisfaction with it.

It should equally be said, if we are to understand fully the discursive context of this poem, however, that during the 1790s anxieties about the political objectives of Methodism were countered by an alternate interpretation, first put forward by the methodist ministry, but later identified with Elie Halévy's *England in 1815*, that instead of being a revolutionary religious movement Methodism was actually a stabilizing and counter-revolutionary force. The eulogy delivered at Wesley's funeral stressed "the leavening influence of Methodism in a politically restive situation."[21] As Bernard Semmel has observed, citing Joseph Sutcliffe's *Review of Methodism* (1805), "This theme was repeated again and again in Methodist sermons which assumed that, not only was Methodism in good part responsible for spawning Britain's new industrial growth, but it was the means by which 'vast groups of loose and disorderly men, subject as they have been to sudden stoppages in trade, to exorbitant advances of provisions, have been governed almost without mobbing and confusion.' No longer were there 'very serious riots among colliers and manufacturers' as in times past."[22] Methodism could be seen as a religion of control, a means of socializing, civilizing, and governing a certain populace ("vast groups of loose and disorderly men") that might otherwise resist government. William Wilberforce, in his influential *Practical View of the Prevailing Religious System of Professed Christians* (1795), makes a similar claim for the importance of Evangelicalism, a practical, vital Christianity. Wilberforce hopes that through the moral instruction and improvement of "the rising generation . . . an antidote may be provided for the malignity of that venom which is storing up in a neighbouring country." By inculcating the doctrines of Christianity, he argues, evangelical pastors have tended "directly as well as indirectly, to the maintenance of the cause of order and good government." They cultivate "a considerable degree of fervour and animation" to counter the impotence of Christianity as "a mere system of ethics"; but at the same time they restrain these passions "within due bounds."[23]

Since Wordsworth's fragmentary "[Essay on Morals]" indicates that *The Recluse* was initially conceived as a project that would counter an abstract "system of ethics" with a politically effective moral rhetoric, it should not surprise us that he would be interested in these highly charged political debates concerning the role that impassioned language plays in governing the lower classes or inciting them to violence. In a letter accompanying his gift of the 1800 *Lyrical Ballads* to Wilberforce, he portrays himself as "a Fellow-labourer with you in the same Vineyard, acting under the perception of some one common truth and attributing to that truth the same importance and necessity" (*EY* 685). Rather than belonging to the class of small property owners or "statesmen" idealized in the poem *Michael*, "men of respectable education who daily labour on their own little properties" and who could be understood in terms of the georgic conception of a harmony between the laboring poor and nature, Peter Bell is closer to what later came to be known as the *classe dangereuse*. These people, who lacked property, who often lived in areas "crowded with population" (*EY* 314), and who had been uprooted by industrialization and land enclosure, no longer could claim any affective link to a certain locality. Written when the power and alienation of this class was just beginning to be recognized and feared, *Peter Bell* shows Wordsworth's awareness of and sympathy for the reality of working-class despair, unrest, and civil violence and his desire to address the political issues raised by them.

How is this large and nomadic population of people, given to violence and enthusiasm, to be governed? What kind of education suits the social position and intellectual needs of these English sansculottes? How is an English Revolution to be avoided?[24] Beginning with an image of revolutionary terror in its most brutal form—Peter mercilessly beating a defenseless creature in the woods—Wordsworth attempts to show how, through a discipline of imagination, Peter (and, by extension, his class) can be made a useful member of society, one who does "that which lawful is and right" (1,199).[25] The poem can thus be seen as a conservative critique of those historical processes, notably industrialization, enclosure, and increased economic commercialism, that had given rise to a large population of displaced laborers, peddlers, and beggars, who were migrating to the cities and were not susceptible to the socializing influences of nature ("A primrose by a river's brim / A yellow primrose was to him / And it was nothing more" [218–20]) and all too susceptible to "whatever vice / The cruel city breeds" (274–75).[26] Furthermore, it represents a postrevolutionary poetic manifesto about how these people are to be governed and social revolutions are to be avoided: religion, nature, and poetry are seen as the means by which the spread of revolution to England is to be prevented and social stability promoted.

The poem indicates Wordsworth's ambiguous political position: between one class, which he believes has no time to appreciate nature and therefore stands outside of the discipline of imagination, and another class, represented by those listening to the tale (among them a squire and an Anglican vicar), which shows little knowledge of the role that nature and supernatural narratives have historically played in the exercise of control. Another distinctive element of Wordsworth's political makeup is that he identifies with both these classes. The excesses in his depiction of Peter Bell as a predatory loner, a "savage character," and a criminal indicate the anxiety with which he looked on a large class of dissatisfied people that made up the ranks of the methodist church. In a letter to Francis Wrangham, written in March 1809, he asks, "With the Methodists on one side, and the Catholics on the other, what is to become of the poor Church and people of England, to both of which I am most tenderly attached?" (*MY* 1:313). Yet equally importantly, Wordsworth, who also had no property during the 1790s and was among the socially and politically discontented, had little difficulty recognizing aspects of himself in people like Peter Bell. Thus he could say, even as late as 19 October 1831, "I am as much Peter Bell as ever" (*LY* 2:439). *Peter Bell* should not be read as a distanced political treatise, then, but instead as one of the poet's earliest reflections on the relationship between poetry and violence, one in which he draws on the ambiguous, contradictory status of Methodism as a medium for addressing his contradictory sense of his own poetic authority. In it, Wordsworth first developed what was to become his great postrevolutionary theme: how his own powers as a poet had emerged out of social dissatisfaction, marginalization, violence, and discontent. The "history of Peter Bell" might be said to represent, in an indirect way, Wordsworth's first history of a poet's imagination.

The Progress of Religion

It is probable that one upshot of Coleridge and Wordsworth's decision to remain "habitually silent" on at least "one subject"—that of the historical truth of Christianity—was that the poetry of 1797–98 became the medium of an unacknowledged debate. "We found our data dissimiliar [*sic*]," writes Coleridge, in a letter written just before Hazlitt arrived at Nether Stowey, "& never renewed the subject." Coleridge goes on to suggest that although Wordsworth was skeptical of the revelatory status of the Bible, he recognized its importance as a moral institution. "It is his practice & almost his nature," the younger poet writes, "to convey all the truths he knows without any attack on what he supposes a falsehood, if that falsehood be interwoven with virtues or happiness."[27] Critics have often read *Peter Bell* as an explicit rejoinder to *The Ancient Mariner* and have noted many textual echoes and structural parallels linking the two poems.[28] They have also concluded, on the basis of Wordsworth's comment that *Peter Bell* "was composed under a belief that the Imagination . . . does not require for its exercise the intervention of supernatural agency" and Coleridge's famous discussion of the poetic division of labor in *Lyrical Ballads,* that a major subject of debate was the role of the supernatural in poetry.[29] In this connection, the supernatural ballads of the German poet Gottfried Bürger are most frequently mentioned: as a positive influence on *The Ancient Mariner* and as a form of the supernatural that Wordsworth sought to revise. What has not been recognized, however, is that though the immediate focus of debate was the function of the supernatural in ballads, the underlying, and much more pressing, issue for both poets was theological: the need to redefine the meaning and value of biblical supernaturalism. Prompted by *The Ancient Mariner,* Wordsworth, in *Peter Bell,* reflected on the historical meaning of the Christian gospels and set out to redefine, in anthropological and political terms, the validity of salvific narrative. Throughout the eighteenth century, the anthropological importance of religion was well known, as is indicated by Vico's assertion that "among all peoples the civil world began with religion" (*New Science* 7). Equally importantly, poetry and religion, as Robert Lowth suggests, were intimately linked in their origins: "If the actual origin of Poetry be inquired after, it must of necessity be referred to Religion" (*Sacred Poetry of the Hebrews* 1:37). Wordsworth's interest in biblical narrative should thus not be seen as separate from his reflection on the origin and ends of poetry.

It is surprising that no one has ever noted that *Peter Bell* puns on one of the most famous of Enlightenment skeptics, Pierre Bayle (often called Peter Bayle in England). Bayle is generally considered the founder of the rationalist criticism of the Bible and myth popularized by the Enlightenment. His *Dictionnaire historique et critique* (1695–97), which Coleridge drew from extensively as he composed *The Wanderings of Cain, Christabel,* and *The Ancient Mariner,* was the great sourcebook of Enlightenment skepticism and impiety, one of the most popular works of the eighteenth century.[30] In support of an essentially fideistic theological position, Bayle demonstrated throughout the *Dictionary,* in articles that were considered scandalous, that the claims of Christian revelation are fundamentally incompatible with reason (to judge the Bible strictly by reason would be to reduce it to absurdity) and that religious beliefs are not necessarily linked to rational moral conduct. Wordsworth's allusion to Pierre Bayle suggests that *Peter Bell* is a response to the skeptical tradition of biblical interpretation ushered in by the *Dictionary*, which focuses on the political function of biblical narrative and on how to balance the contrary demands of enlightenment and faith: "If perchance your faith should fail / Look up and you shall see me soon" (9–10). Where Bayle uses commentary as a medium of critical argument, however, Wordsworth writes his own version of a biblical narrative, at once a salvific tale and a hypothetical history of religion. What Peter Bell discovers over the course of this lonely summer night is what Western society discovered over the course of its history: his passage from a "crude metaphysics," a religion grounded in violence, magic, and superstition, to one that recognizes the importance of love and human society, recapitulates the historical origins and development of Christianity.

"What spell so strong as guilty Fear!" (first edition, line 152): Peter's theodicy of imagination illustrates the Enlightenment argument, drawn from classical sources, that "fear created the first gods in the world" ("primos in orbe deos fecit timor"). Cicero's use of the idea is typical and shows to what degree the incidents that Peter misinterprets on his educative journey—an eery cry, a leaf that apparently has been dogging his steps, a trail of blood, an ass's smile, a subterranean rumble, a barking dog—belong to this discourse: "The awe inspired by lightning, storms, rain, snow, hail, floods, pestilences, earthquakes and occasionally *subterranean rumblings,* showers of stones and *raindrops the colour of blood,* also landslips and chasms suddenly opening in the ground, also *unnatural monstrosities human and animal,* and also the appearance of meteoric lights and what are called by the Greeks 'comets', and in our language 'long-haired stars', such as recently during the Octavian War appeared as harbingers of dire disasters, and the doubling of the sun . . . all of which alarming portents have suggested to mankind the idea of the existence of some celestial and divine power."[31]

Hobbes revived this idea in *Leviathan*, slanting it specifically toward psychopathology and a discourse on the imagination. He writes: "They [people] that make little, or no inquiry into the natural causes of things, yet from the fear that proceeds from the ignorance itself, of what it is that hath the power to do them much good or harm, are

inclined to suppose, and feign unto themselves, several kinds of powers invisible; and to stand in awe of their own imaginations; and in
time of distress to invoke them; as also in the time of an expected
good success, to give them thanks; making the creatures of their own
fancy, their gods . . . This fear of things invisible, is the natural seed
of that, which every one in himself calleth religion; and in them that
worship, or fear that power otherwise than they do, superstition" (*English Works* 3:93). For Hobbes, the gods are "creatures of . . . fancy,"
fictions engendered by fear. The difference between religion and superstition, then, is only a matter of point of view. There are "as many
gods, as there be men that feign them" (3:96). After Hobbes, the fear
theory became the most popular of eighteenth-century psychological
explanations of the origin of the gods and can be found in most
Enlightenment accounts of primitive religion. "It was fear which
created gods in the world," writes Vico, "not fear awakened in men
by other men, but fear awakened in men by themselves" (*New Science*
120).

The Enlightenment generally used the fear theory in two ways.
First, the psychological explanation, which linked the origin of religion
and despotism to the least admirable of human emotions, justified the
philosophe's critical detachment and skepticism regarding the claims
of revealed religion. Second, it supported arguments for more rationalistic theologies. Skeptics and Deists repeatedly asserted that the
history of religion, whether or not it was providentially determined,
could be seen as a progress from the rudimentary ideas of God en-
tertained by savages and children, ideas grounded in fear of an imagined invisible Father, to a more rational and intellectual theology
recognizing the design of creation. The Church of England responded
with a compromise position, indebted to Locke, by stressing the rea-
sonableness of Christianity and revealed religion as a knowledge that
all nations are progressing towards, though all have not yet reached.

Wordsworth's use of this religious and anthropological paradigm as
one of the major keystones of his aesthetics is quite clear. The claims
made in *Peter Bell* (that a brute can learn that "the heart of man's a
holy thing" [1,312]), in *The Prelude* (that there is a "wisdom and spirit
of the universe" that sanctifies the human mind through a "discipline
/ [Of] both pain and fear" [1.428–40]), and in *Home at Grasmere* (that

what "in stealth by nature was performed / Hath Reason sanctioned"
[MS. B, lines 941–42]) reflect the same movement from a "ministry
of fear," linked to childhood, the early stages of society, and the lower
classes, to a more philosophical religion, in which a providential purpose and pattern can be discerned in the world. What is unique about
Wordsworth's history of religion is that he does not treat fear and
superstition as errors, but instead as positive forces. Thus, in contrast
to Bayle's famous claim that a society of atheists could be as moral as
a society of Christians, Wordsworth, with his eye on the French republic, sets out a dynamic anthropology, in which fear and ignorance
are a necessary part of the development of religious ideas—"Most
fearful work for fearful ends" (959). This position has its immediate
source in Coleridge's "Destiny of Nations," where the fears engendered by a superstitious imagination are given a central role in the
emancipation of mankind:

> For Fancy is the power
> That first unsensualises the dark mind,
> Giving it new delights; and bids it swell
> With wild activity; and peopling air,
> By obscure fears of Beings invisible,
> Emancipates it from the grosser thrall
> Of the present impulse, teaching Self-control,
> Till Superstition with unconscious hand
> Seat Reason on her throne.   [80–88]

The tale of Peter Bell is the story of how the crude and "dark" imagination of an itinerant potter, by "peopling" the world with "Beings
invisible," is disciplined and unsensualized, brought through the ministry of "obscure fears" to an awareness of "new delights," of love and
charity. Yet unlike *The Ancient Mariner,* where this history is providentially determined, *Peter Bell* traces, as Hume would have argued, "the
origin of religion in human nature"—in the "ordinary affections of
human life."[32] It indicates that the progress of religion is less a man-
ifestation of God's active intervention than of the power of a "crude
metaphysics" to scare its subjects into gentler fictions and modes of
civil government.

David and Balaam

Though formally divided into three parts, *Peter Bell* imitates, in language, imagery, and themes, the two-testament structure of the Bible:
Parts First and Second parallel Old Testament myth, while the new
Christian orientation of Part Third, which Wordsworth liked best, is
announced, in the same manner as Milton indicates a shift of perspective in books 3, 7, and 9 of *Paradise Lost,* by a new invocation.
Since Part First has already been examined, I will primarily focus on
the final two parts of the narrative.

   Like many Enlightenment histories of religion, *Peter Bell* explicitly
links the beginnings of religious experience with superstition in its
crudest form. For Peter, who had "never felt / The witchery of the soft
blue sky" (234–35), witchcraft and superstition will initiate him into
the disciplinary world of the imagination. When the ass first refuses
to budge on his summons, Peter decides that it is possessed: "Some
ugly witchcraft must be here!" (first edition, line 452). But Peter is
not a person much alarmed by magic: "A Witch is playing in my sight /
Her desperate tricks but what care I" (MS. 5, 23ʳ), he declares, as his
brutality progressively takes on the character of a denial and exorcism
of magic. When the ass finally does move, by falling to its knees, Peter
is ecstatic and feels that he has at last gained possession of it:

> Quoth Peter "I shall have you now
> Now I shall have you safe & sound["]
> To Peter it was like a token
> That some curst magic spell was broken."   [MS. 1, 21ʳ]

Yet "spells" are not "broken" that easily. When the ass still refuses to
do his bidding, Peter concludes, in a canceled passage, that "the devil's
in him" and that more violence is necessary, so "with more fierce &
furious blows" he attacks "the harmless beast" (MS. 1, 22ʳ). But now
his violence is motivated by increasing anxiety that he must either
break the spell or fall victim to it:

> Whether to chear his coward heart
> Or that he felt a wicked chain
> Twined round him like a magic spell,
> Upon my faith I cannot tell,
> But to the work he fell again.   [506–10]

Peter does, indeed, become bewitched: he falls under the "spell" of "guilty Fear," when he begins to imagine powers greater than himself and summons up the supernatural as an explanation of his "wicked dealing." "No doubt the devil in me wrought," he asserts, as "ten thousand ugly apprehensions / Of eyes and ears the black inventions / The soul of Peter are deceiving" (MS. 1, 31^r). Witchcraft represents Peter's first encounter with the "Spirits of the Mind," conjured up from below, and they will continue to haunt him in the various pre-monitory signs he sees on his journey, in the ass's grin, "uglier far than death and sin / And all the devils together" (1,019–20), and in the subterranean devil, the result of Peter's misunderstanding that miners are at work underground.

Magic, violence, and religion are thus closely bound up with each other in Wordsworth's conception of origins. His use of Old Testament myth in the poem brings out this connection, especially in his pat-terning of Peter Bell's life on the story of two well-known Old Testa-ment prophets. The first of these is derived less from the Bible than from Bayle's "David," a notorious article in the *Dictionary* that had been singled out by the Walloon Church Consistory in Rotterdam for censorship and that crystallized, as Walter Rex has observed, "the eighteenth-century's image of the prophets of the Old Testament and of the God who was supposed to have inspired them."[33] In it, Bayle argues that there is no connection between the greatness, the piety, and the holiness of David, the man most "after GOD's own Heart" (*Dictionary* 2:605), and his moral character and conduct. Bayle delights in enlarging upon those aspects of David's life that do not accord with a rational concept of moral equity or justice. Having noted that it is generally believed, that David's "Adultery with *Bathsheba,* the Murder of *Uriah,* and the Numbering of the People, are the only Faults he can be charged with," Bayle adds that "there are many other things in his Life that deserve Censure. He is a Sun of holiness in the Church: he there diffuses, by his Writings, a fruitful Light of Consolation and Piety, which cannot be enough admired; but that Sun had it's Spots" (2:608–09).

A lengthy list follows of David's failings, foremost among these being his ruthless political opportunism, "in some respects, like that of the *Ottomons*" (2:612), his violent behavior, and his lechery, adultery, and polygamy. Bayle's description of David's dealings with a landowner named Nabal, of Carmel in Maon, is typical: "Now let us deal plainly: Is it not manifest, beyond Contradiction, that *David* was about to do a very criminal Action? He had no right to the Goods of *Nabal*, nor any Authority to punish him for his Incivility. He was roving up and down the World with a Gang of trusty Friends: He might, indeed, have asked some Gratuity of those who could afford it; but if they refused, he ought to have taken it patiently, and he could not compel them to it by Military Execution, without plunging the World again into the dreadful Confusion, which they call the State of Nature, where no Law obtained but that of the stronger" (2:607n). David is here represented as a violent leader of a gang of banditti or free-booters who, "roving up and down the World," threaten others to extort goods from them. Such actions, Bayle insists, properly belong to "the State of Nature." In another example, Bayle tells how David, "with his little Band of Six hundred bold Adventurers," used the town of Ziklag as a base for frequent incursions into the surrounding countries, where he "killed, without Mercy, both Men and Women. He left nothing alive but Cattle, which was the only Booty he returned with" (2:606n). To this already long list of violent excesses are added David's adultery, promiscuity, and polygamy, which Bayle argues "cannot well be excused." With characteristic understatement, the sage of Rotterdam declares that "we cannot say, with regard to the Pleasures of Love, that he took much pains to mortify Nature" (2:608).

Since David was traditionally revered as a saint, a prophet, the author of the Psalms, and a typological antecedent of Christ, Bayle's criticism was viewed as outright impiety and gave rise to heated controversy.[34] It seemed that he was condemning the Old Testament prophets as criminals and barbarians, pointing out the irrationality of Old Testament ethics, and showing that the God of the Jews was a God of cruelty and injustice. As Walter Rex observes, "At the end of the article at least one point has been scored with the utmost clarity: that this great figure from the Old Testament, the venerated ruler of the Jews, the ancestor of Christ (some believed), whose psalms were reverently sung in all the Calvinist Churches, had committed terrible crimes from the beginning of his rule to its end" (198–99). The article was thus "a triumphant demonstration of the barbarity of the moral foundations of Christianity" (*Pierre Bayle and Religious Controversy* 255).

Peter Bell shares with his textual ancestor many similarities: both are portrayed as "wild" men, roving the countryside, taking whatever they can find; both are men of great violence, passion, and lawlessness; both are polygamists; both are typologically linked to Christ ("he two and thirty years or more / Had been a wild and woodland rover" [176–77]). Wordsworth even employs the characteristic stylistic devices of the *Dictionary*, notably the use of an ostensibly artless author consistently saying more and less than he would like to say, a style in which the argument continually gets lost in digression (or, at least, appears to do so to the outsider).[35] He also is in agreement with Bayle's description of the barbaric origins of primitive Christianity, for he tells of a time when "poets fearlessly rehears'd / The wonders of a wild career" (first edition, lines 129–30). However, rather than arguing, as Bayle and his Enlightenment followers did, either that there is no connection between religious ideas and moral conduct or that reason and revelation are fundamentally irreconcilable, *Peter Bell* demonstrates that it was through the violence of a superstitious imagination that religious ideas were first revealed to early humans and they made the transition from barbarism to a world of Christian love. The great miracle of the story of David is that even though he was a bandit, an adulterer, and a man of passion, he became a prophet and a poet. Peter is not, like David, a great poet, but he is a primitive storyteller, and, as I will later argue, Wordsworth does link his own poetic origins to him. From an anthropological perspective, then, the stories of Peter and David can both be seen as originary myths, which display how prophecy, born from violence, becomes socialized through supernatural narratives of its own making. Here, too, is a political myth, which I will return to in chapter 6, that explains how revolutionary radicalism is transformed into poetry.

Wordsworth's exploration of the connection between violence and prophecy is further elaborated in his use of a second Old Testament myth—the story of that most unlikely of sorcerers and prophets, Balaam the son of Beor (Numbers 22–24). In Christian tradition, Balaam is a complex figure, part mercenary villain, part clown, part seer. Yet his prediction that "there shall come a Star out of Jacob, and a Sceptre shall rise out of Israel" (Numbers 24:17) gave him a privileged place among the gentile prophets, as the founder of the Magi, those who anticipated and sought out Christ. "Comming to Curse," writes Milton in *Articles of Peace*, Balaam "stumbled into a kind of Blessing."[36]

He enters the history of the Israelites during their encampment on
the plains of Moab, near the end of their forty years of wandering.
The account is essentially in two segments. Balak, the Moabite king,
seeing the Israelites encamped on the plains of Moab, sends an em-
bassy to Balaam in Ammon, requesting that he come to curse them.
Initially Balaam refuses, having received a divine injunction not to
curse the Israelites, but after the request is repeated (and God gives
his temporary blessing) he agrees and sets out on his journey to Moab
the next morning. The second part of the story, consisting primarily
of seven prophetic effusions, does not overtly influence the structure
of *Peter Bell*, except as it suggests that the narrative is about the genesis
and confirmation of prophecy. In the first part, we are informed that

> God's anger was kindled because he went: and the angel of the
> LORD stood in the way for an adversary against him . . .
>
> And the ass saw the angel of the LORD standing in the way, and
> his sword drawn in his hand: and the ass turned aside out of the
> way, and went into the field: and Balaam smote the ass, to turn
> her into the way.
>
> But the angel of the LORD stood in a path of the vineyards, a
> wall *being* on this side, and a wall on that side.
>
> And when the ass saw the angel of the LORD, she thrust herself
> unto the wall, and crushed Balaam's foot against the wall: and he
> smote her again.
>
> And the angel of the LORD went further, and stood in a narrow
> place, where *was* no way to turn either to right hand or to the
> left.
>
> And when the ass saw the angel of the LORD, she fell down
> under Balaam: and Balaam's anger was kindled, and he smote
> the ass with a staff.

Here we see the same strange mixture of repetition, violence, and low
comedy that is so characteristic of *Peter Bell*. Three times the ass turns
away from the angel, and three times Balaam, blind to the divine
figure's presence, beats the ass, the third time with a stick. At this
point a strange thing happens, the only other instance in the Bible
being that of the talking serpent: moved by the Lord, the ass turns to
Balaam and asks, "What have I done unto thee, that thou has smitten
me these three times?" Unlike Peter Bell, who is at least slightly dis-

composed, first when the ass cries out in a long and harsh bray, and
later when it turns its head and grins at him, Balaam is not at all fazed
by the ass's speech. As Robert Alter has observed in his excellent
discussion of the thematic patterning of the story, Balaam "responds
as though he were accustomed to having daily domestic wrangles with
his asses":[37]

> And Balaam said unto the ass, Because thou hast mocked me:
> I would there were a sword in my hand, for now would I kill thee.
> And the ass said unto Balaam, *Am* not I thine ass, upon which
> thou hast ridden ever since I *was* thine unto this day? was I ever
> wont to do so unto thee? And he said, Nay.

Only then does the Lord open Balaam's eyes:

> He saw the angel of the LORD standing in the way, and his sword
> drawn in his hand: and he bowed down his head, and fell flat on
> his face.
> The angel of the LORD said unto him, Wherefore hast thou
> smitten thine ass these three times? behold, I went out to with-
> stand thee, because *thy* way is perverse before me:
> And the ass saw me, and turned from me these three times:
> unless she had turned from me, surely now also I had slain thee,
> and saved her alive.

Prostrate before this vision, a man "falling *into a trance,* but having his
eyes open" (Numbers 24:4), the irate seer finally repents his violence:
"And Balaam said unto the angel of the LORD, I have sinned; for I
knew not that thou stoodest in the way against me: now therefore, if
it displease thee, I will get me back again" (22:34).[38]

Peter Bell shows a similar interest in the sources of vision. But where
the Bible resorts to a notion of supernatural agency as the source of
vision and speech, Wordsworth consistently explains the origin of the
supernatural in psychological terms, as the product of a combination
of imagination, ignorance, and fear. When Peter, looking into the
waters, sees what he takes to be a spectre and, giving "a loud and
frightful shriek . . . back he falls just like a stone" (584–85), we discover that the unseen figure, whose presence the ass has been attempting to communicate, is a dead man, not an angel. When he hears
an eery cry and then sees the ass turn off the road to follow "right

upwards from the hollow / That lamentable noise to follow," he feels
the "conviction strange" that he is about to suffer a spectral "visitation
worse than all" (798–804); we find out, however, that the ass is following the cry of the dead man's son Robin. The culminating "miserable
vision" (1,185) that Peter sees of two "wraiths" by the roadside, his
past self and his dying Highland wife, reworks once more Balaam's
encounter with the angel. The Old Testament sources are reinforced
by the parallelism between this girl's death and that of Israel's wife,
Rachel, who "died and was buried by the side of the road" after giving
birth to a child she named Benoni, the "son of my sorrow" (Genesis
35:18–19).[39] This is the name that the Highland girl had given to her
unborn child. John E. Jordan has observed that the appearance of
these spectral visions, called "swarths" in Cumberland, were often
thought to presage an individual's death.[40] Old Testament prophecy
is thus brought to a conclusion in folklore and with our recognition
that if Peter is to deal with a guilt now fully recognized, he must die
a spiritual death in order to be reborn.

Primitive Salvific Narrative

Peter's encounter with the methodist preacher, immediately after his
vision of the two "wraiths," signals the poem's shift, first announced
in the invocation of Part Third, from Old Testament theology to New
Testament themes and metaphors. Mary Jacobus has demonstrated in
detail the extent to which Wordsworth found in methodist conversion
narratives "a formula for redemption with exactly the popular cur-
rency he needed to rival Coleridge's traditional metaphor, the spiritual
voyage" ("*Peter Bell* the First" 226).[41] It should be added that their
popularity among the poor and uneducated increased their anthropological value. Wordsworth uses the conversion narrative in the same
manner that Coleridge uses the Ancient Mariner's tale, both as a myth
or fable expressing the primary and popular symbolic elements that
constitute primitive Christianity—the appearance of the "wondrous
word" (946), the importance of love, and the glad tidings of the resurrection—and as a chronicle or recapitulation of its genesis. Just as
Methodism, as a religion popular among the poor and illiterate and
employing itinerant preachers, could be seen as having conformities

with the early Church, so too conversion narratives could provide a key to understanding the original power of the Christian gospel and its impact on the lower classes. As in accounts of wild children, where despite the fact that language already exists, their progress toward it could be used as an abstract of the origin of language, Peter is being converted to a Christianity that already exists (for the narrator, his audience, the reader, and even for one of his wives). Nevertheless, as he comes to feel and believe in the spirituality of an institution that previously had no meaning for him, as he constructs and recounts a story that has conversionary force, he can demonstrate and epitomize how Christianity first came into being. His link to these origins is suggested by his name. He is a "bell" who is "turned to iron soon" (567)—at one point, Wordsworth perhaps even toyed with the idea of calling him "Be[a]ter Bell" (MS. 2, 1ʳ). Also, he is the namesake of Simon Peter, the rock or foundation of Christianity.[42] For Christ declared, "Thou art Peter, and upon this rock I will build my church" (Matthew 16:18). The history of his conversion can thus be read as a history of the psychological origins of Christianity, as Balaam becomes Peter, David becomes Christ—a progress that will not depend on "the intervention of supernatural agency" (Dedication, *Peter Bell* 41), but instead on a symbolic advance, a progress of mind, from Old to New Testament myth. "What education is to the individual man," writes Lessing in his "Education of the Human Race," "revelation is to the whole human race."[43]

One could examine in detail the events that give rise to an idea of redemption in Peter's mind, beginning with his guilty reflection on the "bleeding wound" (916) of the ass and followed by his recollection of his past misdeeds, the encounter with the spectre of the Highland girl, his hearing of the "joyful tidings" of the evangelical preacher, and his New Birth. However, since it is the idea of resurrection that essentially distinguishes Christianity from Judaism, the origin of this notion should be the focus of our attention. In Parts First and Second, a groundwork of typological prefigurings of this idea is laid, but Peter misreads them. The first of these is of Peter reawakening from a swoon that seemed "as if his life were flown" (first edition, line 575). Later, when the ass, gaunt and "almost wasted to the bone" (670), "strait with a transition tragic . . . Up from the ground . . . doth rise," Peter mistakenly equates its rise with "the touch of magic" (623–25).

The spectral emergence of the dead man out of the waters of the stream is also understood in supernatural terms:

> He pulls, he pulls, and pulls again,
> And he whom the poor ass had lost,
> The man who had been four days dead,
> Head-foremost from the river's bed
> Uprises like a ghost.   [651–55]

Since the "uprising" from a "bed" of "the man who had been four days dead" clearly reworks the story of Lazarus, it indicates the tale's progressive movement toward a Christian framework of interpretation. John tells us that when Christ arrived near Bethany, Lazarus "had *lain* in the grave four days already." As soon as Mary, Lazarus's sister, "saw him, she fell down at his feet, saying unto him, 'Lord, if thou hadst been here, my brother had not died.'" Jesus went to the tomb, which was "a cave, and a stone lay upon it," ordered that the stone be removed, and "cried with a loud voice, Lazarus, come forth," whereupon Lazarus appeared (John 11:32–44). The difference, of course, between the two episodes is that the drowned man *stays* dead: his is a failed resurrection, which is reaffirmed when Robin, searching for him, echoes the Lazarus story. "Sobbing / Beside the entrance of a cave" (739–40), unable to enter it, he cries "aloud, 'come, come to me, / I cannot come to you'" (764–65), the reason being, as the first edition makes clear, that the boy's call is directed not toward the living, but toward "the silent dead! / His father!" (685–86).

In Part Third, the idea of Christian resurrection is first introduced obliquely when Peter, attempting to assuage his conscience, claims that "'tis plain . . . This poor man never but for me / Could have had christian burial" (1,003–05). Later the narrator recalls Christ's entrance into Jerusalem:

> 'Tis said, that through prevailing grace
> He not unmov'd did notice now
> The cross upon thy shoulders scored
> Meek beast! in memory of the Lord
> To whom all human-kind shall bow;
>
> In memory of that solemn day
> When Jesus humbly deign'd to ride

> Entering the proud Jerusalem,
> By an immeasurable stream
> Of shouting people deified.   [first edition, lines 1,021–30]

Wordsworth deftly links this passage metaphorically to the earlier episode of the dead man in the stream by describing Christ's entrance into Jerusalem as an immersion into "an immeasurable *stream* / Of shouting people." As Matthew declares, Christ went to Jerusalem to "suffer many things of the elders and chief priests and scribes, and be killed, and be raised again the third day" (Matthew 16:21). When Peter arrives at the dead Father's home, the mother, thinking that her husband has returned, runs out of the cottage, only to find that the man on the ass is "another." Echoing Mary's meeting with Christ in the story of Lazarus, the narrator describes how

>   instantly upon the earth
> Beneath the full moon shining bright,
> Just at the ass's feet she fell,
> And from the ass poor Peter Bell
> Dismounts in most unhappy plight.
>
> What could he do?

Peter has once more been placed in the position of having to deal with death, for "the woman lay / Dead, as it seemed, both breath and limb." Peter is "confused," but guided by a newfound sympathy (and the "full moon shining bright"), "He raised her up and while he held / Her body propped against his knee / She waked" (1,250–63). In what represents an extraordinary humanization of the Christian gospel, Wordsworth, by echoing the language of the New Testament in the phrase "He raised her up," places Peter both in the position of Christ and in that of a witness to the resurrection, the "joyful tidings" (1,208) of the New Testament. "To scenes like these he was not used, / 'Twas altogether new to him" (1,259–60).

Peter Bell can be seen, then, as a secularized Easter narrative, a gospel story, which leads Peter to a specific Wordsworthian conception of resurrection, to the discovery that

> The heart of man's a holy thing,
> And Nature through a world of death

Breathes into him a second breath
Just like the breath of spring.   [1,312–15]

Putting aside, for the moment, the notion of "natural resurrection,"
we should nevertheless notice that the poem's conclusion is also patterned on the gospel narratives. It can hardly be a coincidence, for
instance, that the poem ends, as do the four Gospels, with a journey
"two hours ere the break of day" (1,369) to find the body of a dead
man, or that Peter is accompanied by a neighbor named Matthew
Sim[ps]on (1,367–69), his name linking him to both the evangelist
and the apostle. That Peter begins his story immediately after the wife
has figuratively undergone a resurrection also suggests that the narrative has an apostolic significance. In fact, while Peter is telling his
tale, the woman "upon a stone—sits" (1,316), at once recalling the
angel who "came and rolled back the stone from the door [of the tomb
of Christ], and sat upon it" (Matthew 28:2) and linking the tale metaphorically to Christ's words "Thou art Peter, and upon this rock I
will build my church." *Peter Bell* shows the conformities between conversion narratives and the early Christian Gospel, suggesting that such
miracles need not be seen as part of "a history only of departed
things," but can be recognized, if we only look around us, as "a simple
produce of the common day" (*Home at Grasmere*, MS. D, 803–08).

Yet if Peter's tale is a sacred narrative, it is an unusual one, because
it is imbedded in what is obviously a bad poem, delivered by "an inept
village Milton" (Jordan, *Peter Bell* 16) who is in difficulties from the
start. Offering a crude tale to a crude muse, a strange brew of low
comedy and rough violence, the narrator seems less a poet in the high
prophetic tradition than a garrulous sorcerer's apprentice, attempting
to conjure up the powers of a subterranean muse, the "Spirits of the
Mind" who inhabit the "wayward world" of magic. His is a "high
argument" (971–80), one that would rival Milton's "great Argument"
(*Paradise Lost* 1.24) on human origins and ends, if only he knew where
it was going.

Peter Bell is an interpolated tale, a form that explicitly focuses on the
role of interpretation in the telling and reception of stories. When,
for instance, the narrator declares that " 'Tis said, that through prevailing grace, / [Peter] not unmov'd did notice now / The cross" (first
edition, lines 1,021–23), he admits that he is not the author of the

tale, but only "relat[ing] the tale / Of Peter Bell the Potter" (134–35).
"I've play'd, I've danced with my narration" (981), he declares, as if
he were a modern-day David, dancing before the Ark of the Covenant.
The interpolations that arise during the reception of the tale are
equally clear, especially in the earlier versions of *Peter Bell*, in which
the villagers enter more actively into the interpretation and shaping
of the story. The most significant of these occurs at the beginning,
when, through the concerted efforts of Mistress Swan, little Bess, and
the Squire, the narrator is forced to start again. Other examples might
be cited—for instance, the comic debate sponsored by the news that
Peter "had a dozen wedded wives":

> "Oh monster!" cried the Parson's Lady;
> "Poor fellow!" echoed Stephen Otter;
> "Poor fellow! say you?" Mistress Swan,
> I do assure you such a man
> Was Peter Bell the Potter.   [250–55]

Or consider the narrator's digression occasioned by Bess's fear that
he is telling a ghostly supernatural ballad (731ff.), or his allusion to
Mr. Swan's use of tobacco (1,013–15). These incidents draw our attention to the dynamics of storytelling and suggest that the poem is
concerned with the phenomenon of oral narrative, how stories are
transmitted and shaped as they are passed from one village to the
next.

   The poem's focus on oral narrative draws on romantic ideas about
the ballad tradition. However, its imitation of Christian salvific narrative suggests that other considerations also influenced Wordsworth,
notably contemporary debates over the truth value and historicity of
the Gospels, discussions occasioned by the publication of Lessing's
"New Hypothesis Concerning the Evangelists Regarded as Merely Human Historians" (1778).[44] Lessing's primary hypothesis is that the Gospels were not original texts, but were translations of an earlier "written
collection of narratives concerning Christ's life and teaching, which
arose out of orally transmitted stories of the apostles and all those
people who had lived in association with Christ" (*Lessing's Theological
Writings* 66). This written collection, which he calls the Gospel of the
Nazarenes, was not the work of a single author, but was instead com-
piled by many anonymous persons, who freely drew upon, enlarged,

abbreviated, or altered the oral narratives of the primitive Christian milieu, those stories that had been passed down "from the mouths of credible people who had lived with Christ" (67). Lessing suggests the diversity of these original sources: "There were stories which originated from all eleven apostles; many of them were quite true but were not sufficiently useful for the later Christian world. There were stories which originated only from Christ's women associates, of which it was in part doubtful whether they had always understood correctly the wonder-man whom they so loved. There were stories which could only have come from his mother, from people who had known him in his childhood at the house of his parents; and however reliable they were, what help could they be to the world, which had enough to learn of what he did and said after entering upon his teaching office" (75). Lessing goes on to argue that the Synoptics were not the only translations of the original Gospel of the Nazarenes, but instead were the versions that came to be favored and were canonized over the course of time.

This view of the primitive Gospels as oral narratives and of the apostles as "poor, deprived, ill-educated men, subject to accesses of superstitious fear and reverence . . . primitive bards telling a tale destined to be repeated over and over again, and winning an audience in the most unlikely places," was of enormous importance to both Wordsworth and Coleridge, who mentions Lessing's essay as early as 1796.[45] Recent studies have persuasively shown that Coleridge was engaged, during the late 1790s, in a project greatly influenced by his knowledge of the German Higher Criticism, represented by such figures as C. G. Heyne, Alexander Geddes, J. D. Michaelis, and J. G. Eichhorn: that of finding a new basis for Christian faith through a reinterpretation of biblical narrative as universal myth. As E. S. Shaffer has demonstrated, Coleridge planned, in his epic poem "The Fall of Jerusalem," to show how all religions and cultures, having originally fallen away from a primal monotheistic faith, were reunited and fused together through the life and death of Christ: "Jew and Babylonian, Greek, Roman, and Egyptian, Christian and Mohammedan yet to be born, were conquered by and absorbed into Christianity in the great symbolic metropolis of the East that stood for the enduring significance of that life and that death" (*"Kubla Khan" and "The Fall of Jerusalem"* 37). Jerome J. McGann and Leslie Brisman have extended

Shaffer's ideas, especially to *The Ancient Mariner*. McGann has suggested that the poem imitates "a culturally redacted literary work" that illustrates, through its fictional character as a story that has undergone successive interpretations, interpolations, retellings, accretions, and redactions, the gradual but constant growth and articulation of religious experience. As it depicts the transition from a world of superstition and miracle to one grounded in human love ("He prayeth best, who loveth best / All things both great and small" [614–15]), *The Ancient Mariner* can be read as a history of the origin and development of Christianity, from its beginnings in the oral narratives of the wandering, ill-educated, superstitious apostles, to its more sophisticated realization as doctrine and received text. Writes Leslie Brisman: "It is the events and course of things in a poem—the *history* of revelation and the historicity of the narrative movement from miracle to moral—that constitute the glory of scripture and literature."[46]

We are now in a position to recognize that the oft-noted structural similarities between *Peter Bell* and *The Ancient Mariner*, which Wordsworth emphasized through parody and allusion, reflect their shared interest in the genesis and meaning of salvific narratives; both poems suggest that religious experience originates in the crude oral superstitions of Lessing's rude, wandering apostolic milieu and develops as these stories are repeated, written down, and reinterpreted. It is worth noting that *Peter Bell*, like *The Ancient Mariner*, is a circular narrative, which links the figure of Peter "crippled sore in his narration" (1,275) to the narrator who, "with visage pale, / And sore too from a slight contusion," delivers his "promised tale" to "cover [his] confusion" to a pious group around his "stone table" (139–55). The history of Peter Bell thus leads up to that moment when the poet tells his tale in the garden. This emphasis on the connection between past and present storytelling indicates that the poem is as much concerned with the genesis and history of the narrative first told by Peter as it is with the events narrated in it. We should recall that Christ was by an "immeasurable stream / Of shouting people deified" (first edition, 1,029–30), that is, by a tradition of Christian believers. The poem even provides its own history of reception: Wordsworth bases *Peter Bell, A Tale in Verse* on an oral ballad called "the tale / Of Peter Bell the Potter" (134–35), related by a naive village poet (a "heartless [instead of a "grey-beard"] loon" [67]). The oral sources of this ballad have been lost in time, but

they can ostensibly be traced back to an original redemptive narrative
first told by (the singer/prophet/apostle) Peter Bell. Wordsworth's emphasis on the limitations of his narrator and his suggestion that the
tale is told as a "cover" for "confusion" parallel the emphasis of Lessing
and the Higher Criticism on the intellectual limitations of those who
first received the Christian revelation, people grappling with a mystery. *Peter Bell* reinterprets the history of Christianity as a history of
the manner in which a circle of people, spread across time, have lis-
tened to, understood, and transformed a certain kind of narrative—
"the wonders of a wild career" (first edition, line 130). It is perhaps
for this reason that Wordsworth, in an early manuscript of the poem,
toyed with the idea of indicating the sacred status of the story by twice
placing the name Peter Bell in close juxtaposition with the word
"amen" (MS. 2, 1ʳ) and why, as Hazlitt testifies, "he announced the
fate of his hero in prophetic tones" (*Complete Works* 17:118).

Like Coleridge, Wordsworth mythologizes biblical narrative. But
where Coleridge asserts the primacy and centrality of Christianity, as
it came to be embodied by Jerusalem, Wordsworth supplies an alternate center that allows for cultural diversity by tracing all religious
beliefs back to a primal source in the mysteries of a mind that shapes
itself out of its contact with nature. Embedded in Peter's journey
through the forest is a history of religions, as the "rocks that tower on
either side" are transformed by his imagination into "a wild fantastic
scene":

> Temples like those among the Hindoos,
> And mosques and spires and abbey windows
> And castles all with ivy green.   [826–30]

But more important than any history of religious displacement is the
fact that the landscape is shown to have generated multiple religious
institutions—Hindu temples or Moslem mosques, or the spires and
windows of abbeys. The numerous classical allusions in the poem,
which Geoffrey Durrant has noted, from the opening reference to
Pegasus and the subsequent identification of the limping poet as a
modern-day Hephaestus, serve a similar purpose, suggesting that *Peter
Bell* synthesizes all religions as it returns them to their origin in the
imagination's encounter with nature.[47] By emphasizing the common
and popular origins of this story, as a ballad and a conventional meth-

odist conversion narrative, by indicating that miracles do not depend on "the intervention of supernatural agency" (Dedication), and by showing that the sacred develops as a progress of mind in which "crude Nature work[s] in untaught minds," Wordsworth shows us that biblical narratives, whether popular or sacred, are not important because of a divine origin, but because they document "the laws and progress of belief " (*Prelude* 7.298–99) and lead us through discipline to feel the holiness of the heart's affections.

The Gospel of Nature

Like "The Idiot Boy," *Peter Bell* is a poem in which comedy is the medium of sophisticated argument. The humor of *Peter Bell* is not only indebted to mock epic and to a comic vision of the Old Testament account of Balaam, but is probably also very much influenced by anti-methodist literature, by magazine poems such as "The Methodist" (1766), which includes the following attack on methodist preachers:

> The *Fishermen* no longer set
> For *Fish* the meshes of their Net,
> But catch, *like Peter, Men of Sin,*
> For *catching* is to *take them in.*

Within a context of comic satire, Wordsworth nevertheless found, by positing the conformities between the methodist reawakening of the spirit among the poor and marginal classes of England and the primitive world of the gospel narratives, a way to observe, to re-experience, and thus to link his poetry to the origins of Christianity. Christianity's vital message did not reside in the past, but was being continually re-enacted among the lower classes of society. Wordsworth is concerned less with the historical veracity of the Bible than with its power as story to remake or refashion its audience. Methodist conversion narratives demonstrate in more radical terms the fundamental capability of all narratives to transform and discipline the self, to *resurrect* new selves out of old ones. The history of the Bible as a sacred narrative is thus made an emblem of all imaginative narratives, which progressively discipline the imagination, civilizing, humanizing, and socializing otherwise violent selves, as these narratives themselves undergo imagi-

native transformation, passing from fables, to oral conversion
narratives, to myths, and finally to sacred texts.

In *Peter Bell,* nature has the status of a sacred text, which remains
inactive without the intervention of the imagination:

> Nature ne'er could find the way
> Into the heart of Peter Bell.
>
> In vain, through every changeful year
> Did Nature lead him as before. [214–17]

Nature "leads" Peter in the same way as a text leads its reader: it
provides the preconditions of a progressive imaginative reading and
interpretation that will transform him and, by so doing, transform
how nature appears to him. The nature that consequently appears at
the end of the poem, which "Breathes into him a second breath / Just
like the breath of spring" (1,314–15), is one that has been *brought into
being* over the course of Peter's journey, through his having learned
how to interpret it in a specific way, now responding to things that
previously he ignored. Nature educates through its capacity for progressive multiple readings, each reflecting the intellectual development of the individual and making possible the passage from the fear
of nature to the love of man. In the fragmentary essay "[The Sublime
and the Beautiful]," Wordsworth claims that "as we advance in life,
we can escape upon the invitation of our more placid & gentle nature
from those obtrusive qualities in an object sublime in its general character; which qualities, at an earlier age, precluded imperiously the
perception of beauty which that object if contemplated under another
relation would have been capable of imparting" (*ProseW* 2:349).
Though the sublime and the beautiful coexist simultaneously in nature, they do not exist in the same way for the mind, which is affected
first by the "obtrusive qualities in an object sublime" and only later by
a more "placid and gentle nature." Drawing on writers such as Robert
Lowth and Hugh Blair, who argued that the poetry of the Old Testament is a direct expression of the ancient Hebrews' everyday relationship with nature, *Peter Bell* reinterprets the Bible as a mythic
history of mankind's progressive understanding of nature. From this
perspective, the poem is not so much an imitation of the Bible as a
complementary or rival interpretation of the history documented by
the Bible of primitive mankind's changing understanding of nature.[48]

Part Third, as quite literally a "gospel of nature," can thus stand to the violent "world of death" from which Peter has emerged in the same manner as New Testament love stands to Old Testament prophecy, because both represent in mythic terms the same anthropological development—the wedding of the mind to nature.

Peter Bell celebrates the human heart. But it is also a political manifesto, for Wordsworth is claiming that in modern society nature, and a poetry grounded in nature, are to perform the same socializing roles that were originally performed by the Bible and myth. As long as Peter stood outside of nature, he stood outside of social or moral control. Discipline begins to be exercised from the moment that he begins to see himself as a figure in a "plot," when he discovers that "there is some plot against me laid" (437). From then on Peter gets caught up in his own reading of nature, and through this entanglement is taught the value of language, sympathy, family, religion, and society.

We can see, then, that Wordsworth's turn to nature was not motivated from a desire to avoid or evade politics, but from the belief that nature and the narratives it supports have historically been the very medium of political argument and social control. What he feared most was that governmental policies, which did not recognize the social importance of nature, had given rise to a large, marginal class of ungovernable people who were a likely source of revolutionary activity—a subject I will return to in chapter 6.[49] In the 1800 preface he assigns two major causes for what he sees as a return of contemporary society "to a state of almost savage torpor." He points out that a decade of revolutionary and counter-revolutionary struggles, "the great national events which are daily taking place," has combined with "the encreasing accumulation of men in cities" to produce a volatile situation: the "uniformity" of the work of these people gives rise to "a craving for extraordinary incident," that is to say, despair, hopelessness, and the pent-up anger of people like Peter Bell lead to a desire for violence and radical change, "which the rapid communication of intelligence hourly gratifies." The literary situation is no better. The major writers of the English tradition, Wordsworth observes, "are driven into neglect by frantic novels, sickly and stupid German Tragedies, and deluges of idle and extravagant stories in verse" (*ProseW* 1:128). *Peter Bell* represents Wordsworth's first major attempt to deal in aesthetic and political terms with this "deluge."

FOUR

A "Word Scarce Said"
At the Crossroads of
Hysteria and Witchcraft

Old Susan, she who dwells alone,
Is sick, and makes a piteous
moan,
    As if her very life would
    fail.

    There's not a house
    within a mile,
    No hand to help them in
    distress;
    Old Susan lies a-bed in pain,
    And sorely puzzled are the
    twain,.
For what she ails they cannot
guess.
["The Idiot Boy" 19–26]

Susan Gale's strange disease and unusual cure have received little critical attention from readers of "The Idiot Boy"—so little, in fact, that no one has felt it worth clarifying what her illness actually is. The doctor never arrives to give a diagnosis, so descriptions of her sickness, from Southey's term "indisposed" to Danby's "imaginary illness" and "psychological bed-riddenness," have been decidedly vague.[1] For most readers, her illness is psychosomatic and of relative unimportance, except as a comic device that occasions Johnny's mock epic quest. Like Betty Foy's terrors, Susan's disease would seem to be but another instance of "Female Wit" at work creating "mighty Contests" from "trivial Things."[2] Nevertheless, in the 1800 preface to *Lyrical Ballads*, speaking of both "The Idiot Boy" and "The Mad Mother," Wordsworth places the workings of the female imagination at the center of these poems when he states that they trace "the maternal passion through many of its more subtle windings" (*ProseW* 1:126).

It is not by chance that Susan, like many other women whom Wordsworth wrote about at this time, is described as "she who dwells alone" (19). In Wordsworth's reference to "maternal passion" (either "connubial or parental" [*MY* 1:336], as he later notes) and its "subtle windings," one can discern the figural survival of the traditional medical discourse on hysteria. For centuries, in highly metaphoric descriptions of female physiology, medicine had explained the disease in terms of "unnatural states" of the womb—the hungry up-and-down wanderings and complicated windings of the uterus, or the poisonous and corrupt "vapors" rising from a diseased womb.[3] Hysteria (or the Mother, the Incubus, spleen, vapors) was usually accompanied by a sensation of "suffocation," pressure felt on the chest or a choking feeling in the throat. But it was also known for its mimetic powers, its protean mimicry of other diseases. "The shapes of *Proteus,* or the colours of the *chameleon,* are not more numerous and inconstant, than the variations of the hypochondriac and hysteric disease," writes the Edinburgh doctor Robert Whytt.[4] Significantly, the imagination is rarely absent from these discussions. As Edward Jorden, who reintroduced the ancient notion of hysteria as a sex-linked disease, writes: "We doe observe that most commonly besides the indisposition of the bodie: here is also some Melancholike or capricious conceit . . . which being . . . removed, the disease is easily overcome."[5] As neurology supplanted humoral psychology in the seventeenth century, the uterus was less frequently mentioned in connection with hysteria, even as the imagination gained in importance. Now physicians began citing the strange and powerful effects of a combination of passion and strong imagination on the weak nerves and bodies of women. "Women are more subject than Men to Diseases arising from the Passions of the

Mind," writes the Italian physician Georgi Baglivi, "and more violently affected with them, by Reason of the Timorousness and Weakness of their Sex." Treatment consists, therefore, in reducing "the disorderly Motions of the Imagination to their Primitive Regularity."[6]

This link between hysteria and the imagination, as well as its fashionable popularity among the wealthy, led to its being frequently satirized throughout the eighteenth century. "Vapourish people are perpetual subjects for diseases to work upon," remarks Robert Lovelace. "*Name* but the malady, and it is *theirs* in a moment."[7] Susan's psychosomatic illness, therefore, should not be seen apart from a context of satire.[8] Yet even so, the disease was also of considerable interest to doctors and philosophers, who saw in it a profound and disturbing proof of the body's compliance with the promptings and demands of the imagination. Hysteria had become an exemplary disease of the imagination. Through the observation of women afflicted by it, the powers of the imagination and bodily imitation were made visible to the eye, not as abstract principles, but as forces "monstrous and terrible to beholde" seen palpably operating on women's bodies, behavior, and speech (Jorden, *Suffocation of the Mother* 2).

Though eighteenth-century medicine was primarily mechanistic in orientation, its interest in psychopathology brought it into close proximity with poetic concerns. As L. J. Rather has observed, physicians commonly ascribed (partly because of inadequate physiological knowledge) "as much or more in the way of bodily change to the emotions or 'power of the imagination' than would all but the most convinced proponents of the psychological causation of disease today."[9] In describing various diseases of the imagination, their force and effects, their causes and cures, medicine developed a complex and extensive discourse on the imagination and on suggestion, association, sympathy, and imitation. "It appears almost incredible," Peter Shaw writes in *The Reflector* (1750), "what great Effects the Imagination has upon Patients."[10] Medicine was rich in spectacular accounts of individuals possessed by their imaginations, and these cases imparted to its discourse on the imagination a strangeness, vivacity, and concreteness that exercised a profound, if rarely acknowledged, influence on philosophy and literature. Where the modern doctor sees a tubercular condition, the eighteenth-century doctor saw the wasting power of melancholy and nostalgia.[11] In the obsessive ravings of madmen, the fits of epileptics, the convulsions of religious enthusiasts, the rage of the hydrophobic, but most of all in the strange bodily afflictions caused by melancholy, spleen, or hysteria, physicians set aside physical causes and diagnosed the sublime and threatening presence of a diseased imagination.

This horizon of inquiry, I believe, more than satire, underlies Susan Gale's appearance in "The Idiot Boy." In this chapter, I would like to examine how the medical and philosophical discourse that made hysterical women victims of the workings of a powerful imagination also made them, for Wordsworth, a key to unlocking the mysteries of "a mind beset / With images, and haunted by itself " (*Prelude* 6.179–80). Just as Freud, a century later, turned to "hysterical women" as a scientific point of departure for psychoanalysis, Wordsworth also found in these women a medium of speculative argument, a means for observing and forcefully delineating, as he notes in connection with *Lyrical Ballads,* the manner in which "language and the human mind act and react on each other" (*ProseW* 1:120). In seeking a language to describe and understand his own imagination, Wordsworth turned not only to the contradictory discourse on Methodism and the extraordinary powers of methodist preaching, but also to the figure of the "hysterical woman" who inhabited medical discourse.

The Witch/Hysteric

Wordsworth was writing at a time when a knowledge of medicine was understood as a prerequisite for empirical speculation. Locke's *Essay,* by combining ethics and physiology, had placed medical theory at the center of philosophical debate so that, by the end of the eighteenth century, as Hans-Jürgen Schings has shown, the "philosophical doctor" had become a popular literary type.[12] It should not surprise us, then, that Coleridge and Wordsworth decided in 1798 to visit Germany, where Coleridge met Johann Friedrich Blumenbach, the famous anthropologist and comparative anatomist, and Wordsworth sought to furnish himself "with a tolerable stock of information in natural science" (*EY* 213). Nor would it have been unusual for a poet, seeking material for *The Recluse,* to have turned to Erasmus Darwin's *Zoönomia.* In late February or early March 1798, Wordsworth urged

the printer Joseph Cottle to send him this encyclopedic medical treatise *"by the first carrier"* (*EY* 199; author's emphasis). Though approximately two weeks later Dorothy wrote that these volumes had
answered Wordsworth's purpose, it was not until 9 May, at least two
months later, that they were finally returned (*EY* 214–15, 218).

It is probably an exaggeration to say, as does James Averill, that
Wordsworth drew from *Zoönomia* the associationist theory of perception that earlier critics, such as Arthur Beatty, attributed to David
Hartley.[13] It would have been very difficult for anyone educated at
Cambridge during the late eighteenth century *not* to be conversant
with the subject.[14] Nevertheless, *Zoönomia* was an influential work.
Wordsworth found in it a powerful demonstration of the speculative
uses of the "case history." Arranged under classificatory headings,
often amounting to little more than an anecdote, a few words, or a
short paragraph, the case histories that form so large a part of *Zoönomia* are more than just examples or illustrations. They play an integral
role in Darwin's speculations on human nature and represent the
basic figural medium of his discourse, the place where his own often
highly speculative theories about association and human development—ideas that led to the book's being singled out by the *Anti-Jacobin*
for censure in 1798—could be illustrated and demonstrated. In the
"case history" Wordsworth found a mode of writing that could be
adapted to poetic as well as philosophical argument, one well suited
to the observation, dramatic display, and interpretation of the workings of the imagination. Yet it should also be stressed that he was
aware of its shortcomings. Commenting on George Crabbe's poetry,
Wordsworth writes, in 1808, that "the Muses have just about as much
to do [with "mere matters of fact"] as they have with a Collection of
medical reports, or of Law cases" (*MY* 1:268). Though medical and
philosophical cases provided Wordsworth with a vocabulary for taking
up poetic, moral, and philosophical concerns, they represented a discursive form that could not enter his poetry without substantial revision.

The very fact that no critic has felt called upon to identify Susan
Gale's illness is a gauge to Wordsworth's success in transforming the
case history. Just as his representation of Johnny in the poem redefines
popular and medical conceptions of idiocy, Wordsworth replaces the
objectivity and detachment claimed by the case history with the ob-

servations of a comic narrator and asks the reader to laugh, yet sympathize, with Susan's dilemma. Since this is probably not the first time this lonely spinster has suffered from such complaints, we can see her sickness as at once a neighborhood calling card and a symptom of her need for love. Simultaneously her therapy reflects the concerns that made the observation of hysterical women a staging ground for a broader inquiry into the powers of imagination and poetic language. It begins early in the poem, shortly after Betty leaves in search of her son:

> And Susan now begins to fear
> Of sad mischances not a few,
> That Johnny may perhaps be drowned;
> Or lost, perhaps, and never found;
> Which they must both for ever rue.   [177–81]

"Present fears / Are less than horrible imaginings" (*Macbeth* 1.3.137–38). Susan, in ignorance of what is happening to Johnny, imagines the direst of situations:

> Long time lay Susan lost in thought;
> And many dreadful fears beset her,
> Both for her Messenger and Nurse;
> And, as her mind grew worse and worse,
> Her body—it grew better.
>
> She turned, she tossed herself in bed,
> On all sides doubts and terrors met her;
> Point after point did she discuss;
> And, while her mind was fighting thus,
> Her body still grew better.
>
> "Alas! what is become of them?
> These fears can never be endured;
> I'll to the wood."—The word scarce said,
> Did Susan rise up from her bed,
> As if by magic cured.   [412–26]

Here mental terror is substituted for bodily pains: the "dreadful fears" and "doubts and terrors" conjured by Susan's imagination replace the pains of hysteria. This therapy expresses a traditional idea that disease is a product of the idle mind.[15] Yet the logic of this transference, central to Wordsworthian poetics, is also partly explained by Edmund Burke, who argues that pain and fear have a common physiological basis and "act upon the same parts of the body, and in the same manner, though somewhat differing in degree . . . The only difference between pain and terror, is, that things which cause pain operate on the mind, by the intervention of the body; whereas things that cause terror generally affect the bodily organs by the operation of the mind suggesting the danger."[16] In Susan's case, this metaphoric displacement is not based, as Burke argues, on a physiological mechanism, but instead on the fact that pain and terror represent alternate modes of imaginative activity. Therapy consists in a rechanneling of the imagination so that instead of speaking unconsciously, in bodily symptoms and physical pain, it finds expression in images and symbols. The poet's task, akin to the psychoanalyst's, is that of alleviating physical suffering by providing the imagination with language. Not surprisingly, it finds its conclusion in a "word scarce said," whereupon Susan rises "as if by magic cured."

The narrator's declaration that this cure works like "magic" requires us to address another feature of the history of hysteria: its close link to witchcraft. Though Betty Foy and Susan never *say* what they believe is causing Susan's pains, one strong possibility that they are not likely to have discounted is that she is bewitched. In a world still inhabited by "goblins," "ghosts," and "wandering gipsy-folk" (226–30) who threaten to steal straying children, diseases that had no natural explanation or remedy were frequently suspected as having supernatural causes. In his *Displaying of Supposed Witchcraft* (1677), John Webster complains that "in all its parts in the North of *England* . . . the common people, if they chance to have any sort of the Epilepsie, Palsie, Convulsions or the like, do presently perswade themselves that they are bewitched, fore-spoken, blasted, fairy-taken, or haunted with some evil spirit, and the like."[17] The villagers' reluctance to verbalize their suspicions does not indicate an absence of witchcraft, but instead reflects the deeply felt anxiety and the distrust of the performative powers of words that are characteristic of societies in which magic is practiced. When words can wound and cure, when they are no sooner said than they become realities, speech is not used lightly and some things are best left unsaid. Betty can sit for hours in "a sad quandary," because "there's *nobody to say* / If she must go, or she must stay!" (168–70, my emphasis). But "at the first word that Susan said" (184), her mind is made up and she is off in search for her son, partly to prevent Susan from finishing her sentence "'God forbid it should be true!'" (183). In like manner, Susan can deliberate "point after point," attempting to rationalize the doubts and terrors meeting her "on all sides," but it is not until she declares, "'I'll to the wood,'" that she is able to "rise up from her bed, / As if by magic cured." Betty and Susan consider her cure a miracle, cause for as "merry meeting / As ever was in Christendom" (430–31). But readers are provided with an alternative explanation, that this case demonstrates the psychological basis of magic.

It is important to recognize that hysteria played a major role in the demystification of witchcraft. The first great victory of modern psychiatry, in fact, was its transformation of the witch and her victim into melancholy or hysterical women. Edward Jorden reintroduced the concept of hysteria after attending the 1602 trial of Elizabeth Jackson for having bewitched Mary Glover. *A Briefe Discourse on the Suffocation of the Mother,* written to counter the influence of King James's *Daemonologie,* aimed to show that cases of demonic possession were really attributable to the "varietie" and "strangenesse" of the symptoms of hysteria.[18] The work was indebted to Reginald Scot, who had earlier argued that witchcraft had its source in the confused imaginations of melancholy women, often brought on by menopause.[19] A "strong imagination" combined with a "strange event," John Cotta suggests, has "intangled many a poore spinster in a thicker string then her cunning could untwist, to save the cracking of her neck."[20]

Despite the obvious differences between the medical discourse on hysteria and witchcraft beliefs, both discourses generally were applied to the same marginalized individuals—unmarried women, most frequently widows and spinsters, though occasionally also young unmarried women, especially poor women living on the margins of villages. What changed in the transformation of a witch into a hysteric was not the person, rarely even the way she was treated, but the explanatory system within which that individual's difference was understood. Both modes of explanation also applied the same pressures on women to conform to sanctioned ideas about the need for family life. As H. C. Midelfort notes in discussing witchcraft in renaissance Germany, "The structure of society was so completely geared to the family that persons without families were automatically peculiar, unprotected, and suspect. Widows in particular were defenseless until they remarried. So were spinsters. For this reason, husbands urged their wives to remarry if death should separate them."[21] Freud offered the same advice to hysterics. These two considerations—the fact that a witch and a hysteric are the *same* person interpreted differently, and the resulting association (even interchangeability) between witchcraft and hysteria, as modes of explanation that emphasize the powers of a strong imagination—are of central importance to Wordsworth's representation of witches in "The Three Graves," "The Mad Mother," "Goody Blake and Harry Gill," and "The Thorn." In these poems isolated or abandoned women come to serve as the empirical medium for recovering the original workings of the imagination and exploring its power to produce such weird forms of delirium and bodily symptoms that they might appear to be "under the dominion of spells" (William Harvey, *On Parturation* 542).

"The Three Graves"

Though the sphere of supernatural agency was certainly diminished by the transformation of the witch into a hysterical woman, the realm of the imaginary agency was greatly expanded. No longer primarily an object of superstition, but instead a concern of physicians, the witch could enter into case histories as part of the empirical discourse on the powers of the imagination. It is in this ambiguous form, as a figure inhabiting a liminal zone between supernaturalism and medical discourse, that the witch appears in Wordsworth's poetry. In the fragmentary "Three Graves," which he began in 1797 and which was later taken up by Coleridge, the manner in which psychopathology, superstition, and poetry converged on the witch/hysteric is clear.

In his note, Coleridge stresses the link between psychopathology and witchcraft that gave rise to the poem. Based on an actual incident ("positive facts, and of no very distant date"), the poem would have provided "a striking proof of the possible effect on the imagination, from an idea violently and suddenly impressed on it."[22] It would have followed, he declares, "the progress and symptoms of the morbid action on the fancy" in three women, each recognizably a type of woman customarily prone to hysteria or accusations of witchcraft—a lonely widow "bordering on her fortieth year"; her daughter Mary, a "barren wife"; and Ellen, a "maid forlorn."[23] Even Edward, who is the object of their rivalry, catches the sickness. His surprise upon hearing the widow's proposal of marriage, Coleridge tells us, combined with "the effect of horror which he felt, acting as it were *hysterically* on his nervous system," makes him fling "her from him and burst into a fit of laughter" (268, my emphasis). Wordsworth writes that the rejected widow, furious, frustrated, and embarrassed, falls to her knees and, resorting to witchcraft, curses both her daughter and future son-in-law, angrily taunting them:

> "I am a woman weak and old
>   Why turn a thought to me?
> What can an aged mother do,
>   And what have ye to dread?
> A curse is wind, it hath no shape
>   To haunt your marriage bed."   [*Poems,* lines 196–201]

As he would later do in the case of Susan, Wordsworth uses this situation to emphasize the performative powers of language. "A curse is wind"; a word is as transitory as breath; it has "no shape," no substance. Yet the mother knows that her words can invoke spirits, the earthly "Spirits of the Mind," and imagination.

There is no reason to doubt Coleridge's claim for the factual basis of the poem. As Pierre Bayle observes, cases in which newlyweds came to believe that their marriage-bed was bewitched were quite common: "I could not restrain myself from making you recall something which is without doubt very common in your province, and which visibly demonstrates what the imagination can accomplish. Several men are unable to consummate their marriage and believe that this impotence is the effect of a spell. From then on, the newlyweds regard each other with an evil eye, and their discord descends sometimes into a most horrible enmity: the sight of one makes the other shiver. What I tell you here are not old wive's tales, but certain and incontestable facts which only too often come into the sight and ken of all the neighbors in the provinces, where much faith is put in the traditions of witchcraft."[24] Bayle demystifies witchcraft, telling us that these superstitions supply us with a "visible demonstration" of "what the imagination can accomplish." "An imagination that is alarmed by the fear of a witch's spell," he writes, "can overthrow the animal economy and produce those extravagant symptoms that exasperate the most expert medical doctors" (*Réponse* 3:559). Initially functioning as explanations and excuses for "impotence," these beliefs lead inevitably to suspicion, "discord," and, finally, "most horrible enmity" between the newlyweds; the imagination invests the "evil eye" with real power and "the sight of one makes the other shiver."

"The Three Graves" probably would have told a similar story, in which a young couple's belief in a curse prevents them from having sexual relations (she remains a "barren wife") and progressively leads to mutual enmity. Upon first hearing the curse, Mary believes that "the bed beneath her stirred" (*Poems* 157). And Coleridge, aware that "the common opinion is that witches visit this evil service upon newlyweds by pronouncing certain words during the nuptial benediction" (*Réponse* 3:561), describes Mary imagining her mother cursing her:

> And when the Vicar join'd their hands,
>   Her limbs did creep and freeze:
> And when they prayed, she thought she saw
>   Her mother on her knees.   [lines 240–43]

When Mary leaves the church, just as her feet touch the "mossy track" (a symbol that reappears in "The Thorn"), she falls victim to hysteria, the "Suffocation of the Mother":

> The shade o'er-flushed her limbs with heat—
>   Then came a chill like death:
> And when the merry bells rang out,
>   *They seemed to stop her breath.*   [247–55, my emphasis]

Though the subsequent "progress and symptoms of the morbid action on the fancy" (*Complete Poetical Works* 1:269) of Mary remains incomplete, Ellen's case, also fragmentary, is similar and provides more clues concerning the direction the poem would have taken.

It is of the essence of the mother's curse, itself expressive of a love born from her having "fed upon the sight" of the young lovers' "'course of wooing,'" that the young couple should also find itself repeating the original love triangle.[25] Ellen, "at whose house / Young

Edward woo'd his wife" (316–17), also falls in love with Edward and, after likewise being cursed by the mother, becomes a rival lover. "They clung round him [Edward] with their arms," Coleridge writes, "Both Ellen and his wife" (379–80), the latter now reduced to a common noun. And when Edward cries,

> Dear Ellen did not weep at all,
>   But closelier did she cling,
> And turned her face and looked as if
>   She saw some frightful thing.   [385–88]

We later discover that Mary is the "frightful thing" that Ellen sees clinging "on his breast." In Ellen's imagination, Mary has become a diabolical double of the mother:

> And with a kind of shriek she cried,
>   "Oh Christ! you're like your mother!"   [446–47]

This doubling is essential to the working out of Edward's curse, for symbolically Edward *does* marry "the mother," as is clear in his reference to Mary in his nightmare—"A mother too!" (522). The progress of Ellen's hysteria is fragmentary: the curse appears to have produced a "sore grief . . . haunting in her brain" (428–29); she grows "thin" (430) and suffers from "convulsion" (437). However, in an isolated fragment, we are given an extraordinary representation of madness and Wordsworth's most explicit representation of a case of bodily possession. Ellen's body becomes the stage for melancholy's appearance as nightmarish spectacle:

> And she was pinched and pricked with pins,
>   And twitched with cord and wire;
> And starting from her seat would cry,
>   "It is a stool of fire."
>
> And she would bare her maiden breast,
>   And if you looked would shew
> The milk which clinging imps of hell
>   And sucking daemons drew.   [*Poems* 206–13]

Ellen's morbid extravagance, her belief that she is being "pinched and pricked with pins" and her display of milk flowing from her "maiden breast," evokes the bodily histrionics of the witch trials. As if her

breasts were "witches teats," those insensible protruberances where
the witch fed her familiars and which were discovered by pricking the
body "with pins," Ellen displays what she takes to be the *indicia* of
possession. Perhaps her breasts do actually give milk. If so, this can
be seen either as a symptom of her desire to be a mother, and thus
an illustration of the powerful workings of the imagination, or possibly, since we lack the intervening narrative, as an indication that she
has indeed become one, her madness arising, perhaps, because she
has been abandoned by her lover (Edward?) or has lost her child.
Though either interpretation is possible, the ambiguity is not without
significance, for we will see this problematic interpretive framework
repeated in "The Mad Mother" and "The Thorn."

Witchcraft and the Discipline of Charity

Wordsworth's reasons for abandoning "The Three Graves" are not
clear; he later claimed that Coleridge made it "too shocking and painful, and not sufficiently sweetened by any healing views" (*PW* 1:374).
In the spring of 1798, however, he began three other witchcraft
poems—"Goody Blake and Harry Gill," "The Mad Mother," and "The
Thorn." These can be understood as attempts to solve the problems
posed by the failure of the earlier poem: how to modify the detached
language of the case history without relinquishing the ability to take
up the speculative questions, relating to the imagination, that had
found their locus in descriptions of witch/hysterics. "Goody Blake and
Harry Gill," a "true story" (as the subtitle indicates) of a farmer in
Warwickshire falling victim to witchcraft, is one of the first of the
poems written for *Lyrical Ballads*.[26] Drawn almost verbatim from the
copy of *Zoönomia* that Wordsworth borrowed from Cottle in early
March, from the section dealing with *mania mutabilis*, its structural and
stylistic proximity to the medical case history is apparent. In the 1800
preface, Wordsworth declared that he "wished to draw attention to
the truth that the power of the human imagination is sufficient to
produce such changes even in our physical nature as might almost
appear miraculous. The truth is an important one; the fact (for it is
a *fact*) is a valuable illustration of it" (*ProseW* 1:150). As in "The Three
Graves," then, the poem uses the psychopathology of witchcraft as a

key to demonstrating the power of the imagination to shape and organize ("as if by magic") even bodily processes. It examines the psychical construction of a witch—the process whereby old women are made
into witches by the imaginations of their accusers—and the fearsome
disciplinary power that arises from this fiction. Instead of being told
by an objective narrator, the story of Harry Gill's illness is recounted
by a villager, perhaps a farmer, who is not removed from the world
of superstition and gossip that make witches and bewitchings possible.

The tale is a simple one. Harry, a "lusty drover" (17), suspects that
the old weaver Goody Blake has been pilfering kindling from his
hedge over the course of the winter, so he decides to catch her in the
act. On a particularly cold night, after lying in wait for her behind a
barley rick, he hears her busily filling her apron with twigs. Like a
predatory animal, he "softly creeps" down the hill, and stands "behind
a bush of elder" watching her. (Again, we see a reworking of the
"primitive encounter.") When Goody Blake has finished gathering
sticks, he "springs" on her and "fiercely" grabs and shakes her, crying
"'I've caught you then at last!'" (79–92). The implied sexual aggres-
sion and the satisfaction of violent desire is barely suppressed; Harry,
like Peter Bell, takes pleasure in unrestrained violence and uncon-
tested possession ("Every Jack must have his Gill"). The old cottager,
overcome by the ferocity of the attack, falls to her knees (like the
mother in "The Three Graves"), and, as a last resort, "her withered
hand uprearing" (97), prays that if Harry cannot sympathize with
others' suffering, he should feel it physically:

> "God! who art never out of hearing,
> O may he never more be warm!"
> The cold, cold moon above her head,
> Thus on her knees did Goody pray.   [99–102]

Goody Blake may indeed believe her words summon up divine powers
(even the victims of social ostracism make whatever use they can of a
stereotype). But it is clear that they function without the authority of
supernatural agency, beneath a bare and vacant heaven, its only in-
habitant the "cold, cold moon." They depend instead upon the imagination of her *human* auditor, who "heard what she had said: / And
icy cold he turned away" (103–04).

Harry falls victim to a self-made fiction. "Old and poor" (21), "housed alone" (36), living outside the village "on a hill's northern side" (30), a nocturnal creature whose crimes, though petty, take place at night, Goody Blake easily fits the traditional stereotype of the witch. Erasmus Darwin even said she looked "like a witch in a play" (*Zoönomia* 2:359), and Southey, in his review of *Lyrical Ballads* in *Critical Review,* wrote that the poem was likely to "promote the popular superstition of witchcraft" (200). All that is needed, therefore, is for her "prayer" to follow the conventional pattern of admonitory magic for Harry, already cold from his long nightwatch "in frost and snow" (71), to be convinced that it is his ill luck to have stumbled onto a witch and to be filled with icy horror.[27] The resulting bizarre illness confirms his belief:

> 'Twas all in vain, a useless matter,
> And blankets were about him pinned;
> Yet still his jaws and teeth they clatter,
> Like a loose casement in the wind.
> And Harry's flesh it fell away;
> And all who see him say, 'tis plain,
> That, live as long as live he may,
> He never will be warm again.   [113–20]

Harry's disease manifests a double relation. It is an *accusation*, and thus a projection of his own cold-heartedness upon the old woman. Yet it is also a form of *punishment* and thus reflects, at the level of his body, the inceptive stages of conscience and guilt, the recognition that he has violated the law of charity. As historians of witchcraft, such as Alan Macfarlane and Keith Thomas, have suggested, witchcraft accusations reflected social ambivalence toward Christian charity. Joseph Addison stresses the same point in his reflections on witchcraft: "When an old Woman begins to doat, and grow chargeable to a Parish, she is generally turned into a Witch, and fills the whole Country with extravagant Fancies, imaginary Distempers, and terrifying Dreams. In the mean time, the poor Wretch that is the innocent Occasion of so many Evils begins to be frighted at her self, and sometimes confesses secret Commerces and Familiarities that her Imagination forms in a delirious old Age. This frequently cuts off Charity from the greatest Objects of Compassion, and inspires People with a Malevolence towards those poor decrepid Parts of our Species, in whom Human

Nature is defaced by Infirmity and Dotage."[28] Paralleling the manner in which Johnny was transformed into a supernatural threat to property, this old woman, suffering extreme poverty and deprivation ("old and poor; / Ill fed she was, and thinly clad" [21–22]), is "turned into a Witch" by those who would deny her charity. Yet Wordsworth insists in these poems that the imagination has its own moral logic, for even when the witch-hunter never learns charity (we might note that when the tale is told Goody Blake has long since been dead) such cold-heartedness is punished by the mind's guilty and terrified recoil from the sublime threat of his own projections and conjurations.

"The Mad Mother"

"The Mad Mother," one of the most powerful and least understood poems of *Lyrical Ballads,* places major demands on a reader, because in it Wordsworth not only draws on the genre of the "case history," using a deserted woman, driven insane by melancholy and loss, as a vehicle for examining the relationship between the imagination and passion, but also radically transforms and disrupts its narrative structure. The case history form hardly extends beyond the first stanza, which provides relevant biographical information:

> HER eyes are wild, her head is bare,
> The sun has burnt her coal-black hair;
> Her eyebrows have a rusty stain,
> And she came far from over the main.
> She has a baby on her arm,
> Or else she were alone:
> And underneath the hay-stack warm,
> And on the greenwood stone,
> She talked and sung the woods among,
> And it was in the English tongue.

At this point, instead of using the neutral, objective tone of reportage preferred by physicians, Wordsworth shifts to dramatic monologue and depicts the woman's madness from within; the woman's case history as *she* sees and understands it, a history not yet fully disentangled from delirium.[29] The resulting poem, as it moves ambiguously between intense and conflicting emotions of love, anger, and fear, constitutes an extraordinary psychological portrait of the melancholy of the "witch/hysteric."

The woman's monologue is spoken in a rare moment of lucidity brought about by the child's suckling at her breast. As James H. Averill has noted, Wordsworth drew the idea of the child's power to alleviate insanity from *Zoönomia* (*Poetry of Human Suffering* 156), in which Darwin writes: "Where the cause is of a temporary nature, as in puerperal insanity, there is reason to hope, that the disease will cease, when the bruises, or other painful sensations attending this state, are removed. In these cases the child should be brought frequently to the mother, and applied to her breast, if she will suffer it, and this *whether she at first attends to it or not*; as by a few trials it frequently excites the storgè, or maternal affection, and removes the insanity, as I have witnessed" (2:360, my emphasis).

The possibility that an insane woman might not be conscious of the suckling child during the period when it is drawing her out of her delirium provides Wordsworth with the premise for a descent into madness. He focuses on that moment when the child's face, which had been submerged by the supernatural phantasms of the woman's mind, is suddenly and joyfully recognized by the woman. Like someone just awakened from a dream, the woman remembers the instant when the face of the child suddenly appeared, displacing the fiendish faces of the creatures of her insanity:

> "A fire was once within my brain;
> And in my head a dull, dull pain;
> And fiendish faces, one, two, three,
> Hung at my breast, and pulled at me;
> But then there came a sight of joy;
> It came at once to do me good;
> I waked, and saw my little boy,
> My little boy of flesh and blood;
> Oh joy for me that sight to see!
> For he was here, and only he."   [21–30]

"My little boy, / My little boy," she exclaims, happy in seeing "that sight of joy," *her* child "of flesh and blood," suckling at her breast. But her joy in seeing that "he was here, *and only he*" is also one of having

escaped a supernatural nightmare, in which she was possessed, like
Ellen of "The Three Graves," by the "fiendish faces" of incubi "hanging" and "pulling" at her breast. It is crucial to recognize that in both
her mad and lucid moments, she is looking at her suckling child, yet
in her madness his face goes unrecognized and is instead transformed
and multiplied into the horrific faces of diabolic imps. We are thus
given, in the woman's transition from madness to lucidity, a dramatic
representation of the movement, which we traced in discussing the
primitive encounter, from the supernatural phantasms of the primitive mind to natural vision.[30]

Wordsworth is not depicting a case of possession, but instead a
disease—the Incubus or Nightmare, as it was often called. "Sleepers,"
Burton writes in the *Anatomy of Melancholy,* "by reason of humours, &
concourse of vapours troubling the phantasy, imagine many times
absurd & prodigious things, & in such as are troubled with Incubus,
or witch-ridden (as we call it); if they lie on their backs, they suppose
an old woman rides, & sits hard upon them, that they are almost stifled
for want of breath, when there is nothing offends but a concourse of
bad humours, which trouble the phantasy."[31] Like Fuseli's reclining
woman in *The Nightmare,* a popular painting that Wordsworth is likely
to have known (if not through an engraving, through one of the many
political parodies of it done during the 1780s and 1790s—for instance,
those by Thomas Rowlandson, Robert Newton, and Temple Webb),
the woman, "almost stifled for want of breath," has fallen victim to
her "phantasy" and in her delirium (perhaps because of the weight of
the child) has imagined that she was ridden by the devil's incubi.[32]
When the child's suckling and caresses free her from the Incubus,
loosening "something at my chest," she is able to breathe once more:

> "Oh! press me with thy little hand;
> It loosens something at my chest;
> About that tight and deadly band
> I feel thy little fingers prest.
> The breeze I see is in the tree:
> It comes to cool my babe and me.   [35–40]

The child's love "cools" her "blood" and "brain" (32) (the breast/fire
antithesis we saw at work in the fragment on Ellen's hysteria) and

makes possible her perception of "the breeze ... in the tree" that "comes to cool my babe and me."

The willingness of witches to confess, Reginald Scot argued, is not evidence of guilt, but a sign of their melancholy imaginations: "The force which melancholie hath, and the effects that it worketh in the bodie of a man, or rather of a woman, are almost incredible. For as some of these melancholike persons imagine, they are witches and by witchcraft can worke woonders, and doo what they list: so doo other, troubled with this disease, imagine manie strange, incredible, and impossible things" (*The Discoverie of Witchcraft* 3.9:30). The mother's melancholy gives rise to a similar inability to distinguish what is real from what is unreal in her past, whether the "fiendish faces" of her delirium are memories (and she, a witch) or only imaginings. Given her tangled confusion about her past, the existence of a child presents a distressing problem. Who is its father? And how is she to establish its paternity? Seeking evidence of his parentage, whether he is the offspring of a natural or infernal "father," the woman anxiously scrutinizes his face, hoping to discover the image of the father. As she becomes progressively more sane, the child's face becomes increasingly human. She begins to sort out her past. "'I am thy father's wedded wife'" (72), she joyously affirms, as she remembers the "poor man" (78) who deserted her, their marriage, and "*his* sweet boy" (75, my emphasis), the issue of their union. However, just at the moment when she begins to hope to "live in honesty" (74) and to "pray / For him that's gone and far away" (79–80), the child finishes suckling, and the mother begins to relapse into madness:

> "My little babe! thy lips are still,
> And thou has almost sucked thy fill.
> —Where art thou gone, my own dear child?"   [83–85]

In that terrible pause, after the end-stopped declaration of the end of the child's nursing and before the mother's pathetic call for her lost child, her son's origins have once more fallen into doubt as he increasingly takes on the devilish face of the incubus:

> "What wicked looks are those I see?
> Alas! alas! that look so wild,
> *It never, never came from me:*

If thou art mad, my pretty lad,
Then I must be for ever sad."   [86–90, my emphasis]

"When a woman yields to an incubus," writes Norman Cohn, "she imperils her eternal salvation."[33] To be "for ever sad," forever melancholy, is to be forever a witch, unable to pray, in league with the devil, embraced not by a wedding band but by the "tight and deadly band" of the Incubus.

Since the child's "face," like the face of the child reflected in the water of the pond in "The Thorn," is a projection, the fact that it has two faces—as child or imp—suggests that the mother is attempting to deal with an unconscious emotional ambivalence, her contradictory feelings of love, anger, and resentment toward the Janus-like husband who loved and abandoned her.[34] Like the women Freud diagnosed as having hysteria, she suffers "from reminiscences," her symptoms being "residues and mnemic symbols of particular (traumatic) experiences."[35] Her language consequently has a contradictory aspect, as each image is structured by displacement and overdetermination. Her breast is the confused seat of her love for both the child and its "father" (he who "cares not for my breast"[61]). This confusion between maternal and sexual love, in which each is displaced onto the other, also extends to her delirium where it engenders, in a supernatural register, the father's demonic counterparts. The child, who is the symbolic locus of these ambivalences and, like a projective screen, "doth gather passion from his mother's eye" (*Prelude* 2.243), is not removed from them.[36] One of the more poignant tensions in the poem, resulting from this ambivalence, is her fear that if indeed she is a witch, then she is also probably capable of infanticide. As Scot observes, it was generally believed that witches usually killed "infants of their owne kind," often using them to make "witches salve," the "ointments whereby they ride in the aire" (*The Discoverie of Witchcraft* 1.4:5, 3.1:23) and escape harm. The mother's attempts to comfort her child—"lovely baby, do not fear! / I pray thee have no fear of me . . . I cannot work thee any woe" (15–16, 20)—express her own anxiety. And the protection she offers also is not without its dark ironies:

"And do not dread the waves below,
When o'er the sea-rock's edge we go;
The high crag cannot work me harm,

Nor leaping torrents when they howl;
The babe I carry on my arm,
He saves for me my precious soul."   [43–48]

The child is all that stands between the mother and damnation, and
she would save it; but to do so, to prevent the "sea-rock's edge," the
"high crag," and "leaping torrents" from doing her child and herself
harm, she would need the powers that only witchcraft and the witch's
ointment can give.

  The concluding stanza of the poem intensifies the poignancy of a
mother's agonizing desire to hold onto her son, her sanity, and her
"precious soul." Her solution is to seek escape in the woods:

"Oh! smile on me, my little lamb!
For I thy own dear mother am:
My love for thee has well been tried:
I've sought thy father far and wide.
I know the poisons of the shade;
I know the earth-nuts fit for food:
Then, pretty dear, be not afraid:
We'll find thy father in the wood.
Now laugh and be gay, to the woods away!
And there, my babe, we'll live for aye."   [91–100]

For a single woman with child, as the sad case of Martha Ray makes
plain, the forest is a refuge from villagers' "taunts" (71) and, as "tried"
suggests, possible prosecution. The progress of the witch/hysteric is
one of increasing movement away from society, back to a state of
wildness ("I'll build an Indian bower" [55]). Yet because "the wood"
is also where witches held their sabbats, murdered their bastard children, and engaged in orgies with the devil, it is a refuge that is likely
to increase the villagers' suspicions, as well as her confusion. She would
live on "earth-nuts," yet she also knows "the poisons of the shade"—
one of the arts of witchcraft. The final lines of the poem, in which
laughter and gaiety are closer to hysteria than joy, fully dramatize the
confusion and anguish of this melancholy woman, hoping to find "thy
father in the wood."

The Making of a Witch

Some called it madness; such indeed it was,

. . . .

If prophesy be madness; if things viewed
By poets of old time, and higher up
By the first men, earth's first inhabitants,
May in these tutored days no more be seen
With undisordered sight.   [*Prelude* 3.147–55]

For Wordsworth, abnormal psychology was not without its "prophetic" aspects. If "things viewed / By poets of old time" and "By the
first men, earth's first inhabitants" cannot be seen "with undisordered
sight," then in the "disorder" of the witch/hysteric, older than Christianity, one might still observe the original powers of primitive imagination and trace the origin and progress of those institutions based
upon it. The madness that placed these women at the geographical
margins of society, in proximity with wild nature, also placed them at
its historical edges. As Coleridge's note to "The Three Graves" indicates, the poem was not primarily concerned with the psychopathology
of witchcraft, but sought to show that the powers of the primitive
imagination were not restricted to "savage or barbarous tribes," but
could still be observed among the poor and uneducated in country
villages: "I had been reading Bryan Edwards's account of the effects
of the *Oby* witchcraft on the Negroes in the West Indies, and Hearne's
deeply interesting anecdotes of similar workings on the imagination
of the Copper Indians (those of my readers who have it in their power
will be well repaid for the trouble of referring to those works for the
passages alluded to); and I conceived the design of shewing that instances of this kind are not peculiar to savage or barbarous tribes, and
of illustrating the mode in which the mind is affected in these cases"
(*Complete Poetical Works* 1:269). In "The Thorn" anthropological inquiry and "prophesy" are affiliated in a similar fashion, as the "madness" of Martha Ray provides an empirical vehicle for an experimental
account of the genesis of language, poetry, and myth.[37]

As a synthesis of the dramatic perspectives of both the witch and
her accuser, the poem is Wordsworth's most sophisticated representation of the witch/hysteric and of the conflict between medical and
supernatural modes of explanation.[38] It has not been recognized that
the poem is not contemporary, but describes actions that took place

in the remote past. It should be read as a literary ballad (probably modeled, as de Selincourt points out, upon a ballad from David Herd's *Ancient and Modern Scottish Songs*), ostensibly written during the latter half of the seventeenth century, when witchcraft beliefs existed alongside the newly emerging methods and procedures of the New Science.

For twenty years, Martha Ray, a woman loved, then jilted by Stephen Hill, has haunted a lonely spot high in the mountains outside the village. Nobody actually knows why:

> Now wherefore, thus, by day and night,
> In rain, in tempest, and in snow,
> Thus to the dreary mountain-top
> Does this poor Woman go?
>
> . . . .
> I cannot tell; I wish I could;
> For the true reason no one knows.   [78–81, 89–90]

But everyone in the village has an opinion. Some hold that this "poor Woman," whose situation is even more extreme than that of the Mad Mother, is suffering from hysteria or melancholy, "a fire . . . kindled in her breast" (120) by her abandonment:

> Her state to any eye was plain;
> She was with child, and she was mad;
> Yet often was she sober sad
> From her exceeding pain.   [127–30]

To increase her misery and madness, she has lost her child (by miscarriage or stillbirth). Others in the village interpret her case differently and suspect her of being both an infanticide and a witch. "Some," who "remember well" (152), say she "would up the mountain often climb" (154) "full six months" (122) after she went mad, approximately when the child was due. "If a child to her was born" no one knows, or "if 'twas born alive or dead" (148, 150) cannot "*with proof* be said" (148–51, my emphasis). But all that winter when, late at night, "the wind blew from the mountain-peak" frequented by Martha Ray and when these villagers sought the safety of the "churchyard path," they heard the wild cries of what seemed a meeting of the "living" and the "dead":

For many a time and oft were heard
Cries coming from the mountain head:
Some plainly living voices were;
And others, I've heard many swear,
Were voices of the dead.   [159–63]

These may have been Martha Ray's cries, distorted by the wind; but
since their source is "the mountain head," a usual site for nocturnal
sabbats, it is not surprising that these villagers concluded that she had
entered into a compact with the devil and murdered her child at the
sabbat.

It is significant that though these villagers suspect Martha Ray, they
never legally accuse her. As Alan Macfarlane has noted, witchcraft
accusations were rarely spontaneous, spur-of-the-moment charges
made by individuals, but instead reflected a community consensus,
reached over a long period of time: "Witchcraft suspicions tended to
move in an ever-widening ripple through the village, the final accusation being based on a general consensus of opinion which rested on
the mutual exchange of fears through gossip . . . Counter-action
against witches was a village affair in its later stages. Not merely the
concern of an individual, it mobilized a number of emotional forces
in the parish . . . When enough proof was accumulated, and the village
was united, the prosecution could occur" (*Witchcraft* 110–12). With a
subtle understanding of the social dynamics of witchcraft accusations,
Wordsworth depicts the atmosphere of suspicion and doubt, the constant rumor, gossip, and debate that preceded, often for many years,
a village's reaching consensus and initiating legal action against a
witch. In this instance, general agreement has not been reached.

The superstitious people in the village believe that enough evidence
can be found to justify legal action and have made "an oath that she
/ Should be to public justice brought" (221–22). "I've heard," says the
old mariner, "the moss is spotted red / With drops of that poor infant's
blood" (210–11), but he finds it difficult to accept that Martha Ray is
an infanticide. The villagers also believe they know where the child
was buried, knowledge they have gained by resorting to a form of
"crystal-gazing," one of the more popular forms of "white magic" used
by cunning folk to recover treasure and stolen goods or to reveal the
future. In mirror-magic the client or, more commonly, a "scryor" (usu-

ally a young boy), by looking into a reflecting surface, such as a mirror, beryl, swordblade, or basin of water, would conjure a figure (devil or angel) who would assist him, often in the search for buried treasure. As Scot observes, this figure often took the "faire forme of a boy of twelve yeares of age," who then would be asked "if there be anie treasure hidden in such a place N. & wherin it lieth, and how manie foot from this peece of earth, east, west, north, or south" (*Discoverie of Witchcraft* 15.16:245–46). In "The Thorn," the villagers also conjure a child, but Wordsworth, no more a believer in mirror-magic than Scot was, makes it clear that what is reflected by the surface has been projected upon it by their imaginations:

> Some say, if to the pond you go,
> And fix on it a steady view,
> The shadow of a babe you trace,
> A baby and a baby's face,
> And that it looks at you;
> Whene'er you look on it, 'tis plain
> The baby looks at you again.   [214–20]

Assured of the location of the child's grave, the villagers set out to recover "the little infant's bones" (223), the "treasure" buried beneath the hill of moss. And these would have been enough to justify an accusation, for, as Jean Bodin argued: "If anie womans child chance to die at hir hand, so as no bodie knoweth how; it may not be thought or presumed that the mother killed it, except she be supposed a witch: and in that case it is otherwise, for she must upon that presumption be executed; except she can proove the negative or contrarie. Item, if the child of a woman that is suspected to be a witch, be lacking or gone from hir; it is to be presumed, that she hath sacrificed it to the divell: except she can proove the negative or contrarie" (Scot, *Discoverie of Witchcraft* 2.5:14). Proof of infanticide was tantamount to proof of witchcraft, especially when combined with a history of suspected witchcraft, the responsibility resting with the accused to "proove the negative or contrarie." As in "Goody Blake and Harry Gill," however, Wordsworth seeks to show that the violence of primitive superstition enforces its own kind of charity; the imagination is governed by its own dialectical and humanizing discipline. When the villagers began digging for "proof " (151), "instantly the hill of moss / Before their eyes began to stir!" (225–26). Fearful of what this sight might portend, they decided to let matters stand. Though Martha Ray has escaped legal prosecution, there is nothing optimistic about the conclusion of the poem. Like many women who eventually were convicted of witchcraft, she still remains within the pale of suspicion, ostracized from the community and a continual object of fear, hostility, gossip, and debate.

This conflict and uncertainty are clearly manifested in the mind and language of the narrator, whose "superstitious imagination" is, as Parrish has cogently argued, "the subject of the poem" (*Art of the "Lyrical Ballads"* 100, 99).[39] Geoffrey Hartman sees in this "slow and teasing narrative" the exposure of "a mind shying from, yet drawn to, a compulsive center of interest."[40] This center is his earliest memory, a primal scene of terror that happened before he had a language to describe it. While climbing among the hills, when the old sailor first came to this seaside village and had not yet "heard of Martha's name" (173), he was caught in a terrible storm:

> 'Twas mist and rain, and storm and rain:
> No screen, no fence could I discover;
> And then the wind! in sooth, it was
> A wind full ten times over.
> I looked around, I thought I saw
> A jutting crag,—and off I ran,
> Head-foremost, through the driving rain,
> The shelter of the crag to gain;
> And, as I am a man,
> Instead of jutting crag, I found
> A Woman seated on the ground.
>
> I did not speak—I saw her face;
> Her face!—It was enough for me;
> I turned about and heard her cry,
> "Oh misery! oh misery!"   [177–91]

Seeking a rock, he came upon what seemed an isolated woman, her body so close to the earth that she had almost become part of it, suffering, like mad Lear, the brunt of the storm.

In his anxious effort to explain its effect upon him, the old sailor vacillates between two systems of explanation, from the "hinterland

of broad folk attitudes" (Danby, *Simple Wordsworth* 60), the superstitions that give rise to storytelling, to an almost compulsive emphasis
upon ethnographic description and scientific measurement, the experimentalism of the New Science. Arising after he had "turned
about," these explanatory systems have the status of screen memories.
Not only do they stand in for this original event, but they have become
so linked to it that the sailor, despite his sense of the insufficiency of
his language, is unable to separate what he originally saw from its
subsequent reconstruction in memory.

"Sea-faring folk," Herder observes, "still remain particularly attached to superstition and the marvellous. Since they have to attend
to wind and weather, to small signs and portents, since their fate depends on phenomena of the upper atmosphere, they have good reason
to heed such signs, to look on them with a kind of reverent wonder
and to develop as it were a science of portents."[41] To a superstitious
sailor—a perfect subject for a study, as Wordsworth writes in his note
to "The Thorn," "of the general laws by which superstition acts upon
the mind" (*PW* 2:512)—the connection between the storm, the pond,
and a woman, seated on the ground, repeating the words "Oh misery!
oh misery!" almost as if they were part of a spell, would have been
obvious. For centuries, *tempesterii,* claiming the power to raise winds
and storms, had haunted seaports and cajoled money out of sailors
hoping for safe voyages. "Begone, ye slaves!" Rivers says to the companions of the Female Beggar in *The Borderers,* "or I will raise a whirlwind / And send you dancing to the clouds like leaves" (1797–99
version, lines 245–46). Among the superstitious, Scot declares, "a clap
of thunder, or a gale of wind is no sooner heard, but either they run
to ring bels, or crie out to burne witches" (1.1:1).[42] Storms could be
raised in a number of ways. However, as Norman Cohn observes, the
technique often "consisted of beating, stirring or splashing water. A
pond was ideal for the purpose, but if none was available it was enough
to make a small hole in the ground, fill it with water or even with
one's own urine, and stir this with one's finger."[43] Having come upon
what seemed a lonely woman beside a pond in such a storm ("A wind
full ten times over"), engaged in the incantatory repetition of words,
the sailor is not without fears that he, like Harry Gill, has stumbled
upon a witch.

Except for his repeated mention of her "scarlet cloak," the old mariner does not describe Martha Ray, so it is not certain whether her physical appearance corresponds to the stereotype of the witch. In fact, Wordsworth's major criticism of Sir George Beaumont's painting of "The Thorn" was that "the female figure . . . is too old and decrepit for one likely to frequent an eminence on such a call" (*PW* 2:512).[44] Yet it is significant—in ways that support Parrish's contention that the sailor did not actually see Martha Ray, only "a gnarled old tree hung with moss" (*The Art of the "Lyrical Ballads"* 101)—that though she perhaps does not resemble a witch, the thorn does. "Toothless" (*PW* 2:240n), "old and grey," with "knotted joints," this "wretched thing forlorn" (adjectives also used in connection with Martha Ray)

> looks so old
> In truth, you'd find it hard to say
> How it could ever have been young.   [1–9]

Like the woman, the thorn struggles against "a *melancholy* crop" (my emphasis):

> Up from the earth these mosses creep,
> And this poor Thorn they clasp it round
> So close, you'd say that they are bent
> With plain and manifest intent
> To drag it to the ground;
> And all have joined in one endeavour
> To bury this poor Thorn for ever.   [16–22]

This is "hysterica passio," the "climbing sorrow" (*King Lear* 2.4.57), the suffocating clasping "so close" that we saw earlier in "The Mad Mother." In Wordsworth's well-known description of the origin of ancient myths, in book 4 of *The Excursion,* he suggests that they originate from the imagination's being "lord / Of observations natural" (4.707–08). In "distant ages of the world," he writes, "Withered boughs grotesque, / Stripped of their leaves and twigs by hoary age," became "lurking Satyrs, a wild brood / Of gamesome Deities" (4.847, 879–86). "The Thorn" shows how the mythology of witchcraft—perhaps born from a person's "observing, on the ridge of Quantock Hill, on a stormy day, a thorn which . . . had often [been] passed in calm and bright weather" (*PW* 2:511) without being noticed—subsequently comes to be applied to individuals.

Witchcraft and the Language of Passion

All of the witchcraft poems direct our attention toward the manner in which marginal individuals become the focus of various modes of fictionalization and stereotyping. Yet even as they do so, they reflect that process themselves. Whether the image of Martha Ray compulsively repeating her few words "Oh misery! oh misery! / Oh woe is me! oh misery!" (65–66) was a fiction engendered by the winds or by the sailor's memory, it nevertheless provided Wordsworth with a staging ground for an inquiry into the origin of human language and myth.

In his note to the poem, Wordsworth stresses the intrinsic connection between language and passion. "Words, a Poet's words more particularly, ought to be weighed in the balance of feeling, and not measured by the space they occupy upon paper," he insists. "For the Reader cannot be too often reminded that Poetry is passion," for both have their genesis in language. Thus, the history of poetry is also a "history or science of feelings" (*PW* 2:513); the progress of poetic language is a document of the mind and passions of man from antiquity to the present. Both poetry and passion, Wordsworth argues, are born and develop within the interplay between "the deficiencies of language" and linguistic "repetition":

> An attempt is rarely made to communicate impassioned feelings without something of an accompanying consciousness of the inadequateness of our own powers, or the deficiencies of language. During such efforts there will be a craving in the mind, and as long as it is unsatisfied the speaker will cling to the same words, or words of the same character. There are also various other reasons why repetition and apparent tautology are frequently beauties of the highest kind. Among the chief of these reasons is the interest which the mind attaches to words, not only as symbols of the passion, but as *things*, active and efficient, which are of themselves part of the passion. And further, from a spirit of fondness, exultation, and gratitude, the mind luxuriates in the repetition of words which appear successfully to communicate its feelings. [*PW* 2:513]

The poverty of language among uneducated people or in primitive societies makes repetition necessary. Wanting the proper word, the mind "craves" adequate expression and takes pleasure "in the repetition of words which appear successfully to communicate its feelings." And from this repetition ensue pattern and form.

To support this theory Wordsworth refers to "innumerable passages from the Bible, and from the impassioned poetry of every nation," thus drawing our attention, as Murray Roston has noted, to the late eighteenth-century interest in Hebrew poetics, especially to the idea of "parallelism" developed by Robert Lowth. Roston's overly rigid conception of antiphonic structure and the biblical tradition, however, leads him to argue that "*The Thorn* contains no visible trace of biblical form."[45] By so doing he misses just how unique an experiment the poem really is. In his *Lectures on the Sacred Poetry of the Hebrews*, Lowth is typical of the eighteenth century in viewing Hebrew poetry as "the only specimens of the primeval and genuine poetry" (1:50). His work belongs to the eighteenth-century anthropological project, whose parameters were later greatly widened by William Jones's *Asiatic Researches*, of using, as Herder notes, these "most ancient records of the human mind and heart . . . the simplest forms, by which the human soul expressed its thoughts," as a means for shedding light on the mind and ways of seeing of early mankind.[46] In "The Thorn," Wordsworth uses Hebrew poetry as a model for writing an experimental primitive ballad aimed at dramatizing the primitive origins of poetry.

Organized by a loose parallelism of words and phrases rather than by meter, biblical poetry, as Lowth recognized, aims at an accumulation of meaning through repetition: "In Hebrew the frequent or rather perpetual splendour of the sentences, and the accurate recurrence of the clauses, seem absolutely necessary to distinguish the verse: so that what in any other language would appear a superfluous and tiresome repetition, in this cannot be omitted without injury to the poetry" (*Sacred Poetry of the Hebrews* 1:101). In Psalm 114, for instance, the pattern is clear:

> The sea saw, and fled;
> Jordan turned back:
> The mountains leaped like rams;
> The hills like the sons of the flock.
> What ailed thee, O Sea, that thou fleddest;

Jordan, that thou turnedst back:
Mountains, that ye leaped like rams;
And hills, like the sons of the flock?
At the presence of the Lord tremble thou Earth;
At the presence of the God of Jacob!
Who turned the rock into a lake of waters;
The flint into a water spring.   [*Sacred Poetry of the Hebrews* 2:35]

Metrical phrasing is achieved through the use of the caesura, which breaks the line into two symmetrical or complementary hemistiches. The parallelism thus established is then expanded to paired-line repetitions or distichs, each repeating verbal and semantic units. These pairs fall into larger symmetrical strophes; the first four lines, in the declarative mode, are repeated by the next set of four lines in the interrogative. An alternating pattern of strophes is thus established, of historical declaration and causal questioning, which finds its resolution in the last strophe, where the "presence" of God and his powers are affirmed. The piling up of parallel and antiphonal words and meanings—making "things . . . answer to things, and words to words, as if fitted to each other by a kind of rule or measure"—makes possible an intensification of feeling in the face of a felt deficiency in language's ability to image divinity (*Sacred Poetry of the Hebrews* 2:34).

It is not my purpose to do an extensive formal analysis of "The Thorn." However, a cursory examination of the basic formal elements of the poem will suggest its extraordinarily intricate antiphonal structure, of alternating strophic units of question and answer:

"But what's the Thorn? and what the pond?
And what the hill of moss to her?
And what the creeping breeze that comes
The little pond to stir?"
"I cannot tell; but some will say
She hanged her baby on the tree;
Some say she drowned it in the pond,
Which is a little step beyond:
But all and each agree,
The little Babe was buried there,
Beneath that hill of moss so fair."   [199–209]

The "responsive form" of the stanza is built upon one strophic unit (set off by quotation marks and formed by the repetition of "what['s] the . . . ?") followed by a responsive strophe of "some . . . say / She hanged" and "Some say she drowned." As in Psalm 114, the pattern of question and response seeks to signify what eludes representation— in this case, the enigmatic proximity of passion and death. The sailor uses the hemistich—"I cannot tell"—at an emphatic place between the two strophes (a formal device he uses elsewhere in order to vary line repetition, for instance, in lines 4, 9, 15, 20, and 31). More frequently, however, his narrative proceeds in hemistiches, as in "But what's the Thorn? and what the pond?", the caesura establishing parallels and echoes within each line. Numerous examples might be cited: "There is a Thorn—it looks so old" (1); "No leaves it has, no prickly points" (7); "'Tis three feet long, and two feet wide" (33, 1798 version); "A beauteous heap, a hill of moss" (36); "I cannot tell; I wish I could" (89); "Nay rack your brain—'tis all in vain" (103, 1798 version); "More know I not, I wish I did" (144); "'Twas mist and rain, and storm and rain" (177); and in his climactic encounter with Martha Ray, "I did not speak—I saw her face" (188).

For the most part, the narration is patterned in tristrophic stanzas:

> Now wherefore, thus, by day and night,
> In rain, in tempest, and in snow,
> Thus to the dreary mountain-top
> Does this poor Woman go?
> And why sits she beside the Thorn
> When the blue daylight's in the sky
> Or when the whirlwind's on the hill,
> Or frosty air is keen and still,
> And wherefore does she cry?—
> Oh wherefore? wherefore? tell me why
> Does she repeat that doleful cry?   [78–88]

The stanza is structured by three interrogative strophes. Two of these appear in similar forms in other stanzas (lines 71–74, 100–03), and thus set up interstanzaic parallels. Each strophe has its own internal verbal and semantic repetitions, as in the syntagmatically ordered "thus . . . In rain, in tempest, and in snow, / Thus . . ." Yet each also echoes the other. For instance, the "daylight," "whirlwind," "frosty air," and "hill" of the second strophe repeat the first strophe's "day," "tempest," "snow," and "mountain-top." The last strophe picks up the "wherefore . . . Does this poor Woman go?" of the first strophe and expands it into two parallel phrasings ("wherefore does she cry?" and "wherefore? wherefore? . . . Does she . . . cry?"). As the narrator turns increasingly to the problem of repetition, his questioning both enacts and raises the fundamental issue of the poem, the attempt to understand the psychological and practical necessities underlying linguistic repetition.

At the center of both the old mariner's narration and his memory is Martha Ray's lament, a prototype of language working to give suffering form:

> Oh misery! oh misery!
> Oh woe is me! oh misery!   [65–66]

If we view this encounter as another reworking of the primitive encounter, now between a "man" and a "witch," and if we see the language that arises from this encounter as a representation of the origin of language, as I believe we should, what is striking is that language, even at its origin, is characterized by the play of pleasure and insufficiency. Martha's repetition of "Oh misery! oh misery!" suggests that she too speaks within the necessities imposed upon her by the poverty of language: with few words at her disposal, and these primarily interjections—"beyond doubt," as Hugh Blair argues, "the first elements or beginnings of Speech" [*Rhetoric and Belles Lettres* 1:102])—she clings to the words that best approximate her pain. Strikingly, this clinging not only produces repetition but also generates a new phrase, "Oh woe is me!" as an assonantal variation of "Oh misery!" This movement, at once linguistic and cognitive, from interjection to statement, passionate expression to rudimentary reflection, epitomizes, in miniature, the conventional eighteenth-century understanding of the origin and progress of human language. It consists of the "decomposition" of the initial expression into smaller discursive units, reflecting ideas first put forward by Condillac and later taken up by Maupertuis, Rousseau, and Diderot, on the importance of decomposition for the emergence of thought.[47] "If a thought has no succession in the mind," Condillac argues, "it does have succession in discourse, where it is decomposed into as many parts as the ideas it contains. Therefore we are able to

observe what we do in thinking, we can render account of it to ourselves; we can consequently learn to conduct our reflection" ("Discours
préliminaire," *Oeuvres philosophiques* 1:403b).

Supporting Bialostosky's contention that Wordsworth's poetry
should be understood as a "poetics of speech" (*Making Tales* 19), Martha Ray's passion and the old sailor's comprehension of the trauma
he once experienced are inseparable from their experiments in the
art of speaking. Significantly, *poetry* is born from this repetition; Martha Ray's anguish takes a symmetrical, anaphoric form, a distich, broken into four parallel hemistiches by caesuras. Her passion does not
stand separate, then, from this progress in language; words "are of
themselves part of the passion" (*PW* 2:513). She repeats a second "Oh
misery!" because she senses a pleasure and mitigation of pain, as well
as a deficiency in expression. Mixed with painful passions is the pleasure of speaking them. "In describing any passions whatsoever, which
are voluntarily described," Wordsworth declares, "the mind will upon
the whole be in a state of enjoyment" (*ProseW* 1:148), and out of this
chain of repetitions is built up the fabric of repetitions and gaps that
constitute poetic language and human passion in their primal forms.

The Poet at the Crossroads

As a major figure in Wordsworth's mythology of origins, the lonely
witch/hysteric provided him with a figural and empirical means for
imagining in palpable terms the genesis of language and culture. Possession in its most extreme forms was manifested in the dispossessed,
in the power that recoils on those who look on others with fear-
enchanted eyes. To represent the witch/hysteric was not to describe
her melancholy with clinical detachment, but instead to confront and
possibly to fall victim to a being largely of one's own creation. Wordsworth's representations posit a different, more emotionally charged
stance toward her than the evaluative stance of medicine. "I never
heard of such as dare," the old sailor of "The Thorn" tells us, "approach the spot when she is there" (98–99).

In the later poetry, this relationship changed, following two trajec-
tories. First, Wordsworth increasingly distanced himself, socially and
imaginatively, from these women: no longer seen at close range, they

were less threatening and he had less sympathy for them. Second, as
Wordsworth shifted away from observing others toward observing
himself, the encounter with witch/hysterics gave way to the recollection
of those moments in his past when it seemed that he drank from the
same daemonic cup. The witch/hysteric was an ambivalent figure of
the power of the primal or savage imagination, the bestower of both
trauma and language, but she was progressively displaced by an
equally threatening and fascinating power—Wordsworth's own imagination. In the remainder of this chapter, I would like to examine how
his concept of poetic authority derived from the combined distancing
and displacement of these women.

Resolution and Independence presents a starker, more patriarchal conception of poetic origins, and a more general effacement of the female
imagination, as Wordsworth rewrites the supernatural origins of poetry in more masculine terms, as madness within himself and the
leech-gatherer. Yet the preoccupation with melancholy and magic, and
the presence, after a terrible tempest, of the leech-gatherer—stirring
and "conning" the muddy waters of a pond "as if he had been reading
in a book" (line 81), wearing "a Cloak, the same as women wear" (*PW*
2:238n), his body, through sickness or pain, "bent to a hoop"—still
betray, though in a far more concealed fashion, the poem's debt to
the discourse on witchcraft.[48] "Poor Susan," a poem probably written
between September 1798 and 18 July 1800, draws once more on the
link between medical hysteria and the imagination to argue for the
importance of nature as a basis of sexual and moral health.[49] Charles
Lamb, even without recognizing the echo in "what ails her?" to the
case of Old Susan in "The Idiot Boy" ("For what she ails they cannot
guess," line 26) and to "Goody Blake and Harry Gill" ("What is't that
ails young Harry Gill?" line 2), had no difficulty recognizing the
poem's sources in the discourse on hysteria. He points out the significance of a word like *vapour* in this context: "There was quite enough
to stamp the moral of the thing never to be forgotten. 'Fast volumes
of vapour' &c."[50] Susan suffers, as David Simpson has observed, from
"forced celibacy," the common condition of all servant girls in England
at this time.[51] Her absence from nature makes her susceptible to "a
note of enchantment," but witchcraft is now no more than a hysterical
reverie—"volumes of vapour." In "The Solitary Reaper," the "experimental" concerns that first interested Wordsworth in the speech of

isolated women are present, yet the poem aims at subsuming the woman's status as imaginative threat in order to celebrate her civilizing powers. "Single," "solitary," "alone" in the field, hers is still "a melancholy strain" of "natural sorrow, loss, or pain," or of "old, unhappy, far-off things," a primordial song whose power over the listener is prelinguistic, for it is sung in a language unknown to him. "O'er the sickle bending," she emblematizes the conjunction of death and poetry. But now her song speaks of the fertility of the female voice and womb, "for the Vale profound / Is overflowing with the sound." Like language, which was believed to have been born "among Arabian sands," her song moves northward, breaking "the silence of the seas / Among the farthest Hebrides" and connecting the ancient past with the present.[52] The lonely witch has been displaced by the solitary agricultural laborer; her unfulfilled desire now takes the form of a love song and a harvest requiem heard by a passerby. Through this encounter, the poet renews the contact between his own song and its origins; having done so, however, he continues his journey, carrying in his heart the music "long after it was heard no more."

Among the poems that Wordsworth included in the *Memorials of a Tour on the Continent, 1820* is a sonnet entitled "On Approaching the Staub-bach Lauterbrunnen." Because of the sonnet's late date of composition (between November 1820 and November 1821), it can serve to indicate the closing trajectory of Wordsworth's poetry on witch/hysterics. Drawing partly on Dorothy's *Journal*, Wordsworth conveys, in the opening quatrain, his astonishment on hearing a wild choral song raised by a handful of female beggars on his approach to Staubbach Waterfall:

> UTTERED by whom, or how inspired—designed
> For what strange service, does this concert reach
> Our ears, and near the dwellings of mankind!
> 'Mid fields familiarised to human speech?—   [*PW* 3:171]

Disoriented and surprised, the poet wonders how such a "strange service" could exist in such close proximity to society. In the 1822 note to the poem, the primal status of this "concert" is further emphasized. "The vocal powers of these musical Beggars may seem to be exaggerated; but this wild and savage air was utterly unlike any sounds I had ever heard; the notes reached me from a distance, and on what oc casion they were sung I could not guess, only they seemed to belong, in some way or other, to the Waterfall—and reminded me of religious services chanted to Streams and Fountains in Pagan times" (*PW* 3:474).[53]

In the second quatrain, which enjambs into a spillover fifth line, Wordsworth links the mendicants' song to myth and the supernatural:

> No Mermaids warble—to allay the wind
> Driving some vessel toward a dangerous beach—
> More thrilling melodies; Witch answering Witch,
> To chant a love-spell, never intertwined
> Notes shrill and wild with art more musical.

The manner in which Wordsworth idealizes and distances himself from these women and the threatening power of their song is striking: instead of being sirens, they are beneficial mermaids, naiads of the waterfall; instead of being wind-witches, they "allay the wind" and engage in an enchanting love-spell, conjured up by "Witch answering Witch." Distance and idealization go together. Dorothy Wordsworth, who was much closer to these women, had a different response to their song. "*I* was close to the women when they began to sing," she writes, "and hence, probably it was that I perceived nothing of *sweetness* in their tones. I cannot answer for the impression on the rest of the party except my Brother, who being behind, heard the carol from a distance" (*DWJ* 2:118n).

In the "turn" of the concluding five lines, Wordsworth shows the extent to which he has repudiated the earlier poetics of marginality:

> Alas! that from the lips of abject Want
> Or Idleness in tatters mendicant
> The strain should flow—free Fancy to enthral,
> And with regret and useless pity haunt
> This bold, this bright, this sky-born, WATERFALL!

Where Wordsworth, in the 1790s, would have interpreted this song as an expression of the struggle of the dispossessed against "abject Want," in the 1820s he sees social need, now viewed as idleness dressed as beggary, as a blemish that can only "enthral" the "free Fancy" as it "haunt[s]" a "sky-born, Waterfall," with "Regret" and "useless pity."

The other trajectory of Wordsworth's witchcraft poetry is towards the discovery of these powers within himself. One of the best examples of this inward turn is the "spot of time" that tells of the death of Wordsworth's father. Though the death itself is described in the simplest and barest of terms, simply as "he died" (*Prelude* 11.365), the two parallel clauses introducing the event evoke the authority and immediacy of supernatural intervention ("ere I to school returned," "ere I had been ten days / A dweller in my father's house") and transform a coincidence—that the child successfully returned home while his father did not—into a mysterious "chastisement." As Mary Moorman notes, John Wordsworth, on his return from a remote corner of Cumberland, "lost his way in the darkness on Cold Fell and was obliged to spend a winter night shelterless on a fell side, with the result that he arrived home in the grip of mortal illness" (Moorman 1:68). It is important to notice that though the child imagines that he is being punished, he does not at first know why; only later does he find a reason when he calls

> to mind
> That day so lately past, when from the crag
> I looked in such anxiety of hope.   [369–71]

The true focus of the episode, then, is not so much the death of the father as the child's explanation of it.

One thing generally true of witchcraft beliefs is that they have traditionally played a major role in explaining strange and otherwise unaccountable deaths. As E. E. Evans-Pritchard has argued, witchcraft may not be particularly useful for explaining a single chain of events, but it does help to explain the *coincidence* of two chains of causation.[54] It is not difficult, for instance, to understand either the series of events that led to John Wordsworth's death or that made Wordsworth's homecoming possible. What Wordsworth as a child wanted to understand is what linked these two series, why he was chosen to live at exactly the same time his father was marked for death. And it is here that witchcraft emerges as an explanatory system.

We can be quite certain why the child thought that his visit to this lonely spot was somehow connected to his father's death:

> There was a crag,
> An eminence, which from the meeting-point

Of two highways ascending overlooked
At least a long half-mile of those two roads,
By each of which the expected steeds might come—
The choice uncertain. Thither I repaired
Up to the highest summit. 'Twas a day
Stormy, and rough, and wild, and on the grass
I sate half sheltered by a naked wall.
Upon my right hand was a single sheep,
A whistling hawthorn on my left, and there,
With those companions at my side, I watched,
Straining my eyes intensely as the mist
Gave intermitting prospect of the wood
And plain beneath.   [11.349–63]

Of all the places that humans have traditionally feared and avoided, the crossroads or "meeting of the ways" is one of the most sinister. Oedipus killed his father Laius "in a place where three roads meet," and, as Leslie Brisman has cogently argued, there is an oedipal conflict at work in Wordsworth's transcription of the event: a singular "point of origins," the killing of the father, is re-enacted by the poet as he moralizes on this primal memory of standing at the crossroads.[55] One might generalize this argument further by noting that inasmuch as the crossroads is a figure of choice, Wordsworth is recounting a rite de passage, closely linked to his notion of the genesis of his own poetic authority.

There is an even darker side, however, to the figure of the "poet at the crossroads" that closely links this episode to the witchcraft poetry. Crossroads were also spots traditionally associated with social outcasts and the damned; it was there that suicides were buried, parricides were left to rot, and murderers were gibbeted: "Damned spirits all, / That in crossways and floods have burial" (*Midsummer Night's Dream* 3.2.382–83). In the Penrith Beacon episode, which immediately precedes this "spot of time," Wordsworth drew upon his childhood memories of a gibbet that stood at a crossroads that he had daily passed on his way to the Hawkshead grammar school. In *An Unpublished Tour,* he imagines the effect that this place, called Gibbet Moss, would have had, a century earlier, upon a passerby: "At that time the marshy ground at the head of this lake used to resound with the doleful cry of the Bittern . . . This sound, blending with the whistling of the Hawk repairing hither from distant crags & the croaking of the carrion Crow & the Raven attracted by the suspended corpse, must have made a dismal chorus for the ears of Passengers, while the circumstances of the murder were yet fresh in memory, approaching along the several lanes which meet near the point where the gibbet stood"(*ProseW* 2:333–34). Like other crossroads gibbets, the one at Gibbet Moss was believed to be haunted and the local people avoided it even during daylight. We might thus say that there is a metonymic link between the two "spots of time" of book 11, as the poet places his own cross-roads story "near the point where the gibbet stood."

It should be added that the crossroads were places where demonic powers were felt to be especially strong. One went to the crossroads to meet devils or demons; they were places where magic was practiced; and it was believed that witches met there for sabbats. In 1324 Dame Alice Kyteler confessed that she had killed cocks at a crossroads for "an insolent fiend" named Robert Artisson, tearing them limb from limb and using their entrails for magical compounds.[56] The notorious *Malleus Maleficarum* provides the following account by a male witch of how he raised hailstorms and tempests:

> And this is how we go to work: first we use certain words in the fields to implore the chief of the devils to send one of his servants to strike the man whom we name. Then, when the devil has come, we sacrifice to him a black cock at two cross-roads, throwing it up into the air; and when the devil has received this, he performs our wish and stirs up the air, but not always in the places which we have named, and, according to the permission of the living God, sends down hailstorms and lightnings. [140]

Jeffrey Burton Russell recounts the story of Catherine Delort, who was persuaded by her lover to make a pact with the devil. They went to a crossroads at midnight, where

> they built a fire, putting on it the remains of human bodies they had taken from a cemetery. She cut her left arm and let a few drops of her blood fall onto the burning mess, while speaking strange words which she did not now remember. Thereupon a demon named Berit appeared in the shape of a purplish flame,

which evidently conferred upon her the power to do all kinds of maleficium. Following her pact with Berit, Catherine would fall into a deep sleep every Saturday night, during which she would be transported to the witches' assembly.[57]

The structural similarity between these confessions suggest that we might speak of a "crossroads narrative" that exhibits the following pattern: an individual visits a crossroads, a supernatural figure (frequently a "servant" of the devil) is summoned, a ritual sacrifice takes place (often with cocks), and the pact thus made endows the person with certain magical powers, notably the power to be transported from one place to another (for the purpose of sabbats).

If we read the episode of "Waiting at the Crossroads" in the light of these narratives, it can be seen that rather than being a confession, as many have argued, of a child's impatience to return home and of his strange sense of guilt over his father's death, Wordsworth's account of how he climbed with "anxiety" and "hope" a crag situated at "the meeting-point / Of two highways" represents a radical reshaping of the conventional crossroads narrative. And inasmuch as this passage draws its authority from witchcraft, echoes of "The Thorn" lead a shadowy existence in this passage. The old sailor, having "climbed the mountain's height" to "view the ocean wide and bright," is caught in a terrible storm and runs for the shelter of a "jutting crag," only to find that it is "a Woman seated on the ground." But now the gothic supernaturalism of the witchcraft poems has all but disappeared, leaving only the latent signs of the witch's continuing presence in the crag, the wind "stormy, and rough, and wild," and the "whistling hawthorn," later described as "the one blasted tree" (377). We are never given a satisfactory explanation why, "the day before" (345) the servant was to arrive, Wordsworth went out to this lonely spot, or what he did there or hoped for (with such "anxiety"), or whom he expected to see, as he

> watched,
> Straining my eyes intensely as the mist
> Gave intermitting prospect of the wood
> And plain beneath.

We do know, however, that he believed that something had happened that gave him great powers and that they were paid for with (or caused) his father's life. As Brisman has observed, to feel guilty about his father's death "is to feel guilty of a witchcraft-like arrogation of power" (*Romantic Origins* 314). And like Martha Ray, he too began to haunt the spot.[58]

Unlike conventional crossroads narratives, however, this one is played out entirely in the sphere of the imagination. Now Wordsworth does not "often . . . repair" to the site to meet a servant or a stranger, but instead to see a mist "which on the line of each of those two roads / Advanced in such indisputable shapes." He returns there to "drink / As at a fountain" a potion of "spectacles and sounds." There is probably an echo, in these lines, of Hamlet's dialogue with his dead father:

> Angels and ministers of grace defend us!
> Be thou a spirit of health, or goblin damn'd,
> Bring with thee airs from heaven, or blasts from hell,
> Be thy intents wicked, or charitable,
> Thou com'st in *such a questionable shape*
> That I will speak to thee.   [1.4.39–43, my emphasis]

Wordsworth's crossroads narrative intimates a ghostly encounter, not with a father, but with an "unfather[ing] vapor" (*Prelude* 6.527), and the pact that was struck on "that day," which Wordsworth repeatedly returned to as a source of power, was not with a devil, but with his own imagination. Here he discovered that his own mind was "beset / With images, and haunted by itself " (*Prelude* 6.179–80). No longer needing real horses, either to go home or to return to the crossroads, Wordsworth could claim that in "this later time," especially "at *midnight,*" when the "storm and rain / Beat on my roof," but even during the day, "unknown" to him, he was transported, like a witch, back to that "crag" by his imagination. The power that was once mediated by the witch/hysteric has now been appropriated by the poet, as he finds the source of the crossroads' sinister performative powers in the darkness and mystery of his own imagination.

PART THREE

Death

FIVE

The History of Death

Where Christian theology under-stood death in moralistic terms, as a punishment for sin or as a debt and tribute due unto nature (as Prince Hal says to Fal-staff, "thou ow-est God a death" [1 *Henry IV*, 5.1.126]), romantic poets most frequently view death as a cultural phenomenon, which derives its specific character and coloration from human beings. Theirs is not the story of how death came into the world as a condition, but instead how it came into being as an idea. Since we cannot experience death and also describe it, it is necessarily primarily a product of representation. Romantic poets cultivated this insight and turned their attention to the diversity of ways in which human beings, past and present, when faced with this unknowable gap, have filled it with heavenly and spectral worlds, building up elaborate fictions on the basis of surmise.

The importance of death in Wordsworth's poetry has long been recognized, and some of the best and most searching criticism has drawn
our attention to it. Nevertheless, the anthropological importance of this
idea has only briefly been remarked.[1] The intellectual nature of death
can easily be seen in Wordsworth's early poetry—for instance, in a passage originally intended for *An Evening Walk,* where he asserts that the
children who play beside a church graveyard lack "mortal minds." Death
has "no power oer their particular frames," because they little realize,
"in their wild mirth," "how near / Their sensible warm motion" is allied
"to the dull earth that crumble[s] at their side" (*PW* 1:6–7n). If Wordsworth had left it at that, if he had said no more than that children lack
an idea of death, he would have been voicing an Enlightenment commonplace. However, in 1798, as he began writing poems for *The Recluse,*
he began to explore in greater depth the anthropological significance of
the idea of death. The resulting poems, from "We Are Seven" to *The
Excursion,* constitute a major philosophical project, that of a general history of death.

Enlightenment Histories of Death

When Wordsworth began to write a history of death, he was not initiating
a new kind of inquiry, but instead confronting an already existing genre
of writing, whose general outlines need to be known if we are to understand his distinctive concerns. It was the Enlightenment that first transformed death into an idea, making it one of the fundamental distinctions
between human beings and animals.[2] Voltaire, for instance, having recourse to the idea of a wild child, claims that "the human race is the
only one that knows it must die, and it knows this only through its
experience. A child brought up alone and transported to a desert island
would have no more idea of death than a cat or a plant."[3] An animal
does not fear death, writes Rousseau, because one "can desire or fear
things only through the ideas one can have of them . . . and knowledge
of death and its terrors is one of the first acquisitions that man has made
in moving away from the animal condition" (*Discourses* 116). Though the
recognition that death and its terrors were "acquired" ideas did not
lessen its mysteries, it did make death a major focus of eighteenth-century speculation on origins. It made it reasonable to inquire into the

genesis and history of these ideas; to examine the different ways in which
death is expressed in social institutions, practices, customs, myths, and
rituals; and to explore the connection between death and religious notions, such as immortality, the afterlife, Hell and the Underworld. A
genre of inquiry thus came into being concerned with the genesis and
transformation of ideas about death and the afterlife.

Though Locke did not write such a history, his assertion that all ideas
have their origin in sensation or in the reflection on sensation provided
a general answer to how such an inquiry might proceed. In book 3 of
the *Essay,* he suggests that words document the ideas of "the first Begin-
ners of Languages," so etymology can serve as a medium for inquiring
into their original ideas and guessing "what kind of Notions they were,
and whence derived." The most abstruse and spiritual ideas, Locke argues, names "which stand for Things that fall not under our Senses,"
can be traced back to their beginnings in sensible ideas. "*Spirit,* in its
primary signification, is Breath," he writes, "*Angel,* a Messenger"
(3.1:403). This model of the gradual evolution of spiritual ideas out of
concrete, sensory impressions through abstraction and greater linguistic
sophistication governed empirical accounts of the origin of death and
the afterlife during the eighteenth century. It suggested that our ideas
of death, like other primitive ideas, first came from the sphere of sensory
impressions and our rudimentary reflection on them.

Lowth's *Lectures* illustrate how Lockean empiricism informed these
histories. Claiming that "the incorporeal world" had its origin in "things
corporeal and terrestrial" (1:163), Lowth argues that the ancient Hebrews' understanding of death emerged from their reflection on the
condition and location of the bodies of the dead. As ignorant as the rest
of mankind about "the actual state and situation of the dead" (1:158–
59), yet unable, because of their lack of "that subtilty of language, which
enables men to speak with plausibility on subjects abstruse, and remote
from the apprehension of the senses," the Hebrews derived their ideas
of death and the afterlife, Lowth stresses, from "what was plain and
commonly understood concerning the dead, that is, what happened to
the body." Since it was observed that "after death the body returned to
the earth, and that it was deposited in a sepulchre . . . a sort of popular
notion prevailed among the Hebrews, as well as among other nations,
that the life which succeeded the present was to be passed beneath the
earth" (159–64). In Lowth's view, the early Hebrews' idea of the soul

was but a ghostly version of the condition of the body after death, while
the dark world of Sheol, the descriptions of the souls inhabiting it, and
the journeys of the dead to the pit were but poetic or metaphysical
elaborations on the location and disposition of the body in the grave.
What happened to the soul in the next world had its metaphoric and
imagistic origin in what happened to the body in this one. Lowth's argument is typical of the empiricist discourse on death because it claims
that, despite our increased linguistic sophistication in talking about death
and immortality, the key to all our metaphors for death, the material
substratum from which they all fundamentally derive, is to be found in
what we see happening to or what we do with the bodies of the dead.
To decipher religious myths about death and immortality, then, we need
only recognize that the nexus of all spiritual imagery is the corpse; all
narratives about life after death can be reduced to and derive their
formal organization from a primal confrontation, which every culture
and every individual repeats, with the bodies of the dead. The history
of death, then, is the history of our organization, displacement, and
metaphoric embellishment of this encounter, through language and funerary rituals.

In the *New Science*, Vico asserts an equally close connection between
the empirical condition and disposition of the dead, and primitive ideas
about the soul and the afterlife, as "words are carried over from bodies
and from the properties of bodies to signify the institutions of the mind
and spirit" (78). Claiming that *"humanitas"* derives "first and properly
from *humando*, burying" (8–9), Vico makes the fact that humans are the
only animals that bury their dead a first principle of the *New Science*. "All
nations," he writes, "barbarous as well as civilized, though separately
founded because remote from each other in time and space, keep these
three customs: all have some religion, all contract solemn marriages, all
bury their dead . . . From these three institutions humanity began among
them all" (97).[4] This principle forms the basis of his project of writing a
"scientific" genealogy of the Underworld. For the first poets, he argues,
the lower world had only one deity, the water of the perennial springs,
called Styx, by which the gods swore. In keeping with the limitations of
their corporeal imaginations, these poets could not envision a heaven
any higher than the mountain summits, while the "first lower world" was
no deeper "than the source of the springs" (271). When the primeval
giants had learned to bury their dead, thus making it possible for them

to stay in one location, to cultivate fields and found cities, the Underworld was deepened to the depth of a grave. To support this claim, Vico refers us to the Old Testament and to book 11 of the *Odyssey*, where the lower world is described as being "no deeper than a ditch" (271). With the growth of cities and agriculture, the Underworld grew more populated, extended over a greater area, and sank to "the depth of a furrow." Finally, as the civilized giants, living in the mountains, sought to distinguish themselves from the uncivilized giants who lived in the valleys and who continued "their infamous promiscuity," the lower world "was taken to be the plains and the valleys [where the uncivilized giants lived], as opposed to the lofty heaven set on the mountaintops" (271). Vico is typical of most eighteenth-century writers in his claim that the Underworld mirrors the world of the living, an insight drawn from Lucretius, who argued that "all those things, which stories tell us exist in the depths of Acheron, are in our life."[5] Religious ideas are thus homologous with social relations: with each gain in mankind's capacity to understand or control the physical environment comes a corresponding deepening and expansion of the capacity to imagine a spiritual realm.

Vico is less concerned with tracing the history of the idea of death per se than with showing its importance as a socializing force. Dismissing Hellenic and Roman philosophers, who used the idea of an Underworld allegorically "for the meditation and exposition of their moral and metaphysical doctrines" (272), he stresses that the idea of the Underworld discovered by Orpheus's descent originally served a more practical purpose by reducing "the wild beasts of Greece to humanity."[6] Among the philosophes generally, for whom "the chief source of moral ideas is the reflection on the interests of society," ideas about the Underworld, conveyed in myths and funeral practices, though ostensibly about the dead, were in fact fictions for the living, a major means by which the Church and State exerted control over human minds.[7] "The pomp," is, indeed, as Wordsworth observes, "for both worlds, the living and the dead" (*Prelude* 12.335–36). This made the idea of death more than an anthropological issue. The important role that it played in the establishment and maintenance of civil and ecclesiastical power also made it a matter of political debate.

One final example of a "history of death," this time drawn from Herder's *Spirit of Hebrew Poetry* (1782–83), will help us to discern, in more detail, the basic pattern of these inquiries, while suggesting an alternative position that was available to Wordsworth. The Seventh Dialogue, which presents a debate between the empiricist Alciphron and the more visionary respondent Euthyphron, begins with Alciphron's claim, which derives from William Warburton's *Divine Legation of Moses Demonstrated,* that the ancient Hebrews totally lacked an idea of the soul.[8] This idea was derived much later, he argues, from Chaldean philosophy and was "superadded to the simple traditions of antiquity. In the account of Adam, in Job, in the Psalms, there is nothing of it" (1:164). Alciphron then proceeds to deliver an "historical deduction of the kingdom of the dead" (176), one that seeks to show "at how late a period and how gradually, from what trifling considerations, and these mostly inferences, which infer too much, and proofs, which prove too much, nay, from blind wishes, and obscure presentiments, has man's hope of immortality been produced!" (170). In Genesis, he argues, there is no idea of an afterlife: "Adam was earth, and knew of no immortality. He saw Abel lying in blood; the first death was bewailed, although there was no dead to bewail—yet no angel came to comfort the mourners with the least hope of immortality. His soul was in the blood, and was poured out upon the earth; thence it cried towards heaven, and was buried with the blood. Such was the faith of the first world, and even after the flood. The fathers fell asleep, and their life was ended" (1:170).

In "the first world," the "dead" did not exist; the soul was "in the blood" and "was buried with the blood," the grave reaching no deeper than the depth of the sanguinary pools "poured out upon the earth." Following Lowth, Alciphron stresses that the first idea of a soul arose from the practice of interment, for the grave "was in time shaped into a realm of shades" (170). "In the first conception," he remarks, the realm of the dead "was the grave simply, the abiding and everlasting dwelling place of the dead; only that they [the Hebrew poets] thought of them to be still living in their graves. These therefore they denominated houses, of rest, the dwelling places of endless peace." Death made them "limbless and powerless beings," shadows of their former selves. Nevertheless, the dead were so loved that they were represented as leading an animate though shadowy existence in the grave. They coexisted with the living. It is this world that gave rise to the literary dialogues with and journeys to the dead, where persons are represented "as visiting the graves of their friends like dwelling places, conversing with them, while yet in their graves, and watering the dust of their dwellings, or planting them with herbage" (173).

As a disciple of the Enlightenment, Alciphron also interprets the origin of the Underworld in political terms: the world of the dead mirrors the rise of social inequality among the living. The "house" of the dead, he argues, was originally an egalitarian institution that erased social differences because it was inhabited by rich and poor alike in "perfect equality." In time, however, this "house" expanded into a "kingdom" of fathers and, in turn, into an "empire" of the dead. It was the Flood, Alciphron argues, that "gave the first great occasion for the poetical representation of an empire of the dead . . . Thus it was the Rephaim, the giants, who groan and wail beneath the waves, whose voice perchance was thought to be heard in the roaring billows, and whose restless motion was felt in the earthquake and the storm at sea. But these were the most ancient and gigantick inhabitants of the empire of death" (175). By the time the Book of Job was composed, these traditions had weakened, so that the Empire of the Giants became a silent congregation of the dead. After this, the subterranean realm received its first king, Belial, and Sheol became his palace.

Euthyphron, as he responds to Alciphron's "historical deduction," does not so much deny its validity as point out its incompleteness. Like all empiricist accounts of death, it is too much dominated by the melancholy shadow of the grave. Euthyphron anticipates Wordsworth by claiming that mankind's early ideas of immortality were not merely derived from the state and condition of the dead, nor simply allegories of social relations, nor solely coercive fictions aimed at assuring control over a savage, undisciplined populace; they were also expressions of the continuities felt between the self and nature. As the priest of "The Brothers" declares, "The thought of death sits easy on the man / Who has been born and dies among the mountains" (lines 182–83). One need only cast one's eyes upward to the stars, Euthyphron declares, to see "the book of immortality which God unseals and spreads open to us" (176). Think of the morning as a symbol of resurrection, he argues, or of sleep as an image of death. The dark empiricist view of death, which draws all its imagery for the afterlife from the grave, must be balanced by more positive conceptions that have their origin in our response to the beauty and order of nature.

It is significant, as will become clearer when we examine "Lucy Gray," that Euthyphron, in support of this claim, cites the story of Enoch. In Genesis, Enoch's disappearance is represented as a mystery:

> And Enoch lived sixty and five years, and begat Methuselah:
> And Enoch walked with God after he begat Methuselah three hundred years, and begat sons and daughters:
> And all the days of Enoch were three hundred sixty and five years.
> And Enoch walked with God: and he *was* not; for God took him.
>
> [5:21–24]

The myth offers us no clues concerning what happened to Enoch, and this reticence powerfully conveys the perplexity with which the ancient Hebrews conceived of death. Alciphron attempts to dismiss it as a "fragment perhaps of an ancient song" and as a veiled way of talking about someone "who had prematurely died" (176–77). Euthyphron, following Warburton, counters that even though the idea of a soul was not articulated until a later date, the story of Enoch nevertheless occupies an important place in a history of death, because in it one can recognize the first *intimation* of immortality.[9] Later, it would become "more distinctly impressed" by the Chasidim, and then confirmed by the translation of Elijah, in which we are given an eye-witness account: "And it came to pass, when the LORD would take up Elijah into heaven by a whirlwind, that Elijah went with Elisha from Gilgal . . . And it came to pass, as they still went on, and talked, that, behold, *there appeared* a chariot of fire, and horses of fire, and parted them both asunder; and Elijah went up by a whirlwind into heaven" (2 Kings 2:1, 11). Out of the rudimentary beginning of a man who had disappeared without a trace had developed the intimation, then a doctrine of immortality, and finally the idea of "Paradise, the dwelling of the fathers, and a perpetual banquet of joy in Abraham's bosom" (184).

Preburial Death

We can see, then, that when Wordsworth began to write intensively on the subject of death, in 1798, there already existed a recognizable Enlightenment discourse that saw death and the afterlife as ideas that had their origin in the empirical body and the grave. These inquiries provided him with a paradigm within and against which he wrote a series of poems focusing on specific stages in the development of these ideas. Set within this context, Wordsworth's famous dictum that we are naturally unable "to admit the notion of death as a state applicable" to our being (*PW* 4:463) represents a radical departure from Enlightenment thought, which had assumed that the idea of immortality, like the idea of death itself, was too sophisticated for the primitive mind and developed later. For Wordsworth, the notion of immortality, our first religious idea, is derived not from the grave, but from life; rather than providing us with the symbolic materials for an idea of afterlife, our empirical knowledge of the dead robs us of this belief, leaving poetry the task of finding a linguistic means for us to recover from this mortal theft. The history of death is thus a dialectic, built upon the conflict between ideas of immortality, drawn from the continuities of nature, and our empirical knowledge of the dead.

The child's utter rejection of the idea of death as annihilation finds its greatest spokesperson in one of Wordsworth's most loved heroines, the "wildly clad" little eight-year-old of "We Are Seven." She is at once Wordsworth's domestic "wild child" and his new Eve, her hair, like her predecessor's in *Paradise Lost* (4.305–08), "thick with many a curl / That clustered round her head." With powerful lyrical condensation, the poem can be said to re-enact Milton's scene of the Fall. Now, however, the tempter who would bring death into the world is not Satan, using flattery, but a catechist, who seeks to make the girl accept an abstract dualism that kills: "But they are dead; those two are dead! / Their spirits are in heaven!" Wordsworth's revision of the Fall is also a rereading of Rousseau's *Emile,* which was a frequent subject of conversation in the months immediately preceding the composition of *Lyrical Ballads,* when Wordsworth and Coleridge were considering contemporary educational theories. There Rousseau teaches us how to use reason to coerce children into accepting that death applies to them:

> NURSE Do you remember the time when your mother was a girl?
> LITTLE GIRL No, nurse.
> NURSE Why not, since you have so good a memory?
> LITTLE GIRL Because I was not yet in the world.
> NURSE Then you have not always been alive?

LITTLE GIRL No.

NURSE Will you always be alive?

LITTLE GIRL Yes.

NURSE Are you young or old?

LITTLE GIRL I am young.

NURSE And is your grandmother young or old?

LITTLE GIRL She is old.

NURSE Was she once young?

LITTLE GIRL Yes.

NURSE Why isn't she young anymore?

LITTLE GIRL Because she got old.

NURSE Will you get old like her?

LITTLE GIRL I don't know.

. . . .

NURSE But, still, do you believe you will live forever?

LITTLE GIRL When I am very old, very old . . .

NURSE Well, then?

LITTLE GIRL Finally, when one is so old, you say that one has to die.

NURSE Will you, then, die sometime?

LITTLE GIRL Alas, yes.[10]

In "We Are Seven," it is the adult who needs to be educated. Words-worth's Eve does not fall to the seductive logic of her Rousseauist ca-techist. Instead, drawing on the language of the Old Testament—"All flesh *is* grass" (Isaiah 40:6)—she boldly points to her brother's and sister's graves—"Their graves are green, they may be seen"—as proof that death is not radically discontinuous with life. The grave need not be imagined as a site of phantasms and terror, nor death as an empty self-devouring allegory, a "vast unhide-bound Corpse" (*Paradise Lost* 10.601). Instead, she imagines her dead brother and sister as quietly joining her in an evening meal, listening to her songs, and silently watching her knit and play. She teaches us that death is not a private but a communal state, that it can be simple, close (only "twelve steps or more from my mother's door"), and familiar—a "tame death," to quote Philippe Ariès, who ar-gues that it is "the oldest death there is" (*The Hour of Our Death* 28). A major aspect of our enjoyment of the poem lies in our vicarious, perhaps atavistic, sense that we do not necessarily have to be fallen, that death will not come into the world unless we admit it as an idea. Yet the debate structure of the poem tells us that this childhood denial of death, this "high instinct" (*Intimations Ode*), is a fragile state that needs more than simply dogmatic assertion if it is to be maintained in later years.

Readers have often taken this child to be a spokesperson for a "natural" idea of death, as if her position were totally devoid of any cultural support. Yet her use of biblical language suggests that her notion of death is not so much a natural one as a very old one, as old as the Orient. It can be traced back to the time, described by Herder, when the Underworld was no larger than a "house" and the living coexisted and conversed with the dead. What adds to the power of the poem is Wordsworth's recognition that this idea of death was about to disappear from England, to be replaced by the more hierarchical conceptions offered by her interrogator.

An extraordinary aspect of the experimentalism of 1798 was that Wordsworth, having recognized the cultural preconditions of a "tame death," set out in a number of poems, including the early "spots of time" fragments of MS. JJ of the *Prelude,* to imagine what death might have been like *before* there were families, communities, or graves. A major poem in this regard is the "Complaint of a Forsaken Indian Woman." The poem has not been well liked. On one hand, its sources in the observation and reflection on savage nations are all too explicit, for it was drawn directly from Wordsworth's reading in Samuel Hearne's *Journey from Hudson's Bay to the Northern Ocean* (1795). On the other hand, it has generally been assumed that the poem is simply an exercise in primitivist sentimentalism, a conventional "complaint" in one of the more execrable of literary genres, the "dying Indian song," its exoticism a stimulant to jaded sensibilities, its goal to engage our sympathy by displaying the pathos of an Indian dying, with stoic fortitude, alone in the northern wilderness of Canada.[11] Most readers, unwilling to read the poem as a critique of this genre, have agreed with Carl Woodring's assessment that it remains "at the level of commonplace" and that the woman is a stock exotic figure, overlaid with sentimentalist and primitivist associations.[12]

In the 1800 preface, Wordsworth did not emphasize the poem's sentimentalism, but instead its experimentalism, as an illustration of "the manner in which our feelings and ideas are associated in a state of excitement . . . by accompanying the last struggles of a human being at the approach of death, cleaving in solitude to life and society" (*ProseW*

1:126). Why Wordsworth chose to write about an isolated and abandoned Copper Indian dying in the northern wilderness of Canada requires little conjecture.[13] What must have struck him, as he read Hearne's account of how an Indian woman, "without much ceremony . . . was left unassisted, to perish above-ground" (202), was that here was a society that neither buried its dead nor engaged in any ceremonies relating to their final disposition. Arguing that "a custom apparently so unnatural is perhaps not to be found among any other of the human race" (203), Hearne observes that "the Northern Indians never bury their dead, but always leave the bodies where they die, so that they are supposed to be devoured by beasts and birds of prey; for which reason they will not eat foxes, wolves, ravens, &c. unless it be through mere necessity" (341). In the *Essays upon Epitaphs,* citing William Camden's *Remaines Concerning Britain,* Wordsworth stresses that "never any . . . neglected burial but some savage nations; as the Bactrians, which cast their dead to the dogs; some varlet philosophers, as Diogenes, who desired to be devoured of fishes; some dissolute courtiers, as Maecenas, who was wont to say, ' . . . I'm careless of a grave:—Nature her dead will save'" (*ProseW* 2:49–50). For a poet familiar with the anthropological link between burial and metaphysics, Hearne's observations provided an extraordinary opportunity to explore, with empirical support, the idea of death in a preburial society.

Hearne adopts an empiricist view when he writes that the Copper Indians are unlike their southern neighbors because they are "utterly destitute of every idea of practical religion" and have no "idea of a future state" (343–44). This utter this-worldliness is also manifest in Wordsworth's depiction of the woman's "grave-site." She has been given everything she needs for existence in this world—food, water, a fire, furs, things that now bring her "no joy" (17)—yet she has been left nothing to assist her in a future life or any journey she might undertake as a dead soul. Nor has a special site been marked out to receive her remains. No respect is shown her body, which has been left to perish above ground, prey to wolves and scavengers. Wordsworth explains this lack of concern in his *Essays upon Epitaphs,* where he argues that our respect for the bodies of the dead arises from an intimation of immortality. "We respect the corporeal frame of Man," he writes, "not merely because it is the habitation of a rational, but of an immortal Soul" (*ProseW* 2:52). Since this society has no conception of the soul, it has left the woman

completely unprepared, either materially or linguistically, to think of
death as anything other than complete annihilation. But Wordsworth,
as he confronted the Enlightenment, did not simply illustrate Hearne's
text. Instead, the "Complaint" radically reinterprets his arguments by
showing how an intimation of immortality precedes and is at odds with
the stoicism of the woman's society.[14] It presents a speaker who is struggling to articulate an idea of a soul and an afterlife that would ameliorate
the fear of death, and yet who lacks the symbolic means that other
societies have devised for this purpose. Without burial rituals to guard
and preserve her body after death, without narratives and writing to
preserve her memory, without myths about the afterlife to assist her,
without a family or a society to support her, in a cold and bleak nature
that, contrary to Herder's nature, allows mankind no freedom beyond
the daily struggle for the necessities of life, she nevertheless tries to affirm
her "high instincts." Here we are given a woman who antedates the New
Eve of "We Are Seven" because she inhabits a nature that has not yet
been shaped into an adequate human environment. Lacking the symbolic means to make her intimation of immortality concrete, she nevertheless tries to articulate her ideas with the language at her disposal: she
represents death through *things* and through what her senses inform her
about changes of state, in the sky, her fire, her food, her water, and her
body. But the harsh environment in which she is dying offers her no
assistance.

The poem opens with the woman's recollection of a dream she had
in which she saw and heard the sights and sounds of the aurora borealis,
yet lived:

> In sleep I heard the northern gleams;
> The stars, they were among my dreams;
> In rustling conflict through the skies,
> I heard, I saw the flashes drive,
> And yet they are upon my eyes,
> And yet I am alive . . .

This image of a violent heaven of strange flashing fires and "rustling
conflict" may be a projection into a metaphysical realm of the harsh
realities of her own society, but it nevertheless allows her to hope she
will "see another day" after her body has "die[d] away." In comparison
with her tribe's own conception of the northern lights, which are called

"*Ed-thin*," or "Deer," after the crackling electrical sparks a deer skin makes when stroked on a dry night, her dream is prophetic. It anticipates the rudimentary metaphysical ideas of the southern Indians, who understand these lights and sounds as "the spirits of their departed friends dancing in the clouds" (346n).

The idea of a future life, however, depends upon a notion of a soul, and when the woman looks to the fire, now in ashes, attempting to understand how her identity might exist through time and change, she is perplexed and cannot see how her "death" can be any different from that of the fire:

> My fire is dead: it knew no pain;
> Yet is it dead, and I remain:
> All stiff with ice the ashes lie;
> And they are dead, and I will die.

Her hope that her "pain" might distinguish her life from that of the fire is short-lived; she comes to the conclusion that "she" must die with her body.[15]

It should not surprise us that this woman does not conceive of her mind and body in the same way as we do. Robert Langbaum first noted the strangeness of this woman's mind, pointing out how difficult it is for us to sympathize with her when there is "no core of character that is beyond what the speaker says" (*Poetry of Experience* 72). Rather than being a weakness, this lack is, in fact, one of the poem's great successes. Wordsworth represents someone who conceives her body not as an organic totality, but instead as an aggregate of parts. Her limbs have a discrete life and identity of their own ("When ye were gone my limbs were stronger" [25]; "When from my arms my Babe they took" [33]; "he stretched his arms, how wild!" [39]). She inquires into the life and death of her body with the same detachment with which she reflects on the condition of the fire: "I cannot lift my limbs to know / If they have any life or no" (64–65). Similarly, rather than seeing *through* her eyes, as if they were windows of the soul, she describes seeing in a distanced manner, as impressions registered *upon* her eyes: "I saw the flashes drive, / And yet they are upon my eyes."[16] The absence of a "core of personality," of a psyche, suggests, as will become clearer in discussing the "spots of time," that the idea of death plays a key role in the psychological constitution of the self.

Instead of a private, psychological definition of the self, this woman understands it as an amalgam of societal status and parental duties. Death is consequently less a physical phenomenon than a social and familial loss. "Alone, I cannot fear to die," she asserts, for being isolated and forgotten is a far greater death than the termination of life: "Methinks 'tis strange I did not perish / The moment I was left behind" (*PW* 2:475). Yet her society has no place for the dead; instead, it cuts them off from the living and forgets them. The woman's desire to be part of her tribe even in death and her feeling that she could die "with happy heart" if she could die with her child "close to me," indicates how important it is for humans to transform death into a social and familial institution. In the *Essays upon Epitaphs,* Wordsworth observes that though we naturally believe that "some part of our nature is imperishable . . . the wish to be remembered by our friends or kindred after death, or even in absence is . . . a sensation that does not form itself till the *social* feelings have been developed, and the Reason has connected itself with a wide range of objects" (*ProseW* 2:50). The "Complaint" shows us that the development of customs relating to the dead are closely linked to the development of society and a nature shaped by human hands.

Stanza 5 speculates on the emotions that originally gave rise to the practice of writing epitaphs, if not also (because the Copper Indians do not write) to writing itself:

> "O wind, that o'er my head art flying
> The way my friends their course did bend,
> I should not feel the pain of dying,
> Could I with thee a message send;
> Too soon, my friends, ye went away;
> For I had many things to say."

Epitaphs are bound up with the desire of the dead to continue to speak to the living after their words can no longer be carried by breath or on the winds. The "pain of dying," for this woman, is the pain of being forgotten. In a rejected passage, having sensed that it is somehow unjust that "one beloved, forlorn, / Should lie beneath the cold starlight," she hopes that by not following her people she has at least succeeded in marking out the spot where she died:

> I might have dropp'd, and died alone
> On unknown snows, a spot unknown.

> This spot to me must needs be dear,
> Of my dear Friends I see the trace.
> You saw me, friends, you laid me here,
> You know where my poor bones shall lie,
> Then wherefore should I fear to die?   [*PW* 2:475–76]

Wordsworth decided not to include this passage, probably because it allowed for too much optimism in a poem about a woman's faltering attempt to think her way beyond the metaphysical limitations of her culture. Instead, the poem ends in failure, with the woman unable to formulate a sustaining idea of immortality. Yet her "complaint" does, in negative terms, speak for spiritual needs that her society has not yet found the symbolic means to satisfy. The poem thus teaches us something about the importance of burial and writing by showing us what it would be like to die without them.

"Lucy Gray" and the Mythic Understanding of Death

Though Wordsworth is often viewed as a poet primarily concerned with monumentalizing death, in epitaphs and tombs, it should equally be stressed that, as part of his representation of the history of death, he also sought to recover the voices of the unburied dead, those voices that can only be heard, like the complaint of the forsaken Indian woman, in "the motions of the winds" and that have their abode "in the mystery of words" (*Prelude* 5.620–21). Though the mythic aspects of the "Lucy poems" have often been noted, the tendency of readers to conflate the speaker(s) of these poems with Wordsworth and to conclude that he was making a cryptic personal confession while under intense psychological pressure in Goslar, Germany, has prevented them from recognizing these poems as innovative experiments in the mythic representation of death. Like the "Complaint," these poems enact a primal linguistic struggle to deal with death, only now the emphasis is not on the person who dies, but on the speaker who is left behind. Lucy is presented as prehuman and prelinguistic: she dies, as Geoffrey Hartman has observed, "at the threshold of humanization" (*Wordsworth's Poetry* 160). In Wordsworth's anthropology, someone must have died before us to set in motion the linguistic practices that make us human. Lucy is that someone.

In "Strange fits of passion," a poem whose sources in Peter Bell's nocturnal ride on the ass are explicit, Wordsworth shows how a lover, by arbitrarily associating the slow, plodding movement of his horse with time and his beloved Lucy with the moon, suddenly comes to an awareness of the possibility that she might be dead. As in the "Waiting at the Crossroads" episode of *The Prelude,* natural symbols and events take on a premonitory status in retrospect. Love and guilt thus become fused in the narrator's sense that he was implicated in her death. In "A slumber did my spirit seal," Wordsworth shifts from premonitions to myth, as he represents how death might have appeared to a mind grappling for the first time with "human fears." Death remains a mystery, and the narrator, unable to discriminate living from inanimate things, struggles to understand the nature of this change:

> She seemed a thing that could not feel
>   The touch of earthly years.
>
> No motion has she now, no force;
>   She neither hears nor sees;
> Rolled round in earth's diurnal course,
>   With rocks, and stones, and trees.

The narrator's vision of the afterlife, like that of the dying woman of the "Complaint," could hardly be cruder, or more marvelously strange and terrible. His is a world in which the corpse governs the imagery of the afterlife, even as the process by which the dead are spiritualized is rudimentary: what has been immortalized is not a spirit, but the body, which rolls interminably, as a "thing" hardly different from "rocks, and stones, and trees," in an elemental material nature. Significantly, the idea of death as a slumber that seals the spirit for a reawakening appears as an alternative not taken. "She dwelt among the untrodden ways" is more obviously an epitaph, and its literary sources in pastoral elegy are more easily recognized. Where in "Strange fits of passion" the description of Lucy as looking "every day / Fresh as a rose in June" evokes antithetically an image of her present state as a decaying corpse, this poem transforms Lucy into "a violet by a mossy stone," a pastoral version of the grave. However, this form of pastoral ultimately fails to solace the speaker, who is left with the painful awareness of her loss.

"Three years she grew in sun and shower" is the most ambiguous of the poems in the series. Though it is often anthologized, no one seems to have recognized that the story of Nature's plan to raise Lucy is *not* a description of her growth, but instead a consolatory fiction that seeks to explain her sudden death at the age of "three" ("Three years she grew ... Then Nature said ... / Thus Nature spake ... She died"). Here death is not portrayed as a Grim Reaper, but instead as "Nature," a benevolent parental figure who wants to make Lucy into "a Lady of my own." In this pantheistic vision, Lucy is transformed into a genius loci, an expression of the "law and impulse" of nature. But this idea of the afterlife as a "happy dell" is no more successful than any of the others in dealing with death. In the final stanza, as the speaker reflects on the myth he has created, he notes that he can silently sympathize with what Lucy has become—"this heath, this calm, and quiet scene"—but the rhetoric of a pastoral afterlife breaks down, leaving him with the memory of irredeemable loss—"the memory of what has been, / And never more will be."

Even from this sketchy summary, it should be obvious that this series of lyrics explores the primitive idea of death. "Lucy Gray" belongs to this series; it differs from the other poems in that Wordsworth shifted from lyric to myth, drawing directly from classical and biblical sources for his understanding of the genesis of myths concerning the afterlife. The poem's sources in the ballad tradition, in Robert Anderson's "Lucy Gray of Allendale" (1798) and Percy's *Reliques*, especially "The Children in the Wood," have long been recognized.[17] What has not been noted is that Wordsworth, as he recounted how Lucy's parents, following her footprints, are brought to an abrupt impasse in the recognition of her disappearance, was explicitly modeling the poem on the story of Enoch. The echo of the verse "And Enoch walked with God; and he was not; for God took him" is quite obvious in the lines

> They followed from the snowy bank
> Those footmarks, one by one,
> Into the middle of the plank;
> And further there were none!

Wordsworth presents us with a primal myth—Lucy was and then she "was not"—and, like the story of Enoch, we can read it either as a veiled account of a premature death or as a mysterious disappearance. A modern-day Alciphron might point to the Fenwick note to the poem in order to argue that Lucy actually drowned in the stream, but it should be stressed that the poem does not provide this information and instead leaves us, like the parents on the bridge, in a state of surmise. At the center of the poem is this primal mystery, and the poem is generated through its documentation of the successive interpolations of this myth. These interpolations progressively spiritualize and immortalize Lucy (she "will never more be seen" [line 12], she is "in heaven" [42], she is a "living child" [58]). We are thus given a history of the idea of death that does not proceed referentially or chronologically, but instead resides, like the series of "translation" narratives in the Bible, in the history of interpretations that this story has given rise to. In discovering these sedimented, interpolative layers, we see how a commonplace event, which can be explained without reference to supernatural intervention, has been taken up and revised over the course of its history by an interpretive community, and has come to form the basis of a faith in an afterlife. And as readers, we too take our place in that history as we employ alternative explanatory systems to deal with this death. Thus, the poem is about the "translation" of Lucy Gray in both a spiritual and a textual sense; it shows how an original, mysterious event comes, through successive retellings and interpretations, to serve as an "intimation of immortality."

"Lucy Gray" is a syncretic myth of origins, for in it Wordsworth also reworks classical ideas about the afterlife. In the poem's concluding interpolation, we are given an explicit version of the Orpheus myth. Lucy, "upon the lonesome wild . . . trips along, / And never looks behind; / And sings a solitary song" (60–63), as if she were both the dead Eurydice and the poet Orpheus, continually bringing herself back from the Underworld through song, on the one condition that she "never look[s] behind."[18] Yet it should be stressed that the concluding Orpheus myth is itself an interpolation. This suggests that the original myth is *pre*-Orphean, an anticipation or presentiment of ideas that were only later given symbolical coherence through the idea of a journey to the Underworld. This story is not, then, simply an imitation of the myth of Orpheus: through the notion of the conformities between contemporary village life and the archaic past, we are provided with an interpretive framework for understanding how the Greek myth came into being.

The poem is structured in terms of three quests: Lucy's, for her mother; the parents', to retrieve Lucy; and the narrator/reader's, for "the sweet face of Lucy Gray." Each of these articulates with greater clarity and concreteness the topos of the classical *catabasis*, the downward journey to the silent realm of the dead. In the first of these—Lucy's search for her mother—the Orphean quest is played out among the living and, interestingly, it is the Orphean figure who dies in the process. Words-worth shows us how the language of myth can be found in everyday rural images that have been modified by the imagination. If the image of Lucy carrying a lantern intimates the dark journey into the Under-world, or if we see in that moment when "the Father raised his hook, / And snapped a faggot-band" a shadowy premonition—indeed, a pro-totype of the Christian imagery—of death, these are ideas that we bring to the narrative and which take on this meaning retrospectively, when Lucy has been broken from her family. Lucy's is a failed catabasis, be-cause she does not seem to know where the Underworld is. Wandering "up and down," like the "Children in the Wood," she does not know that her journey should be a *descent*.

In the second journey the roles are reversed, as the parents seek to retrieve their dead daughter, now symbolically a Eurydice. Significantly, unlike Lucy's journey, theirs begins after they have arrived at an idea of death and after the "storm" of nature that Wordsworth, echoing the "Complaint," associates with primal nature. Having wandered all night, "far and wide" without a "guide" (36)—the figure that will subsequently play such an important role in these journeys—they see, at daybreak from a hill overlooking a moor, a "bridge of wood, / A furlong from their door." As in "Strange fits of passion," where a commonplace object becomes unconsciously linked with the idea of death, the bridge and the river become associated with all that separates and prevents them from retrieving their child, and they accept her death: "They wept—and, turning homeward, cried, / 'In heaven we all shall meet.'" Yet it is at this moment, which echoes the final lines of *Paradise Lost*, that the mother sees Lucy's footprints, and the two begin a rudimentary descent in search of her: "Then downwards from the steep hill's edge / They tracked the footmarks small . . ." The bridge initially seems to offer them convey-ance, thus giving us an insight into that stubborn unwillingness of the human mind to accept death that underlies the Orpheus myth. Yet mid-way the footprints suddenly vanish and the two can go no further. Though one might easily identify the river and the bridge with the classical imagery for the Underworld—with Styx and the gate that di-vides the living from the dead—Wordsworth's real intention is to show the everyday empirical sources out of which the myth of Orpheus and the classical Underworld came into being. "Two things must surprise us about the so-called underworld of classical times," Michael G. Cooke has written. "One, it was not very deep, not far at all from everyday, walking-around life. And two, it didn't even need to be down, or *under*; the dead (or the daring) went *out* beyond the limits of the recognized, constituted, incorporated world into the dimensions of shades."[19] "Lucy Gray" shows us the Otherworld before it becomes an Underworld, when it was still on the earth's surface, no deeper than the depth of a stream, no further from the living than the other side of a country bridge.

With the failure of the parents' quest, we are brought, in the culminating and framing interpolation, to a new idea of the Orphean journey, which makes myth itself the medium of Lucy's immortality. Here the Orphean myth is most explicit, as song takes on its traditional Orphic power over death. Lucy becomes a genius loci, a spirit of the stream who "o'er rough and smooth . . . trips along, / And never looks behind." Like the dismembered head of Orpheus, singing as it floated down the river Hebrus, Lucy has become the embodiment of an immortality achieved through time. In a poem whose polemical basis lies in its avoidance of the language of the Underworld, a poem that draws its idea of immortality not from the grave, but from the surface of the earth, from the flowing brook and the solitary "whistling" (64) wind, Lucy has been translated into a "solitary song." She can be "a living child" only if she does not look behind. In the death that lies in this look, a death not only for Lucy, but also for the reader (who also occupies the position of Eurydice), Wordsworth returns us to the fundamental argument posed by the Enlightenment, one that his poetry confronted and sought to displace: that the death that kills is the death we derive from the body, from seeing the faces of those who have died before us.

Though "Lucy Gray" is based on an unusual situation, it nevertheless can serve as a prototype for Wordsworth's basic rhetorical strategy in dealing with death: the absence or disappearance of Lucy's corpse, combined with our inability to place her physically in the grave, prevents us from locating her symbolically in the Underworld and frees us to imagine her afterlife in ways that our senses deny us. One of Wordsworth's many unburied dead, Lucy is free to wander where she will, for she has no place, except in song. Translated into myth, she is an intensely spiritualized being, a figure heard in the sounds of the wind and brooks. As such, she is a type of all the preburial dead, whose "dim abode" is the "distant winds" and whose voices make up the "ghostly language of the ancient earth" (*Prelude* 2.328–29).

The "Spots of Time" and the Genesis of Burial

The forsaken Indian woman's repeated assertion that her friends will remember the "spot" where she died is closely linked to the genesis of a series of short autobiographical sketches, which have come to be known as the "spots of time" passages. Three of these, which tell of the child's encounter with a drowned man, his discovery of a gibbet below Penrith Beacon, and "Waiting at the Crossroads," were written as a unit. Two others, the Boy of Winander episode and "Nutting," are closely related. All were written at Goslar, around the time of the Lucy poems. In these poems, we see how Wordsworth's belief in the conformities between the child and savage peoples—that as "a five years' child" he had "stood alone / Beneath the sky, as if I had been born / On Indian plains . . . A naked savage" (*Prelude* 1.291–304)—allowed him to transfer to his child-hood the modes of inquiry that had traditionally focused on native life. These passages, therefore, do not represent a departure from the concerns we have been examining, but instead the appearance of a new subject for these inquiries.

All these poems return us to a world where—at least for the child—there are not yet any graves, where memories of the dead are still linked to "spots" marked out in the landscape. Each can thus be said to explore the dark prehistory of death. Each shows us how the human mind is born out of its confrontation with death and how the same symbolic activities that create graves and bind the unburied dead to the soil also create minds that can serve as burial sites for the past. An examination of two of these passages will allow us to discern the essential character-istics of this transference.

In the Boy of Winander episode (originally written as an autobio-graphical narrative), Wordsworth describes a frequently repeated event, how "many a time" a solitary child, divested of language and culture so that he can re-enact a primal scene in the history of mankind, would

> stand alone
> Beneath the trees or by the glimmering lake,

And there, with fingers interwoven, both hands
Pressed closely palm to palm, and to his mouth
Uplifted, he as through an instrument
Blew mimic hootings to the silent owls
That they might answer him.   [*Prelude* 5.393–99]

Drawing on conventional notions of the onomatopoeic origin of language, Wordsworth reworks the primitive encounter. No longer the effect of the repeated encounter of two wild children, it now derives from
the child's mimetic encounter with nature. Wordsworth focuses upon
the "skill" and repetition ("many a time") required to make articulate
sounds, the actual physical mechanisms of sound articulation—the exact
disposition of the fingers, palms, and hands, their positioning next to
the mouth, and the precise blowing "as through an instrument"—that
have to be learned before the child can imitate or mimic the natural
cries of the owls. Where the owls' "shout[s]," "quivering peals," "long
halloos," and "screams" are limited by the physiological conformation of
their vocal organs, the boy shows an advance over nature by using his
hands to produce "mimic hootings." Within the theoretical perspective
of eighteenth-century language theory, which makes the existence of a
flexible tongue a late stage in the history of speech, the Boy of Winander's recourse to his hands in order to articulate sounds (as if he had
not yet learned to use his tongue) and his dependence upon intonation
("varying . . . tones of voice") in his hootings suggest that this episode
also contributes to a hypothetical history of the process by which the
child is ushered into language.

As Wordsworth observes in the note to "The Thorn," we derive a
pleasure from repetition; the mind "luxuriates in the repetition of words
which appear successfully to communicate its feelings" (*PW* 2:513). This
pleasure incites the old sailor to repeat his tale, Peter to continue to
attack the ass, and the Boy of Winander to reiterate his mimic hootings,
with each echo setting up a pattern of anticipation and response:

And they would shout
Across the wat'ry vale, and shout again,
Responsive to his call, with quivering peals
And long halloos, and screams, and echoes loud,
Redoubled and redoubled—concourse wild
Of mirth and jocund din.   [5.399–404]

What also contributes to the yield of pleasure in this game is the delight that arises from the child's discovery of the mastery that language gives him over nature and absent things. It is a narcissistic language game, a version of the "*fort / da*" game analyzed by Freud in *Beyond the Pleasure Principle*: the otherwise silent owls, by responding immediately to the child's imitations, affirm his sense of sovereignty. But more than pleasure is at stake. As Geoffrey Hartman has noted, the dominant effect of this episode is that of "a mysterious and supervening thought of death" (*Wordsworth's Poetry* 20). The child's actions are in deadly earnest, even if he is no more aware of their true function than was Peter Bell, for coincident with language comes an inchoate notion of the meaning of death and absence. Even before he has imagined his own death, the child has acted it out by proxy, figuratively investing his identity or "voice" in the absent owls, only to hear it brought back to him as an echo.[20] And before he is even fully conscious of this presentiment of death, he glories in the feeling of immortality, the miracle of miracles, his ability to recall himself perpetually, through language, out of the mute silence of an otherworld.

Like the two previous poems, the opening section of the Boy of Winander episode depicts a time when the Otherworld was still aboveground and death but a short journey across a "wat'ry vale."[21] To speak to the Otherworld, one had only to shout across the waters. This paradoxical dialogue, however, does not last. When the child is suddenly confronted with a "deep silence" that cannot be surmounted, death, as disruption, makes its presence felt, so gently that it comes as a "shock of mild surprize":

> sometimes in that silence, while he hung
> Listening, a gentle shock of mild surprize
> Has carried far into his heart the voice
> Of mountain torrents; or the visible scene
> Would enter unawares into his mind
> With all its solemn imagery, its rocks,
> Its woods, and that uncertain heaven, received
> Into the bosom of the steady lake.   [5.406–13]

In this magnificent scene, the mind of the boy, still unaware of death, becomes the perceptual ground or inscape where burial, not yet localized, is enacted on a cosmic scale, as a still "uncertain heaven" is "received into the bosom" of a "steady lake."

Dying had been going on long before "death" was ever remembered, so language is less a deferral of death than its medium. By ushering language into being, the boy introduces the very possibility of a history of death and of the elegiac narrative that sets his own death within that history. This is the true fate that we feel attaches to his death, a fate implicit in the past tense of the opening line "There was a boy." In the second part of the poem, we learn that the "boy was taken from his mates, and died / In childhood ere he was full ten years old." Words-worth emphasizes the location of the grave:

> Fair are the woods, and beauteous is the spot,
> The vale where he was born; the churchyard hangs
> Upon a slope above the village school,
> And there, along that bank, when I have passed
> At evening, I believe that oftentimes
> A full half-hour together I have stood
> Mute, looking at the grave in which he lies.

Verbal repetition (the "wat'ry vale" becomes "the vale where he was born"; the churchyard "hangs / Upon a slope" just as the boy had "hung listening") reinforces the structural parallelism between the two parts of the narrative: in each case, someone seeks to enter into an evening dialogue with the silent dead. Yet this parallelism also emphasizes the historical transformation that has taken place in the idea and medium of death—the anthropological distance between the child's and the man's conceptions of death. In the poem's two sections, we thus see epitomized two major statements in Wordsworth's history of death, as the historical appearance of the grave changes the idea of death. In the second section, death is monumentalized. Burial has made it possible for the dead to go underground, to "slumber" in a place that is now understood as a communal condition, a "silent neighbourhood of graves" (5.427–28), itself a reflection of the village life that surrounds it. Where the differentiation of states had earlier proceeded along a horizontal axis, across the waters, it is now registered vertically: there is an "ascending" movement from the lower worlds, represented by the silence of the sleeping dead and the children of the rural school—whose "gladsome sounds" should not obscure our recognition that they are also "mad at their sports like

withered leaves in winds"—to the embodiment of religious life, a new
"lady" replacing "the bosom" of nature that first received the dead, the
"village church" that sits "on her green hill, forgetful of this boy / Who
slumbers at her feet." Language has also gained in complexity and sophistication; the ecstatic hootings of the child have been replaced by the
epitaphic and elegiac writing of the poet. Born in an age too late to
make the Orphic claim that language can cross the gap separating the
living from the dead, the poet nevertheless uses his narrative to accommodate this silence, to link himself to the boy and his intimation of
immortality, and to give death, through writing, a local habitation and
a name.

The Boy of Winander illustrates a central feature of Wordsworth's
anthropology of death: that the dead receive a dual burial, in earth and
in narratives. Language and burial can thus be seen not only as two of
the most important social and socializing human institutions, but also as
complementary symbolic mediums that came into being at approximately the same time for the same purpose—to deal with death by reas-
serting symbolically our original belief in immortality. Graves idealize the
dead by placing them out of sight, by using nature to modify their
sublime powers, and by placing them together, so that they are no longer
alone, but can be conceived as a community. The dead are also buried
in narratives. No longer able to speak themselves, to be active agents in
the world and in language, they depend upon others for their continued
existence. Just as the dead first inhabited the winds and only later received a specific monumentalized location, so too the dead in narratives
follow a similar progress from winds, to village stories, to epitaphs.

Wordsworth indicates the close relationship between burial and language in his discussion of the Boy of Winander episode, in the preface
of 1815: "I have begun with one of the earliest processes of Nature in
the development of this faculty [the imagination]. Guided by one of my
own primary consciousnesses, I have represented a commutation and
transfer of internal feelings, co-operating with external accidents, to
plant, for immortality, images of sound and sight, in the celestial soil of
the Imagination" (*ProseW* 3:35n). A striking feature of this description
is that Wordsworth portrays the mind as a psychic equivalent of the
earth, a "celestial soil," while perception is metaphorically equated with
the practice of burial, "plant[ing] for immortality, images of sound and
sight." Mental categories are thus metaphorically understood in material

terms, so that the development of memory is seen as analogous to that
of burial. The "spots of time," which we can now recognize as psychic
internalizations of the issues raised by the "Complaint of a Forsaken
Indian Woman," explore the mind's discovery of this connection, when
in retrospect it comes to see itself as a burial ground, where "objects and
appearances, / Albeit lifeless then," are

> doomed to sleep
> Until maturer seasons called them forth
> To impregnate and to elevate the mind.   [*Prelude* 1.621–24]

Immediately following the Boy of Winander passage in the 1805 *Prelude* is Wordsworth's description of how, in "the very week" that he came
to Hawkshead, he witnessed the retrieval of a drowned man from Esthwaite Water (5.426). This episode explores further the child's developing
understanding of death by depicting his first encounter with the corporeal dead. Since the discovery and subsequent burial of James Jackson
did not, in fact, occur at this time, but instead happened a month after
Wordsworth's arrival at Hawkshead (Reed *EY* 47–48), it is clear that
these two events are being synchronized, to make the poet's story of
being "first transplanted" or rooted to the Vale coincident with Jackson's
death and burial (1799 *Prelude* 1.260). "A person does not belong to a
place until there is someone dead under the ground," declares José Ar-
cadio Buendia, the fictional patriarchal founder of Macondo, in *One
Hundred Years of Solitude*.[22] Wordsworth shares this belief in the socializing
power of death. Communities are built in the face of death, which links
otherwise solitary individuals to one another and binds them to place.

The episode offers us three perspectives on death, as we progress
from the "half-infant thoughts" of the child "roving up and down
alone" like a postdiluvian solitary, "seeking I knew not what"; to that
of the child as spectator in a crowd, anxiously watching for the emergence of the "dead man" from the lake; to that of the poet recollecting
this experience and communicating it to others (*Prelude* 5.454–70).
Like the Boy of Winander passage, the narrative focuses on the discovery of the Underworld. Wordsworth links the progress of the idea
of death to the progress of language and the institution of burial.
From the "green peninsulas," "shaped like ears," which seem to make
inroads into the shapeless lake, to the "unclaimed garments telling a
plain tale," to the company "sound[ing]" the waters "with grappling-

irons and long poles," the emergence of a spectral underworld is bound up with learning to see the world through language. This is especially true when the child, looking across the water, through the "gloom" of twilight, sees a "heap of garments," akin to a burial site, on the far shore:

> Long I watched,
> But no one owned them; meanwhile the calm lake
> Grew dark, with all the shadows on its breast,
> And now and then a fish up-leaping snapped
> The breathless stillness.   [5.462–66]

Wordsworth describes the suspended moment when the child, his gaze carried over to the other shore, has an intimation of the Underworld. The water grows dark and spectral "shadows" begin to play "on its breast." Then fishes, the traditional conveyers of the dead, come from below to disturb the surface of a now "breathless stillness." The premonitory aspects and phantasmal qualities of the scene do not so much derive from what Wordsworth is actually seeing as from what he knows has happened. The intimation of a world just out of sight, below the earth's surface, is realized when, next day, out of the dark waters of the lake,

> At length, the dead man, 'mid that beauteous scene
> Of trees and hills and water, bolt upright
> Rose with his ghastly face, a spectre shape—
> Of terror even.   [5.470–73]

Wordsworth does not describe the burial of the drowned man, though this is the obvious reason for the search. Instead, he concentrates on the manner in which the *image* of the dead man rose in his mind— on death, not as a condition, but as an idea:

> And yet no vulgar fear,
> Young as I was, a child not nine years old,
> Possessed me, for my inner eye had seen
> Such sights before among the shining streams
> Of fairyland, the forests of romance—
> Thence came a spirit hallowing what I saw
> With decoration and ideal grace,

> A dignity, a smoothness, like the works
> Of Grecian art and purest poesy.   [5.473–81]

In this passage, more than in any other, we are shown that there are no primal encounters; they exist only hypothetically. Death is always already a cultural idea. The sight that rose before the nine-year-old child's eye was not a purely empirical figure, but instead a phantom "of texture midway betwixt life and books" (*Prelude* 3.613) who emerged as much out of the "shining streams" of the child's romance-struck mind as he did out of the waters of the dead lake. Many readers have been disturbed by the metamorphosis of the drowned man into a "literary image" and have concluded that it indicates a lack of sympathy on Wordsworth's part.[23] But the issue here is not one of choosing between fact and fiction, but of choosing between fictions— between whether our ideas of death are to be governed solely by the eye, by "the impression of death" we receive "from the outward senses" (*ProseW* 2:51), or are also to be shaped by the "inner eye," which allows the corpse to undergo a sea-change in language. In fact, the ghastliness of the corpse, which many critics have taken as a true image of death, is as much a poetic figure as the alternate sculptural representation of its "ideal grace."

Let me instead suggest that the collision in this passage between two ideas of death reflects Wordsworth's explicit effort to address a central feature of the Enlightenment discourse on death: its critique of the role that the fear of death plays in human life. The philosophes willingly admitted that this fear served a rational purpose, for "the human species could not be preserved, had not nature inspired us with an aversion towards it."[24] But they also stressed that the history of death was one of an excessive civil and ecclesiastical exploitation of this fear, as a means of social control. "All human institutions, all our opinions," writes the Baron d'Holbach, "conspire to augment our fears and to render our ideas of death more terrible and more revolting."[25] Oft repeating the Platonic maxim "that those who pursue philosophy aright study nothing but dying and being dead," the philosophers of the Enlightenment set out to teach others how to die by providing them with the alternate, rationalist idea—that the dead are beyond death, so "la mort n'est rien."[26] Writes d'Holbach: "It is the want of power to form an idea of death that makes man dread it; if

he were to form a true idea of it, he would cease from then on to fear
it" (*Système de la nature* 1:225). Central to their project was an extensive
critique of the important role that the imagination played in the genesis of a fear of death. Abraham Tucker, in the *Light of Nature Pursued,*
argues, for instance, that "the melancholy appearance of a lifeless
body, the mansion provided for it to inhabit, dark, cold, close and
solitary, are shocking to the imagination; but it is to the imagination
only, not the understanding; for whoever consults this faculty will see
at first glance, that there is nothing dismal in all these circumstances."[27] If human beings were to learn once more how to die in
peace, the understanding would have to replace the dangerous and
empty phantasms of the imagination, linked as they were to the body,
to the ceremonies surrounding dying, to funerary rituals, and to the
entire Church apparatus of Hell, damnation, and demons.

Lessing's essay "How the Ancients Represented Death" suggests that
rather than seeking to replace the imagination with the understanding, mankind should seek an alternative to the Christian way of imagining death. In the essay, Lessing shows dramatically that, contrary to
his contemporaries' assumptions, classical antiquity had not represented death as a figure of terror—a skeleton or Grim Reaper—but
instead as a healthy young boy, the brother of Sleep. As a caption to
the frontispiece illustration of death standing over a corpse, Lessing
cites Statius's *Thebais*: "Nullique ea tristis imago" ("And to none does
this shape seem sorrowful"). The essay gave rise to an extensive controversy, not only because it constituted an exceptional historical study
of the representation of death in antiquity, but also because it showed
that what had been taken to be a natural and universal attitude toward
death was instead the result of a specific way of representing it that
had come into being when Christianity displaced an earlier and more
positive viewpoint. Having criticized Christianity for having "banished
the ancient cheerful image of Death out of the domains of art," it left
its readers with a challenge: to rid the world of "the terrible skeletons,
and again . . . [take] possession of that other better image."[28]

Whether or not Wordsworth's introduction of the uncharacteristic
metaphor of Hellenic art into the 1804 revision of the Drowned Man
passage indicates that he was now familiar with Lessing's essay, it
nevertheless suggests that he too took up the Enlightenment challenge
to create a new idea of death.[29] Displacement, however, operates in a

different manner, for rather than denying the terror of death, Wordsworth makes it part of the education of the mind, as it moves from
the sublime to the beautiful. Rather than seeking to replace the imagination with reason, the task of this episode and other poems in the
series is to show how the imagination plays a productive role in spir-
itualizing death.

More characteristic is the conclusion to the 1799 version of the passage, which concentrates on the drowned man's burial (and "resurrection," as the Christian image of "garments" implies) in the poet's
mind:

> I might advert
> To numerous accidents in flood or field,
> Quarry or moor, or 'mid the winter snows,
> Distresses and disasters, tragic facts
> Of rural history, that impressed my mind
> With images to which in following years
> Far other feelings were attached—with forms
> That yet exist with independent life,
> And, like their archetypes, know no decay.   [1.279–87]

Replanted in Wordsworth's imagination, the drowned man has become one of many stories, "tragic facts / Of rural history." The world
of the dead, it would seem, is not only a "silent neighbourhood of
graves" (*Prelude* 5.428), but also an aggregate of narratives, a community inhabiting the ear (not of Esthwaite Water, but of the poet),
and it is in this "celestial soil" that the dead are transformed. Like
their "archetypes," the actual bodies of the dead in the grave, they
become "forms" that no longer engender fear and sublimity, but "exist
with independent life" and "know no decay."

Intimations of Immortality

The *Intimations Ode* represents, in two senses, a culminating statement
in Wordsworth's history of death. First, the odic form allowed him to
present this history in a more discursive, generalized, and synoptic
manner than was possible in the shorter lyrics and narratives. Second,
the poem is itself presented as a moment in that history, as "a summa,

a culmination and extension of all that has gone before it" (Ferguson, *Language as Counter-Spirit* 98). Where the previously discussed poems depicted various stages in the history of death, without reflecting on them, the *Ode* articulates a "philosophy of death." It presents a wisdom that emerges in the twilight of that history, when death has been recognized as an object of thought. Its task is to show us how the mind, in recollecting the forms that death and the afterlife have taken over time, can build upon the ruins of pastoral elegy and Christian dogma a new kind of "faith that looks through death," even when these previous ideas have lost their vitality and have themselves passed away. Unlike a universal history of spirit like Hegel's, however, Wordsworth's philosophy of death is not an achievement of abstraction, but instead emerges from a concrete autobiographical situation, in the felt losses of the speaking poet.

The adopted persona is consequently an important aspect of the poem, one of its great successes. To appreciate the nature of that achievement, however, one must first understand the broad historical scope of the poem, which Wordsworth indicated in the first published version by including an epigraph from Virgil's Fourth Eclogue, "paulo maiora canamus" ("let's sing a nobler song"). Peter J. Manning has demonstrated that many of "the puzzles of the Ode" are "deliberate and rooted in convention" and reflect the distinctive ways in which Wordsworth revises "the eclogue, and . . . the rich tradition that arose from its interpretive crux of the babe as either a particular, real child or a mythic symbol."[30] He notes that where Virgil's is a public poem, prophesying the birth of a divine child who will usher in the return of a golden age and race, Wordsworth's is a more private poem that relinquishes the world of action and of adult sexuality and places the pastoral myth of a golden age once more in the past. It should be added that this epigraph also functions as a historical marker. The Fourth Eclogue was popularly known as the "Messianic Eclogue," because Christian commentators had reinterpreted the speaker's vague and enigmatic reference to the coming of a divine child as a prophecy of the birth of Christ. Its mysteries, like those of the myth of Enoch, consequently came to be viewed as being historically appropriate to the limited understanding of Virgil as a "virtuous pagan moving toward revelation but never vouchsafed it" ("Wordsworth's Intimations Ode and Its Epigraphs" 538). The words "paulo maiora canamus"

were given a world-historical significance, as a prophecy of the end of
the classical age ("The last great age the Sibyl's song foretold / Rolls
round: the centuries are born anew!") and an "intimation" of a new
poetry that would come into being with the birth of Christ. Through
his choice of epigraph, Wordsworth thus indicates the *Ode*'s sources
in and reflection on a tradition that traced itself back to these words
and saw in them an intimation of the new idea of death ushered in
by Christ.

When "let's sing a nobler song" is interpreted as Wordsworth's own
poetic assertion, however, it suggests that the *Ode* is also marking the
end of that tradition and is seeking to find a new basis for a belief in
immortality. Though it has been treated as a humanized nativity ode,
in which "the birth of the god which Wordsworth celebrates is his,
and anyman's, rather than the birth of Christ" (Ferguson, *Language
as Counter-Spirit* 107), the poem is less a celebration of a birth than a
graveside elegy for the twilight of an age. Instead of contemporaneity
and presence, we feel the vast distance that separates the speaker from
his Virgilian and Christian origins; time, change, and loss have become the ground of poetic voice. Through a series of metaphoric
recognitions of death (in the "past away" of stanza 2, the "where is it
now?" of stanza 4, the "die away" of stanza 5, and the grave-like world
of custom, "heavy as frost, and deep almost as life," of stanza 8), the
poet passes from the vacancy, doubt, and grief of a Good Friday of
spirit to the discovery of the resurrectional powers of the mind—"O
joy! that in our embers / Is something that doth live." In a world shad-
owed by "the darkness of the grave," the poet now discovers "truths
that wake, / To perish never." "Know ye not, that so many of us as
were baptized into Jesus Christ were baptized into his death?" writes
Saint Paul. "Therefore we are buried with him by baptism into death:
that like as Christ was raised up from the dead by the glory of the
Father, even so we also should walk in newness of life" (Romans 6:3–
4).

When Wordsworth replaced the "paulo maiora canamus" epigraph
with the subtitle "intimations of immortality from recollections of
childhood" and the passage from "My Heart Leaps Up," he was not
so much indicating a changed focus as shifting, as we have seen in
other instances, to a complementary mode of anthropological argument.[31] In the Fenwick note to the *Ode,* Wordsworth drew attention

to the link between the metaphysics of the child and the anthropological idea of "intimations" as it had developed in biblical exegesis: "I
used to brood over the stories of Enoch and Elijah, and almost to
persuade myself that, whatever might become of others, I should be
translated, in something of the same way, to heaven" (*PW* 4:463). This
complementarity between the life of the individual and the cultural
history of humankind allows the speaker to make the claim that he
stands in the same relation to his childhood as Christian theology
stands to the Old Testament and classical myth (Plato and Virgil).
Thus, the *Ode* is at once a very personal poem, which speaks of private
losses and anxieties about the future, and one that sets these losses
and fears within the larger context of an anthropological history of
death, self-consciously dramatizing, through the speaker's personal
development, the historical evolution of a language that can make
these losses meaningful.

The *Ode* can be divided into three parts. The first four stanzas,
written in March 1802, constitute what might be called the problematic of the poem, encapsulated in the lines, "Whither is fled the visionary gleam? / Where is it now, the glory and the dream?" It should
be noted that Wordsworth initially appears to have been reluctant to
employ the anthropological models that he customarily used to address origins, for the poem remained a fragment until March 1804.
Nevertheless, he drew on them at that time: needing somewhere to
begin, an Archimedean "point whereon to rest his machine" (*PW*
4:464), he joined, in stanzas 5 through 9, the Platonic pre-existence
myth with a "hypothetical history," using the child as an empirical
figure of origins. We are told how the child, "among his new-born
blisses," is "fretted" by his mother's kisses and derives "light" or intellectual power from his father's eyes. Drawn out of his "dream of
human life," he is socialized and encouraged to take his place in the
world of language and action. "A wedding or a festival, / A mourning
or a funeral," unto these he gives his heart and "frames his song."
Later, in a metaphor that recalls the Boy of Winander and eighteenth-
century language theory, he learns to "fit his tongue / To dialogues
of business, love, or strife." Life is ultimately reduced to a theatrical
vocation, as if human identity were simply a matter of "endless imitation."

From Coleridge's *Biographia Literaria* onward, the representation of

the deaf and mute child in stanza 8 has remained a crux of interpretation:

> Thou, whose exterior semblance doth belie
>   Thy Soul's immensity;
> Thou best Philosopher, who yet dost keep
> Thy heritage, thou Eye among the blind,
> That, deaf and silent, read'st the eternal deep,
> Haunted for ever by the eternal mind,—
>   Mighty Prophet! Seer blest!
>   On whom those truths do rest,
> Which we are toiling all our lives to find;
> Thou, over whom thy Immortality
> Broods like a Day, a Master o'er a Slave,
> A Presence which is not to be put by;
>   To whom the grave
> Is but a lonely bed without the sense or sight
>   Of day or the warm light,
> A place of thought where we in waiting lie.   [1807 version]

In this extraordinary passage, whose syntax suggests the immense
philosophical burden that Wordsworth placed on the child, he is depicted as being fundamentally a contradictory being: a "best Philosopher" or visionary prophet, who "deaf and silent, read'st the eternal
deep," yet someone who is also unable to comprehend or speak what
he sees because he lacks language. The "truths" that "we" who inhabit
language "are toiling all our lives to find" "*rest*" upon him, as presences
"not to be put by"; but they are not *known* by him and he "blindly"
relinquishes them. To this child, the grave is but "a lonely bed," a
"place of thought," where, denied "sense or sight / Of day," we "waiting lie." Death, then, is a kind of intellectual darkening, a blinding;
moving among us, the child is an "eye among the blind."

   Coleridge used this passage to illustrate what he saw as a characteristic Wordsworthian fault of using "thoughts and images too great
for the subject." "In what sense," he asks, "can the magnificent attributes, above quoted, be appropriated to a *child*, which would not make
them equally suitable to a *bee*, or a *dog*, or a *field of corn*; or even to a
ship, or to the wind and waves that propel it?" (*BL* 2:136–40). Coleridge is being somewhat disingenuous here, because an obvious dif-

ference between the child and things in nature is that though he begins without language, he acquires it, thus advancing from "*mute* dialogues with [his] mother's heart" (*Prelude* 2.263, my emphasis) to speaking and writing. This may represent a "splendid paradox" (2:141), but it expresses our paradoxical relation to nature. Equally importantly, in not distinguishing Wordsworth's "deaf and silent" child from any other part of nature, Coleridge ignores the poem's sources in eighteenth-century speculation on deaf and mute individuals.

Until the late eighteenth century, congenital deafness was, as Samuel Johnson declared, "the most desperate of human calamities," because it represented an almost insurmountable obstacle to a child's intellectual and social development.[32] To be born deaf was, in almost all cases, to be mute, and the want of language was a far greater handicap than the loss of hearing. Denied education, treated as an idiot or a monster, barred from conveying property by contract or will, the deaf-mute endured utter privation. Roch-Ambroise Sicard, successor to Charles-Michel de l'Epée as director of the National Institution for Deaf-Mutes in Paris, explains the condition of the deaf in terms of their exclusion from language: "We express . . . ideas with spoken sounds and evoke them in the minds of others by impressions on their hearing; we combine ideas and fix them in our minds by means of words. Now because no sound can affect the deaf person's hearing (he has none) and because he consequently has no symbols for fixing and combining his ideas, it is evident that no original idea can remain in his mind and that no unfamiliar idea can reach him. Hence the total communication gap between him and other people—there he is alone in nature with no possible use for his intellectual faculties, which remain inactive and lifeless unless some kindly hand happens to pluck him from this deathlike sleep."[33]

In the midst of society and among those who speak, the deaf-mute nevertheless was "alone in nature." When Sicard asserts that the deaf person must be "plucked" from a "deathlike sleep" of the intellect, he is echoing Condillac's description of the Wild Child of Lithuania, whose "first state . . . was a sleep interrupted only by dreams" (*Treatise* 226). Deaf-mutes were closely linked to wild children in the speculative thought of the Enlightenment. In fact, as Diderot had argued in the *Letter on the Deaf and Dumb,* the major difference between the two was that deaf-mutes actually existed, unlike "those fictional beings who exhibit no sign of culture" (*Oeuvres* 1:354). With only gestures at their disposal, deaf-mutes became popular empirical figures in speculation about human beginnings. Degérando explicitly linked them to savages, writing that "we cannot recommend too strongly to the explorers for whom these reflections have been prepared, that they should become particularly acquainted with the methodical signs used so successfully by citizen Sicard to establish his first communication with deaf-mutes. For the deaf-mute is also a Savage, and Nature is the only interpreter to translate for him the first lessons of his masters" (*Observation of Savage Peoples* 72).

During the latter half of the century, as a result of the great successes of the abbé de l'Epée in educating the congenitally deaf, it became possible, without recourse to miracles, for deaf-mutes to learn and communicate with those who hear. As Oliver Sacks has observed, an astonished world learned that the deaf were "infinitely educable." It was a "wonderful circumstance—how a despised or neglected minority, practically denied human status up to this point, emerged suddenly and startlingly upon the world stage."[34] The first anthropological society, the Société des Observateurs de l'Homme, fully cognizant of Jean-Marc Itard's educational work with the Wild Boy of Aveyron (discovered in 1798), did not miss the speculative opportunities offered by deaf-mutes. Degérando, who also wrote a book on educating them, remarks that "no more curious spectacle has been offered to the regard of the metaphysician than that of deaf-mutes from birth." He further suggests that they provide a means "of apprehending in their principles the generation of our ideas, of appreciating with exactitude the influence of signs." "All the correspondences that we have established between the generation of ideas and the progress of signs is proved," he continues, "by the history of a deaf-mute."[35] Not surprisingly, Jean Massieu, who had learned to speak under the direction of the abbé Sicard in 1798, was asked to deliver an autobiographical sketch of his childhood at one of the first meetings of the society. And when he did so in 1800, he was questioned, among other things, about his ideas of death prior to his arrival at the National Institution for Deaf-Mutes:

What idea did you have then of death?

> I thought that it was the cessation of movement, of sensation,
> of *ingestion,* of the sensitivity of the skin and the flesh.
> Why did you think that?
> I had seen a dead person.
> Did you think that you would live forever?
> I believed that there was a celestial land and that the body was
> eternal.

These responses, which set an empirical conception of death against
a primal belief in immortality, were duly recorded and published by
the secretary, Louis-François Jauffret and, later by the abbé Sicard as
an appendix to his *Théorie des signes.*[36]

I have drawn attention to the "experimental" discourse on the congenitally deaf to suggest that the appearance and function of the child
in the *Ode* is much more complex, and far more indebted to Enlightenment philosophy, than has generally been realized. I do not want
to suggest that the child actually *is* a deaf-mute, but instead that he
represents, in his "deaf and silent" state, a naturalization and domestication of this figure of empirical inquiry. In fact, one can still discern
traces of the discourse on savages in Wordsworth's reference to him
as a "six years' Darling of a pigmy size" (86). Set, like his philosophical
counterparts, in a hypothetical history, he performs a similar speculative role as a link to human origins. Yet it is not enough to recognize
this discursive tradition. We should also recognize that the metaphoric
paradoxes and broken syntax of the passage express Wordsworth's
struggle to make this genre of inquiry say something different. When
such individuals had become the ventriloquistic dummies of empirical
philosophers, how was one to insist on their otherness? When all truth
had been reduced to *spoken truth,* how was one to speak of a world
that exists only for those who cannot speak?

Wordsworth's answer to this epistemological problem, as we have
seen in other instances, is to make the observation of these individuals
itself a dramatic structure that emphasizes the limitations not only of
those observed, but also of those who do the observing. Thus, all
knowledge is not reduced to those who speak. Wordsworth is not
arguing that we can know what those "truths" are that "rest" upon
the child, only that we can know that there are experiences that we
have forgotten and can no longer recover, ways of seeing that we can

no longer see, ways of being linked to nature and to others that we
have lost. Recent studies of the poem, drawing on Johnston's land-
mark essay, have recognized that the "fountain light of all our day,"
the "master light of all our seeing," is not "something" that can be
recovered, but is instead the remembrance of a vanishing or a forgetting. "*All* he [the poet] remembers of his immortal state," writes
Johnston, "is that he has forgotten it." As Paul Fry has eloquently put
it, "The main point is . . . that memory harbors phantoms."[37] The
figure of the child in the *Ode,* like other marginal figures who "hold /
A silent station in this beauteous world" (*Prelude* 12.51–52), does not
speak to us directly, but instead through his *otherness.* He reminds us,
if only figuratively, that we are not what we once were, that we harbor
phantom selves.

Another reason why it is important to emphasize the poem's dramatic structure is that the speaker is also represented as a marginal
figure—as a blind poet. Cleanth Brooks first noted the shift, in
stanza 3, "from sight to sound," from the eye to the ear. After a detailed discussion of how sound pervades this stanza, in the birds' songs,
"the tabor's sound," the "timely utterance," the echoing hills, and the
cataracts that blow "their trumpets from the steep," he concluded that
the speaker's appeal to the Child of Joy to "shout round me, let me
hear thy shouts, thou happy Shepherd-boy!" is that of "a blind man
trying to enter the joyful dawn world."[38] The blind poet and the deaf
child thus represent two poles in a continuum, and each completes
the other. Like the child, the blind poet is a paradoxical figure. He
speaks of the losses that come with language and social life ("The
things which I have seen I now can see no more"). He shows us that
we are imprisoned in language, a world constructed in words; if we
are to see at all, it must be through language. Only after he has "heard
the call" of the children playing, can he "see / The heavens laugh with
you in your jubilee." Rather than an ecstasy of sight—"I see, I see,
with joy I see!"—the poet's participation is auditory: "I hear, I hear,
with joy I hear!" Yet significantly, even as the blind poet recognizes
the failure of language to mediate vision adequately, he engages in a
visionary struggle to make language once more meaningful, to renew
a tradition that has become a grave, a weight of custom "heavy as
frost, and deep almost as life." I want to return to this issue, but
because the Enlightenment representation of marginality figures so

largely in this poem, a brief examination of how Wordsworth's blind poet differs from his empirical precursors will be of value.

If, as eighteenth-century writers had argued, our customary ideas about death and the afterlife have their origin in sensation—in what we *see* happening to dead bodies—it was reasonable to ask whether blind people, whose ideas of death can only come from what they have *heard* about death, might not have a different idea of death and the future life than those who see. The most famous and controversial of these cases, one that led to its author being jailed, was Diderot's account of the death of the Oxford mathematician Nicholas Saunderson, in his *Letter on the Blind for the Use of Those Who See*. Diderot's discussion of the life of Saunderson serves as part of a larger demonstration "that the state of our organs and our senses has a great bearing on our metaphysics and morals, and that even the most purely intellectual ideas . . . closely depend on the conformation of our bodies" (*Lettre sur les aveugles* 12). If all ideas have their origin in the senses, then a person lacking sight should have radically different moral and metaphysical notions from one who sees. "How different," writes Diderot, "are the morals of a blind person from ours! How different again would those of a deaf person be from those of a blind person! And how imperfect would a being with an extra sense find our morality, to say nothing worse" (14). For Diderot, the observation of blind people is a powerful vehicle of criticism because it allows him to disrupt and call into question our customary tendency to assume that we all inhabit the same world and share the same God. Yet the critical power of the blind is achieved by emphasizing their difference, by marginalizing, dehumanizing, and alienating them. Having stressed their extreme abhorrence of theft (less because they are stolen from than because they are themselves unable to steal) and their lack of modesty, Diderot "suspects blind people in general of inhumanity. To a blind person, what difference is there between a man urinating and a man bleeding in silence?" (13). Since our humanity is so closely bound up with our ability to sympathize with those who suffer and die, the blind are removed from the community of mankind; the idea of death, which should link them to others, actually alienates them, because they do not understand it as anything more than a function of nature.

Though a severe handicap, blindness is not without some advantages. Sensory deprivation constitutes a form of abstraction, which assists the mind in reducing ideas to their clearest and most definite forms, because it is neither confused by the richness and complexity of sensory experience, nor enslaved by the imagination. "If the imagination of a blind person is nothing other than the faculty of recalling and combining the sensations of palpable points; and that of a man who sees, the faculty of recalling and combining visible or colored points, it follows that the person born blind perceives things in a much more abstract manner than we do, and that in purely speculative questions he is perhaps less liable to be fooled" (19). In Diderot's hands, Saunderson becomes a monument to reason dwelling in darkness, struggling alone towards abstract truth, without the distractions and dogmas imposed by the eye and augmented, to the point of terror, by the imagination. In a famous passage of the *Essay Concerning Human Understanding*, Locke argues that the fear of darkness is not a natural condition, but arises from bedtime stories told by "foolish" maids to innocent children: "The *Ideas* of *Goblines* and *Sprights* have really no more to do with Darkness than Light; yet let but a foolish Maid inculcate these often on the Mind of a Child, and raise them there together, possibly he shall never be able to separate them again so long as he lives, but Darkness shall ever afterwards bring with it those frightful *Ideas,* and they shall be so joined that he can no more bear the one than the other" (2:397–98). Diderot's blind man, having lived with darkness all his life, is not susceptible to the melancholy powers of the imagination, superstition, and ecclesiastical ceremony, so he can face death rationally, without the fears that possess the seeing.[39]

For the Enlightenment, the deathbed scene was the final test of philosophical principles and an expression of the completion of a good life. Jacques-Louis David's *Death of Socrates* (1787), for instance, was considered the supreme artistic achievement of the age (fig. 3). Saunderson's death, which scandalized the French religious orthodoxy, became a notorious figure of the "bonne mort." On the point of death, Saunderson showed little regret in dying. He summoned the clergyman Gervase Holmes to his bedside. There they debated the existence of God, and Saunderson proved himself literally blind to the "argument by design." "I have been condemned to pass my life in darkness," he declared. "And you cite prodigies that I do not in the least understand, and which can only be proof for you and for others like you. If you want me to believe in God, you must make me touch him" (40).

Fig. 3. Jacques-Louis David, *The Death of Socrates* (1787). Oil on canvas. The Metropolitan Museum of Art, Wolfe Fund, 1931. Catharine Lorillard Wolfe Collection (31.45). All rights reserved, The Metropolitan Museum of Art.

Having reduced theology to "prodigies," having insisted that it be grounded in touch, Saunderson elaborated an evolutionary theory of nature, in which the blind are likened to monsters (one of the more obvious indications that this is not Saunderson but Diderot speaking), after which he fell into delirium, cried out in a scandalous parody of Christ's last words, "O God of Clarke and of Newton, take pity on me!" (44), and died. Diderot's account of the death of Saunderson, like most of these cases, is a fiction. Yet Saunderson's death illustrated how death might be confronted philosophically, with a mind freed from the despotic powers of the imagination and eye.

In taking up the persona of a blind poet, Wordsworth was countering the Enlightenment on its own terms by using one of its characteristic empirical figures. Like Diderot, Wordsworth insists on the difference, almost the incommensurability, between the metaphysical systems of the seeing mute child and the speaking blind poet. But where Diderot makes Saunderson an isolated emblem of dispassionate reason, an understanding that has not fallen victim to the terrors of the imagination, Wordsworth, drawing on Milton's poetic use of his own blindness in the invocations to *Paradise Lost,* adopts a voice that mediates between visionary or prophetic illumination and our common darkened human condition. The blind poet is a figure of the *engraved* mind, one that came into being in death—"in darkness lost, the darkness of the grave" (117). But the blind poet brings comfort, as he speaks of our common human fears and shows us that, through language and the imagination, we can see beyond loss, suffering, and death.

In *The Excursion,* the Wanderer recalls the story of a blind dalesman who would advance alone to the very brink of a precipice, yet would be "timely warned . . . Protected, say enlightened, by his ear" (7.494–95). "Enlightened, by his ear": he is the embodiment of what human beings, guided by language, can achieve: "by science led, / His genius mounted to the plains of heaven" and he "discoursed of natural or moral truth / With eloquence, and . . . authentic power" (7.505–13). The Wanderer, drawing a religious as well as an epistemological argument from blindness, exclaims that "faculties [here also read "souls"], which seem / Extinguished, do not, *therefore,* cease to be." In such "a marvellous spectacle" can be found

A type and shadow of an awful truth;
How, likewise, under sufferance divine,
Darkness is banished from the realms of death,
By man's imperishable spirit, quelled.   [517–30]

For Wordsworth, this blind man has learned how to transfer the visionary sense from the eye to the ear ("to the mind among her powers of sense / This transfer is permitted" [521–22]), from sight to words. Since another word for "transfer" is "metaphor," he symbolizes a new ground for metaphysical faith in language—not in touch, as was the case with Saunderson ("If you want me to believe in God, you must make me touch him"), and not in sight, as is the case with the child, who has no need of "any interest / Unborrowed from the eye" ("Tintern Abbey" 82–83).

In the figure of the blind poet struggling to see once more through words, Wordsworth found a means of linking the themes of death and resurrection with the poetic issue of remaking language. If the dead reside as much in language as in the grave, then a far greater death occurs when language is no longer a celestial soil but a grave of custom, "heavy as frost, and deep almost as life." Stanza 2, with its singsong catalog of conventional poetic images, now hollow from overuse ("The Rainbow comes and goes, / And lovely is the Rose"), dramatizes how easily poetic language can lose its power to evoke a living glory and can become cliché. As Helen Vendler has suggested, its culminating statement that "there hath past away a glory from the earth" is an "ironic echo" of Christ's prophecy in Matthew 24:35: "Heaven and earth shall pass away, but my words shall not pass away."[40] Christ's faith in the permanence of his words would certainly have had personal significance to Wordsworth, who, during the spring of 1802, had undergone, as Jared R. Curtis has argued, a period of crisis.[41] Equally importantly, however, this allusion suggests that this personal crisis is being used in ways similar to the purposes served by the "paulo maiora canamus" epigraph, to give intense expression to a larger cultural problem—that of the life and death of tradition. From this perspective, the graveside that the poet stands beside at the opening of the poem can be said to be as much the graveside of metaphor as that of life. The figure of the blind poet, struggling with words that no longer allow him to see a glory now "past away," dramatizes Wordsworth's belief that a tradition and poetry, which had its origin in Virgil's prophecy, had become ossified and needed to be remade.

From this perspective, the theme of resurrection that informs the poem is less a theological than a poetic and cultural issue. The faith that ultimately supports the poet is one that has been achieved through the symbolic resources of language. The *Ode* represents a humanization of the language of *The Book of Common Prayer,* notably the Easter liturgy and the requiem services for the dead. It celebrates the historical appearance of this language and provides a philosophical reflection on the power that it has given us over the empirical idea of death. In the concluding stanza, in the phrase "Another race hath been, and other palms are won," there is an allusion to 1 Corinthians 9:24–25: "Know ye not that they which run in a race run all, but one receiveth the prize? So run, that ye may obtain. And every man that striveth for the mastery is temperate in all things. Now they *do it* to obtain a corruptible crown; but we an incorruptible."[42] But where

Saint Paul argues that we must relinquish earthly goals for the life of the spirit, Wordsworth grounds the divine in man, in "natural" rather than Christian "piety," in "the human heart by which we live," "its tenderness, its joys, and fears." It is in this remaking of the liturgy through the figure of the blind poet that Wordsworth finds a way to give meaning to what has been lost. Thus, he can return in the final stanza to the imagery that opened the poem, the "Fountains, Meadows, Hills, and Groves," and find new meaning in them. Though he admits that "the radiance which was once so bright / Be now for ever taken from my sight," he has nevertheless found a new power, in "thoughts that spring / Out of human suffering." These thoughts do not escape the darkness of "mortal minds," for even "the Clouds" and the "setting sun" seem to have entered into a "watch o'er man's mortality." Nor do they escape the grave, for they have come into being with it. But they do lead to the recognition that even if the poet is mortal and his poetry a "poor earthly casket of immortal verse" (*Prelude* 5.164), he nevertheless participates, as all poets do, in revitalizing the past and thus renewing the "celestial soil of the Imagination" (*ProseW* 3:35). Wordsworth's history of death does not lead, then, to the rationalistic idea of an empty and therefore harmless death, but instead to the progressively more sophisticated notion that death is as deep as language and, consequently, those who would go beyond it must struggle with "thoughts that do often lie too deep for tears."

The Deaf Dalesman of *The Excursion*

In book 7 of *The Excursion* (and also as a conclusion to the *Essays upon Epitaphs*), Wordsworth turned from figurative deafness to the case of Thomas Holme, one of the greatest of his solitaries. A man who lost his hearing early in childhood, Holme achieved, in his "loneliness of soul" (403), an independence of mind and spirit:

> by the solace of his own pure thoughts
> Upheld, he duteously pursued the round
> Of rural labours.   [417–19]

Though Holme's life is idealized, we nevertheless can see in Words-

worth's description how terrible it is to live in a world of utter silent-
ness, cut off from friends, and even the right to hold property:

> For himself,
> All watchful and industrious as he was,
> He wrought not: neither field nor flock he owned:
> No wish for wealth had place within his mind;
> Nor husband's love, nor father's hope or care.   [423–27]

Lacking a wife and children, Holme was still loved by his older brother's family for his "gentle manners," "peaceful smiles," and "slow-
varying countenance." But his true friends were his books:

> ready comrades whom he could not tire;
> Of whose society the blameless Man
> Was never satiate. Their familiar voice,
> Even to old age, with unabated charm
> Beguiled his leisure hours.   [440–44]

Holme found "society" in these "ready comrades," who did not "tire"
of him (as one assumes others might have) and spoke to him in a
"familiar voice."

Wordsworth describes Holme as passing out of life almost as quietly
as he lived it; "a few short steps / Of friends and kindred" are all that
were needed to bear him to "the profounder stillness of the grave"
(465–68). The unusual use of the comparative of *profound* indicates
that death is less a change of state, than a completion of his essential
condition. If, as Wordsworth declares in the *Intimations Ode,* our "noisy
years seem moments in the being / Of the eternal Silence," the deaf
never fully leave that stillness. Holme's life, always seen against the
backdrop of the mute grave, thus has the power to reflect this silence
back upon the living:

> the scythe he swayed;
> And the ripe corn before his sickle fell
> Among the jocund reapers.   [421–23]

Holme's life thus comes to epitomize our fundamental relation to
death.

In death Holme recovers the aural connection to nature that was
denied him in life:

—And yon tall pine-tree, whose composing sound
Was wasted on the good Man's living ear,
Hath now its own peculiar sanctity;
And, at the touch of every wandering breeze,
Murmurs, not idly, o'er his peaceful grave.   [477–81]

Wordsworth provides a theological justification for the claim that these sounds murmur "not idly" over Holme's grave: in death "the assembled spirits of just men" are "made perfect, and from injury secure" (453–54). But there is another reason, which is very much bound up with his poetics of death. From a linguistic perspective, the fundamental difference between the living and the dead is that whereas the former can be agents of speech and can actively represent themselves and others, the latter relinquish this power to become the object of others' speech and writing. The living are bound together by speaking and listening, the dead by being spoken about, in gossip, books, and stories. Death is a transition, then, from being a private speaker to being a public "spoken." This is why the deaf man, though denied by his "sad privation" (476) full membership in human society, regains in death what he lacked in life. Holme passes from seeking "*ready* comrades" to being one of their number. His intensely private silence gives way to communal speech, and his individual impairment no longer matters.

Because Holme's deafness made him dependent on others to speak for him, even in life he epitomized the condition of the mute dead, whose continuing life resides in what others say about them. Holme's death, then, is not so much a contradiction of his life as its completion. The narrative is remarkable for its calm tranquillity. To us, Holme is our "ready" comrade, and we seem to read about him in the same silence that he communicated with his "ready comrades" and the world. Thus, his story, even if it is delivered orally by the Pastor, provides us with a certain perspective on their storied lives; we see them in a writerly fashion, against the backdrop of eternal silence. We too must eventually depend on others' voices for our continued existence, and our lives are also stories whose authorship we control for but a short while, and even then not wholly. Our lives must also be relinquished to the community, private life giving way to public narrative. Wordsworth's representation of Holme is, indeed, his own *Let-*

ter on the Deaf and Dumb for Those Who Can Hear. But unlike Diderot, he begins with Holme's marginal status only to go beyond it, not by making him more like those who hear, but by making the reader recognize the degree to which he shares the same condition. The speaking are only the *not yet* mute; the isolation of the deaf man is but a more extreme form of their own isolation and their own "sad privations," which will finally be lost in their dual burial, in the earth and in narratives.

PART FOUR

The History of the Earth

SIX

"A Power Like One of Nature's"

The Geological History
of Revolution

*Paradise and groves
Elysian, fortunate islands,
fields like those of old
In the deep ocean—wherefore
should they be
A History, or but a dream,
when minds
Once wedded to this outward
frame of things
In love, find these the growth
of common day?
I, long before the blessed hour
arrives,
    Would sing in solitude the
    spousal verse
Of this great consummation, would pro-
claim—
Speaking of nothing more than what we
are—
How exquisitely the individual Mind
(And the progressive powers perhaps no less
Of the whole species) to the external world
Is fitted; and how exquisitely too—
Theme this but little heard of among men—
The external world is fitted to the mind;
And the creation (by no lower name*

Can it be called) which they with blended might
Accomplish: this is my great argument.

[*Home at Grasmere*, MS. B, lines 996–1014]

These lines have long been recognized as a major declaration of the
"great argument" of *The Recluse*. Echoes of the high visionary language of Milton and the plot and imagery patterns of apocalyptic
thought are apparent, as M. H. Abrams has demonstrated.[1] But we
should also realize that this passage is one of the first great statements
of an *environmental* theory of human life, and this language makes
Wordsworth's vision unique. His enduring concern is not with the
mind or nature in isolation, but with how human powers and respon-
sibilities manifest (and have manifested) themselves over time in our
active engagement with nature—with

> the very world which is the world
> Of all of us, the place in which, in the end,
> We find our happiness, or not at all.   [*Prelude* 10.725–27]

To many readers, the above may sound commonplace. Yet obvious
things often are not well understood. By and large, contemporary
critics have shown little interest in knowing what environmental theory
was during the latter part of the eighteenth century and how Wordsworth might have responded to it.[2]

As Clarence J. Glacken has eruditely demonstrated, Western environmental thought, from antiquity to the nineteenth century, focused
on three general questions: "Is the earth, which is obviously a fit environment for man and other organic life, a purposefully made creation? Have its climates, its relief, the configuration of its continents
influenced the moral and social nature of individuals, and have they
had an influence in molding the character and nature of human culture? In his long tenure of the earth, in what manner has man
changed it from its hypothetical pristine condition?"[3] These questions
in turn gave rise to three general ideas: 1) the idea of a "designed
earth" or "creation" expressly made for human beings; 2) the idea of
"environmental influence"—that the mind is shaped, to some degree,
by climate and soil; and 3) the idea of human "geographical agency"—
that human beings, since the beginning of time, have not only adapted
themselves to nature, but also transformed it. This third idea, which

emerged during the eighteenth century, was of enormous importance, as it led to the recognition that human beings play as great a role in shaping the earth's surface as winds, rivers, tides, and other physical forces.

If we turn back to the Prospectus to *The Recluse,* we can see that it takes up these three fundamental ideas of environmental theory and organizes them into two interacting histories, which, with "blended might," form a third. The first, a history of "environmental influence," would have shown how the human mind is fitted "to the external world." It would present both an education of the "individual Mind" and an anthropological history of the human race, "the progressive powers perhaps no less / Of the whole species." This *history of mind* was to have been complemented by a *history of the earth,* an account of how, through human geographical agency, the face of "the external world is fitted to the mind." Wordsworth stresses that this "theme" is "but little heard of among men." One might add that it is rarely mentioned in Wordsworth studies. He goes on to say that these two histories would constitute dialectically the larger history, which is the true epic argument of *The Recluse,* of how a truly human environment came into being (the topos of the Lake District): how the "progressive powers" of human beings have shaped and, in turn, been molded by, a changing and developing nature, to accomplish a new "creation (by no lower name / Can it be called)." Wordsworth shifts the notion of a "designed earth," a "creation" fit for mankind, from its customary position as an origin to that of a historical product, a "great consummation" achieved by the reciprocal blending of human and natural agency.

The absence of a concept of environmental discourse may not seem all that important, but it has led to a fundamental misreading of Wordsworth's poetry, which treats nature as if it were a stable, ahistorical phenomenon, opposed to mind. Wordsworth's nature is not simply an object of thought, nor a vehicle through which the mind finds itself. It is as much a historical phenomenon as the mind, and the role that human environments have played in shaping human minds is no less extraordinary for Wordsworth than the geological agency of human beings, those "diminutive giants," as Herder called them, who descended "from the mountains, to subjugate the earth, and change climates with their feeble arms" (*Outlines of a Philosophy of the History of Man* 176). It is not meditation that links the mind to nature, but instead human environments, which mediate this relationship in physical and aesthetic terms. Wordsworth is an environmental historicist. The true subject of *The Recluse* is not that of the mind coming to self-consciousness, but instead the story of how, through the "blended might" of human and natural agency, a certain kind of environment came into being that has allowed the mind and nature to achieve their greatest potential.

Because Wordsworth's environmental historicism represents a sophisticated response to eighteenth-century theories of the interaction of human beings and nature, which are not well known, a brief examination of this context will be of value. During the latter half of the century, the point of departure for most environmental thought was Montesquieu's deterministic claim, in the *Spirit of the Laws* (1748), that climate and soil have a major influence on the moral and physical characteristics of nations and their political institutions. For Montesquieu, "the empire of the climate is the first, the most powerful, of all empires" (299). Citing a famous experiment he performed on the effects of heat and cold on a sheep's tongue, Montesquieu concluded that major physiological differences existed between the people of northern regions, who were strong, vigorous, courageous, and of sluggish passions, and those of the south, who were weak, lethargic, timorous, and (because of the sensitivity and delicacy of their organs of sensation) driven by extreme passions. Different climates produce people with different wants, so social, political, and cultural differences can be understood as responses (appropriate or inappropriate) to these needs.

Montesquieu accorded soils a similar power in shaping the moral characteristics and laws of nations. "The goodness of the land, in any country, naturally establishes subjection and dependence," he argues, because a barren earth encourages humans to be industrious, sober, courageous, and inured to hardship, as they are forced "to procure by labour what the earth refuses to bestow spontaneously." Other indications of Montesquieu's strongly deterministic bent might be cited, for instance, when he asserts that "the barrenness of the Attic soil established there a democracy; and the fertility of that of Lacedaemonia an aristocratic constitution" (271–73). One should equally recognize, however, that, at least regarding land surfaces, Montesquieu showed an awareness that human beings can and do change their physical environments: "Mankind by their industry, and by the influence of good laws, have rendered the earth more proper for their abode. We see rivers flow where there have been lakes and marshes: this is a benefit which nature has not bestowed; but it is a benefit maintained and supplied by nature . . . Thus, as destructive nations produce evils more durable than themselves, the actions of an industrious people are the source of blessings which last when they are no more" (274–75).

The idea that "soil" is not a simple given, but instead a "more proper . . . abode" for mankind because of human "industry" and "laws," was of major importance to eighteenth-century writers, because it directly linked the physical environment of a society with its political institutions. "Countries are not cultivated in proportion to their fertility, but to their liberty," declared Montesquieu, going on to note that one sees "in most ages deserts in the most fruitful parts, and great nations in those where nature seems to refuse everything" (272). The discourse on climate and soils thus became strongly linked with politics, a connection that I suspect has much to do with the rising importance of English landscape painting during the years leading up to and following the French Revolution. Far from just commemorating landscapes, these paintings also celebrate the social institutions that have created them. Similarly, as in Volney's *Ruins of Empires* or Shelley's "Ozymandias," the popular representation of the desert wastes of the Middle East indicated, even more than the vanity of earthly kings, the enormous power of despotic governments or "destructive nations" to lay waste nature. Montesquieu's position in regard to the politics of the environment is unequivocal: "Those countries which the industry of man has rendered habitable, and which stand in need of the same industry to provide for their subsistence, require a mild and moderate government" (273–74).

Enlightenment philosophers were probably the first to recognize that the most dramatic document of the history and power of the human mind is the earth itself. As George Marsh notes, the "transforming power" of human life is "more clearly demonstrable in the influence man has thus exerted upon superficial geography than in any other result of his material effort."[4] One of the most important matrices of eighteenth-century speculation about the hypothetical history of the earth's physical environment came from the comparison of the Old and New Worlds. As Glacken has observed, there was a striking contrast "between long-settled Europe (many of whose lands had been under the plow for centuries, whose forests had been cut to make way for grain fields, vines, orchards, or villages, towns, and cities, many of whose rivers had now become tractable—their courses deepened and straightened—and were attended, as by bridesmaids, by many small canals) and the relatively virgin areas of the colonies of North America" (*Traces on the Rhodian Shore* 657). Though this contrast was just as obvious to Columbus, it was not until the eighteenth century that the radical difference between these two landscapes came to be seen as largely the result of human agency, of the varying lengths of time that each continent had been settled and of the different degrees of control that their inhabitants had exerted over their respective environments. The difference between the two worlds thus became an emblem of the immense amount of human labor that, over ages, had gone into making Europe a habitable world for human beings. Writes Buffon: "In every country where the number of men is too inconsiderable for forming and supporting polished societies, the surface of the earth is more unequal and rugged, and the channels of rivers are more extended, irregular, and often interrupted by cataracts. The Rhône and the Loire would require the operation of several ages before they became navigable. It is by confining and directing the waters, and clearing the bottoms of rivers, that they acquire a fixed and determinate course. In thinly inhabited regions, nature is always rude, and sometimes deformed."[5]

Underlying this comparison of "natures" was a comparison of cultures. "Compare the small savage nations of America with our great civilized peoples," declares Buffon. "Contemplate at the same time the state of the earth that these nations inhabit. You will easily judge the insignificance of these men by the paltry impression that their hands have made on their soil . . . These unpolished nations, large and small, only burden the globe without relieving it, starve it without assisting it, destroy it without improving it, using everything without renewing anything."[6] For Buffon, as for Wordsworth, nature is "marvellously seconded" by human agency, which brings it to a state of perfection. Given mankind's charge to remake nature, Buffon reads the relative merits of individual societies through the relative merits of their nat-

ural environments: savage nations, he concludes, are a "burden" to
the earth.

Buffon's comments are not limited to physical considerations, but
extend to questions about mankind's proper aesthetic environment.
"Wild nature is hideous and dying; it is I, I alone, who can render it
agreeable and alive . . . It is cultivated nature that is beautiful!"
(*Oeuvres philosophiques* 34). This combination of aesthetic theory and
physical geography, which is characteristic of late eighteenth-century
thought, is equally obvious in William Robertson's *History of America*:
"When we survey the face of the habitable globe, no small part of that
fertility and beauty, which we ascribe to the hand of Nature, is the
work of man. His efforts, when continued through a succession of
ages, change the appearance and improve the qualities of the earth.
As a great part of the ancient continent has long been occupied by
nations far advanced in arts and industry, our eye is accustomed to
view the earth in that form which it assumes when rendered fit to be
the residence of a numerous race of men, and to supply them with
nourishment" (1:256). A comparison of the two continents made it
clear that the "fertility" and "beauty" of Europe were attributable less
to nature than to human "efforts," "continued through a succession
of ages," which had changed "the appearance" and improved "the
qualities of the earth." Since the land features of America were ostensibly the same as those that the first Europeans had originally encountered and learned to control, philosophers could see America as
a concrete image of what the landscape of Europe had once been. At
the same time, by recognizing the differences between the two continents, they were able to conceive the vast geographical transformations that had affected their own "ancient continent." The settlement
of America thus took on the character, both literally and metaphorically, of a repetition of the original making of the European continent.
But where ages had been necessary to make Europe a truly human
environment, the American settlers, with their new system of government, were achieving similar results in generations.

Like many other writers, Robertson also called attention to the difference in the climates of the two regions. Though Europe and the
northern regions of America roughly occupied the same latitudes, it
was obvious that the winters in the New World were much colder and
the weather more variable than in Europe. Robertson admitted that

many physical factors contributed to this difference (among these, trade winds, ocean currents, altitude, and so on). But he concluded, somewhat guardedly, that *culture* lay at the basis of these climatic differences. In fact, he went on to suggest that "the progress of culture and population" was likely eventually to "mitigate the extreme rigour of the climate in the more northern districts of America" (1:251). Behind this extraordinary claim was the discovery, little known nowadays, that the climate of America had actually changed markedly in the years immediately following its settlement by the Europeans. Hugh Williamson, in a paper read before the American Philosophical Society in 1770, first noted this "very observable change of climate," as the winters in Pennsylvania had become warmer and the summers more temperate.[7] He concluded that this alteration had been brought about by the settlers, as they cleared woods, drained marshes, channeled river courses, and increased the amount of cultivated land. What was happening in America was little short of astonishing: not only had a relatively small number of ill-equipped human beings radically transformed a landscape, but they had also begun to change its climate.[8] As the American agriculturalist Jared Eliot declared, though the first settlers "were destitute of Beasts of Burthen or Carriage" and were "unskill'd in every Part of Service to be done: It may be said, That in a Sort, *they began the World a New.*"[9] As Horace Bushnell put the issue, "Not all the winds, and storms, and earthquakes, and seas, and seasons of the world, have done as much to revolutionize the earth as he [man], the power of an endless life, has done since the day he came forth upon it, and received, as he is most truly declared to have done, dominion over it."[10]

It can be said, then, that by the end of the eighteenth century it had become possible to claim, as did James Dunbar, that "soil and climate, if not altogether foreign to the mind, are, like the mind, susceptible of improvement, and variable, in a high degree, with the progress of civil arts" (*History of Mankind in Rude and Cultivated Ages* 342). A "history of the earth" was thus possible, one that would show how the physical landscape, through a combination of geological forces and human activity, had become a proper environment for human beings. The intertwining of these two kinds of history, of the mind and of the earth—an interconnection that is central to Wordsworth's *Recluse* project—also allowed environmental theory to play a major role in eighteenth-century speculation about human origins. If soil, terrain, and climate were important factors in the establishment of physical, racial, cultural, and national differences among humans, then it was necessary, if one was to understand the primitive mind and its institutions, first to reconstruct the climatic and geological forces that had operated in remote antiquity, shaping the world and the minds of early mankind. "What can we determine with certainty respecting the *origin* and *nature of Man*, without knowing his *history*?" asks Jean André Deluc in his *Elementary Treatise on Geology*. How can we know any thing of the *history of Man*, except we know sufficiently the *history of the planet* which he inhabits?—How can we learn the *history of this planet*, without studying the *monuments of its revolutions*, and all that Natural Philosophy can discover to us of their causes?"[11] Hypothetical reconstructions of the landscape, geography, and environment of the primeval world thus began to appear in these writings as a major mode of anthropological explanation. And like other empiricist philosophical forms, these primitive landscapes occupy a middle ground between fiction and fact, as imaginative elaborations on available scientific knowledge, often with a view to reconciling Genesis and geology. On one pole were the expansive "theories of the earth" of Thomas Burnet, William Whiston, and John Woodward, which even in their own day were accused of being "philosophical romances"; on the other, the highly imaginative hypotheses of the philosophes, notably Boulanger, Diderot, and Buffon. Scientific or not, these works provided a system of images and a theory of primeval forces operating in the distant past that were taken up by moral philosophers as they sought to understand early social institutions.

Geology and Revolution

Near the beginning of the Revolution Books of *The Prelude* an unusual event occurs that I want to use as a point of departure for discussing Wordsworth's use of geological metaphor. The poet describes how, having just arrived in France in 1791, he visited the crumbling remains of the Bastille. Emphasizing the contrast between what he saw, as he sat in "the open sun" where "silent zephyrs sported with the dust," and what he sought, Wordsworth tells us that he picked a stone

out of the rubbish (9.63–64). He admits to having felt "strong incum-
bencies" as he sat looking at the rock, but nevertheless confesses, "I
looked for something which I could not find, / Affecting more emotion
than I felt." So he pocketed the stone, as if it were no more than a
souvenir or relic of revolution and he just a tourist or pilgrim, and
set out to see a sight that moved him much more—the sentimental
depiction of revolution in Charles le Brun's painting *The Repentant
Magdalene,* which was then being displayed at the Carmelite Convent
of Paris.[12] Few readers are likely to see anything particularly odd in a
poet finding more significance in a painting than in a rock. However,
it is a fact of some historical interest that Wordsworth, like Keats
confronting the Grecian urn, tried to read this stone, believing that it
could tell him something profound about the nature of the revolution
that had just occurred.

To Wordsworth's contemporaries the relationship between reading
rocks and reading revolutions would have been quite obvious. We
should recognize that prior to the events that took place in America
and France during the latter part of the eighteenth century, "revolution," both in word and concept, was less frequently encountered in
political theory than in astronomy, geometry, geography, and especially geology.[13] By the 1790s, geology had assumed the status of *the*
preeminent science of revolution. First, it constituted a science of interpretation. As Roy Porter has observed, it had developed ways of
reading, out of the mute landscape, the story of "great revolutions,
decay and restoration, the struggle of titanic Earth forces."[14] Cuvier
makes a typical claim for the interpretive powers of the geologist when
he argues, "Every part of the globe bears the impress of these great
and terrible events so distinctly, that they must be visible to all who
are qualified to read their history in the remains which they have left
behind."[15] Ramond de Carbonnières, from whose commentary on
William Coxe's *Travels in Switzerland* Wordsworth drew extensively in
Descriptive Sketches, makes a similar claim: "This country exhibits, in
the different ages of its mountains, a picture sublimely terrible of the
vicissitudes of nature, her slow operations, her sudden freaks, and her
dreadful disasters. On these rocks, generated and decayed in the
course of more than thirty centuries, these carcases of mountains,
hurl'd into the vallies which they formerly overlooked, and buried

under huge masses of ice, the curious observer will read with amazement the annals of the world, and the history of its revolutions."[16]

John Playfair describes the earth as "the theatre of many great revolutions" and argues that the proper object of geology is "to trace the series of these revolutions, to explain their causes, and thus to connect together all the indications of change that are found in the mineral kingdom." He notes "the immense violence which . . . accompanied the formation of mineral veins . . . which our imagination erroneously paints as the abode of everlasting silence and rest."[17] To the geologist, the earth was a silent "archive," its various land forms, as Deluc had argued, "the *monuments of its revolutions*."[18] In addition to providing the interpretive means for reading revolutions out of the silence of stones, geology also constituted an extensive and developed *theory* of revolution. In the various "theories of the earth" that were published over the course of the eighteenth century, early geology sought to clarify the laws governing the revolutions of the earth. Perhaps not surprisingly, it should be added, these theories were much debated during the revolutionary decade, and England and France each developed alternate theories of geological revolution. French geologists, having just done away with the ancien régime, argued that geological change was violent and sudden, and that the history of the world was a history of the supersession and extinction of worlds. English geologists, on the other hand, oscillated between two positions—Hutton's Burkean view, that what we call geological revolutions are actually the effects of slow changes occurring over vast periods of time; and scriptural geology, which claimed that the biblical account of creation and deluge was compatible with science.[19]

As Alan Liu has persuasively argued, the Revolution Books of *The Prelude* thematize and re-enact the young English republican poet's "perpetual confusion about the kind of thing the Revolution is and the kind of language appropriate to describe it" ("Shapeless Eagerness," 5). In these books, Wordsworth struggles to go beyond "star[ing] and listen[ing] with a stranger's ears" (9.55), beyond looking on the scenes of revolution

> as doth a man
> Upon a volume whose contents he knows

> Are memorable but from him locked up,
> Being written in a tongue he cannot read,
> So that he questions the mute leaves with pain,
> And half upbraids their silence.   [10.49–54]

I would suggest that a central story told in these books is that of how Wordsworth learned to read social revolution in terms of the language of geology. Contemporary catastrophist geology, with its depiction of immense forces that radically shaped human life and the face of nature, provided him with a system of images useful for depicting the enormous changes that had taken place in France. Equally importantly, inasmuch as these books describe Wordsworth's struggle to create a theory of revolution, we can see how geology allowed him to make sense of these events by giving them a direction and a law.[20] When the poet arrived in Paris, the revolutionary landscape had become as silent as a geologic formation. "The first storm was overblown," he declares, "And the strong hand of outward violence / Locked up in quiet" (*Prelude* 9.109–11). Wordsworth's initial inability to "unlock" this silence, to read the stone as a monument of revolution and thus to go beyond the illusory quiet of the revolutionary scene, can be seen as an interpretive failure that sets the Revolution Books in motion.[21]

Most Enlightenment theories of the earth are directionalist in orientation: that is, they argue that the geological and physical forces affecting the earth's surface have changed over time and that the more sublime features of the earth's surface (high mountain ranges, huge gorges, and so on) cannot be explained in terms of present-day environmental forces, which have lessened considerably. More violent and catastrophic physical powers needed to be invoked in order to understand the formation of the early world. In these texts, the early postdiluvian world is drawn in sublime language, as being continually shaken by catastrophic upheavals, widespread volcanic action, earthquakes, enormous storms, and repeated inundations. These physical events, it was believed, had had a traumatic impact on the mind and beliefs of primitive humans, giving a determinate character to early civil governments and religions.

Buffon's *Epochs of Nature* (1778), a work that was widely read during the period, illustrates how these early geological theories of the earth supported speculation about the psychology of primitive mankind. Buffon argues that the earth, originally a molten mass separated from the sun by the collision of a comet, had undergone seven revolutionary "epochs," each governed by the progressive cooling of the earth. In the first and second epochs, the earth took its spherical form and the great mountain chains, the "primary" or "primeval" mountains, were formed. By the third epoch, the earth was no longer hot enough to vaporize all the water, and the atmosphere let loose torrents that completely flooded the earth, except for the highest summits of the primary mountains. It was in these boiling seas, as they gradually cooled, that life had its beginning, and with it the sediments and deposits that would later form much of the earth's crust. In the fourth epoch, the seas began to retreat, triggering a period of intense volcanic activity that raised the sea floor upwards, creating the continents. During the fifth epoch, land animals appeared, first in the northern regions, because the lands in the south still burned and remained deserts; in the sixth, the continents separated, as vast regions sank once more beneath the seas. It was this world, still shaken by earthquakes, volcanoes, and floods, that greeted the first humans, born high in the steppes of Asia, who ushered in the seventh and last epoch: "The first men, witnesses of the still recent and very frequent convulsions of the earth, having only the mountains for asylums against the inundations, chased frequently from these same asylums by the fires of volcanoes, trembling on ground that shaked beneath their feet, naked in spirit as well as in body, exposed to the injuries of all the elements, victims of the fury of ferocious animals, whose prey they were, all equally impressed with the sentiment of melancholy, all equally impressed with the sentiment of melancholy, all equally pressed by necessity— did they not seek promptly to unite, first to defend themselves through numbers, and then to aid each other and work in concert to make dwellings and weapons?" (*Oeuvres philosophiques* 187a). Continually threatened by massive physical forces and prey to the fury of animals, early humans, in their terrible isolation, suffered from intense melancholy and madness, which left an indelible impression on their memories and their civil and religious institutions. "These men, profoundly affected by the calamities of their first state, and still having before their eyes the ravages of floods, the fires of volcanoes, the chasms opened by the shaking of the earth, preserved an enduring and nearly eternal memory of the calamities suffered by the world: the idea that it must be destroyed by a universal deluge or by a general conflagration" (187b).

For Buffon, as for Boulanger, from whom he drew many of these ideas, one had only to imagine this primitive landscape and draw conclusions about early mankind's traumatic response to it in order to have a key to primitive mythology.[22] It explained early human beings' reverence for certain mountains, like Ararat, that had provided them with asylum from the floods, and their terror of others that had "burst with fires more terrible than thunder" (188a); it affirmed that the myths concerning the war of the Titans or the sinking of Atlantis were not empty fictions, but apocalyptic renderings of geological events that had actually taken place in remote antiquity; it provided clues to the origin of the idea of an angry and vengeful god; and, finally, it provided an explanation, which Wordsworth was to draw on extensively in the Revolution Books of *The Prelude,* of the origin of despotic governments. For the philosophes, all artistic or social expressions of the sublime could be seen as re-enactments of a primal postdiluvian trauma, now repressed, that had played a central role in the psychical and social development of mankind.

In the Revolution Books, Wordsworth uses ideas of primitive landscape, postdiluvian trauma, and their impact on the early formation of society to write his own history of how a postrevolutionary, rather than a postdiluvian, society emerged out of the wholesale violence and ruins of a revolutionary decade. Landscape thus functions as a medium of political and anthropological argument. His progressive discovery of the conformities between these two worlds is the major argument of these books.

After leaving Paris and moving to Orléans, Wordsworth was still unable to understand the revolution. He writes:

> I scarcely felt
> The shock of these concussions, unconcerned,
> Tranquil almost, and careless as a flower
> Glassed in a greenhouse, or a parlour-shrub,
> When every bush and tree the country through,
> Is shaking to the roots.   [9.86–91]

Here France is portrayed as undergoing seismic "shock[s]" and "con-

cussions," felt "the country through" and threatening all organic
growth. In explaining his "indifference" to these events—how he, like
Peter Bell, could walk unconcerned through a world that was shaking
beneath his feet—Wordsworth argues that he was "unprepared / With
needful knowledge" (91–93).²³ The "master pamphlets of the day"
provided only a "meagre soil" out of which "half-insight . . . grew wild"
(9.97–99). He describes one of the royalists, "blighted" and "mastered"
by the times:

> At the hour,
> The most important of each day, in which
> The public news was read, the fever came,
> A punctual visitant, *to shake this man* . . .   [156–59, my emphasis]

Rather than providing a "culture" for human life, reading the "public
news" engendered fever and madness. Wordsworth declares that "the
soil of common life was at that time / Too hot to tread upon" (9.169–
70). The land "swarmed with passion," and became "a plain / Devoured by locusts," a desert:

> Carra, Gorsas—add
> A hundred other names, forgotten now,
> Nor to be heard of more; yet were they powers,
> Like earthquakes, shocks repeated day by day,
> And felt through every nook of town and field.   [9.178–83]

To a degree, the metaphors associating France with a burning desert,
"devoured by locusts" and quaking under the verbal eruptions of revolutionary journalist-politicians, now forgotten, allude to Milton's description of Hell in *Paradise Lost*. Furthermore, they are part of the
standard arsenal of the poetic sublime. Yet equally importantly, we
should see that the revolutionary environment is being depicted as a
primitive landscape undergoing immense geological changes. Compare the above passage, for instance, with Boulanger's description of
the early postdiluvian world:

> What would be our thoughts if we were no more to receive light
> from the extinguished sun; if the sublimely concerting powers of
> nature were to be rendered forgetful of their harmony, and
> dashed into a new chaos? if the seas were to deluge the earth? if

the earth was to rise up against them? what would our exclamations be, were we to see a thousand fiery volcanos break forth on
every side? if we were to behold fire, sulphur, and bitumen vom-
ited in torrents from the torn entrails of convulsed mountains? if
most of the continents, all shattered were to sink under us? what
ultimately would be our thoughts if the now human beings were
to find themselves in the midst of so many terrifying scenes, and
such universal desolation? there needs neither philosophy nor
metaphysics to form a conjecture. [*The Origin of Despotism* 28–29]

Even as one notes the close similarities between Boulanger's primeval world and Wordsworth's depiction of revolutionary France, an
obvious difference between the two is that Wordsworth is not describing a physical environment, but is instead employing the language of
"climate" and "soils" to depict a culture or society that has returned
to origins. Just as eighteenth-century environmentalist theorists had
argued that the quality of a country's soil and climate is directly linked
to its government ("Those countries which the industry of man has
rendered habitable, and which stand in need of the same industry to
provide for their subsistence, require a mild and moderate government" [Montesquieu, *Spirit of the Laws* 273–74]), Wordsworth claims
that language, as the *soil* of culture, also requires moderate government. The incendiary language of French politicians made them like
primeval volcanoes. Through the repeated shocks of revolutionary
ideology, France had been returned to its violent and barren beginnings.

Wordsworth claimed that he had a special "sense" for seeing "into
past times as prophets look / Into futurity" (*PW* 2:480). Over the
course of the Revolution Books, we learn (along with the young poet)
the source of this prophetic power: in his belief that in France he had
walked in a world that, in the sphere of culture, had returned to
the world's postdiluvian origins. Thomas Paine had made a similar
claim for the original status of America: "The case and circumstances
of America present themselves as in the beginning of a world; and
our enquiry into the origin of government is shortened, by referring
to the facts that have arisen in our own day. We have no occasion to
roam for information into the obscure field of antiquity, nor hazard
ourselves upon conjecture. We are brought at once to the point of

seeing government begin, as if we had lived in the beginning of time"
(*Rights of Man* 185). Wordsworth shares with Paine the belief that
unlike earlier political theorists, whose inquiries "into the origin of
government" were based on "conjectural histories" or the study of "the
obscure field of antiquity," his generation had been afforded the opportunity of actually "seeing government begin, as if we had lived in
the beginning of time." Instead of looking to America as an empiri-
cally observable image of social origins, however, Wordsworth saw in
France a different kind of beginning. This imaginative establishment
of anthropological conformities is a key to the structure of *The Prelude*.
It suggests that we understand the poem in terms of Wordsworth's
attempt to dovetail politics and anthropology: to use anthropology to
unlock the mysteries of a revolutionary decade and, reciprocally, to
use his experience of the French Revolution as an empirical basis for
talking about human origins. From book 6, where it seemed that
France was "standing on the top of golden hours, / And human nature
seeming born again" (6.353–54), to book 10, when revolutionary
hopes turned to superstition and terror, political history and anthropological narrative mutually reinforce one another as Wordsworth
draws out the conformities between the present and the prehistoric
past.

In book 10, in the climactic episode of the Revolution Books, Wordsworth describes that visionary moment, central to his poetry, when he
became conscious of the conformities between the present and the
past. The setting of this vision is important; it takes place in a room
"high and lonely, near the roof / Of a large mansion or hotel" (10.57–
58), a precarious shelter, like the high-mountain asylums described by
Enlightenment philosophes. Writes Boulanger: "There have been
aeras when man looked upon himself as the object of the hatred and
vengeance of irritated nature. There was an end of all society, mankind being obliged to wander, as chance directed, upon the ruins of
the world, and as driven by those plagues that seemed to persecute
him, being then destitute of succours, of subsistence, and of comfort;
if wretched mortals then retired to the mountains, the crumbling
mountains sunk from under their feet; if they were fugitives upon the
plains, the waters hastened to overtake and drown them" (*The Origin
of Despotism* 20).

What Wordsworth discovers, as he thinks of the September massacres separated from him by less than a month, is that he is no safer, in this violent revolutionary world, than were early humans as they sought to escape earthquakes and deluges. He suddenly realizes "most deeply in what world I was" (10.56). Human culture can undergo revolutions that are just as devastating as the revolutions of the earth, the hurricanes, deluges, and earthquakes described by geologists:

> The horse is taught his manage, and no star
> Of wildest course but treads back his own steps;
> For the spent hurricane the air provides
> As fierce a successor; the tide retreats
> But to return out of its hiding-place
> In the great deep; all things have second birth;
> The earthquake is not satisfied at once.   [1850 *Prelude* 10.78–84]

In this heightened state of reverie, achieved by reading the recent massacres through "tragic fictions, / And mournful calendars of true history," Wordsworth, having "wrought upon" himself, comes to a realization that culture is in continual revolution: "all things have second birth." In little more than two years, he had seen the "glorious course" of revolution—the "triumphal arcs," the "great spousals," the "dances of liberty" ("hand in hand danced round and round the board . . . round and round the board they danced again" [6.363–412]— show a different face, as from Arras issued a dictator, as the Place de Carousel was "heaped up with dead and dying" (10.48), as France returned to a state of nature and became "a place of fear . . . Defenceless as a wood where tigers roam" (10.80–82).

In the remainder of book 10, Wordsworth describes his return to England, the shock he received when it declared war on France, and how both societies re-emerged from the ruins of "postdiluvian" destruction, a "loathsome charge" that "burst and spread in deluge through the land" (10.438–39). The book culminates in one of Wordsworth's greatest prophetic visions, his account of how he heard of the death of Robespierre while riding on Leven Sands:

> As I advanced, all that I saw or felt
> Was gentleness and peace. Upon a small
> And rocky island near, a fragment stood
> (Itself like a sea rock) the low remains

(With shells encrusted, dark with briny weeds)
Of a dilapidated structure, once
A Romish chapel, where the vested priest
Said matins at the hour that suited those
Who crossed the sands with ebb of morning tide.
Not far from that still ruin all the plain
Lay spotted with a variegated crowd
Of vehicles and travellers, horse and foot,
Wading beneath the conduct of their guide
In loose procession through the shallow stream
Of inland waters; the great sea meanwhile
Heaved at safe distance, far retired. I paused,
Longing for skill to paint a scene so bright
And cheerful, but the foremost of the band
As he approached, no salutation given,
In the familiar language of the day,
Cried, "Robespierre is dead!"   [1850 *Prelude* 553–73]

"In the familiar language of the day": unremarkable language, yet remarkable in its suggestion that if we were reading this passage correctly we should have expected this man to speak in a different tongue. Beginning with what would have been a common sight—a group of morning travelers being guided at low tide across Leven Sands, on the route from Cartmel to Ulverston—Wordsworth indicates the visionary status of this prospect by echoing, in his description of how "the plain / Lay spotted with a variegated crowd / Of vehicles and travellers," Adam's prophetic vision of the descendents of Cain: "He look'd and saw a spacious Plain, whereon / Were Tents of various hue" (*Paradise Lost* 11.556–57). Where Adam, however, is given a glimpse into futurity, Wordsworth's vision rolls backward into past times, to see this scene as being constantly repeated in human history. He explicitly recalls the period prior to the English Reformation, when "those / Who crossed the sands with ebb of morning tide" gave thanks for having made the dangerous crossing at "A Romish chapel, where the vested priest / Said matins." There are echoes of Exodus, of the escape and deliverance of Israel from the persecutions of Pharoah. More remarkably, however, in describing these people wandering over a wide "plain" of "sands" and "wading" in "procession" through the ebbing waters to a sacred rock to give thanks for deliverance, while the "great sea" heaves at a distance, Wordsworth returns us to human origins, in the period immediately after the Flood. Though ostensibly an everyday event, Wordsworth makes the scene at Leven Sands an emblem of a history of ritual that extends back, through the ceremonies of the Catholic Church and the story of Exodus, to the earliest of sacred festivals—those of the survivors of the Deluge. A remark by Boulanger can gloss this passage: "In the island of Samothracia, there was [sic], in the time of Diodorus Siculus, annual festivals of this kind, which they then celebrated by going up on the tops of high mountains, to thank the gods for the ancient deliverance from the waters of the deluge. I am satisfied, that the idolatrous worship, which has been paid to so many mountains, was no more than consequences of that grateful acknowledgement which the nations had preserved for the asylums whereupon the wrecks of the human race were saved" (*The Origin of Despotism* 62). In the Leven Sands passage, Wordsworth provides a similar account of the historical origins of the sacred as a commemoration, in Boulanger's words, of "the revolutions of nature, whether occasioned by water or fire" (*The Origin of Despotism* 62). His description of the chapel as being "like a sea-rock . . . with shells encrusted, dark with briny weeds," transposes a product of human labor into something that is akin to nature.

In what became the conclusion to book 10 of the 1850 *Prelude*, Wordsworth repeats Adam's exclamations concerning the justice of God, now manifest in history:

> Great was my glee of spirit, great my joy
> In vengeance, and eternal justice, thus
> Made manifest. "Come now, ye golden times,"
> Said I, forth-breathing on those open sands
> A hymn of triumph, "as the morning comes
> Out of the bosom of the night, come ye . . ."   [*Prelude* 10.539–44]

Though Wordsworth goes on, in the rest of book 10, to trace his later confusions and anxieties as he attempted to develop a rational theory of morals, the episode at Leven Sands completes the link between catastrophist geology and revolutionary politics. Once established, the directionalist model of geological development, with its movement from the sublime to the beautiful, could then provide him with a pattern of social change. "From this time forth in France, as is well known," Wordsworth declares, "Authority put on a milder face" (567–68).

Landscape and Postdiluvian Trauma

In arguing that Wordsworth found in catastrophist geology a compelling system of imagery for talking about human environments undergoing enormous changes, I do not want to claim that this poetry is not indebted to apocalyptic thought. But Enlightenment geology shifted its emphasis by placing apocalypse at the beginning rather than the end of time. By suggesting that apocalyptic imagery originated in the never-forgotten impression that primitive nature had had upon the minds of human beings, the Enlightenment viewed apocalyptic fictions as products of metaleptic reversal, of putting first things last. In Wordsworth's poetry, apocalyptic imagery has a similar primal status, and is always structured as a return to an original, prehuman environment in which man is separated from nature, with a consequent unleashing of the powers in nature that human life has sought to control.

One of the best examples of this apocalyptic metalepsis is the Dream of the Arab episode in book 5 of *The Prelude*. Since the relationship between geology and revolution in this dream has already been examined in detail by Ernest Bernhardt-Kabisch, I want to focus here on the integral connection between the psychic landscape of the dream-vision and the notion of postdiluvian trauma. Initially, in the prologue to the dream, Wordsworth seems to be setting out a radical dichotomy between the historicity of human culture and the permanent, unchanging essence of nature.[24] Even if nature were to undergo apocalyptic destruction, "wrenched throughout" by the "inward throes" of earthquakes and volcanoes or suffering under fire "sent from far to wither all / Her pleasant habitations," the "living presence" would "still subsist / Victorious" through revolution and would not suffer the extinction of any of its forms; "composure," "kindlings," and "morning" would "presage" "a returning day" (5.29–36). This would not, however, be the case with "the consecrated works of bard and sage, / Sensuous or intellectual, wrought by men" (41–42). "Where would they be?" he asks (41–44). Once lost, the great achievements of human labor, built up "through length of time" and aspiring to "unconquerable life" (9–20), cannot be recovered. Human beings, traumatized by these catastrophic events, would "survive / Abject, depressed, forlorn, disconsolate" (26–27).

Having voiced these fears to a philosopher friend, Wordsworth discovers that his friend has felt "kindred hauntings" (55), occasioned by thoughts that, like the waters of the Flood, "to height unusual rose" (61). The ensuing apocalyptic dream, then, is the expression not of personal but of universal anxieties, like those described by Buffon, who speaks of our preserving "an enduring and nearly eternal memory of the calamities suffered by the world: the idea that it must be destroyed by a universal deluge or by a general conflagration" (*Oeuvres philosophiques* 187b). In the dream, the philosopher re-enacts this primal fear, as he finds himself in an "Arabian waste, / A desert," sitting "there in the wide wilderness / Alone upon the sands. Distress of mind . . . growing in him" (71–75). This is no ordinary landscape, but a world where human life has made little difference. In another instance of the reworking of a "primitive encounter," the philosopher describes his joy in meeting a wandering Bedouin, mad and anxious lest the distant "glittering light" be "the waters of the deep / Gathering upon us" (5.129–31). As P. J. Marshall has observed, desert Arabs, throughout the eighteenth century, were "in particular . . . thought to be embalmed specimens of a remote past still living in the present."[25] In *The Universal History* (1744) it is claimed that "the customs, manners, and genius, of the *Arabs,* except in matters of religion, are in effect the same at this day that they were betwixt three and four thousand years ago."[26] Given these assumptions, it should not surprise us that Wordsworth would represent this wandering Bedouin as a survivor from an earlier world, still suffering from the trauma of that

> day of vengeanc[e] when the sea
> Rose like a giant from his sleep and smote
> The hills, and when the firmament of heav[en]
> Rained darkness which the race of men beheld
> Yea all the men that lived & had no hope.[27]

Like the other marginal figures we have so far discussed, this man enters Wordsworth's writing as a vehicle of anthropological speculation and self-discovery. Since the world seen "by the first men, earth's first inhabitants, / May in these tutored days no more be seen / With undisordered sight" (*Prelude* 3.153–55), the encounter makes it possible for him to link his own melancholy *postrevolutionary* "hauntings" with the *postdiluvian* trauma of the world's first men and their anxiety about the impending return of the Flood.

The quixotic Arab's quest to bury (and thus preserve) in the desert sands the primary elements of human culture—a stone, which he says is Euclid's *Elements,* and a shell, which sounds a prophetic ode foretelling "Destruction to the children of the earth / By deluge now at hand" (98–99)—has received much attention. Various sources have been put forward, among these a dream of Descartes, Josephus's *History of the Jews,* and Ovid's *Metamorphoses.*[28] To this lengthy and plausible list, let me add another. Vitruvius, in the sixth book of *De architectura,* gives a famous account of the philosopher Aristippus, who, when shipwrecked on a strange coast, suddenly observed "geometrical diagrams" drawn upon the sand (fig. 4). Vitruvius writes that he "shouted to his companions: 'There are good hopes for us; for I see human footsteps!' Forthwith he made for the city of Rhodes and came straight to the gymnasium," where he took up philosophical topics directly. When his companions, anxious to return home, asked him if he wished them to convey any messages, he enjoined them to say "that men should provide for their children wealth and travelling equipment of such a kind, that, even after shipwreck, it can swim to land along with its owners. For those are the true safeguards of life which are immune from the stormy injustice of Fortune, the changes of politics and the ravages of war."[29]

In a section of *The Prelude* dealing with the importance of books and education, one that begins with anxious questions about whether any human product can withstand eventual destruction, Aristippus's insistence on the value of learning as the only "true" safeguard against shipwreck, ill fortune, political changes, and war would have had a special significance. The philosopher in the Dream notes with joy the "strange freight / Which the newcomer carried through the waste" (84–85). The situation, however, is not without humor, because instead of carrying "travelling equipment" that might "swim to land along with its owners," the Arab rides a camel and carries a stone and shell, which he is about to bury in the desert. Yet here, in a deeper sense,

Fig. 4. Frontispiece to David Gregory's edition of Euclid's *Opera* (Oxford, 1703). Courtesy of the New York Public Library.

the two stories are linked. Where Aristippus saw the geometrical figures drawn in the sand as "human footsteps," as signs that marked
the presence of civilized human beings, the mad Arab hopes to preserve geometry by returning it to the sands from which it originally
arose.

As Bernhardt-Kabisch has noted, the stone and shell are not only
cultural artifacts, but are also "igneous rock and aquatic fossil . . . the
basic building materials of all geological formation" ("The Stone and
the Shell" 485). This close affiliation between stone and shell, geometry and poetry, suggests that the disjunction that we saw between
culture and nature in the prologue was only apparent. Nature is neither more nor less subject to destruction than books. After an apocalyptic deluge (political or geological, it makes no difference), nature
would survive, but it would be a barren desert—just stones and shells.
The task of making nature once more habitable to human beings is
as difficult as that of recovering "poetry and geometric truth / (The
knowledge that endures)" (5.64–65). In fact, they are the same activity, as is indicated by Wordsworth's comment, in the *Guide Through the
District of the Lakes,* on the valley of Wastdale, whose "little chapel and
half a dozen neat dwellings scattered upon a plain of meadow and
corn-ground intersected with stone walls apparently innumerable"
have taken on the appearance of "an array of mathematical figures,
such as in the ancient schools of geometry might have been sportively
and fantastically traced out upon sand" (*ProseW* 2:172). Wordsworth's
environmental historicism made nature as much a product of human
labor as art is. His consistent conflation of nature and culture, as we
also saw in the case of the "Romish chapel" and "sea rock" rising from
the sands of the Leven estuary, does not indicate confusion, then, but
instead a profound recognition that the things of nature and the
things of mind are inseparably linked.

Geology and Primitive Word Gathering

Both the Revolution Books and the Dream of the Arab episode describe poetry as being fundamentally bound up with postdiluvian/
postrevolutionary trauma, in the anxious, conservative response of
poets to the violence of the Deluge. In the Arab's mad attempt to

preserve the stone and shell from destruction, we might see a figure
of the primal poet as the antithesis of the revolutionaries of book 9,
whose seismic shocks and concussions made "the soil of common life
. . . Too hot to tread upon" (9.169–70). As poets "share [in] that maniac's anxiousness" (5.160), as they struggle against the deluge in the
combined activity of preserving what can be salvaged from destruction
and of retrieving what has been lost in the sands of time, they take
from the sea the very ground they stand on. Geological directionalism
made its greatest contribution in providing Wordsworth with a model
for understanding the relationship between revolution and poetry in
his own life. Though the mad Arab and the revolutionary may seem
totally at odds with one another, they actually represent antithetical
aspects of the same process. In a geological universe, destruction provides the materials of new creation. This model gave rise to a specific
conception of poetic vocation, set out most clearly in *Resolution and
Independence,* in which the poet, engaged in youth with the sublime
revolutionary activity of breaking down traditional institutions, becomes, with age, the means by which these institutions are recovered
and preserved so that they can serve as the "soil" or "asylum" of
mankind in subsequent periods of revolution.

   Written in the months immediately following the negotiation of the
Treaty of Amiens in March 1802, *Resolution and Independence* reflects
on the preceding revolutionary decade. Marjorie Levinson has recently shown the extent to which the *Intimations Ode* recounts the
change that took place in Wordsworth's conception of nature, as the
gladness of a revolutionary dawn gave way to the twilight of a more
sober political vision, signed and sealed by the Treaty of Amiens.[30]
This change is even more explicit in *Resolution and Independence,* which
speaks of hope quickly darkening into despondency and disenchantment:

> But, as it sometimes chanceth, from the might
> Of joy in minds that can no further go,
> As high as we have mounted in delight
> In our dejection do we sink as low.   [22–25]

Underlying this anxious meditation on the course of revolution is a
fear that runs through much of Wordsworth's poetry that poetic lives,
like those of Burns and Chatterton, follow a similar pattern: poets

"begin in gladness; / But thereof come in the end despondency and madness" (48–49). *Resolution and Independence* is very much a poem about poetic vocation, about how Wordsworth shaped his poetic life so that his earlier "revolutionary" joys and fears could be seen as playing a formative role in the development of a "resolutionary" poet.[31]

The poem is divided into three major sections. The first seven stanzas link the landscape to the early postdiluvian world and describe the poet's melancholy. Stanzas 8 through 11 depict his encounter with the leech-gatherer. The final nine stanzas present a "scene of instruction," in which the poet undergoes a ritualistic initiation into his vocation. Wordsworth first constructs a myth of origins, then places himself within it, formulating a notion of what poetry is by identifying himself with his imagined primeval precursors and affirming the conformities between his own situation and what they confronted in the distant past.

Though we can be quite certain that the "old remembrances" (20), the "fears and fancies" that came upon Wordsworth that morning, "Dim sadness—and blind thoughts, I knew not, nor could name" (27–28), refer, at least in part, to the trauma of the French Revolution (the "recent deluge" [*Prelude* 10.619]), what is distinctive about Wordsworth's approach to these concerns is that he sets them within the context of a hypothetical history. The "plashy earth" has only just emerged from the previous night's terrible rains, which "came heavily and fell in floods"; the air is redolent with mist and "filled with pleasant noise of waters." Milton's brooding dove even appears to register a new beginning. The tense-shift of stanza 3 ("I was a Traveller then upon the moor") introduces human memory and places the scene into an indefinite past, thus encouraging us to see the conformities between the situation of the poet, wandering alone on a dreary waste, and a postdiluvian solitary. Reading backwards, from the poet's experience into the hypothetical past, we learn that early postdiluvians were unable to participate completely in the ecstasy of an animal kingdom rejoicing in the morning because they were unable to forget past destruction.

Though Wordsworth portrays his encounter with the leech-gatherer as a chance happening, as "something given," it is clear, within the rhetorical structure of the poem, that this meeting does not happen by accident. We are not given a reportorial rendering of his and Dorothy's actual encounter with a wandering Scottish mendicant near Dove Cottage, but instead a figure set in a radically revised environment, as an answer to the questions relating to vocation that were raised in the first section:

> Who will not wade to seek a bridge or boat
> How can he ever hope to cross the flood?
> How can he e'er expect that others should
> Build for him, sow for him, and at his call
> Love him who for himself will take no heed at all?[32]

Standing on the margins of "a pool bare to the eye of heaven," itself part of a dreary visionary landscape, a "naked wilderness" (*PW* 2:237n), the already transformed leech-gatherer undergoes a further metamorphosis that increases his conformity and link to antiquity— he becomes "the oldest man . . . that ever wore grey hairs" (56).

As in the Discharged Soldier episode, Wordsworth focuses less on the man himself than on how he is figuratively transformed in the eyes of the watching poet. This is especially true in the following canceled passage:

> My course I stopped as soon as I espied
> The Old Man . . .
>   a minute's space I guess
> I watch'd him, he continuing motionless:
> To the Pool's further margin then I drew;
> He being all the while before me full in view.   [*PW* 2:237n]

A. W. Thomson has cogently argued that the poem recounts the progressive humanization of the leech-gatherer, as Wordsworth eventually demystifies his initial figurations of the old man so that he can begin to appear "as a human being." Significantly, these transformations are also organized as a twofold anthropology: the Lamarckian evolutionary scheme, which shows how a "huge stone" becomes a "thing endued with sense," then a "sea-beast," and then a "Man . . . in his extreme old age," is coordinated symbolically with a history of the poet's imagination, a dramatization of perception that displays how "the old man as he essentially is—his *gestus,* or essential attitude," slowly emerges from the passion-enchanted eyes of the solitary wanderer who observes him.[33] Wordsworth emphasizes the fictionalizing and textualizing procedures of seeing in both the savage and the anthropologist, deconstructing the interpretive frameworks of those who observe, while simultaneously making the history of this deconstruction itself part of an anthropological history of mind as it moves from superstitious to factual fictions.

It has not been recognized that these metaphoric transformations project the leech-gatherer's geo-genealogical origins far back into the distant past, to the time of the Deluge. Initially, he appears as an "erratic boulder":

As a huge stone is sometimes seen to lie
Couched on the bald top of an eminence;
Wonder to all who do the same espy,
By what means it could thither come, and whence;

. . . .

Such seemed this Man.   [57–64]

Martin J. S. Rudwick has stressed the importance of these erratic blocks, "often perched on hill-tops and showing no relation to the present drainage system," in the geological thought of the time. "Such phenomena," he observes, "clearly witnessed to a discontinuity between the present and the geologically recent past; they implied a period of conditions very different from those of the present day. What agencies could have been responsible for these spectacular effects? It was no use appealing to the magnitude of geological time, for no amount of time could shift boulders the size of houses by the agency of the processes now at work in the areas concerned. Moreover, the organic world seemed to have been affected as radically as the inorganic: as Cuvier had shown, the 'diluvial' gravels yielded a whole fauna of extinct mammalia. The only plausible explanation was that a violent rush of water had swept suddenly over the relevant land-areas, causing both the transport of erratic blocks and the annihilation of the indigenous fauna."[34] By metaphorically associating the leech-gatherer with an erratic boulder "from some far region sent," Wordsworth enters into contemporary debates about whether there actually was a flood and sides imaginatively with the diluvianists.

From a "huge stone," the leech-gatherer passes into

    a thing endued with sense:
Like a sea-beast crawled forth, that on a shelf
Of rock or sand reposeth, there to sun itself;

Such seemed this Man, not all alive nor dead,
Nor all asleep—in his extreme old age.   [61–65]

In the preface to the 1815 *Poems,* Wordsworth singled out this passage as an example of the modifying powers of the imagination and argued that it displayed a two-stage movement: "The stone is endowed with something of the power of life to approximate it to the sea-beast; and the sea-beast stripped of some of its vital qualities to assimilate it to the stone; which intermediate image is thus treated for the purpose of bringing the original image, that of the stone, to a nearer resemblance to the figure and condition of the aged Man; who is divested of so much of the indications of life and motion as to bring him to the point where the two objects unite and coalesce in just comparison" (*ProseW* 3:33). The closest thing to this intermediate image of a "sea-beast" assimilated to a "stone" is a fossil; Wordsworth even indicates the strata, "a shelf / Of rock or sand," in which this petrified "sea-beast" is to be found. Geoffrey Hartman has perceptively noted that this old man is "a relict of the spiritual flood . . . a 'sea-beast' stranded by the ebbed tide."[35] We might add that he is meant to provide not only an empirical link to a catastrophe that took place "in times long past" (69) but also, because the fossilized remains of extinct animals in "diluvial gravels" were frequently introduced in support of diluvianism, another proof that such an event actually took place.[36]

The second stage of this metamorphosis, in which the image of a rock/sea-beast and a man "unite and coalesce in just comparison," is certainly one of the oddest images in Wordsworth's poetry. The transformation of the man into an amphibian, moving between water and land, probably owes something to the traditional image of man as the "great amphibian" located temporally, spiritually, and genealogically between worlds. "Thus is Man that great and true *Amphibium,*" writes Thomas Browne, "whose nature is disposed to live, not onely like other creatures in diverse elements, but in divided and distinguished worlds."[37] The strangeness of the leech-gatherer's dress, described in a canceled passage of the poem, might also have contributed something to the image:

Fig. 5. *Ça n'durra pas toujours.* Engraving. Courtesy of the Bibliothèque Nationale Estampes.

And, furthermore, he had upon his back,
Beneath his cloak, a round and bulky Pack;
A load of wool or raiment, as might seem;
That on his shoulders lay as if it clave to him.   [*PW* 2:238n]

The "round and bulky Pack" concealed beneath this isolated wanderer's cloak "cleaves" to him almost as if it were part of his body. The
image of the leech-gatherer, bent by the weight of this pack, would
have evoked the revolutionary image of the laboring poor, typified, for
instance, in the engraving entitled *Ça n'durra pas toujours* (fig. 5), in
which an aristocrat and a priest, holding sword and Bible, stand watching a peasant slowly passing by, weighed down by a heavy burden.
Wordsworth stressed the social orientation of the poem in an 1802

letter to Sara Hutchinson: "I cannot conceive a figure more impressive than that of an old Man like this, the survivor of a Wife and ten children, travelling alone among the mountains and all lonely places, carrying with him his own fortitude, and the necessities which an unjust state of society has entailed upon him" (*EY* 366–67). Whether or not the pun in the word *entailed* was intended (Wordsworth was talking about a sea-beast/man), there is profound irony in the use of a term that refers to the limitation of an inheritance to a specified and unalterable succession of heirs being applied to the poor.[38]

Wordsworth superimposes on this metaphysical and political iconography the language of geology: either he is a strange fossil "sea-beast" that once "crawled forth" onto "a shelf / Of rock or sand," or a primeval mountain or "eminence" that stands in the ebbing waters of the Flood. He is thus symbolically linked to the French revolutionary volcanic journalists of *The Prelude*. But unlike these politicians, this old man has achieved his weighty, almost dormant bulk through suffering a "constraint of pain, or rage / Of sickness felt by him in times long past" that "cast" (with the emphasis on sculptural molding) "a *more than human weight* upon his frame" (my emphasis). When Wordsworth reads the pain and violence of the man's past through his silent, stony features, he is not only reading a man's life, marked in a "body . . . bent double, feet and head," but also deciphering the revolutions that have given rise to "a huge stone." (We are thus brought back to the opening of book 9 of *The Prelude*.) Through this dual reading, one of Wordsworth's greatest conflations of nature and culture, the man's individual life is equated symbolically with earth's revolutions. In the letter to Sara Hutchinson, Wordsworth stresses the supernatural aura of the old man: "A person reading this Poem with feelings like mine will have been awed and controuled, expecting almost something spiritual or supernatural—What is brought forward? 'A lonely place, a Pond' 'by which an old man *was*, far from all house or home'—the figure presented in the most naked simplicity possible" (*EY* 366). A figure of postrevolutionary restoration, the leech-gatherer, like the ruined Chapel Island monastery of Leven Sands, which also stands amid the ebbing waters of the Flood, has become a sacred refuge in the waste of a postdiluvian world.

In the third section of the poem, Wordsworth describes how this sacred status was achieved. We learn that the old man's strength de-

rives from the manner in which he has learned to deal with pain and
trauma. We are given a man engaged in one of the earliest of human
occupations, gathering a bare subsistence from nature. Standing on
"the margin of that moorish flood" (74), he

> the pond
> Stirred with his staff, and fixedly did look
> Upon the muddy water, which he conned,
> As if he had been reading in a book.   [78–81]

Following the practices of the "cunning men" or "leeches," who still
practiced their magic and medicine in remoter regions of the English
countryside during the eighteenth century, the leech-gatherer draws
from the dark (bloody?) waters both the crude instruments of a rudimentary medicine—the leeches used to draw off blood and hu-
mors—and the primary medium of primitive magic, an order of
words.[39] Not only does he "fixedly" look "upon the muddy water," but
he "reads" it, as if it contained the muddy detritus of an original
language. Drawing out words, like leeches, by carefully "conning"
them, he reads himself out of nature, making himself into a monument, by gathering up what remains of the buried and dispersed book
of the mad Arab. Like contemporary geologists, who believed that all
land formations had their "origin at the bottom of the sea," from shells
and sediment, "the collection of sand and gravel, of shells, of coralline
and crustaceous bodies, and of earths and clays variously mixed, or
separated and accumulated," Wordsworth treats culture as a dynamic,
cyclical process in which language, the "soil" of human life, is broken
down by revolutionary activity only to be brought together again by
the poet in what amounts to a form of rudimentary "word-gather-
ing."[40] The primitive poet thus complements the revolutionary, each
playing his part in the cycle that governs revolutions in all things. The
poet passes from the volcanic violence of revolutionary activity to act
in concert with nature toward the production of beauty and order. In
Resolution and Independence, we see how this combination of aesthetic
and geological directionalism gave Wordsworth a pattern to which he
returned in *The Prelude* for understanding the revolutionary decade
and his role within it.

It is perhaps not surprising that this painstaking process of "word-
gathering" extends to the leech-gatherer's difficulties of speech. The

old man chooses his words slowly and carefully, as if his mind were a
sea out of whose "disordered" turbulence the materials of creation
need to be drawn, one after the other, in measured phrases:

> A gentle answer did the old Man make,
> In courteous speech which forth he slowly drew . . .
>
> . . . .
>
> His words came feebly, from a feeble chest,
> But each in solemn order followed each,
> With something of a lofty utterance drest—
> Choice word and measured phrase, above the reach
> Of ordinary men; a stately speech;
> Such as grave Livers do in Scotland use,
> Religious men, who give to God and man their dues.   [85–98]

Dorothy confirms that the man's linguistic difficulties arose from his
having "been hurt in driving a cart, his leg broke, his body driven
over, his skull fractured. He felt no pain till he recovered from his
first insensibility" (*DWJ* 1:63). Despite the various symbolic overlays
that submerge the leech-gatherer's genealogy, we can see that he belongs to that group of marginal individuals who, through sickness,
have been reduced to a state of nature and can now epitomize, having
regained their speech, the transition from nature into culture. His
mind, like the scattered book, submerged and dispersed by the waters
of the Flood, is reconstructed in "lofty utterance" in the same manner
as the curative leeches are drawn from the pools left by the Deluge.
In the first version of the poem, the analogy between the gathering
and exchange of words and of leeches is more explicit. Asked what
he does for a living, the leech-gatherer replies:

> This is my summer work in winter time
> I go with godly Books from Town to Town
> Now I am seeking Leeches up & down
> From house to house I go from Barn to Barn
> All over Cartmell Fells & up to Blellan Tarn.[41]

Gathering and dispensing words and leeches "from Town to Town,"
the leech-gatherer makes a meager living, as wandering mendicant,
primitive "leech," or physician and poet.

   The therapeutic process—between the poet and the leech, the poem and the reader—is based upon a process of verbal exchange. In the poem's original version, Wordsworth assumed that this process was immediate and uncomplicated: he hoped that a direct transcription of the leech-gatherer's words would produce the same effect upon his readers as they had originally had upon him. In his response to Coleridge's and the Hutchinson sisters' complaints about the tediousness of the man's story, he returns to the aesthetics of "The Thorn": "It is in the character of the old man to tell his story in a manner which an *impatient* reader must necessarily feel as tedious. But Good God! Such a figure, in such a place, a pious self-respecting, miserably infirm . . . Old Man telling such a Tale!" (*EY* 367). Though Wordsworth, in revising the poem, deleted most of the leech-gatherer's speech, he did not do so without resistance, and the final version includes a metafictional critique of his audience. He depicts their tedium in the ill attention of an "impatient" poet. The irony of approaching someone who is standing knee-deep in a pond and, after declaring that "this morning gives us promise of a glorious day," asking him "What occupation do you there pursue?" is lost on this speaker. Perhaps, too, we see in the leech-gatherer's "flash of mild surprise" a commentary on both the speaker's obtuseness and his philosophical preoccupations. Initially, the poet allows the words of the leech-gatherer to escape him and, like the leeches, to re-enter the stream: "But now his voice to me was like a stream / Scarce heard; nor word from word could I divide" (107–08). Having lost the words through neglect, the poet once more falls victim to melancholy: "My former thoughts returned: the fear that kills; / And hope that is unwilling to be fed" (113–14). "Perplexed, and longing to be comforted," he therefore asks this ancient once more about his vocation: "How is it that you live, and what is it you do?" (119). "With a smile," directed as much toward Wordsworth's audience as the naive poet, the leech-gatherer "did then his words repeat" (120). We can see that the poem is enacting its message, as the old man teaches him that poetry is the activity of "conning" words. Only then are we given a direct citation of the leech-gatherer's speech:

"Once I could meet with them on every side;
But they have dwindled long by slow decay;
Yet still I persevere, and find them where I may."   [124–26]

With the appearance of direct speech, this most elaborate of "primi-tive encounters" comes to its formal conclusion.

The leech-gatherer's tale has a powerful effect upon the poet, for it speaks indelibly of the postdiluvian/postrevolutionary vocation of the poet. It leads Wordsworth to envision him wandering through a primeval landscape, engaged in the hazardous task of gathering a language capable of withstanding madness:

> all troubled me:
> In my mind's eye I seemed to see him pace
> About the weary moors continually,
> Wandering about alone and silently.   [128–31]

Through his encounter with this aged survivor from antique times engaged in a primitive form of medicine, now in decay, Wordsworth found a prototype for the task of a postrevolutionary poet. As an art of collecting, exchanging, and healing with words, as an art that con-geals the verbal detritus of the Flood—shell and stone—once more into rocks of asylum and into the soil of culture, poetry does not move away from politics, but seeks to make revolutionary language and the world that it creates once more into stable ground. In the preface to *Lyrical Ballads*, Wordsworth describes the poet as "the *rock* of defence for human nature; an upholder and preserver, carrying everywhere with him relationship and love. In spite of difference of soil and cli-mate, of language and manners, of laws and customs: in spite of things silently gone out of mind, and things violently destroyed; the Poet binds together by passion and knowledge the vast empire of human society, as it is spread over the whole earth, and over all time" (*ProseW* 1:141, my emphasis).

The Rocky Crag

Wordsworth's primitive landscapes share two major elements. They are sublime and desolate worlds, of sands, naked rocks, rugged land formations, unchanneled waters and headlong torrents. Equally im-portantly, these regions exhibit few traces of human geographical ac-tion. They have not yet been made habitable, and they suffer for it.

The most powerful expression of this suffering is certainly Wordsworth's description of his descent through the Ravine of Gondo:

> The immeasurable height
> Of woods decaying, never to be decayed,
> The stationary blasts of waterfalls,
> And everywhere along the hollow rent
> Winds thwarting winds, bewildered and forlorn,
> The torrents shooting from the clear blue sky,
> The rocks that muttered close upon our ears—
> Black drizzling crags that spake by the wayside
> As if a voice were in them—the sick sight
> And giddy prospect of the raving stream,
> The unfettered clouds and region of the heavens,
> Tumult and peace, the darkness and the light,
> Were all like workings of one mind, the features
> Of the same face, blossoms upon one tree,
> Characters of the great apocalypse,
> The types and symbols of eternity,
> Of first, and last, and midst, and without end.   [6.556–72]

A striking aspect of this passage is that Wordsworth applies to landscape the language of trauma that we have seen him use to describe
the madness of the "earth's first inhabitants" (3.153). "Bewildered and
forlorn," ravaged and "charactered" by the retreating waters of the
Flood, the ancient earth also suffered postdiluvian trauma, figured
by the "sick sight / And giddy prospect of the raving stream." Unchanged since the Flood, this geological remnant of the primeval
world is presented as a "hollow rent," a throaty gorge trying unsuccessfully to speak articulate language; the rocks mutter, the crags
speak "as if a voice were in them," yet they are unable to voice, and
thus control, this pain. This melancholy suggests that the earth has
undergone its own discipline. The "speaking face of earth" (5.12) has
learned to speak, partly by virtue of geological change, but mostly
through human agency. The relationship between human beings and
nature is not, then, one of mutual antagonism, but of two "progressive
powers" (as Wordsworth says in the Prospectus) that act in concert,
with "blended might," to accomplish a new "creation (by no lower
name / Can it be called)" (*Home at Grasmere*, MS. B, lines 1,007–13).

This progressive interrelation is a central argument of *A Guide Through the District of the Lakes*. In the first section, entitled "View of the Country as formed by Nature," which deals primarily with the climate and physical topography of the Lake District, Wordsworth provides a trenchant statement of the directionalist pattern of geological and geographical change operating in nature. "Sublimity," he asserts, "is the result of Nature's first great dealings with the superficies of the earth; but the general tendency of her subsequent operations is towards the production of beauty, by a multiplicity of parts uniting in a consistent whole" (*ProseW* 2:181). This transformation of the sublime into the beautiful is achieved, he argues, by many "*secondary agents of nature*," which are "ever at work to supply the deficiences of the mould in which things were originally cast," introducing intricacy, variety, and richness to the sublime, yet barren, simplicity of primal nature.

Wordsworth mentions erosion and the alluvial deposits laid down by streams and rivers, but it is clear, especially in the second section, entitled "Aspect of the Country as Affected by its Inhabitants," that human beings are the most important of these "secondary agents." There he stresses the enormous changes that have taken place as "the hand of man has acted upon the surface of the inner regions of this mountainous country, as incorporated with and subservient to the powers and processes of nature" (201). The most sweeping of these has been in the vegetation and animal populations of the region. In what represents one of the first examples of a geography of plants, a study of the changes that have occurred in the plant life of a region over an extended period of time, Wordsworth notes that the vast woods that once covered most of the area have all but disappeared. Though oak, ash, birch, Wychelm, white- and blackthorn, alders, willows, and yews can still be seen in native coppices or scattered in lessening numbers in the mountains, not a single Scotch fir, which once had been abundant, has existed in the region "for some hundreds of years" (189).

But human beings control their natural environments by doing more than simply clearing and improving the land for agriculture. They also actively domesticate and substitute different plant or animal species for others, by introducing and then increasing, almost at will, domestic populations of plants and animals, while ridding regions of those flora and fauna that are "wild" or inimical to human economies. Holly, for instance, was used to feed sheep, so these trees "were carefully preserved for that purpose when all other wood was cleared off; large tracts of common being so covered with these trees, as to have the appearance of a forest of hollies" (198). Wordsworth notes the economic basis for the cultivation of trees: the re-establishment of bloomeries in the late seventeenth century "made it the interest of the people to convert the steeper and more stony of the enclosures, sprinkled over with remains of the native forest, into close woods, which, when cattle and sheep were excluded, rapidly sowed and thickened themselves" (201). Foreign tree species have also been introduced: the sycamore, "from Germany, not more than two hundred years ago," followed by "beeches, larches, limes, &c. and plantations of firs" (189) within the previous fifty years. Wordsworth notes similar changes in the animal population, for when "the aboriginal colonists of the Celtic tribes were first driven or drawn" to the region of the lakes, it was inhabited by wolves, boars, wild bulls, red deer, and "the leigh, a gigantic species of deer which has been long extinct" (194). Other examples of the manner in which the inhabitants of the Lake District have transformed their environment might be noted. Present purposes will be served, however, if we recognize the extent to which Wordsworth believes that human environments are, physically and aesthetically, "secondary" creations that displace the sublime "primitive conformation" (178) of the earth. Landscape can thus be seen as a historical product of the interaction of human beings with nature; it documents the ways that they have responded to it with labor, government, and the domestication and management of plant and animal species.[42]

In a more extended study, one would want to examine Wordsworth's account of the progressive deepening and enrichment of that interaction. Such a study would necessarily include a "history of property," for Wordsworth shares with most eighteenth-century writers the belief that the genesis of an idea of property was a necessary precondition for human society.[43] What is distinctive about Wordsworth's project, linking him more closely to Burke than to Locke, is that he is less interested in the changing legal meanings of property than in the ways in which human beings are imaginatively, emotionally, and psychologically rooted to land. In the "spots of time" episodes where the

child steals raven eggs, woodcocks, and a boat, in the violence of "Nutting," in Peter Bell's attempt to steal the ass, Wordsworth works out a
theory of primitive property relations. Though property rights are
easily transgressed in these poems (things appear to be there for the
taking), they are preserved and guarded by the child's guilty and
fearful projection of a nature frequented by "huge and mighty forms"
(*Prelude* 1.424) who remain its jealous, vengeful, "absent owners." The
difference between the world that the child of *The Prelude* inhabits,
with its naked pools, dreary crags, and melancholy beacons (11.320–
21), made more sublime by stormy winds and sleety rains, and that
of *Michael,* "The Brothers," and *Home at Grasmere* is the difference
between a world of rudimentary property relations governed by fear
and supernaturalism, and a more "social" world, in which the value
of things is ultimately bound to the labor or emotional investment (as
in "The Last of the Flock," "Alice Fell," or "Simon Lee") that is put
into things over time.[44] "Land," Wordsworth declared in a famous
letter to Charles Fox, "serves as a kind of permanent rallying point
for . . . domestic feelings, as a tablet upon which they are written which
makes them objects of memory in a thousand instances when they
would otherwise be forgotten. It is a fountain fitted to *the nature of
social man* from which supplies of affection, as pure as his heart was
intended for, are daily drawn" (*EY* 314–15, my emphasis). With the
disappearance of these small tracts, Wordsworth asserted, an entire
range of ideas and emotions was disappearing from human life, to be
replaced by the unpropertied rootlessness and uncultivated feeling
that he associated with cities, notably London.

I would like to turn, in the remainder of this chapter, to a passage
that dramatically illustrates how Wordsworth, as he framed a theory
of his own poetic and psychological development, drew on the directionalist model provided by geological histories of the earth. In book
13, as he prepares to bring to a close his history of "the discipline /
And consummation of the poet's mind" (270–71), he joins the two
powers that have shaped the poem and his life, imagination and "intellectual love":

> Imagination having been our theme,
> So also hath that intellectual love,
> For they are each in each, and cannot stand

> Dividually. Here must thou be, O man,
> Strength to thyself—no helper hast thou here—
> Here keepest thou thy individual state:
> No other can divide with thee this work,
> No secondary hand can intervene
> To fashion this ability. 'Tis thine,
> The prime and vital principle is thine
> In the recesses of thy nature, far
> From any reach of outward fellowship,
> Else 'tis not thine at all.   [185–97]

Originally formed by imagination and "intellectual" love, each sublime in their natures, the self maintains its "individual state," like a solitary mountain at the beginning of creation. "No secondary hand" can "fashion" this primary self, this "work." It is achieved outside of society, "far / From any reach of outward fellowship." Yet like the primitive mountains of early geological thought, this self is imperfect. Human society is required "to supply the deficiences of the mould in which things were originally cast" (*ProseW* 2:181):

> But joy to him,
> O, joy to him who here hath sown—hath laid
> Here the foundations of his future years—
> For all that friendship, all that love can do,
> All that a darling countenance can look
> Or dear voice utter, to complete the man,
> Perfect him, made imperfect in himself,
> All shall be his. And he whose soul hath risen
> Up to the height of feeling intellect
> Shall want no humbler tenderness . . .   [197–206]

The self would seem to pass through its own geological stages, as the primary forces of "intellectual" love and imagination "sow" the "foundations" and "height of feeling intellect" that are completed by the loving friendship of others. The resulting individual is thus enriched, as he becomes filled with a "humbler tenderness," "female softness," "little loves," "delicate desires," "mild interests and gentlest sympathies" (208–10). The female and social passions would seem to be akin

to a verdant cover that makes fertile and beautifies an otherwise barren sublimity.

At this point, as Wordsworth declares what the love of Dorothy has
meant to him, the geological discourse that shapes this passage becomes explicit:

> I too exclusively esteemed that love,
> And sought that beauty, which as Milton sings
> Hath terror in it. Thou didst soften down
> This over-sternness; but for thee, sweet friend,
> My soul, too reckless of mild grace, had been
> Far longer what by Nature it was framed—
> Longer retained its countenance severe—
> A rock with torrents roaring, with the clouds
> Familiar, and a favorite of the stars;
> But thou didst plant its crevices with flowers,
> Hang it with shrubs that twinkle in the breeze,
> And teach the little birds to build their nests
> And warble in its chambers. At a time
> When Nature, destined to remain so long
> Foremost in my affections, had fallen back
> Into a second place, well pleased to be
> A handmaid to a nobler than herself—
> When every day brought with it some new sense
> Of exquisite regard for common things,
> And all the earth was budding with these gifts
> Of more refined humanity—thy breath,
> Dear sister, was a kind of gentler spring
> That went before my steps.   [224–46]

As many of Wordsworth's contemporaries noted, there may have
been some physical basis for the analogy he drew between himself and
a mountain. Benjamin Robert Haydon remarked that "his head is like
as if it was carved out of a mossy rock, created before the flood!"
Henry Taylor claimed that he had "a rough grey face, full of rifts and
clefts and fissures, out of which, some one said, you might expect
lichens to grow."[45] These reactions probably had less to do with a
knowledge of Wordsworth than of his poetry. Throughout his career,
to explain how he had passed from a volcanic revolutionary to a re-

solutionary poet, Wordsworth continually drew on geology and environmental theory. In this passage, as the poem turns back to the correspondent breeze of the Glad Preamble, even the climate of the poem has changed. Love and beauty replace the revolutionary sublime, as the "breath" of his "Dear sister," now a "gentle spring," displaces the "tempest" and "redundant energy" of the poet's earlier "*mount*ings of mind" (1.20, 46). In a slightly grotesque image of feather-warmed domestic cosiness, Dorothy is represented as having "soften[ed] *down*" an "over-sternness" of soul. As the "gifts / Of more refined humanity" are set "budding" over the earth, Wordsworth revises the traditional language of visionary and revolutionary poetics to pay his best compliment to Dorothy. Through her civilizing powers, a new nature had been brought forth in a postrevolutionary waste:

> all grandeur comes,
> All truth and beauty—from pervading love—
> That gone, we are as dust. [13.150–52]

Notes

Introduction

1 Kenneth R. Johnston, in his important full-length study of *The Recluse*, has noted that "there is surprisingly little (relative to the enormous critical literature devoted to Wordsworth's philosophies) for the philosophic system(s) *The Recluse* was to assume" (*Wordsworth and "The Recluse"* [New Haven, 1984], 16). For additional discussions of *The Recluse*, see M. H. Abrams, *Natural Supernaturalism: Tradition and Revolution in Romantic Literature* (New York, 1971), 19–32, 73–80; Beth Darlington's introduction to *Home at Grasmere*, 3–32; Thomas Macfarland, "Wordsworth on Man, on Nature, and on Human Life," *Studies in Romanticism* 21 (1982):601–18; and Jonathan Wordsworth, "On Man, on Nature, and on Human Life," *Review of English Studies* 31 (1980):17–29.

2 See John Alban Finch, "On the Dating of *Home at Grasmere:* A New Approach," *BWS* 14–15; and Reed *EY* 215.

3 On the difficulty Wordsworth encountered in increasing the philosophical importance of the Pedlar, see Jonathan Wordsworth, *The Music of Humanity: A Critical Study of Wordsworth's "Ruined Cottage"* (London, 1969), xiii–xiv, 245–58; and James Butler, introduction to *"The Ruined Cottage" and "The Pedlar"* (Ithaca, N.Y., 1979).

4 *The Structure of Scientific Revolutions* (1962; rpt. Chicago, 1970), 10.

5 *Acts of Inclusion: Studies Bearing on an Elementary Theory of Romanticism* (New Haven, 1979), xv.

6 For Lucretius's impact on the philosophes, see Peter Gay, *The Enlightenment: An Interpretation*, 2 vols. (New York, 1966, 1969), 1:98–105.

7 Lord Kames, *Sketches of the History of Man; considerably enlarged by the last additions and corrections of the author*, 3 vols. (Edinburgh, 1813), 1:1.

8 *The Poems of Alexander Pope*, ed. John Butt (London, 1963), 502.

9 "Memoirs of the Life and Writings of Mr Gray," in *The Poems of Mr Gray* (London, 1775), 192.

10 *Life, Letters, and Journals of George Ticknor,* ed. George S. Hillard, 2 vols.
    (Boston, 1876), 2:167.
11 In the early 1790s, reviewers were enthusiastic about Darwin's "philo-
    sophical poems" and frequently cited his attempt "to inlist Imagination
    under the banner of Science" (*The Botanic Garden; A Poem in Two Parts*
    [Dublin, 1793–96], v).
12 Robert Woof's identification of this source is cited in Michael C. Jaye,
    "William Wordsworth's Alfoxden Notebook: 1798," in *The Evidence of the
    Imagination: Studies of Interactions between Life and Art in English Romantic
    Literature,* ed. Donald H. Reiman, Michael C. Jaye, and Betty T. Bennett
    (New York, 1978), 76–77 n.17.
13 The idea probably first took shape as a scheme of education. In a letter
    to Thomas Poole, dated 5 May 1796, Coleridge proposed a course of
    study divided under the following major headings: "Man as Animal";
    "Man as an Intellectual Being"; and "Man as a Religious Being." This
    synchronic perspective was to have served as the foundation of a seven-
    stage conjectural history of the human race, similar to Knight's, which
    would be patterned on the growth "of the mind." To the four-stage the-
    ory of human progress popularized by the Enlightenment—"Savage,"
    semi-barbarous (or pastoral), agricultural, and "civilized" (here meaning
    "civil")—Coleridge added three others that had also become popular:
    luxury, revolution, and colonial expansion (*STCL* 1:209). In early April
    1797, Coleridge announced that he was planning "a book of Morals in
    answer to Godwin" (*STCL* 1:320), and in December, only months before
    Wordsworth announced *The Recluse,* he returned to the educational pro-
    ject, encouraged that with Thomas Wedgwood's (and, perhaps, Words-
    worth's) help it would be realized (*STCL* 1:361). For a detailed account
    of Wedgwood's scheme, see David V. Erdman, "Coleridge, Wordsworth,
    and the Wedgwood Fund," *Bulletin of the New York Public Library* 60
    (1956):425–43, 487–507.
14 See "The Politics of 'Tintern Abbey,'" *Wordsworth Circle* 14 (1983):10–12,
    and Johnston's "Philanthropy or Treason? Wordsworth as 'Active Parti-
    san,'" *Studies in Romanticism* 25 (1986):371–409. Johnston also discusses
    the similarities between *The Recluse* and John Thelwall's *The Peripatetic;
    or, Sketches of the Heart, of Nature and Society* (*Wordsworth and "The Recluse"*
    11–14).
15 *Wordsworth's Second Nature: A Study of the Poetry and Politics* (Chicago, 1984),
    esp. pp. 216–34.
16 *Wordsworth and the Great System: A Study of Wordsworth's Poetic Universe* (Cam-
    bridge, 1970), 3. For further studies of Wordsworth and natural science,
    see Emile Legouis, *The Early Life of William Wordsworth, 1770–1798: A
    Study of "The Prelude."* tr. J. W. Matthews (1897; rpt. New York, 1965),
    397–418; M. H. Abrams, *The Mirror and the Lamp: Romantic Theory and
    the Critical Tradition* (1953; rpt. London, 1977), 298–312; Lee M. Johnson,

Wordsworth's Metaphysical Verse: Geometry, Nature and Form (Toronto, 1982); James H. Averill, "Wordsworth and 'Natural Science': The Poetry of 1798," *Journal of English and Germanic Philology* 77 (1978):232–46; Hans Eichner, "The Rise of Modern Science and the Genesis of Romanticism," *Publications of the Modern Language Association* 97 (1982):8–30; Charles L. Pittman, "An Introduction to a Study of Wordsworth's Reading in Science," *Furman Studies* 33 (1959):27–60; and William Powell Jones, *The Rhetoric of Science: A Study of Scientific Ideas and Imagery in Eighteenth-Century English Poetry* (Berkeley, Calif., 1966), 213–28.

17 *EY* 454; *Henry Crabb Robinson on Books and Their Writers*, ed. Edith J. Morley, 3 vols. (London, 1938), 1:10; Francis Murray Todd, *Politics and the Poet: A Study of Wordsworth* (London, 1957), 11; *ProseW* 1:126.

18 *Man and Society: The Scottish Inquiry of the Eighteenth Century* (1945; rpt. New York, 1968), 4.

19 *A Treatise of Human Nature*, ed. L. A. Selby-Bigge, 2d ed. (Oxford, 1978), xv.

20 Ian Simpson Ross, *Lord Kames and the Scotland of His Day* (Oxford, 1972), 345.

21 Coleridge described *The Recluse* in similar terms, on 21 July 1832, as a poem that would move from treating "man as man,—a subject of eye, ear, touch, and taste, in contact with external nature, and informing the senses from the mind, and not compounding a mind out of the senses." After surveying "the pastoral and other states of society," it was to have presented "a melancholy picture of the present state of degeneracy and vice," which would serve as proof of the "necessity for, the whole state of man and society being subject to, and illustrative of, a redemptive process" (*Specimens of the Table Talk of the Late Samuel Taylor Coleridge*, ed. H. N. Coleridge, 2 vols. in 1 [New York, 1835], 2:37–38).

22 *Institutes of Moral Philosophy: For the Use of Students in the College of Edinburgh*, 2d ed. (Edinburgh, 1773), 11.

23 For critical studies of early anthropology, see Margaret Hodgen, *Early Anthropology in the Sixteenth and Seventeenth Centuries* (Philadelphia, 1964); George W. Stocking, Jr., "French Anthropology in 1800," in *Race, Culture, and Evolution: Essays in the History of Anthropology* (New York, 1968), 13–41, and *Victorian Anthropology* (New York, 1987), 8–45; Michèle Duchet, *Anthropologie et histoire au siècle des lumières: Buffon, Voltaire, Rousseau, Helvétius, Diderot* (Paris, 1971); F. C. T. Moore's introduction to Joseph-Marie Degérando, *The Observation of Savage Peoples* (Berkeley, Calif., 1969), 1–58; and Paolo Rossi, *The Dark Abyss of Time: The History of the Earth and the History of Nations from Hooke to Vico*, tr. Lydia G. Cochrane (Chicago, 1984), 123–270. For a good selection of early anthropological excerpts, see J. S. Slotkin, ed., *Readings in Early Anthropology* (London, 1965).

24 *The First and Second Discourses*, ed. Roger D. Masters, tr. Roger D. Masters and Judith R. Masters (New York, 1964), 101.

25 It should be stressed that not only was there disagreement about what constituted human nature and the history of the mind, but there was also controversy about whether the structure of the human body and organs had not also undergone a lengthy process of evolution over time. At the beginning of the *Origin of Inequality* Rousseau hints at these possibilities, even as he declines to take them up: "I shall not examine whether, as Aristotle thinks, man's elongated nails were not at first hooked claws; whether he was not hairy like a bear; and whether, if he walked on all fours, his gaze, directed toward the earth and confined to a horizon of several paces, did not indicate both the character and the limits of his ideas" (*Discourses* 104–05).

26 In *An Enquiry Concerning Human Understanding,* Hume develops this idea further: "Records of wars, intrigues, factions, and revolutions are so many *collections of experiments,* by which the politician or moral philosopher fixes the principles of his science, in the same manner as the physician or natural philosopher becomes acquainted with the nature of plants, minerals, and other external objects, by the experiments which he forms concerning them" (*The Philosophical Works of David Hume,* ed. Thomas Hill Green and Thomas Hodge Grose, 4 vols. [1882; rpt. Darmstadt, 1964], 4:64, my emphasis).

27 Rousseau makes the same point when he declares that "to study men, you must regard those around you, but to study man, you must extend your vision, first observing differences in order to discover properties" (*Essai sur l'origine des langues* [Paris, 1970], 516). For the influence of the Royal Society and experimental science upon travel literature, see R. W. Frantz, *The English Traveller and the Movement of Ideas, 1660–1732* (1934; rpt. Lincoln, Neb., 1967).

28 *The History of America,* 2 vols. (London, 1777), 1:268.

29 "A Philosophical Review of the Successive Advances of the Human Mind," in *Turgot on Progress, Sociology and Economics,* ed. and tr. Ronald L. Meek (Cambridge, 1973), 42.

30 *Customs of the American Indians Compared with the Customs of Primitive Times,* ed. and tr. William N. Fenton and Elizabeth L. Moore, 2 vols. (Toronto, 1974), 1:27. Frank E. Manuel examines the notion of "conformities" in *The Eighteenth Century Confronts the Gods* (Cambridge, Mass., 1959), 15–20.

31 As late as 1785, Anders Sparrman, could write (oddly, with slight reservations) that "men with one foot, indeed, Cyclops, Syrens, Troglodytes, and such like imaginary beings, have almost entirely disappeared in this enlightened age" (*A Voyage to the Cape of Good Hope,* ed. V. S. Forbes, tr. J. Rudner and I. Rudner, 2 vols. (Cape Town, 1975–77), 1:35.

32 Cited by Hans Aarsleff, *The Study of Language in England, 1780–1860* (Princeton, 1967), 34, my translation. For my discussion of eighteenth-century language theory I am greatly indebted to this work and to the

same author's *From Locke to Saussure: Essays on the Study of Language and Intellectual History* (Minneapolis, 1982).

33   "Réflexions sur les langues," *Oeuvres de Turgot,* ed. M. Eugène Daire, 2 vols. (Paris, 1844), 2:753. Vico also makes etymology a central part of his New Science: "Etymologies . . . tell us the histories of the institutions signified by the words, beginning with their original and proper meanings and pursuing the natural progress of their metaphors according to the order of ideas, on which the history of languages must proceed" (*The New Science of Giambattista Vico,* 3d ed., tr. Thomas Goddard Bergin and Max Harold Fisch [Ithaca, N.Y., 1968], 105–06).

34   *Making Tales: The Poetics of Wordsworth's Narrative Experiments* (Chicago, 1984), 19.

35   *Oeuvres complètes de Diderot,* ed. J. Assézat, 20 vols. (Paris, 1875–77), 1:351–54.

36   *Oeuvres de M. de Maupertuis,* 4 vols. (Lyon, 1756), 2:394–98. As Aarsleff has noted (*From Locke to Saussure* 191–92), this idea was subsequently taken up by Samuel Formey, the Berlin Academy's secretary, in "Réunion des principaux moyens employés pour découvrir l'origine du langage des idées et des connoissances des hommes," *Historie de l'Academie Royale des sciences et belles-lettres* (Berlin, 1759), 15:367–77. There Formey proposes that a dozen children of the same age be raised without ever having the opportunity to hear language spoken, to observe what effect this might have upon their children. This project was among those taken up by the first anthropological society, the Société des Observateurs de l'Homme, founded in 1799. Louis François Jauffret, in his introduction to a proposed, but never published, volume of the society's proceedings, suggested an experiment, possible only in "a century as enlightened as ours," in which infants would be "placed from their birth in a single enclosure, remote from all social institutions, and abandoned for the development of ideas and language solely to the instinct of nature" (cited in George W. Stocking, *Race, Culture, and Evolution* 16–17). This kind of experiment has a long history and can be traced back as far as Herodotus, who speaks of a similar experiment that was used to determine which nation, Phrygian or Egyptian, was the oldest on earth (*Herodotus,* tr. A. D. Godley, 4 vols. [London, 1931], 1:275–77).

37   For an insightful discussion of the political uses of the tabula rasa metaphor in seventeenth-century utopian texts, see James Ross Holstun, *A Rational Millenium: Puritan Utopias of Seventeenth-Century England and America* (Oxford, 1987), 34–39, 110–15.

38   This awkward sentence is puzzling because it says so much in order to mean so little. If, however, instead of asking what these words *mean,* we ask what they *do,* it is clear that their primary purpose is to insert a "blind man" into the poem. This empirical figure can thus be read as a textual marker indicating the poem's shift, at this critical juncture, toward philosophical statement.

39 *Lettre sur les aveugles,* ed. Robert Niklaus (Geneva, 1951), 32, 11.

40 Coleridge considered Wordsworth's descriptions of marginal individuals as being too close to those used by moral philosophers: "The object in view, as an *immediate* object, belongs to the moral philosopher, and would be pursued, not only more appropriately, but in my opinion with far greater probability of success, in sermons or moral essays, than in an elevated poem" (*BL* 2:130).

41 For a study of Wordsworth's reading in travel narratives, see Charles N. Coe, *Wordsworth and the Literature of Travel* (New York, 1953).

42 "On Ethnographic Authority," *Representations* 1 (1983):123.

43 *The Complete Works of William Hazlitt,* ed. P. P. Howe, 21 vols. (London, 1930–34), 19:11.

44 See especially M. H. Abrams, "Structure and Style in the Greater Romantic Lyric," in *From Sensibility to Romanticism: Essays Presented to Frederick A. Pottle,* ed. Frederick W. Hilles and Harold Bloom (New York, 1965), 533–39; and Marjorie Levinson, *Wordsworth's Great Period Poems: Four Essays* (Cambridge, 1986), 16–18.

45 *The Re-Creation of Landscape: A Study of Wordsworth, Coleridge, Constable, and Turner* (Hanover, N.H., 1984), 58.

46 This figure need not be a holy hermit, but could equally be a wild hermit—an individual reduced, through isolation, to a state of nature. Herder, for example, addressing the question of the origin of language, first cites orangutans and mutes, then argues that "the savage, the hermit living alone in the forest, would have had to invent language for himself, even though he had never spoken it" (*Essay on the Origin of Language,* in *On the Origin of Language,* tr. John H. Moran and Alexander Gode [New York, 1966], 119).

47 See Marjorie Levinson, *Wordsworth's Great Period Poems* 14–57; Jerome J. McGann, *The Romantic Ideology: A Critical Investigation* (Chicago, 1983), 85–88; and Kenneth R. Johnston, "The Politics of 'Tintern Abbey.'"

48 *Two Treatises of Government,* ed. Peter Laslett, rev. ed. (1963; rpt. New York, 1965), 343.

49 *Rights of Man,* ed. Eric Foner (Harmondsworth, Middlesex, 1984), 185.

50 "Eliot, Wordsworth, and the Scenes of the Sister's Instruction," in *Writing and Sexual Difference,* ed. Elizabeth Abel (Chicago, 1982), 53.

51 Cited in Edna Aston Shearer, "Wordsworth and Coleridge Marginalia in a Copy of Richard Payne Knight's *Analytical Inquiry into the Principles of Taste,*" *Huntington Library Quarterly* 1 (1937):73.

52 *The Interpretation of Cultures: Selected Essays* (New York, 1973), 14.

53 *Lectures on the Sacred Poetry of the Hebrews,* tr. G. Gregory, 2 vols. (1787; rpt. New York, 1971), 1:113–14.

54 *The Origin and Progress of Despotism in the Oriental, and other Empires, of Africa, Europe, and America* (Amsterdam [London?], 1764), 25–26.

Chapter 1: Retrospective Tales of
Idiots, Wild Children, and Savages

1   John O. Hayden, "William Wordsworth's Letter to John Wilson (1802): A Corrected Version," *Wordsworth Circle* 18 (1987):38.

2   The narrative was published in the *Bath and Bristol Magazine; or, Western Miscellany* 2 (1833):168–79. Though Poole (aged sixty-eight) indicated that the account was drawn up in March 1797, his memory was clearly at fault on either the month or the year. Previous scholars, believing that "The Somersetshire Tragedy" was written in 1797 rather than, as is now known, sometime between March and 9 May 1798 (as a replacement for the Female Vagrant passage of *Adventures upon Salisbury Plain*), assumed that "John Walford" was written early in April 1797. For a good account of the circumstances surrounding its composition, see William L. Nichols, *The Quantocks and Their Associations*, 2d ed. (London, 1891).

3   Jonathan Wordsworth's "A Wordsworth Tragedy," *Times Literary Supplement* 65 (21 July 1966):642, deserves special attention for its close textual analysis and sensitive presentation of parallels between "John Walford" and "The Ruined Cottage." It includes the extant lines of "The Somersetshire Tragedy" and is the source of my citations. The passages he chooses to establish parallels (significantly, those relating to "silent suffering") were, however, written in the Alfoxden Notebook, probably in March 1798.

4   For a discussion of Wordsworth's use of clothing as an animal covering in "Alice Fell," see David Simpson, *Wordsworth's Historical Imagination: The Poetry of Displacement* (New York, 1987), 180–81.

5   Lines 463–64. Unless otherwise noted, all references to *Peter Bell* are to John E. Jordan's reconstruction of MSS. 2 and 3, in the Cornell Wordsworth series.

6   Hayden, "William Wordsworth's Letter to John Wilson (1802)" 37. See also *EY* 356–57.

7   Wordsworth's parody of Bürger's supernatural balladry, especially of "Lenore," has been fruitfully discussed by Mary Jacobus, *Tradition and Experiment in Wordsworth's "Lyrical Ballads," 1798* (Oxford, 1976), 217–24; Stephen Maxfield Parrish, *The Art of the "Lyrical Ballads"* (Cambridge, Mass., 1973), 86–93; and Geoffrey Hartman, "False Themes and Gentle Minds," in *Beyond Formalism: Literary Essays, 1958–1970* (New Haven, 1970), 290–97. For an illustration of the sentimental representation of idiots, see B. R. McElderry, Jr., "Southey, and Wordsworth's 'The Idiot Boy,'" *N&Q*, n.s. 2 (1955):490–91. McElderry discusses Southey's "Idiot," published in the *Morning Post* on 30 June 1798. The idiot Ned's inability to distinguish between life and death embroils him in a lurid, necrophilic ritual. As in "The Idiot Boy," it is the love of the mother for her son that makes up for his mute helplessness. But this love is easily perverted. When Old Sara dies,

"poor Ned" is unable to understand her death and the funeral. Therefore, after the villagers leave the graveyard (throughout no one seems too concerned about what is now to happen to Ned), he exhumes his mother's coffin and hastens home with it:

> And when he reach'd his hut, he laid
>   The coffin on the floor,
> And with the eagerness of joy,
>   He barr'd the cottage door.
>
> And out he took his mother's corpse,
>   And plac'd it in her chair,
> And then he heapt the hearth, and blew
>   The kindling fire with care.
>
> He plac'd his mother in her chair,
>   And in her wonted place,
> And blew the kindling fire, that shone
>   Reflected on her face:
>
> And pausing now, her hand would feel,
>   And now her face behold,
> "Why, mother, do you look so pale,
>   And why are you so cold?"

After this exhibition of artificial sentimental identification, whose lack of realism thinly covers the turbulent anxiety of broken taboos relating to incest and the dead, the poet wants nothing better than to rid himself of "poor Ned." He quickly appends the expected ending, one that the period reserved for both criminals and idiots, the providential sudden death:

> It had pleas'd God from the poor wretch
>   His only friend to call,
> But God was kind to him, and soon
>   In death restor'd him all.

A notebook entry from 1796–97 suggests that Coleridge also intended to write a poem on an idiot "whose whole amusement consisted in looking at, & talking to a clock, which he supposed to be alive—/the Clock was removed—/he supposed that it had walked off—& he went away to seek it—was absent nine days—at last, they found, almost famish'd in a field—He asked where it was buried—for he was sure it was dead—/he was brought home & the clock it in its place—his Joy—&c He used to put part of every thing, he liked, into the clock-case" (*STCNB* 1, *Text*, entry 212). Coleridge was still planning this poem in September 1802 (*STCNB* 1, *Text*, entry 1,242).

8 For a similar argument concerning madness, see Michel Foucault, *Folie*

et déraison: Histoire de la folie à l'âge classique (Paris, 1961); abridged English translation: Madness and Civilization. A History of Insanity in the Age of Reason, tr. Richard Howard (New York, 1965).

9   An Essay Concerning Human Understanding, ed. Peter H. Nidditch (Oxford, 1975), 2:160–61. For similar distinctions, see Condillac, An Essay on the Origin of Human Knowledge; Being a Supplement to Mr. Locke's "Essay on the Human Understanding," tr. Thomas Nugent (1756; rpt. Gainesville, Fla., 1971), 49–50; and David Hartley, Observations on Man, His Frame, His Duty, and His Expectations, 2 vols. (London, 1749), 1:391–92.

10   Condillac's Treatise on the Sensations, tr. Geraldine Carr (Los Angeles, 1930), xxix.

11   "Account of the Life and Writings of Adam Smith, LL.D.," in Adam Smith, Essays on Philosophical Subjects, ed. W. P. D. Wightman and J. C. Bryce (Oxford, 1980), 292–93.

12   Essay on the History of Civil Society, 3d ed. (Edinburgh, 1768), 7–9.

13   Lectures Concerning History, Read During the Year 1775, in Trinity College, Dublin (London, 1776), 10–11.

14   Antient Metaphysics: or, The Science of Universals (Edinburgh, 1779–99), 3:57.

15   Freudian psychoanalysis represents the culmination of the tendency, clear in Wordsworth's Prelude, to relocate anthropological history within the self. Not surprisingly, Freud, in the History of an Infantile Neurosis (The Standard Edition of the Complete Psychological Works of Sigmund Freud, tr. James Strachey, 24 vols. [London, 1953–73], vol. 17), found empirical support for his description of a "primal scene" by drawing on the memories of a "Wolf-Man," a twentieth-century version of a wild child. He was further tempted to believe that the scene acted out before the boy's eyes—his parents engaged in sexual intercourse more ferarum—dated back to the dawn of history.

16   Mere Nature Delineated: or, a Body without a Soul (London, 1726), 4. For a good account of Peter of Hanover, see Maximillian E. Novak, "The Wild Man Comes to Tea," in The Wild Man Within: An Image in Western Thought from the Renaissance to Romanticism, ed. Edward Dudley and Novak (Pittsburgh, 1972), 183–221.

17   "Ruth" is another "wild-child" poem influenced by the "John Walford" narrative; Wordsworth remarked that it was "suggested by an account I had [not heard] of a wanderer in Somersetshire" (PW 2:509). The poem apparently alludes to the story of Peter of Hanover, as the narrator explains that Ruth was a "slighted child" who went "wandering over dale and hill, / In thoughtless freedom, bold," when her father "took another Mate." Ironically, the Georgian youth she marries received the "wild men's vices" not from nature, but from others.

18   "'The Idiot Boy': Wordsworth Serves out His Poetic Indentures," Critical Quarterly 22 (1980):10.

19   DC MS. 14, 20ᵛ.
20   For a feminist interpretation of the importance of language as contact
     between mothers and children, see Margaret Homans, "Feminist Criti-
     cism and Theory: The Ghost of Creusa," *Yale Journal of Criticism* 1
     (1987):159, 169–72.
21   It is interesting to note that more than a decade after the publication of
     Lyrical Ballads, Coleridge read *An Historical Account of the Discovery and
     Education of a Savage Man* (London, 1802), a translation of Itard's famous
     account of how he educated Victor of Aveyron, a wild child discovered
     in the summer of 1798. (The story was the subject of the film by François
     Truffaut entitled *L'Enfant sauvage.*) Coleridge immediately recognized
     that the case would be "a fine subject to be introduced in William's great
     poem," noting Victor's "restless joy & blind conjunction of his Being with
     natural Scenery; and the manifest influence of Mountain, Rocks, Water-
     falls, Torrents, & Thunderstorms—Moonlight Beams quivering on
     Water, &c on his whole frame—as instanced in his Behaviour in the Vale
     of Monmorency—his eager desires to escape, &c. How deserving this
     whole account of a profound psychological examination / & comparison
     with wild animals in confinement/" (*STCNB* 3, *Text,* entry 3,538). There
     is no indication that Wordsworth knew the story of Victor of Aveyron.
     For a highly sentimentalized contemporary poem on the subject, see "The
     Savage of Aveyron," in *Poetical Works of the Late Mrs. Mary Robinson* (Lon-
     don, 1806).

Chapter 2: First Encounters of the Primitive Kind

1   For a detailed phenomenological discussion of the importance of en-
    counters in Wordsworth's poetry, see Frederick Garber, *Wordsworth and
    the Poetry of Encounter* (Urbana, Ill., 1971).
2   *Du Culte des dieux fétiches: ou, Parallèle de l'ancienne religion de l'Egypte avec
    la religion actuelle de Nigritie* (Paris, 1760), 192–93.
3   "A Defence of Poetry," *Shelley's Poetry and Prose,* ed. Donald H. Reiman
    and Sharon B. Powers (New York, 1977), 481.
4   Bernard Mandeville, *The Fable of the Bees: or, Private Vices, Publick Benefits,*
    ed. F. B. Kaye (1924; rpt. Oxford, 1957), 2:284.
5   For Mandeville's account of the origin of speech, see *Fable of the Bees*
    2:284–94. See also F. B. Kaye, "Mandeville on the Origin of Language,"
    Modern Language Notes 39 (1924):136–42.
6   As is well known, Condillac's *Essay* gave rise, during the latter half of the
    century in France and Germany, to a prolonged discussion of the recip-
    rocal influence of language and thought that reached its peak during the
    1790s with the work of the French Ideologues. For treatments of the
    important influence of Condillac and the Ideologues on Wordsworth's
    ideas about language, see Aarsleff, "Wordsworth, Language, and Ro-

manticism," in *From Locke to Saussure*, 372–81; and Chandler, *Wordsworth's Second Nature*, 216–34.

7 *Oeuvres philosophiques de Condillac*, ed. Georges Le Roy, 3 vols. (Paris, 1947), 1:403b.

8 *The Theory of Moral Sentiments*, ed. D. D. Raphael and A. L. Macfie (Oxford, 1976), 110.

9 Though explicit references to Rousseau are rare in Wordsworth's poetry, the influence has been generally recognized. In addition to those works that Wordsworth would have known, given his fluency in French and interest in the philosophes—for instance, *Emile*, the *Second Discourse*, the *Social Contract*, the *Confessions*, and *Nouvelle Héloïse*—it is also likely that he was familiar with the *Essay on the Origin of Languages*, published in 1781. For a recent examination of Wordsworth's response to Rousseau, see Chandler, *Wordsworth's Second Nature*, esp. pp. 93–119.

10 Shelley makes a similar claim: "Neither the eye nor the mind can see itself, unless reflected upon that which it resembles" ("A Defence of Poetry," 491).

11 Paul de Man reads this passage as a "mock-argument" directed against philosophers who use metalepsis to explain the origin of language, by substituting effects for causes or using categories that are themselves dependent upon the causes they would seek to explain (*Allegories of Reading: Figural Language in Rousseau, Nietzsche, Rilke, and Proust* [New Haven, 1979], 142).

12 In the *Book of Urizen*, Blake also argues that the flood that destroyed the Giants, "of seven feet stature," was not a geological event, but instead a figure for mankind's "narrowing perceptions" (*The Poetry and Prose of William Blake*, ed. David V. Erdman [New York, 1965], pl. 27.38, 47).

13 The close relationship, during the romantic period, between social theory and anthropology made the primitive encounter adaptable to political purposes, as is clear in Blake's revolutionary use of the figure in the Preludium to *America*. In a poem that condenses, as David V. Erdman has observed, "the whole history of man" into a myth "to describe the tremendous change marked by the emergence of the revolutionary spirit," Blake has recourse to the primitive encounter not to describe the origin of language or sympathy in general terms, but to depict the genesis of revolutionary language (*Blake, Prophet Against Empire: A Poet's Interpretation of the History of His Own Times*, rev. ed. [Princeton, 1969], 258). In the violent encounter between the gigantic, nameless, "shadowy daughter of Urthona" and the "hairy youth" Orc, we are shown how a "language of action" engenders the possibility of speech. "Silent she stood as night," Blake writes. "For never from her iron tongue could voice or sound arise; / But dumb till that dread day when Orc assay'd his fierce embrace." Passion melts the woman's "iron tongue," she smiles "her first-born smile," and "then burst the virgin cry," which brings the Preludium

to its conclusion in direct, though ambiguous, speech: "'I know thee, I have found thee, & I will not let thee go; / Thou art the image of God who dwells in darkness of Africa.'"

14 See "Two Early Texts: *A Night-Piece* and *The Discharged Soldier*," in *BWS* 433–37.

15 Herder is typical when he remarks that "almost throughout the whole World, we meet with the most ancient remains of nations and languages, either on mountains, or in the nooks and corners of the land" (*Outlines of a Philosophy of the History of Man*, tr. T. Churchill [1800; rpt. New York, 1966], 17).

16 In the 1850 version, the similarity between the landscape and the early postdiluvian world is more pronounced. "No living thing appeared in earth or air" (4.384), writes Wordsworth, as if this were a nature as yet unpopulated by the animal creation. In *Descriptive Sketches*, the primeval peaks of the Alps are represented as "vacant worlds where Nature never gave / A brook to murmur or a bough to wave . . . Where Silence still her death-like reign extends" (lines 372–76).

17 *Paradise Lost*, in *Complete Poems and Major Prose*, ed. Merritt Y. Hughes (Indianapolis, 1957), 4.172.

18 *The Reveries of the Solitary Walker*, tr. Charles E. Butterworth (New York, 1979), 69.

19 Given the eighteenth-century geological interest in the fossilized remains of what were taken to be giants, it is perhaps not surprising that Wordsworth would associate this giant with a fossil. However, the metaphoric identification of "shade" and "giant," fused in this "tall / And ghostly figure" (124–25), also derives from the etymological connection, emphasized by biblical commentators from Gesenius onward, between the Rephaim, a tribe of Old Testament giants, and the weak, powerless shades of Sheol, both words deriving, it was believed, from a Hebrew verb meaning "to fall asleep," or "to sink down." A further association was made between the Rephaim and the giants destroyed by the Flood. "The place of the damned," as Hobbes notes in *Leviathan*, was "sometimes marked out, by the company of those deceased giants" (*The English Works of Thomas Hobbes*, ed. Sir William Molesworth [1839–45; rpt. Aalen, Germany, 1966], 3:446). Citing Job 26:5 ("Behold the giants [Rephaim] groan under water, and they that dwell with them"), Hobbes argues that "the place of the damned is under the water" (446). In book 8 of *The Prelude*, Wordsworth returned to the figure of the giant in describing how, as a child, "companionless among" the Lake District's highest crags and "solitudes" (8.358), he encountered a shepherd that seemed "in size a giant, stalking through the fog, / His sheep like Greenland bears" (8.401–02).

20 *Wordsworth and the Worth of Words*, ed. John Kerrigan and Jonathan Wordsworth (Cambridge, 1986), 148–49.

21 *The Divine Comedy of Dante Alighieri,* tr. Allen Mandelbaum (Berkeley, Calif., 1982), 1.60–80.

22 Though we do not know which poem was composed first, Coleridge's "Frost at Midnight" also describes a superstitious encounter between the poet and a "stranger." Echoes are numerous: for instance, the "fearful steadiness" of the soldier's form is like Coleridge's description of "the thin blue flame" that "lies on my low-burnt fire, and quivers not."

23 It is worth noting that when this ghastly figure first made his appearance in Wordsworth's poetry, in the *Vale of Esthwaite,* his function as a Virgilian underworld guide was explicit:

> He wav'd again, we entered slow
> A passage narrow damp and low,
> I heard the mountain heave a sigh
> Nodding its rocky helm on high,
> And on we journey'd many a mile
> While all was black as night the while,
> Save his tall form before our sight
> Seen by the wan pale dismal light.   [340–47]

Interestingly, Wordsworth makes this figure an ancient bard: "on one branded arm he bore / What seem'd the poet's harp of yore" (334–35).

24 Wordsworth is here recalling an event that his sister Dorothy described in her *Journal,* dated 27 January 1798: "The manufacturer's dog makes a strange, uncouth howl, which it continues many minutes after there is no noise near it but that of the brook. It howls at the murmur of the village stream" (*DWJ* 1:5). C. F. Stone III has suggested that "this observation . . . could have been the origin of the entire piece" ("Narrative Variation in Wordsworth's Versions of 'The Discharged Soldier,'" *Journal of Narrative Technique* 4 [1974]:37). Strikingly, Wordsworth does not use the words *strange* and *uncouth* to describe the dog's howling, but instead transfers them to the soldier's "uncouth shape" (38) and his "strange half-absence" (143) of speech. The dog also appears to have howled at the murmuring sounds of the soldier.

25 The poem is filled with sounds that seem on the threshold of becoming language. Equally strikingly, these sounds have few sources and seem fashioned out of the same registers, as if nature, reduced to its simplest elements, were capable of producing only variations on a few sounds. The murmuring of the stream, the groans of the soldier, which seem to David B. Pirie a "grotesque parody of communication," and the unceasing howling of the dog merge into one another, almost as if they were variations on a common language of nature (*William Wordsworth: The Poetry of Grandeur and of Tenderness* [London, 1982], 189).

26 "The Use and Abuse of Structural Analysis: Riffaterre's Interpretation of Wordsworth's 'Yew-Trees,'" *New Literary History* 7 (1975):169.

27 Jonathan Wordsworth has suggested that the words "solemn and sub-

lime" (141) allude to the description of Michael in *Paradise Lost* 11.236
(*William Wordsworth: The Borders of Vision* [Oxford, 1982], 15).

28   There has been relatively little criticism of *Peter Bell*. The work of two
     critics stands out: Mary Jacobus, "*Peter Bell* the First," *Essays in Criticism*
     24 (1974):219–42, and *Tradition and Experiment in Wordsworth's "Lyrical
     Ballads," 1798* 262–72; and John E. Jordan, "Wordsworth's Humor," *Pub-
     lications of the Modern Language Association* 73 (1958):81–93; "The Hewing
     of *Peter Bell*," *Studies in English Literature* 7 (1967):561–603; and his edi-
     tion of the Cornell Wordsworth *Peter Bell*. Other useful criticism is pro-
     vided by Geoffrey Durrant, "Wordsworth's 'Peter Bell'—A *Pons Asinorum*
     for Critics," *Wascana Review* 1 (1966):26–42; Frederick Garber, "Words-
     worth's Comedy of Redemption," *Anglia* 84 (1966):388–97; and Melvin
     R. Watson, "The Redemption of Peter Bell," *Studies in English Literature*
     4 (1964):519–30. The relevant nineteenth-century parodies and bur-
     lesques of *Peter Bell* are usefully collected in A. E. H. Swaen, "Peter Bell,"
     Anglia 47 (1923):136–84.

29   See Stephen Maxfield Parrish, *The Art of the "Lyrical Ballads"*; John F.
     Danby, *The Simple Wordsworth: Studies in the Poems, 1797–1807* (London,
     1960); Andrew L. Griffin, "Wordsworth and the Problem of Imaginative
     Story: The Case of 'Simon Lee,'" *Publications of the Modern Language As-
     sociation* 92 (1977):392–409; and Don H. Bialostosky, *Making Tales*.

30   The Squire's cry, "'Hold! . . . against the rules / Of common sense you're
     surely sinning," adopted in 1836, probably refers to the Scottish School
     of philosophy, which became identified with Thomas Reid's *Inquiry into
     the Human Mind on the Principles of Common Sense* (1764).

31   For a fuller examination of the relationship between *Peter Bell* and "John
     Walford," see my article "Wordsworth's Primal Scene: Retrospective
     Tales of Idiots, Wild Children, and Savages," *ELH* 50 (1983):335–42.

32   *Principles of Moral and Political Science*, 2 vols. (1792; rpt. New York, 1978),
     1:27.

33   *Oeuvres philosophiques*, ed. Jean Piveteau (Paris, 1954), 194b. Buffon con-
     cluded that "the training of the dog seems to have been the first art
     invented by man; and the result of this art was the conquest and peaceful
     possession of the earth" ("The Dog," in *Natural History, General and Par-
     ticular, by the Count de Buffon*, tr. William Smellie, 20 vols. [London, 1812],
     4:340–41). The domestic character of the ass needs no argument.

34   *Lectures on Rhetoric and Belles Lettres*, 2d ed. (London, 1785), 1:37.

35   In "To Joanna" the poet, toying with the possibility that he has been a
     witness to "a work accomplished by the brotherhood / Of ancient moun-
     tains" (69–70), tells how a woman named Joanna—like Peter Bell, "slow
     to meet the sympathies of them / Who look upon the hills with tender-
     ness" (6–7)—is taught sympathy through her fear of the uproar of echoes
     created by her laughter. Since echoes engender language, it is not clear
     whether Wordsworth's "naming of the place," his chiseling out Joanna's

name, "like a Runic priest, in characters / Of formidable size" (28–29), is meant to commemorate the experience or show its culmination in writing.

36 "Adam Smith and the Theatricality of Moral Sentiments," *Critical Inquiry* 10 (1984):603.

Chapter 3: The "Wonders of a Wild Career"

1 *The Examiner* (2 May 1819):282–83. Reprinted in *The Romantics Reviewed: Contemporary Reviews of British Romantic Writers,* ed. Donald H. Reiman (New York, 1972), part A, vol. 2:538–39.

2 *Eclectic Review,* 2d ser. 12 (July 1819):66. Reprinted in *Romantics Reviewed,* part A, vol. 1:388.

3 In *Methodism Mocked: The Satiric Reaction to Methodism in the Eighteenth Century* (London, 1960), Albert M. Lyles discusses eighteenth-century antimethodist satires and devotes a chapter to attacks on methodist preachers.

4 David Hempton, *Methodism and Politics in British Society, 1750–1850* (London, 1984), 55.

5 *The Life of Wesley; and the Rise and Progress of Methodism,* 2 vols. (New York, 1820), 1:208. Writes Elie Halévy, "In the semibarbaric provinces, which no one had thought of either civilizing or Christianizing since the Reformation, in the industrial regions in which an ever-denser population, lacking schools and churches, was crowding, thousands were 'converted' by their [preachers'] sermons" (*The Birth of Methodism in England,* tr. and ed. Bernard Semmel [Chicago, 1971], 37).

6 Robert W. Malcolmson, " 'A Set of Ungovernable People': The Kingswood Colliers in the Eighteenth Century," in *An Ungovernable People: The English and their Law in the Seventeenth and Eighteenth Centuries,* ed. John Brewer and John Styles (New Brunswick, N.J., 1980), 126.

7 An anonymous reviewer, perhaps Robert Southey, even went so far as to claim that Methodists constituted a distinct race. "They form a distinct people in the empire," he writes, "having their peculiar laws and manners, a hierarchy, a costume, and even a physiognomy of their own . . . The very character of the English face is altered; for Methodism transforms the countenance as certainly, and almost as speedily, as sottishness or opium. Go to their meeting-houses, or turn over the portraits in their magazines, and it will be seen that they have already obtained as distinct a physiognomy as the Jews or the Gipsies—coarse, hard, and dismal visages, as if some spirit of darkness had got into them and was looking out of them" (review of *Hints to the Public and the Legislature, on the Nature and Effect of Evangelical Preaching,* in *The Quarterly Review* 14, no. 8 (Nov. 1810):480–503.

8 John Walsh observes that "in 1791 to the non-evangelical world the term

'Methodist' was still a blanket title which covered many varieties of 'Enthusiasm'" ("Methodism at the End of the Eighteenth Century," in *A History of the Methodist Church in Great Britain*, ed. Rupert Davies and Gordon Rupp, 2 vols. [London, 1965, 1978], 1:289). On the subject of enthusiasm during the seventeenth and eighteenth centuries, see R. A. Knox, *Enthusiasm: A Chapter in the History of Religion, with Special Reference to the Seventeenth and Eighteenth Centuries* (New York, 1950).

9   *Mystical Bedlam: Madness, Anxiety, and Healing in Seventeenth-Century England* (Cambridge, 1981), 225.

10 *God the Guardian of the Poor and the Bank of Faith* (London, n.d.), 31.

11 *An Attempt to Shew the Folly and Danger of Methodism* (London, 1809), 40.

12 *Life of Wesley* 2:241, 1:214. Heather J. Jackson has brought to my attention that Coleridge, in his marginalia to Southey's *Life of Wesley*, was in essential agreement. Noting the similarities between these bodily states and those recounted by Mesmer and his followers, Coleridge concluded that they were "an actual product of some strange state of the nervous system, utterly unimitable by volition" (*Life of Wesley*, ed. Charles Cuthbert Southey [London, 1846], 2:207–09). See also, in this edition, pp. 1:193; 1:204; 1:257–58; 2:211–12.

13 *The Journal of John Wesley*, ed. Ernest Rhys, 4 vols. (London, 1906), 2:416–17 [14 June 1758]. Wordsworth would probably have been familiar with the role that bibliomancy had played in Wesley's Aldersgate conversion. See *Journal* 1:101–02 (24 May 1738).

14 *Wesley's Veterans: Lives of Early Methodist Preachers Told by Themselves*, ed. Rev. John Telford (London, 1865), 4:12–13.

15 Joshua Marsden, *Sketches of the Early Life of a Sailor*, cited in E. P. Thompson, *The Making of the English Working Class* (1963; rpt. New York, 1966), 368. Mary Jacobus has indicated Wordsworth's interest in this kind of narrative, notably John Newton's *Authentic Narrative of Some Remarkable and Interesting Particulars in the Life of **** (London, 1764), which he might have read as early as 1797 ("*Peter Bell* the First" 226, 240).

16 *A History of England in the Eighteenth Century*, 7 vols. (London, 1892), 3:78. Modern historians have also contributed to the psychopathological interpretation of Methodism as "salvation by hysteria" (Robert Colls, *The Collier's Rant: Song and Culture in the Industrial Village* [London, 1977], 78). E. P. Thompson, who has been foremost among these, argues that Methodism "brought to a point of hysterical intensity the desire for *personal* salvation" (*The Making of the English Working Class* 386). James Obelkevich offers the alternative suggestion that "in a society lacking public forms of diversion, Wesleyan Methodism offered a respectable counterattraction to the beerhouse and village feast on the one hand and a more enjoyable alternative to the parish church on the other" (*Religion and Rural Society: South Lindsey, 1825–1875* [Oxford, 1976], 212). See also W. J. Dawson, who remarks that during his childhood "preachers were the

major stars. In the absence of other excitements, eloquence was the supreme delight" (*Autobiography of a Mind* [New York, 1925], 48).

17 Wordsworth's interest in this issue might have been stimulated by his coming upon Erasmus Darwin's discussion of how "theatric preachers among the Methodists" had produced severe cases of "orci timor," the fear of Hell (*Zoönomia; or, The Laws of Organic Life*, 2 vols. [London, 1794–96], 2:379).

18 For discussions of Methodism during the 1790s, see Hempton, *Methodism and Politics* 55–84; Robert W. Malcolmson, "'A Set of Ungovernable People'"; John Walsh, "Methodism at the End of the Eighteenth Century," and "Methodism and the Mob in the Eighteenth Century," in *Popular Belief and Practice* (Studies in Church History 8), ed. G. J. Cuming and Derek Baker (Cambridge, 1972), 213–17; Bernard Semmel, *The Methodist Revolution* (New York, 1973), 110–36; W. R. Ward, *Religion and Society in England, 1790–1850* (London, 1972), 21–53, and "The Religion of the People and the Problem of Control, 1790–1830"; P. Stigant, "Wesleyan Methodism and Working-Class Radicalism in the North, 1792–1821," *Northern History* 6 (1971):98–116; E. P. Thompson, *The Making of the English Working Class* 350–400; E. J. Hobsbawm, "Methodism and the Threat of Revolution in Britain," in *Labouring Men: Studies in the History of Labour* (New York, 1964), 23–33; and V. Kiernan, "Evangelicism and the French Revolution," *Past and Present* 1 (1952):44–56.

19 *Methodism Unmasked, or The Progress of Puritanism, from the Sixteenth to the Nineteenth Century* (London, 1802), v.

20 From Richard Polwhele, *A Letter to the Rev. Robert Hawker, D. D. Vicar of the Parish of Charles, Plymouth, Occasioned by his Late Expedition into Cornwall.* Cited in the *Gentleman's Magazine* 70 (March 1800):241.

21 Frank Whaling, introduction to *John and Charles Wesley: Selected Prayers, Hymns, Journal Notes, Sermons, Letters and Treatises* (New York, 1981), 57n.

22 Introduction to Elie Halévy, *The Birth of Methodism in England* 20. See also Semmel's *Methodist Revolution* 124–45.

23 *A Practical View of the Prevailing Religious System of Professed Christians, in the Higher and Middle Classes in this Country, Contrasted with Real Christianity* (1795; rpt. London, 1886), 325–27.

24 E. P. Thompson's *Making of the English Working Class* is still the best discussion of the emergence and impact of the idea of the "working class." In *The Dark Side of the Landscape: The Rural Poor in English Painting, 1730–1840* (Cambridge, 1980), John Barrell discusses how landscape painters of this period responded to this new conception of the laboring poor.

25 Wordsworth indicates the political orientation of the poem in the two lines that serve as the epigraph: "What's in a *Name?*" (which echoes Oswald's assertion, in *The Borderers*, "Murder—what's in a word!") and "Brutus will start a Spirit as soon as Caesar" (which alludes directly to republican revolution, through Shakespeare's *Julius Caesar* and through the mention of one of the heroes of the French republic).

26 For an insightful examination of Wordsworth's agrarian idealism, see
    Simpson, *Wordsworth's Historical Imagination,* esp. pp. 56–78.
27 *STCL* 1:410 (18 May 1798). In an earlier letter, to John Thelwall, Cole-
    ridge is more frank and styles Wordsworth "a Republican & at least a
    Semi-atheist" (*STCL* 1:216 [13 May 1796]). In 1803, Coleridge, Hazlitt,
    and Wordsworth entered into "a most unpleasant Dispute" over the "ar-
    gument by design." Coleridge records that "they spoke so irreverently so
    malignantly of the Divine Wisdom, that it overset me" (*STCNB* 1, *Text,*
    entry 1,616).
28 See Jacobus, *Tradition and Experiment* 261–72; Jordan, "The Hewing of
    Peter Bell 566–71; Moorman 1:394; and Thomas McFarland, *Romanticism
    and the Forms of Ruin: Wordsworth, Coleridge, and Modalities of Fragmentation*
    (Princeton, 1981), 74.
29 *Peter Bell* 41. See also *BL* 2:6–7.
30 See Burton Feldman, introduction to the *Dictionary Historical and Critical
    of Mr. Peter Bayle,* 5 vols. (1734–38; rpt. New York, 1984), 1:v–vi. There
    can be little doubt that Wordsworth was familiar with the *Dictionary.* It
    was extremely popular, receiving two separate translations in 1710 and
    1734–38, and was the work "most often found in eighteenth-century
    private libraries" (Elisabeth Labrousse, *Bayle,* tr. Denys Potts [Oxford,
    1983], 48). Also during this period the two poets engaged in collaborative
    composition, so it is likely that their readings were similar.
31 *"De natural deorum" and "Academica",* tr. H. Rackham (New York, 1933),
    137.
32 "Natural History of Religion," in *Philosophical Works* 4:309–16.
33 *Essays on Pierre Bayle and Religious Controversy* (The Hague, 1965), 199.
34 In England, the major participants in this debate were Patrick Delany,
    An Historical Account of the Life and Reign of David, King of Israel (1740;
    rpt. London, 1745); Samuel Chandler, *A Critical History of the Life of David*
    (London, 1746); and Beilby Porteus, *The Character of David, King of Israel,
    Impartially Stated: In a Discourse Preached before the University of Cambridge,
    November 29, 1761,* 2d ed. (Cambridge, 1761?). For an article that is
    sympathetic to Bayle, see the anonymous pamphlet—probably by Peter
    Annet—entitled *The History of a Man after God's Own Heart* (1761). Howard
    Robinson discusses this controversy in "Bayle's Profanation of Sacred
    History," in *Essays in Intellectual History, Dedicated to James Harvey Robinson
    by his Former Seminar Students* (New York, 1929), 147–62. Voltaire's treat-
    ment of David, in his article in the *Philosophical Dictionary* and in the play
    Saul, is even more strident. The parallelism between the story of Peter
    Bell and Voltaire's opening comments on the histories of Saul and David
    suggests that Wordsworth may have drawn as much from Voltaire as he
    did from Bayle: "If a young peasant, in searching after she-asses finds a
    kingdom it is no common affair. If another peasant cures his king of
    insanity by a tune on the harp that is still more extraordinary. But when

this petty player on the harp becomes king because he meets a village priest in secret, who pours a bottle of olive oil on his head, the affair is more marvellous still" (*The Works of Voltaire*, 42 vols. [Paris, 1901], 8:61).

35 E. S. Shaffer has noted that both sides in religious controversy shared a similar style: "The style of the apologists for Christianity partook of the subtle obliquities of their ironic Enlightenment opponents; often both the critical apologists and the Enlightened sceptics ran the same risk of denunciation by the orthodox" (*"Kubla Khan" and "The Fall of Jerusalem": The Mythological School in Biblical Criticism and Secular Literature, 1770–1880* [Cambridge, 1975], 8).

36 *Complete Prose Works*, ed. Don M. Wolfe (New Haven, 1953–), 3:322.

37 *The Art of Biblical Narrative* (New York, 1981), 106. Jordan's essay "Wordsworth's Humor" is still the best treatment of Wordsworth's mixing of "bitter comedy," parody, the mock heroic, satire and seriousness.

38 The allusion to Balaam, in 2 Peter 2:15–16, shows the manner in which the story was taken up by the early Church. Speaking of those who have fallen victim to lust, the author argues that they "have forsaken the right way, and are gone astray, following the way of Balaam *the son* of Bosor, who loved the wages of unrighteousness; but was rebuked for his iniquity: the dumb ass speaking with man's voice forbad the madness of the prophet."

39 The biblical echo is reinforced by the parallelism established between the Highland girl, who in piety walks two miles to the "Kirk . . . twice every Sabbath day" (1,149–50), and one of the dead man's children, not coincidentally named Rachael. When she sees Peter, while on her way to the "chapel" or methodist "meeting-house" (first edition, line 1,051), Rachael echoes the young girl's death cry, "My father! here's my father!" (1,245), and her distress later awakens an infant in the house (1,307–08).

40 See *Peter Bell* 134n.

41 In a letter to Thomas Poole, Coleridge indicates that methodist conversion narratives could provide the model for an affecting autobiography: "I could inform the dullest author how he might write an interesting book—let him relate the events of his own Life with honesty, not disguising the feelings that accompanied them.—I never yet read even a Methodist's 'Experience' in the Gospel Magazine without receiving instruction & amusement: & I should almost despair of that Man, who could peruse the Life of John Woolman without an amelioration of Heart" (*STCL* 1:302 [6 Feb. 1797]).

42 Mario D'Avanzo, in " 'Expostulation and Reply' and the Gospel of Matthew," *CEA Critic* 41 (1979):38–40, has argued that the poem addresses Christian tradition in ways similar to *Peter Bell*, as Wordsworth founds his own gospel of nature on a revisionary reworking of traditional Christian symbols and interpretation, notably the "old grey stone" of the Church.

43 *Lessing's Theological Writings*, tr. Henry Chadwick (Stanford, Calif., 1957), 82.

44   As Hans Frei has observed, the salvific narratives were "the crucial texts for the hermeneutical question in theology toward the end of the eighteenth century" (*The Eclipse of Biblical Narrative: A Study in Eighteenth and Nineteenth Century Hermeneutics* [New Haven, 1974], 64).

45   Shaffer, *"Kubla Khan" and "The Fall of Jerusalem"* 87; see also pp. 30–31. Coleridge wrote to Benjamin Flower on 1 April 1796 that Lessing's "book is not yet translated, and is entitled, in German, 'Fragments of an Anonymous Author.' It unites the wit of Voltaire with the subtlety of Hume, and the profound erudition of *our* Lardner. I had some thoughts of translating it with an answer, but gave it up, lest men, whose tempers and hearts incline them to disbelief, should get hold of it" (*STCL* 1:197).

46   Jerome J. McGann, "The Meaning of the Ancient Mariner," *Critical Inquiry* 8 (1981):51; Leslie Brisman, "Coleridge and the Supernatural," *Studies in Romanticism* 21 (1982):147. See also Anthony John Harding, *Coleridge and the Inspired Word* (Kingston and Montreal, 1985); and James C. McKusick's discussion of the intellectual context of Coleridge's translation of the Song of Deborah, in "A New Poem by Samuel Taylor Coleridge," *Modern Philology* 84 (1987):407–15. McGann has recently returned to this subject in connection with Blake's Illuminated Books, in "The Idea of an Indeterminate Text: Blake's Bible of Hell and Dr. Alexander Geddes," *Studies in Romanticism* 25 (1986):303–24.

47   For a detailed discussion of the classical references in the poem, see Geoffrey Durrant, "Wordsworth's 'Peter Bell'—A *Pons Asinorum* for Critics."

48   Hazlitt insightfully remarks that when Wordsworth originally titled *The Excursion* as a *"Portion* of The Recluse, A Poem," he was employing a term generally used in connection with Scripture, thus implying that his poems should be viewed as "sacred" and worthy of comparison, in their "primitive, patriarchal simplicity, to the historical parts of the Bible" (*Complete Works* 17:59n).

49   The extent of Wordsworth's ambivalence toward people like Peter Bell can be seen in the opening lines of "Andrew Jones," a poem that probably represents a spillover from *Peter Bell*:

> I hate that Andrew Jones: he'll breed
> His children up to waste and pillage,
> I wish the press-gang or the drum
> Would, with its rattling music, come,
> And sweep him from the village!   [*PW* 2:463]

The poem is as much about the political impotence of its speaker, who can only pray that Andrew will be "swept" from the village by a "press-gang" or army recruiter, as it is about Andrew Jones. It indicates the fear (while ironically undercutting it) that such people occasioned, especially as the speaker voices his anxiety that Andrew will "breed" (in an animalistic manner) "his children up to waste and pillage."

Chapter 4: A "Word Scarce Said"

1 *Critical Review*, 2d ser., 24 (Oct. 1798):198; *Simple Wordsworth* 52–54.
2 Pope, *Rape of the Lock* 4.59, 1.2.
3 William Harvey, *On Parturation*, in *The Works of William Harvey, M.D.*, tr. Robert Willis (London, 1847), 542.
4 *Observations on the Nature, Causes, and Cure of those Disorders which have been commonly called Nervous, Hypochondriac, or Hysteric: to which are prefixed some Remarks on the Sympathy of the Nerves*, 2d ed. (Edinburgh, 1765), 96. See also Thomas Sydenham, "Epistolary Dissertation," in *The Works of Thomas Sydenham, M.D.*, tr. Dr. Greenhill (London, 1848), 2:85.
5 *A Disease Called the Suffocation of the Mother* (1603; rpt. New York, 1971), 26.
6 *The Practice of Physick, reduc'd to the ancient Way of Observations, containing a just Parallel between the Wisdom of the Ancients and the Hypothesis's of Modern Physicians* (London, 1704), 179–185.
7 Samuel Richardson, *The History of Clarissa Harlowe*, in *The Novels of Samuel Richardson*, ed. William Lyon Phelps (New York, 1901–02), 4:213.
8 Susan's most notable and strangest antecedents appear in Pope's catalog "of Bodies chang'd to various Forms" by the "*Hysteric* or *Poetic* Fit":

> Here living *Teapots* stand, one Arm held out,
> One bent; the Handle this, and that the Spout:
> A Pipkin there like *Homer's Tripod* walks;
> Here sighs a Jar, and there a Goose-pye talks;
> Men prove with Child, as pow'rful Fancy works,
> And Maids turn'd Bottels, call aloud for Corks.
>
> [*The Rape of the Lock* 4.48–60]

In a society that accorded the female imagination extraordinary powers, it is not surprising that Pope would focus upon its modes and workings, deified by Belinda, to criticize the misuse of the imagination he saw pervading Augustan England.

9 *Mind and Body in Eighteenth Century Medicine: A Study Based on Jerome Gaub's "De regimine mentis"* (Berkeley, Calif., 1965), 17.
10 *The Reflector: Representing Human Affairs, As they Are; and may be improved* (London, 1750), 228.
11 For discussions of the contemporary understanding of psychosomatic illnesses, see Jean Starobinski, "The Idea of Nostalgia," *Diogenes* 54 (1966):81–103; and G. S. Rousseau, "Nymphomania, Bienville and the Rise of Erotic Sensibility," in *Sexuality in Eighteenth-Century Britain*, ed. Paul-Gabriel Boucé (Totowa, N.J., 1982), 95–119. For a study of hysteria, see Ilza Veith, *Hysteria: The History of a Disease* (Chicago, 1965).
12 *Melancholie und Aufklärung: Melancholiker und ihre Kritiker in Erfahrungs-seelenkunde und Literatur des 18. Jahrhunderts* (Stuttgart, 1977), 16–40. See G. S. Rousseau, "Nerves, Spirits, and Fibres: Towards Defining the Ori-

gins of Sensibility," in *Studies in the Eighteenth Century III,* ed. R. F. Brissendon and J. C. Eade (Toronto, 1976), 151.

13   Arthur Beatty, *William Wordsworth, His Doctrine and Art in Their Historical Relations* (Madison, Wis., 1922); See Averill, *Wordsworth and the Poetry of Human Suffering* (Ithaca, N.Y., 1980), 152–66.

14   See Ben Ross Schneider, Jr., *Wordsworth's Cambridge Education* (Cambridge, 1957), 4–17.

15   The notion that disease is caused by idleness is exemplified by the American physician Benjamin Rush's explanation of the positive effect of the American Revolution upon hysterics: "Many persons, of infirm and delicate habits, were restored to perfect health, by the change of place, or occupation, to which the war exposed them. This was the case in a more especial manner with hysterical women, who were much interested in the successful issue of the contest ... It may perhaps help to extend our ideas of the influence of the passions upon diseases, to add, that when either love, jealousy, grief, or even devotion, wholly engross the female mind, they seldom fail, in like manner, to cure or to suspend hysterical complaints" ("An Account of the Influence ... of the American Revolution upon the Human Body," in *Medical Inquiries and Observations,* 3d ed., 4 vols. [Philadelphia, 1809], 1:238).

16   *A Philosophical Enquiry into the Origin of Our Ideas of the Sublime and Beautiful,* ed. James T. Boulton (London, 1958), 132.

17   *The Displaying of Supposed Witchcraft* (London, 1677), 323–24.

18   *The Suffocation of the Mother* 2. Wordsworth's abortive political satire "Imitation of Juvenal" ridicules the *Daemonologie* and suggests that James whetted "his kingly faculties to chase / Legions of devils through a keyhole's space" (*PW* 1:305).

19   *The Discoverie of Witchcraft,* ed. Montague Summers (London, 1930), 3.9:30.

20   *A short discoverie of the unobserved dangers of severall sorts of ignorant and unconsiderate practisers of physicke in England* (London, 1612), 53.

21   *Witch Hunting in Southwestern Germany, 1562–1684: The Social and Intellectual Foundations* (Stanford, Calif., 1972), 185.

22   *The Complete Poetical Works of Samuel Taylor Coleridge,* ed. Ernest Hartley Coleridge, 2 vols. (Oxford, 1912), 1:268–69.

23   *Complete Poetical Works* 268–69; *The Poems,* lines 20–21. Because no complete text is available, those parts written by Coleridge are drawn from *Complete Poetical Works,* while those assigned to Wordsworth are from John O. Hayden's edition, *William Wordsworth: The Poems* (New Haven, 1981).

24   *Réponse aux questions d'un provincial,* in *Oeuvres diverses de M. Pierre Bayle,* 4 vols. (The Hague, 1725–31), 3:561.

25   *Poems,* 56, 52; Coleridge further developed this complex conjunction of magic, possession, sexuality, and mimetic transference in the love triangle of *Christabel,* begun in 1797. Karen Swann, in "'Christabel': The Wan-

have anie power to crie, neither doo my hands serve me to shoove hir awaie, nor my feete to go from hir." Scot reassured the priest that he was not possessed, but "vexed with a disease called *Incubus*, or the mare; and the residue was phantasie and vaine imagination" (*The Discovery of Witchcraft* 4.9:47–48).

33 *Europe's Inner Demons: An Enquiry Inspired by the Great Witch-Hunt* (New York, 1975), 236.

34 The problem posed by the child's bearing the face of the father is a central point of ambivalence in "Lady Anne Bothwell's Lament" (*Reliques of Ancient English Poetry*, ed. Henry B. Wheatley, 3 vols. [London, 1876–77], 2:212). There, the woman, seduced and abandoned, claims that she still loves the boy's father, yet fears that he might grow up to be like him:

> But smile not, as thy father did,
> To cozen maids: nay God forbid!
> Bot yett I feire, thou wilt gae neire
> Thy fatheris hart, and face to beire.

35 *Standard Edition* 11:16.

36 The way in which the figure of the deserted woman images the mother "as hostile and treacherous, in the form of a denying and rejecting Nature, and also as a suffering victim" is profitably examined in psychoanalytic terms by Barbara A. Schapiro, *The Romantic Mother: Narcissistic Patterns in Romantic Poetry* (Baltimore, 1983), 125.

37 Samuel Hearne, *A Journey from Prince of Wales's Fort in Hudson's Bay to the Northern Ocean* (1795; rpt. Rutland, Vt., 1971). Hearne's discussion of the role of the imagination among the Copper Indians occupies a large part of chapter 7, between the two source passages of "The Complaint of a Forsaken Indian Woman," and appears to have played an important, if indirect, role in Wordsworth's understanding of the therapeutic power of the human imagination. Hearne stresses the importance of the imagination in primitive medicine. In fact, among the Indians healing proceeds almost exclusively via the imagination. When a native is sick, "conjurers" are summoned, who "use no medicine either for internal or external complaints, but perform all their cures by charms" (189). In most instances, a lengthy procedure of blowing and sucking upon the afflicted areas of the body suffices. However, in extreme cases, the conjurers construct a "conjuring-house," where they perform what appear to be prodigious feats, swallowing impossible objects (bayonets, long boards, and even cradles), after which the patient is said to be cured by the help of the gods. Hearne later discovered that these deeds were no more than an "ordinary trick," part of the arsenal of "common jugglers" (220). But he had difficulty explaining "the apparent good effect" of the shamans' "labours on the sick and diseased" (220). In one instance, where an Indian was paralyzed completely on one side by a stroke, the deception worked a "truly wonderful" miracle: "When the poor sick man was taken

dering Mother and the Enigma of Form," *Studies in Romanticism* 23 (1984):533–53, has analyzed suggestively the role of hysteria in Coleridge's poetry.

26 Though the poem has not received much serious attention, two studies have profitably examined the role of the narrator: Paul Edwards, "The Narrator's Voice in 'Goody Blake and Harry Gill,'" *English* 19 (1970):13–17; and Don Bialostosky, *Making Tales* 69–74. Mary Jacobus has shown the poem's close affiliation with and subversion of the genre of popular propagandistic ballads, exemplified by Hannah More's *Cheap Repository*. She notes that Wordsworth, instead of seeking to educate the poor, "was asking his literate readers to think about their own code" (*Tradition and Experiment* 239).

27 In religious petition, sacred words were used to intensify the power of the magic. One example, of many offered by Keith Thomas, will suffice to indicate that we need not assume that Goody Blake is without evil intent. Goodwife Veazy, who was considered an expert in the cure of ringworm, tetter-worm, and canker-worm, would proceed in the following manner: "'In the name of God I begin and in the name of God I do end. Thou tetter-worm (or thou canker-worm) begone from hence in the name of the Father, of the Son, and of the Holy Ghost'; after which she applied a little honey and pepper to the afflicted part" (*Religion and the Decline of Magic* [New York, 1971], 179).

28 *Spectator* no. 117, in *Selected Essays from "The Tatler," "The Spectator," and "The Guardian,"* ed. Daniel McDonald (Indianapolis, 1973), 298. See Alan Macfarlane, *Witchcraft in Tudor and Stuart England: A Regional and Comparative Study* (New York, 1970).

29 Robert Langbaum downplays the importance of language in "The Mad Mother" and, therefore, does not feel that the poem is really a dramatic monologue (*The Poetry of Experience: The Dramatic Monologue in Modern Literary Tradition* [New York, 1957], 71–72).

30 The situation echoes that of Mortimer, when he entered the dark dungeon but found himself unable to murder Herbert: "'Twas dark, dark as hell—yet I saw him—I tell thee I saw him, his face towards me—the very looks of Matilda sent there by some fiend to baffle me.—It put me to my prayers—I cast my eyes upwards, and through a crevice in the roof I beheld a star twinkling over my head, and by the living God, I could not do it—" (1797–99 *Borderers*, lines 287–91).

31 *The Anatomy of Melancholy*, ed. Floyd Dell and Paul Jordan-Smith (New York, 1927), 220.

32 In "The Vale of Esthwaite," Wordsworth alludes to the Nightmare, as a "terror shapeless [that] rides my soul" (*PW* 1:278). Reginald Scot recounts a priest's story of his nightly meetings with a succubus: "There commeth unto mee, almost everie night, a certeine woman, unknowne unto me, and lieth so heavie upon my brest, that I cannot fetch my breath, neither

from the conjuring-house, he had not only recovered his appetite to an amazing degree, but was able to move all the fingers and toes of the side that had been so long dead. In three weeks he recovered so far as to be capable of walking, and at the end of six weeks went a hunting for his family" (219). Hearne speculates that the efficacy of symbolic therapy is to be found in the patient's confidence in the conjurer, which leaves "the mind so perfectly at rest, as to cause the disorder to take a favourable turn" (220). As in Susan's therapy, the absorption of the mind in a fiction leaves the body tranquil and free to repair itself. Hearne's account suggests that at one time medicine and poetry were sister arts, as both used the imagination of the patient to manipulate and transform the body, an idea that Wordsworth develops most extensively in *Resolution and Independence*.

The power of symbolic pretence is not, however, without its darker side. When conjurers dislike someone, Hearne writes, "it often proves fatal to that person; as, from a firm belief that the conjurer has power over his life, he permits the very thoughts of it to prey on his spirits, till by degrees it brings on a disorder which puts an end to his existence" (221). As proof of this fact, Hearne confesses that he actually killed a native. His murder weapon: "a rough sketch of two human figures on a piece of paper, in the attitude of wrestling: in the hand of one of them I drew the figure of a bayonet pointing to the breast of the other ... Opposite to those figures I drew a pine-tree, over which I placed a large human eye, and out of the tree projected a human hand" (221). A short time after his public announcement of his intentions, Hearne learned that his intended victim had died, even though he lived more than three hundred miles away. To *make* a design, he suggests, is to *have* a design upon someone. *Real* power resides in the *pretence* of power, so "it is almost absolutely necessary that the chiefs at this place should profess something a little supernatural, to be able to deal with those people" (222n).

38 Averill has argued that Wordsworth's "remarkably dubious" (*Poetry of Human Suffering* 167) allusion to James Hackman's murder of Martha Ray, Basil Montagu's grandmother, on 7 April 1779 was influenced by Darwin's mention of the case in *Zoönomia*, as an illustration of an extreme stage of "erotomania," a "furious or melancholy insanity" (2:365). The close connection between sexuality and hysteria, love and madness, in this case would have been of special interest to Wordsworth. By naming his witch "Martha Ray," he reaffirms that the witch is not the cause, but the victim, of the aggressive imaginings of her accusers. Ironically, Martha Ray was shot as she left a performance of *Love in a Village*.

39 For a subtle interpretation of "The Thorn" as "mental theatre," in which the speaker displays "the dramatic incapacity of experience to explain passion" (282) and of language to encompass the "open site of desire" (283), see Jerome Christensen, "Wordsworth's Misery, Coleridge's Woe:

Reading 'The Thorn,'" *Papers on Language and Literature* 16 (1980):268–86.

40 *Wordsworth's Poetry, 1787–1814* (1964; rpt. New Haven, 1971), 147.

41 "Journal of My Voyage in the Year 1769," tr. F. M. Barnard, in *J. G. Herder on Social and Political Culture* (Cambridge, 1969), 71.

42 Wordsworth's choice of a superstitious seventeenth-century mariner suggests that "The Thorn" is a pastiche of *The Ancient Mariner* aimed at revaluing Coleridge's theory of the supernatural. It is likely that the same passage from Captain George Shelvocke's *A Voyage Round the World by the Way of the Great South Sea* (London, 1726), which Wordsworth recalled when he suggested that the mariner kill an albatross, equally informs his depiction of the old sailor's encounter with a "weather-witch." Having described the terrible weather south of the Straits of le Mair ["the Mare"?], Shelvocke writes that his crew saw no living thing save "a disconsolate black *Albitross,* who accompanied us for several days, hovering about us as if he had lost himself, till *Hatley,* (my second Captain) observing, in one of his melancholy fits, that this bird was always hovering near us, imagin'd, from his colour, that it might be some ill omen. That which, I suppose, induced him the more to encourage his superstition, was the continued series of contrary tempestuous winds, which had oppress'd us ever since we had got into this sea. But be that as it would, he, after some fruitless attempts, at length, shot the *Albitross,* not doubting (perhaps) that we should have a fair wind after it" (72–73). As in "The Thorn," a melancholy sailor's superstitious identification of a natural creature, emerging from the mists, with the cause of tempests invests it with supernatural powers.

43 *Europe's Inner Demons* 153. See also Jacobus Sprenger and Heinrich Kramer, *Malleus Maleficarum,* tr. Montague Summers, ed. Pennethorne Hughes (London, 1968), 139–43.

44 The painting is reproduced as a frontispiece to Hugh Sykes Davies's *Wordsworth and the Worth of Words.*

45 *Prophet and Poet: The Bible and the Growth of Romanticism* (Evanston, Ill., 1965), 172.

46 *The Spirit of Hebrew Poetry,* tr. James Marsh, 2 vols. (Burlington, Vt., 1833), 1:21.

47 "The brush takes time to execute what the eye of the painter embraces at a glance," argues Diderot. To be analyzed or expressed, an idea or sensation must be broken into parts. "The formation of languages required decomposition," he suggests, "but to *see* an object, to *judge* it beautiful, to *feel* an agreeable sensation, to *desire* to possess it, is an instantaneous state of being, what in Greek or Latin is rendered by a single word" (*Lettre sur les sourds et muets,* in *Oeuvres* 1:369). For a discussion of the development of the idea of linguistic decomposition, see Hans Aarsleff, *From Locke to Saussure* 157–58.

48   Prospero, in *The Tempest*, describes the "foul witch Sycorax" as being "with age and envy . . . grown into a hoop" (1.2.258–59). K. M. Briggs observes that "this was often popularly taken as a sign of witchcraft" (*Pale Hecate's Team: An Examination of the Beliefs on Witchcraft and Magic among Shakespeare's Contemporaries and His Immediate Successors* [New York, 1962], 83).

49   Reed suggests that the poem was composed between 29 March 1797 and 18 July 1800 (Reed *EY* 324). Since it was not included among *Lyrical Ballads* and alludes to "The Idiot Boy" and "Goody Blake and Harry Gill," we can probably place its composition closer to the latter date.

50   *The Letters of Charles Lamb, to which are Added Those of His Sister Mary Lamb*, ed. E. V. Lucas, 3 vols. (New Haven, 1935), 2:158 (28 April 1815).

51   Responding to Heather Glen's insightful interpretation of "Poor Susan," in *Vision and Disenchantment: Blake's "Songs" and Wordsworth's "Lyrical Ballads"* (Cambridge, 1983), 102–09, Peter J. Manning, in "Placing Poor Susan: Wordsworth and the New Historicism," *Studies in Romanticism* 25 (1986):351–69, and David Simpson, in "What Bothered Charles Lamb About Poor Susan?" *Studies in English Literature, 1500–1900* 26 (1986):589–612, have developed in greater detail what Charles Lamb meant when he argued that the last verse of the poem, as it was first published in the 1800 *Lyrical Ballads*, "threw a kind of dubiety upon Susan's moral conduct," seeming "to say that poor Susan was no better than she should be, which I trust was not what you meant to express" (2:158). Both articles persuasively show that Lamb was uncomfortable about the possibility that readers might not see Susan as "a servant maid . . . trundling her mop" in the early dawn, but instead as a prostitute. However, Wordsworth did provide his readers with enough information to make the distinction. The "pail" that Susan carries is obviously not just a milk pail, as Lamb's mention of the "mop" suggests. Also, "hysteria" was rarely a complaint that afflicted prostitutes.

52   The south-to-north "progress of poetry" (as well as its east-to-west movement) is suggestively discussed by Geoffrey Hartman, "Blake and the Progress of Poesy," in *Beyond Formalism: Literary Essays, 1958–1970* (New Haven, 1970).

53   Robert Southey, who had visited this spot three years earlier, agreed: "While we were at the waterfall, some half score peasants, chiefly women and girls, assembled just out of reach of the spray, and set up—surely the wildest chorus that ever was heard by human ears,—a song not of articulate sounds, but in which the voice was used as a mere instrument of music, more flexible than any which art could produce,—sweet, powerful, and thrilling beyond description" (*A Tale of Paraguay* [Boston, 1827], 196–97).

54   See *Witchcraft, Oracles and Magic among the Azande* (Oxford, 1937), 63–70.

55   *Romantic Origins* (Ithaca, N.Y., 1978), 314–18.

56 See George Lyman Kittredge, *Witchcraft in Old and New England* (New York, 1958), 94. As is well known, Yeats refers to this incident in "Nineteen Hundred and Nineteen."

57 *Witchcraft and the Middle Ages* (Ithaca, N.Y., 1972), 184.

58 There is a hint of a possible sacrifice in the "single sheep" at the boy's side, but it is the death of the father that introduces him to a "God who thus corrected my desires."

Chapter 5: The History of Death

1 See Frances Ferguson, *Wordsworth: Language as Counter-Spirit* (New Haven, 1977), 29–34; and Thomas Weiskel, *The Romantic Sublime: Studies in the Structure and Psychology of Transcendence* (Baltimore, 1976), 190. For discussions of death in Wordsworth's poetry, see David Ferry, *The Limits of Mortality: An Essay on Wordsworth's Major Poems* (Middletown, Conn., 1959); Geoffrey Hartman, *Wordsworth's Poetry* 19–69; and Richard J. Onorato, *The Character of the Poet: Wordsworth in "The Prelude"* (Princeton, 1971), 69–80, 191–206, 391–93. For recent studies of death, writing, and epitaphs, see Ernest Bernhardt-Kabisch, "The Epitaph and the Romantic Poets: A Survey," *Huntington Library Quarterly* 30 (1967):113–46, and "Wordsworth: The Monumental Poet," *Philological Quarterly* 44 (1965):503–18; Geoffrey Hartman, "Wordsworth, Inscriptions, and Romantic Nature Poetry," in *Beyond Formalism: Literary Essays, 1958–1970* (New Haven, 1970), 206–30; Paul de Man, "Autobiography as De-facement," *Modern Language Notes* 94 (1979):919–30; and Peter J. Manning, "Reading Wordsworth's Revisions: Othello and the Drowned Man," *Studies in Romanticism* 22 (1983):3–28. For a treatment of romantic "dying," see Paul H. Fry, "The Absent Dead: Wordsworth, Byron, and the Epitaph," *Studies in Romanticism* 17 (1978):413–33, and "Disposing of the Body: The Romantic Moment of Dying," *Southwest Review* 71 (1986):8–26.

2 Much has been written on the eighteenth and nineteenth centuries as major turning points in the development of the history of death, notably by Philippe Ariès, *The Hour of Our Death*, tr. Helen Weaver (New York, 1981), and *Western Attitudes Toward Death, from the Middle Ages to the Present*, tr. Patricia M. Ranum (Baltimore, 1974); Edgar Morin, *L'Homme et la mort* (Paris, 1970); David E. Stannard, ed., *Death in America* (Philadelphia, 1975); and Garrett Stewart, *Death Sentences: Styles of Dying in British Fiction* (Cambridge, Mass., 1984). For eighteenth-century studies, see John McManners, *Death and the Enlightenment: Changing Attitudes to Death among Christians and Unbelievers in Eighteenth-Century France* (Oxford, 1981); and Robert Favre, *La Mort dans la littérature et la pensée françaises au siècle des lumières* (Lyon, 1978).

3 Cited by D. J. Enright, *The Oxford Book of Death* (Oxford, 1983), ix. See

also *Voltaire's Notebooks*, ed. Theodore Besterman, 2 vols. (Geneva, 1952), 2:352; and Montesquieu, *The Spirit of the Laws*, tr. Thomas Nugent (New York, 1949), 3.

4 John Weever, whose *Antient Funeral Monuments* Wordsworth cites in his *Essays upon Epitaphs*, recognizing an etymological connection between "burrows" and the suffixes "burgh," "borough," and "bury" used in many town names, claimed that towns were originally built near primitive burial sites (*Antient Funeral Monuments* [London, 1767], 1:vii). In *The Prelude*, Wordsworth describes London as the "burial-place of passions, and their home / Imperial" (8.750–51).

5 *De rerum natura*, ed. Cyril Bailey (Oxford, 1947), 3.978–79. Hobbes's philological claim that the idea of Hell had its origin in a garbage dump on the outskirts of Jerusalem, called Gehenna, is one of the most radical of Lucretian arguments (*English Works* 3:447–48).

6 *New Science* 42; Vico is here recalling the famous lines from Horace's "Art of Poetry" (translated by John G. Hawthorne in *Latin Poetry in Translation* [Boston, 1957]):

> When men lived wild, a spokesman of the gods,
> The sacred Orpheus, scared them from their foul
> And murderous ways; and so the legend says:
> Ravening lions and tigers Orpheus tamed.   [lines 487–90]

7 Hume, "Of the Immortality of the Soul," *Philosophical Works* 4:403.

8 In *The Divine Legation of Moses Demonstrated*, Warburton demonstrated that the early Hebrews lacked notions of the immortality of the soul and of a future life of reward and punishment, and then set out to explain why. Accepting the popular deistic argument that these ideas primarily served a political purpose by frightening otherwise lawless individuals into behaving civilly, Warburton claimed that Moses, the ascribed author of the Pentateuch, knew the political utility of these dogmas and yet, paradoxically, did not reveal them to the Hebrews. The only explanation he could see for such an oversight was that Moses wished to show that the Hebrew people, unlike all other nations, were not held together by human means—by ideology—but instead by divine governance, in a miraculous system continuing from Moses to Christ. Though few of Warburton's contemporaries accepted his arguments for the "divine legation of Moses," his demonstration that the early Hebrews lacked notions of immortality and the afterlife, that "in the Old Testament it [Hades] signified the receptacle of *dead bodies*; in the New, the receptacle of *living souls*," was of enormous importance. He had shown that the idea of death had a history—that it had come into existence at a certain time and that it had changed as Hebrew theology developed (1738–65; rpt. New York, 1978, 4:347n). See also Voltaire's articles "Soul" and "Hell" in the *Philosophical Dictionary*, in *Works* 13:315–16 and 10:21–28; and Lessing, "The Education of the Human Race," in *Lessing's Theological Writings* 83–92.

9   Warburton argues that Moses, in recounting this story, was deliberately
     obscure and concealed the doctrine of a future life from his readers by
     presenting Enoch's "translation" as "only signifying an immature death"
     (4:322). He then compares this account with the later story of the trans-
     lation of Elijah. Warburton argues that "when the latter history was writ-
     ten, it was thought expedient to make a preparation for the dawning of
     a *future state* of reward and punishment, which in the time of Moses had
     been highly improper" (4:322). With the Gospel of Christ, the idea could
     finally be articulated. In Hebrews 11:5, an interpolation of Enoch's story
     makes its true significance clear, as miracle displaces mystery: "By faith
     Enoch was translated that he should not see death; and was not found,
     because God had translated him." In Hebrews this death is no longer a
     puzzling problem, no longer a vague way of talking about a premature
     death or someone's disappearance, but instead can now be seen as a
     proleptic illustration of New Testament doctrine: Enoch's corpse "was
     not found" because he had been "translated" into heaven without ever
     having had to die or "see death."
10   *Emile, or On Education*, tr. Allan Bloom (New York, 1979), 379–80. Words-
     worth cites *Emile* in the essay on the character of Rivers prefaced to the
     1797 version of *The Borderers* (see p. 63 and note).
11   Robert Mayo's remarks are typical: "The poem was greatly admired by
     some readers in its day—partly for this reason [its exoticism], no doubt,
     partly for its popular subject ingeniously modified, partly for its modish
     'complaint' form, and partly because it seemed to present 'a natural de-
     lineation of human passions, human characters, and human incidents'"
     ("The Contemporaneity of the *Lyrical Ballads*," *Publications of the Modern
     Language Association* 69 [1954]:497). See also Mary Jacobus, *Tradition and
     Experiment* 193–94, and F. E. Farley, "The Dying Indian," in *Anniversary
     Papers by Colleagues and Pupils of George Lyman Kittredge* (Boston, 1913),
     251–60. For a contemporary example of this genre, see Thomas Gis-
     borne's "The Dying Indian: An Ode," in *Poems, Sacred and Moral* (London,
     1798).
12   *Wordsworth* (Boston, 1965), 22.
13   Empiricists had drawn attention to such cases before, the classic example
     being Locke's mention of such situations in the opening paragraphs of
     his critique of innate moral sentiments. "And are there not Places where,
     at a certain Age, they kill or expose their Parents, without any remorse
     at all?" he asks. "In a Part of *Asia*, the Sick, when their Case comes to be
     thought desperate, are carried out and laid on the Earth, before they are
     dead, and left there, exposed to Wind and Weather, to perish without
     Assistance or Pity" (*Essay* 1:70–71).
14   For a persuasive interpretation of the poem in terms of the conflict be-
     tween the woman's desire to live and the language of stoicism she derives
     from society, see Stephen Bidlake, "'Hidden Dialog' in 'The Mad Mother'

and 'The Complaint of a Forsaken Indian Woman,'" *Wordsworth Circle* 13 (1982):188–93. A comparison of the "Complaint" with Wordsworth's more conventional description of the savage as one who "encounters all his evils unsubdued; / For happier days since at the breast he pined / He never knew" (*Salisbury Plain,* lines 11–13) indicates the extent to which the poet, in *Lyrical Ballads,* re-evaluated those Enlightenment anthropological commonplaces that he too had taken for granted.

15   Voltaire makes a similar argument in his article "Soul" in the *Philosophical Dictionary,* when he suggests that at first "the soul was taken for the origin and the cause of life, and for life itself. Hence all known nations long imagined that everything died with the body. If anything can be discerned with clearness in the chaos of ancient histories, it seems that the Egyptians were at least the first who made a distinction between the intelligence and the soul; and the Greeks learned from them to distinguish their 'nous' and their 'pneuma'" (*Works* 13:261–62).

16   This conception of sight as only a more extended kind of feeling appears primarily in discussions of blind people who have had cataract operations. For instance, Cheselden, recounting the famous case of a young boy, tells how "when he first saw, he was so far from making any Judgment about Distances, that he thought all Objects whatever touch'd his Eyes, (as he express'd it), as what he felt, did his Skin" (*Philosophical Transactions,* no. 402 [1728], 448). Bruno Snell's well-known discussion of body and mind in Homer's epics provides a useful gloss to "The Complaint." Snell argues that "the Homeric man had a body exactly like the later Greeks, but he did not know it *qua* body, but merely as the sum total of his limbs ... Again and again Homer speaks of fleet legs, of knees in speedy motion, of sinewy arms; it is in these limbs, immediately evident as they are to his eyes, that he locates the secret of life" (*The Discovery of the Mind: The Greek Origins of European Thought,* tr. T. G. Rosenmeyer [Cambridge, Mass., 1953], 8).

17   Strikingly, "The Children in the Wood," which tells of the mysterious disappearance and subsequent death of two children in the wood, also addresses the question of burial. It relates the popular idea that robins, in "piety" for the unburied dead, cover them with leaves:

> No burial 'this' pretty 'pair'
>   Of any man receives,
> Till Robin-red-breast piously
>   Did cover them with leaves.   [*Reliques* 3:175]

In the ballad tradition, even nature abhors the unburied dead. In *Peter Bell,* Wordsworth explores the relationship between burial and the state of nature by naming the son of the dead man Robin and by describing him as being "like a bird," "fed on many a crust of bread," and carrying a hawthorn branch with berries "ripe and red" seeking his father (lines 784, 775, and 752). Wordsworth alludes to "that good and pious deed /

Of which we in the Ballad read" in "The Redbreast (Suggested in a Westmoreland Cottage)" and in *Descriptive Sketches* (1793), where he speaks of a cottage that "The red-breast peace had bury'd . . . in wood" (line 169).

18 Wordsworth translated Virgil's version of the myth between 1788 and 1789. See *PW* 1:283–85.

19 "Women and English Romanticism," *Sacred Heart University Review* 7 (1986–87):3.

20 James Dunbar similarly claims that the pleasure of imitation is the "prime mover, without any further design," that first give rise to language. "Taught by parents, children learn to utter sound, to which afterwards they affix a meaning. Taught by instinct, men utter sound at the beginning, which the understanding afterwards renders more significant. In both cases, the act of the understanding is posterior to a sort of organical impulse" (*Essays on the History of Mankind in Rude and Cultivated Ages* [London, 1780], 85–86).

21 Wordsworth makes use of similar imagery in a *Prelude* passage written during May or June of the following year, where he tells how, having paddled over a "dusky lake" just before "the fall / Of night," he and his confederates left a single friend on a small island to play his flute as they "rowed off gently":

> oh, then the calm
> And *dead still water* lay upon my mind
> Even with a weight of pleasure, and the sky,
> Never before so beautiful, sank down
> Into my heart and held me like a dream.
>
> [*Prelude* 2.176–80, my emphasis]

The passage suggests the Orphean power of music to bridge the gap produced by death.

22 Gabriel García Márquez, *One Hundred Years of Solitude*, tr. Gregory Rabassa (New York, 1971), 22.

23 Susan J. Wolfson, "The Illusion of Mastery: Wordsworth's Revisions of 'The Drowned Man of Esthwaite,' 1799, 1805, 1850," *Publications of the Modern Language Association* 99 (1984):921.

24 Hume, "Of the Immortality of the Soul," *Philosophical Works* 4:405.

25 *Système de la nature, ou, Des loix du monde physique et du monde moral*, ed. M. Mirabaud, 2 vols. (London, 1781), 1:228. See also Rousseau, *Emile* 55.

26 *Phaedo*, in *Opera*, ed. and tr. Harold North Fowler (Cambridge, Mass., 1914), 64a; E. de la M. Glénat, *Contres les craintes de la mort* (The Hague, 1757), 28.

27 Cited by Hazlitt, *Complete Works* 8:327.

28 "How the Ancients Represented Death," in *Selected Prose Works of G. E.*

Lessing, ed. Edward Bell, tr. E. C. Beasley and Helen Zimmern (London, 1890), 225–26.

29 In his letter to Coleridge of 27 February 1799, Wordsworth admits to having "no distinct idea" of the merits of Lessing's work (*EY* 255).

30 "Wordsworth's Intimations Ode and Its Epigraphs," *Journal of English and Germanic Philology* 82 (1983):527. Frances Ferguson has also argued for the importance of the Christian "Pollio" tradition to the *Ode* in *Language as Counter-Spirit* 103–07.

31 Wordsworth's adoption of the Platonic pre-existence myth serves a similar purpose. He explicitly protested against the assumption that he was hoping "to inculcate such a belief." Instead, he argued for the anthropological significance of such ideas as "an element in our instincts of immortality" that has "sufficient foundation in humanity" and can be seen in "the popular creeds of many nations" (*PW* 4:464).

32 *A Journey to the Western Islands of Scotland*, ed. Mary Lascelles (New Haven, 1971), 164.

33 From a *Course of Instruction for a Congenitally Deaf Person* (1799), in *The Deaf Experience: Classics in Language and Education*, ed. Harlan L. Lane, tr. Franklin Philip (Cambridge, Mass., 1984), 85. See also Harlan Lane, *When the Mind Hears: A History of the Deaf* (New York, 1984). Concise summaries of eighteenth-century interest in deaf-mutes can be found in James R. Knowlson, "The Idea of Gesture as a Universal Language in the Seventeenth and Eighteenth Centuries," *Journal of the History of Ideas* 26 (1965):495–508; and Jules Paul Seigel, "The Enlightenment and the Evolution of a Language of Signs in France and England," *Journal of the History of Ideas* 30 (1969):96–115.

34 "Mysteries of the Deaf," *New York Review of Books* 33, no. 5 (27 March 1986):24.

35 *Des signes et de l'art de penser considérés dans leurs rapports mutuels*, 4 vols. (Paris, 1800), 4:452–58.

36 Roche-Ambroise Sicard, *Théorie des signes; ou, Introduction a l'étude des langues*, 2 vols. (Paris, 1814), 2:644. Condillac also cites the story (later translated by P. Templeman and published in the *Gentleman's Monthly Intelligencer* [22 December 1753]) of a man from Chartres who had been born deaf and much later, suddenly and miraculously, had begun to speak. He was questioned by divines, who indicated that "he did not even distinctly know what it was to dye, nor did he ever think about it" (*Essay* 124). In a lengthy appendix to *Elements of the Philosophy of the Human Mind*, originally read before the Royal Society in Edinburgh, Dugald Stewart gives a lengthy account of James Mitchell, a boy born deaf and blind, in which he speaks of the importance of this case "as an object of philosophical curiosity" that would throw "much light . . . on the mental faculties," if a situation were arranged "where an opportunity would be afforded for examining and recording, under the eye of this Society, the

particulars of [the] case" (*Works of Dugald Stewart*, 7 vols. [Cambridge, Mass., 1829], 3:298, 318). Stewart's paper gave rise to a series of letters debating whether or not Mitchell was capable of grieving the death of his father.

37 Johnston, "Recollecting Forgetting: Forcing Paradox to the Limit in the 'Intimations Ode,'" *Wordsworth Circle* 2 (1971):62; Fry, *The Poet's Calling in the English Ode* (New Haven, 1980), 145.

38 *The Well Wrought Urn: Studies in the Structure of Poetry* (New York, 1947), 134–35.

39 In an article on death, Diderot writes that "men fear death like children fearing the dark, only because their imaginations have been frightened by phantoms as empty as they are terrible. The pomp of the last farewells, the tears of our friends, the mourning and the funeral ceremony, the convulsions of the machine breaking down, these are the things that tend to frighten us" (*Encyclopédie, ou, Dictionnaire raisonné des sciences, des arts et des métiers*, new ed. [Geneva, 1779], 32:271).

40 "Lionel Trilling and the *Immortality Ode*," *Salmagundi* 41 (1978):71.

41 *Wordsworth's Experiments with Tradition: The Lyric Poems of 1802* (Ithaca, N.Y., 1971), 3–23.

42 Peter J. Manning notes this echo in "Wordsworth's Intimations Ode and Its Epigraphs," 538.

Chapter 6: "A Power Like One of Nature's"

1 *Natural Supernaturalism* 19–70.

2 The work of David Simpson is a notable exception; see especially *Wordsworth's Historical Imagination* 66, 76–78.

3 *Traces on the Rhodian Shore: Nature and Culture in Western Thought from Ancient Times to the End of the Eighteenth Century* (Berkeley, Calif., 1967), vi.

4 *Man and Nature; or, Physical Geography as Modified by Human Action* (New York, 1864), iv.

5 *Theory of Earth*, in *Natural History*, 1:327–28.

6 *Oeuvres philosophiques*, ed. Jean Piveteau (Paris, 1954), 191a.

7 "An Attempt to Account for the Change of Climate, which has been observed in the Middle Colonies in North America," *Transactions of the American Philosophical Society* 1 (1789):336.

8 William Cronon, distinguishing between macroscopic and microscopic environmental changes, comments that "it was not, as some thought, that the weather itself was changed by clearing, but rather the way landscapes responded to the weather." Even so, he notes that "in one special but important sense destroying the forest changed the very seasons themselves" (*Changes in the Land: Indians, Colonists, and the Ecology of New England* [New York, 1983], 123).

9   *Essays upon Field Husbandry in New England, and Other Papers, 1748–1762,*
     ed. Harry J. Carman and Rexford G. Tugwell (New York, 1934), 7. De
     Crèvecoeur writes in a similar vein: "I think, considering our age, the
     great toils we have undergone, the roughness of some parts of this coun-
     try, and our original poverty, that we have done the most in the least
     time of any people on earth" (*Sketches of Eighteenth Century America,* ed.
     Henri L. Bourdin, Ralph H. Gabriel, and Stanley T. Williams [New Ha-
     ven, 1925], 141).

10   "The Power of an Endless Life," in *Sermons for the New Life* (New York,
     1858), 310.

11   *An Elementary Treatise on Geology,* tr. Rev. Henry de la Fite (London, 1809),
     414.

12   This point is made by Alan Liu in "'Shapeless Eagerness': The Genre of
     Revolution in Books 9–10 of *The Prelude,*" *Modern Language Quarterly* 43
     (1982):7–13. I owe much to this insightful essay and to Ronald Paulson's
     Representations of Revolution, 1789–1820 (New Haven, 1983), esp. pp. 248–
     85.

13   See I. Bernard Cohen, *Revolution in Science* (Cambridge, Mass., 1985),
     xiv; and Hannah Arendt, *On Revolution* (New York, 1963), 13–52.

14   *The Making of Geology: Earth Science in Britain, 1660–1815* (Cambridge,
     1977), 142. For secondary literature on eighteenth- and early nineteenth-
     century geology, see Charles Gillispie, *Genesis and Geology: A Study in the
     Relations of Scientific Thought, Natural Theology, and Social Opinion in Great
     Britain, 1790–1850* (Cambridge, Mass., 1951); Cecil J. Schneer, ed., *To-
     ward a History of Geology* (Cambridge, Mass., 1969); Martin J. S. Rudwick,
     The Meaning of Fossils: Episodes in the History of Paleontology, 2d rev. ed.
     (New York, 1976); A. Hallam, *Great Geological Controversies* (Oxford,
     1983); Nicolaas A. Rupke, *The Great Chain of History: William Buckland
     and the English School of Geology (1814–1849)* (Oxford, 1983); Milton Mill-
     hauser, "The Scriptural Geologists," *Osiris* 2 (1954):65–86; Paolo Rossi,
     The Dark Abyss of Time 3–120; and Marjorie Hope Nicolson, *Mountain
     Gloom and Mountain Glory: The Development of the Aesthetics of the Infinite*
     (Ithaca, N.Y., 1959).

15   *Essay on the Theory of the Earth . . . with Mineralogical Notes, and an Account
     of Cuvier's Geological Discoveries, by Professor Jameson,* tr. Robert Kerr (Edin-
     burgh, 1813), 17.

16   *Lettres de M. William Coxe à M. W. Melmoth, sur l'état politique, civil et naturel
     de la Suisse; traduites de l'Anglois, et augmentées des observations faites dans le
     même pays,* 2 vols. (Paris, 1782), 2:27. For a more detailed discussion of
     the role of geology in the early poetry, see Paul D. Sheats, *The Making of
     Wordsworth's Poetry, 1795–1798* (Cambridge, Mass., 1973), 61–69.

17   *Illustrations of the Huttonian Theory of the Earth* (1802; rpt. Urbana, Ill.,
     1956), 2, 62.

18   Coleridge, wondering whether "every great Epoch whether of the phys-

ical or of the political or of the moral, World" might not begin and end
"in a *Revolution*," likened the earth's surface to a petrified sea: "Over
what petrified Tempest Billows must [not] the Geologist work his way in
the attempt to penetrate beyond the products of . . . the present or human Epoch of this planet" (cited in Trevor H. Levere, *Poetry Realized in
Nature: Samuel Taylor Coleridge and Early Nineteenth-Century Science* [Cam-
bridge, 1981], 170).

19   Roy Porter has suggested that many of the "theories of the earth" written
after the Glorious Revolution, notably those of John Harris, John Keill,
and John Woodward, framed a new idea of geological revolution that
"married Locke to cosmogony" by revising Thomas Burnet's cosmic depiction, in *The Sacred Theory of the Earth*, of a world suffering from ruin
and decay and requiring an apocalypse to be redeemed ("Creation and
Credence: The Career of Theories of the Earth in Britain, 1660–1820,"
in *Natural Order: Historical Studies of Scientific Culture*, ed. Barry Barnes
and Steven Shapin [Beverly Hills, Calif., 1979], 104). Porter has elsewhere argued that there was a similar interlocking of geological and
political theory during the 1790s, as the belief became rampant "in the
age of the French Revolution that Earth science was set fair to undermine
religion and society" (*The Making of Geology* 88). See also Norton Garfin-
kle, "Science and Religion in England, 1790–1800: The Critical Response
to the Work of Erasmus Darwin," *Journal of the History of Ideas* 16
(1955):376–88; I. Bernard Cohen, *Revolution in Science* 208–12. The political aspects of geology are quite obvious in Shelley's "Mont Blanc." See
G. M. Matthews, "A Volcano's Voice in Shelley," *English Literary History*
24 (1957):191–228.

20   Though Wordsworth's familiarity with late seventeenth-century catastrophist "theories of the earth," such as Thomas Burnet's *Sacred Theory
of the Earth*, has long been recognized, not enough attention has been
given to his knowledge of contemporary geological speculation. In addition to Paul D. Sheats's discussion of geology in the early poetry, an
erudite examination of the subject can be found in Ernest Bernhardt-
Kabisch, "The Stone and the Shell: Wordsworth, Cataclysm, and the
Myth of Glaucus," *Studies in Romanticism* 24 (1985):455–90. Marilyn Gaull
discusses Wordsworth's later association with the geologist Adam Sedg-
wick in "From Wordsworth to Darwin: 'On the Fields of Praise,'" *Wordsworth Circle* 10 (1979):33–48. Theresa M. Kelley, in chapter 2 of
Wordsworth's Revisionary Aesthetics (Cambridge, 1988), provides a valuable
examination of Wordsworth's use of stratigraphic maps as analogues of
the mind in *A Guide Through the District of the Lakes*. For a study of the
symbolic character of stones in Wordsworth's poetry, see Marshall
Brown's "Wordsworth's Old Grey Stone," in *Preromanticism* (Stanford
University Press, forthcoming).

21   The situation possibly echoes Gibbon's famous account of the moment

when he conceived the idea for the *Decline and Fall of the Roman Empire* as he "sat musing amidst the ruins of the Capitol while the barefooted fryars were singing Vespers in the temple of Jupiter" (*Memoirs of My Life,* ed. Georges A. Bonnard [London, 1966], 136n). Wordsworth might have known of this passage from John Holroyd, the Earl of Sheffield's edition of the *Miscellaneous Works of Edwin Gibbon, Esq.,* published in 1796.

22   See also the *Correspondance littéraire, philosophique et critique par Grimm, Diderot, Raynal, Meister, etc.,* ed. Maurice Tourneux, 6 vols. (Paris, 1878), 5:363. For eighteenth-century conjectures on the relationship between environment and myth, see Frank E. Manuel, *The Eighteenth Century Confronts the Gods* 129–241.

23   In *Peter Bell,* Wordsworth evokes mankind's fearful response to the primitive world by mediating the "rumbling" work of subterranean miners plying "with gunpowder their trade" through Peter's ignorance of causes.

24   Bernhardt-Kabisch has argued that "it is in order to explore this inexorable historicity of secular, Revolutionary man that Wordsworth adopts the seemingly far-fetched catastrophic perspective—in sharp contrast to the transcendental method employed in the 'Immortality' ode" ("The Stone and the Shell" 464).

25   P. J. Marshall and Glyndwr Williams, *The Great Map of Mankind: Perceptions of New Worlds in the Age of Enlightenment* (Cambridge, Mass., 1982), 128.

26   *The Universal History, from the Earliest Account of Time to the Preface,* 23 vols. (Dublin, 1744–65), 7:244. Rousseau similarly remarks, "During the first dispersion of the human race, until the family was instituted and man had a fixed habitation, there was no more agriculture. People who have no fixed place will not cultivate the earth: such, in former times were the Nomads; the Arabs, living in tents; the Scythians, in their chariots; such, still today, are the wandering Tartars, and the savages of America" (*Essai sur l'origine des langues* 518).

27   "The Ruined Cottage," MS. B, 12ᵛ.

28   See, respectively, Jane Worthington Smyser, "Wordsworth's Dream of Poetry and Science: *The Prelude,* V," *Publications of the Modern Language Association* 71 (1956):269–75; Theresa M. Kelley, "Spirit and Geometric Form: The Stone and the Shell in Wordsworth's Arab Dream," *Studies in English Literature, 1500–1900* 22 (1982):563–82; and Michael Ragussis, *The Subterfuge of Art: Language and the Romantic Tradition* (Baltimore, 1978), 17–34. See also Geoffrey Hartman, *Wordsworth's Poetry* 225–33; J. Hillis Miller, "The Stone and the Shell: The Problem of Poetic Form in Wordsworth's Dream of the Arab," in *Mouvements premiers: Etudes critiques offertes à Georges Poulet* (Paris, 1972), 125–47; Timothy Bahti, "Figures of Interpretation, The Interpretation of Figures: A Reading of Wordsworth's 'Dream of the Arab,'" *Studies in Romanticism* 18 (1979):601–27; and Glenn W. Most, "Wordsworth's 'Dream of the Arab' and Cervantes," *English Language Notes* 22 (1985):52–58.

29   *On Architecture,* tr. Frank Granger, 2 vols. (New York, 1934), 2:3. See the engraving of the story in the frontispiece to David Gregory's edition of Euclid's *Opera* (1703). Wordsworth recalls a similar story in *The Prelude* (6.160–71).

30   *Wordsworth's Great Period Poems* 83–86.

31   It is worth noting that only an *s* stands between an explicitly political poem, which would have been understood as celebrating revolutionary ideology, and the poem as it is usually read. Given the politically charged meaning of a word like *independence,* it is difficult not to hear a semantic echo of its meaning in *resolution* and thus to read the title as "Re[v]olution and Independence."

32   Jared R. Curtis, *Wordsworth's Experiments with Tradition,* 188.

33   "Resolution and Independence," in *Wordsworth's Mind and Art; Essays by William Minto and Others,* ed. A. W. Thomson (Edinburgh, 1969), 189, 196.

34   "Uniformity and Progression: Reflections on the Structure of Geological Theory in the Age of Lyell," in *Perspectives in the History of Science and Technology,* ed. Duane H. D. Roller (Norman, Okla., 1971), 218. In his *Illustrations to the Huttonian Theory,* published in the same year as Wordsworth composed *Resolution and Independence,* John Playfair notes that "the large masses of rock so often met with at a distance from their original place, are one of the arguments used for the *debacle*" (407). Wordsworth also alludes to erratics in *A Guide Through the District of the Lakes,* where he tells how, round the margin of a lake, "huge stones and masses of rock are scattered; some defying conjecture as to the means by which they came thither; and others obviously fallen from on high—the contribution of ages!" (*ProseW* 2:187). For the first explanation of these stones as having been moved by a diluvial current, see Horace Bénédict de Saussure, *Voyages dans les Alpes; précédés d'un essai sur l'histoire naturelle des environs de Genève,* 4 vols. (Neuchâtel, 1779–96), 1:150–51. Charles Darwin describes the great impact that such a stone had upon him: "Old Mr. Cotton in Shropshire, who knew a great deal about rocks, had pointed out to me two or three years previously a well-known large erratic boulder in the town of Shrewsbury, called the 'bell stone': He told me that there was no rock of the same kind nearer than Cumberland or Scotland, and he solemnly assured me that the world would come to an end before anyone would be able to explain how this stone came where it now lay. This produced a deep impression on me, and I meditated over this wonderful stone. So that I felt the keenest delight when I first read of the action of icebergs in transporting boulders, and I gloried in the progress of Geology" (*Autobiography; with his Notes and Letters Depicting the Growth of the "Origin of Species,"* ed. Sir Francis Darwin [New York, 1950], 23).

35   *The Unmediated Vision: An Interpretation of Wordsworth, Hopkins, Rilke, and Valéry* (1954; rpt. New York, 1966), 33.

36   The great "land lizards" or dinosaurs were first discovered in Britain, by
     William Buckland in 1824 and by Gideon A. Mantell in 1825. Previously,
     the sea-saurians, the "Amphibiolithi" described by James Parkinson, were
     the focus of paleontological discussion, from William Stukeley's "Account
     of the Impression of the almost Entire Sceleton of a large Animal in a
     very hard stone," *Philosophical Transactions* 30 (1719):963–68 (an ichthy-
     osaurus); through William Chapman's and J. Wooler's account of a pet-
     rified crocodile in "Fossil skeleton found near Whitby," *Philosophical
     Transactions* 50 (1758):688–91, 786–90; to the famous discovery of a large
     fossil animal (mosasaurus) from the Chalk near Maestricht in Holland
     (1770), described by Petrus Camper in "Conjectures relative to the Pe-
     trifactions Found in St. Peter's Mountain, near Maestricht," *Philosophical
     Transactions* 76, pt. 2 (1786):443–56. "Sea-beast" was about as specific as
     any paleontologist would have been, because these sea creatures were
     seen as standing outside of traditional classifications: "The specimens
     which have been there discovered, have not hitherto warranted the de-
     termining with what species of animal, or even hardly with what genus
     they should be placed." They were nevertheless of major importance to
     diluvianists, because they proved "that the waters of the deluge did cover
     the whole earth . . . leading us to regard the globe we inhabit as one vast
     tomb of a former world" (*Organic Remains of a Former World*, 3 vols. [Lon-
     don, 1804–11], 3:274, 1:256).
37   *Religio Medici*, in *The Works of Sir Thomas Browne*, ed. Geoffrey Keynes, 6
     vols. (London, 1928–31), 1:43.
38   In *The Prelude*, Wordsworth indicates how the sight of the poor was used
     in revolutionary thought as the basis of political action, when he and
     Beaupuy

                              chanced
           One day to meet a hunger-bitten girl
           Who crept along fitting her languid self
           Unto a heifer's motion—by a cord
           Tied to her arm, and picking thus from the lane
           Its sustenance, while the girl with her two hands
           Was busy knitting in a heartless mood
           Of solitude—and at the sight my friend
           In agitation said, "'Tis against that
           Which we are fighting."   [9.511–20]

39   For contemporary ideas about leech-gathering, see Robert N. Essick,
     "Wordsworth and Leech-Lore," *Wordsworth Circle* 12 (1981):100–102.
     The link between leeches, blood, and revolution, emphasized in *The Pre-
     lude* in Wordsworth's reference to those who with "clumsy desperation
     brought / Rivers of blood" and were "swept away," in turn, by "their own
     helper" (10.546–49), is probably a part of the deep symbolic structure

of the poem. Here, however, the patriarchal figure uses his own body to gather the leeches that will cleanse the stream.

40 James Hutton, *Theory of the Earth, with Proofs and Illustrations*, 2 vols. (Edinburgh, 1795), 1:26. As Adam Ferguson observes, "Men at work on the present stock of their language, whether large or narrow, ever contrive to adopt some new form of expression . . . It shews the capacity of man to effect, by degrees that gradual accumulation of signs, on which the progress of language consists" (*Principles* 1:45).

41 Curtis, *Wordsworth's Experiments with Tradition* 194.

42 Wordsworth's use of words such as *scenery* and *view* in describing the Lake District, and his extensive use of the language of the "sublime" and the "beautiful," reflect his debts to traditions of the picturesque developed in guidebooks. But they also indicate that he is less interested in the physical than in the aesthetic aspects of human environments. It is this aspect of Wordsworth's poetry, his consistent rewriting of the eighteenth-century discourse on environmental influence in aesthetic terms, that forcibly impressed John Wilson, when, in 1802, while still at Glasgow University, he wrote a long and effusive letter to Wordsworth praising *Lyrical Ballads:* "May not the face of external nature through different quarters of the globe account for the dispositions of different nations? May not mountains, forests, plains, groves, and lakes, as much as the temperature of the atmosphere, or the form of government, produce important effects upon the human soul; and may not the difference subsisting between the former of these in different countries, produce as much diversity among the inhabitants as any varieties among the latter?" (Mary Gordon, *"Christopher North": A Memoir of John Wilson* [New York, 1863], 28). Wordsworth, in his response to Wilson, enlarged on this point, noting that "how dead soever many full-grown men may outwardly seem to these thi[ngs] they all are more or less affected by them, and in childhood, in the first practice and exercise of their senses, they must have been not the nourish[ers] merely, but often the fathers of their passions" (*EY* 353). To understand the influence of nature on human minds, then, one must go beyond "soils" and "climates" (354) to include the psychological effects of landscape, the ability of "images of danger, melancholy, grandeur, or loveliness, softness, and ease . . . [to] make themselves felt powerfully in forming the characters of the people."

43 Since eighteenth-century writers often considered property even more important to society than language, numerous accounts of the origin of property might be noted. One of the most famous was that of Rousseau, who opens the second part of the *Discourse on the Origin of Inequality* by arguing, "The first person who, having fenced off a plot of ground, took it into his head to say *this is mine* and found people simple enough to believe him, was the true founder of civil society" (*Discourses* 141).

44 Kurt Heinzelman has suggestively argued that Wordsworth set out "to

retrieve economic discourse from its mismanaged and facile rhetorical forms and thus to construct a cogent poetics of labor value" (*The Economics of the Imagination* [Amherst, Mass., 1980], 197).

45 *Autobiography of Henry Taylor, 1800–1875*, 2 vols. (London, 1885), 1:181; *The Diary of Benjamin Robert Haydon*, ed. Willard Bissell Pope, 2 vols. (Cambridge, Mass., 1960–63), 2:148.

Index